W9-BXB-156

Sri Lanka
a country study

Federal Research Division
Library of Congress
Edited by
Russell R. Ross
and Andrea Matles Savada
Research Completed
October 1988

On the cover: Ruwanveli Dagoba, Buddhist shrine built by
Dutthagamani, near Anuradhapura

Second Edition, First Printing, 1990.

Library of Congress Cataloging-in-Publication Data

Sri Lanka: A Country Study.

    Area handbook series, DA pam 550-96
    Research completed October 1988.
    Bibliography: pp. 281-300.
    Includes index.
    1. Sri Lanka. I. Ross, Russell R., 1935-   . II. Savada, Andrea
Matles, 1950- . III. Library of Congress. Federal Research
Division. IV. Series. V. Series: Area handbook series.

DS489.S68   1990   954.93   89-600370

Headquarters, Department of the Army
DA Pam 550-96

For sale by the Superintendent of Documents, U.S. Government Printing Office
Washington, D.C. 20402

Foreword

This volume is one in a continuing series of books now being prepared by the Federal Research Division of the Library of Congress under the Country Studies—Area Handbook Program. The last page of this book lists the other published studies.

Most books in the series deal with a particular foreign country, describing and analyzing its political, economic, social, and national security systems and institutions, and examining the interrelationships of those systems and the ways they are shaped by cultural factors. Each study is written by a multidisciplinary team of social scientists. The authors seek to provide a basic understanding of the observed society, striving for a dynamic rather than a static portrayal. Particular attention is devoted to the people who make up the society, their origins, dominant beliefs and values, their common interests and the issues on which they are divided, the nature and extent of their involvement with national institutions, and their attitudes toward each other and toward their social system and political order.

The books represent the analysis of the authors and should not be construed as an expression of an official United States government position, policy, or decision. The authors have sought to adhere to accepted standards of scholarly objectivity. Corrections, additions, and suggestions for changes from readers will be welcomed for use in future editions.

Louis R. Mortimer
Acting Chief
Federal Research Division
Library of Congress
Washington, D.C. 20540

Acknowledgments

This edition supercedes the *Area Handbook for Sri Lanka* written by Richard F. Nyrop, *et alia,* in 1970. Some parts of that edition have been used in the preparation of the current book, and the authors of *Sri Lanka: A Country Study* are grateful for the seminal work done by the earlier edition's authors. The authors also wish to thank various members of the staff of the Embassy of the Democratic Socialist Republic of Sri Lanka in Washington, D.C. for their assistance.

Various members of the staff of the Federal Research Division of the Library of Congress assisted in the preparation of the book. Richard F. Nyrop made helpful suggestions during his review of all parts of the book. Elizabeth A. Park prepared the telecommunication sections in chapters 3 and 4; Robert L. Worden researched the data used in preparing maps for the book; Carolina E. Forrester checked the content of all of the maps and reviewed the text of the section on geography; and Arvies J. Staton contributed to the figures on military ranks and insignia. David P. Cabitto, Kimberly Lord, and Paulette Marshall did the illustrations; and David P. Cabitto, Sandra K. Ferrell, and Kimberly Lord prepared the graphics. Martha E. Hopkins edited portions of the manuscript and managed editing of the book; Marilyn L. Majeska edited portions of the manuscript and managed production; and Barbara Edgerton and Izella Watson performed word processing.

Others who contributed were Harriet R. Blood, who assisted in the preparation of maps; Mimi Cantwell, Richard Kollodge, Ruth Nieland, and Gage Ricard, who edited portions of the manuscript; Catherine Schwartzstein, who performed final prepublication editorial review, and Shirley Kessel of Communications Connection, who prepared the index. Malinda B. Neale of the Library of Congess Composing Unit prepared camera-ready copy, under the direction of Peggy Pixley. The inclusion of photographs in this book was made possible by the generosity of various individuals and public and private agencies.

Contents

Chapter 3. The Economy 117
John D. Rogers

Chapter 4. Government and Politics 173
Donald M. Seekins

List of Figures

Preface

SRI LANKA: A COUNTRY STUDY replaces the edition of this work published in 1982. Like its predecessor, this study attempts to treat in a concise and objective manner the dominant social, political, economic, and military aspects of Sri Lankan society. Central to the study of contemporary Sri Lanka is the Sinhalese-Tamil conflict, its history, ramifications, and the toll it has taken on the country. For all intents and purposes, the national capital of Sri Lanka is Colombo—the site of its government ministries and foreign embassies. In 1982, however, a new parliamentary complex opened in Sri Jayewardenepura, Kotte, a suburb of Colombo, and the administrative capital was moved there.

Sources of information included books, scholarly journals, foreign and domestic newspapers, and numerous periodicals. Chapter bibliographies appear at the end of the book, and brief comments on some of the more valuable sources recommended for further reading appear at the end of each chapter. A Glossary also is included. Contemporary place names used in this book are those approved by the United States Board on Geographic Names. Measurements are given in the metric system, and a conversion table is provided to assist those readers who are unfamiliar with metric measurements (see table 1, Appendix A).

Country Profile

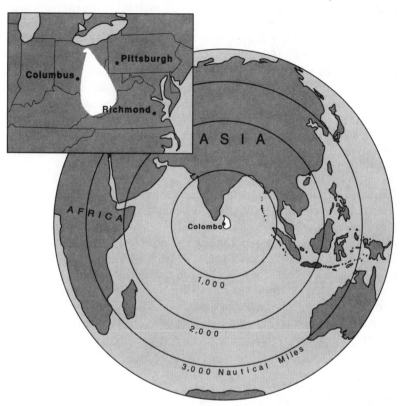

Country

Formal Name: Democratic Socialist Republic of Sri Lanka.

Short Form: Sri Lanka (formerly known as Ceylon).

Term for Citizens: Sri Lankan(s).

Capital: Colombo, located on the southwestern coast.

Administrative Capital: Sri Jayewardenepura since 1982.

Geography

Size: Pear-shaped island 29 kilometers off southeastern coast of India; total area 65,610 square kilometers, of which land area 64,740 square kilometers.

Topography: Irregular, dissected, central massif dominates south; highest elevation Pidurutalagala (2,524 meters) but better-known mountain Adam's Peak (2,243 meters), destination of interfaith pilgrimages. Coastal belt (less than 100 meters elevation) succeeded by rolling plains (100–500 meters elevation) of varying width extends from seashore to foothills of central massif. In northern half of island, topography falls away to rolling plain, relieved only by isolated ridges. Rivers extend radially from central massif to coast; longest Mahaweli Ganga (860 kilometers), which flows in northeasterly direction. About 40 percent of island forested. Coastline regular but indented by numerous lagoons and marked by sandy beaches.

Climate: Equatorial and tropical influenced by elevation above sea level, but marked by only slight diurnal and seasonal variations; temperature in Colombo (at sea level) varies from 25°C to 28°C, and in central massif (site of highest elevations) 14°C to 16°C. Subject to southwest monsoon from mid-May to October and northeast monsoon December to March. Rainfall uneven; divides country climatically into wet zone comprising southwestern quarter and dry zone on remainder of island. Annual precipitation in wet zone averages 250 centimeters; in dry zone precipitation varies from 120 to 190 centimeters.

Society

Population: 14,846,750 (according to 1981 census); 16,639,695 (estimated 1988). Average annual growth rate 1.6 percent; average life expectancy 67.5 years (males 66 years, females 69 years); gender ratio 103.7 males to 100 females.

Ethnic Groups: Sinhalese 74 percent; Tamil 18 percent; Moor (Muslims) 7 percent; others (Burghers, Eurasians, Malay, Veddha) 1 percent. Largest ethnic group divided into low-country Sinhalese (subjected in coastal areas to greater colonial acculturation) and Kandyan Sinhalese (more traditional upland dwellers, named after Kingdom of Kandy, which resisted European encroachments until 1815–18). Tamils divided into Sri Lankan Tamils (on island since early historic times) and Indian Tamils (brought in as plantation labor in the nineteenth century).

Languages: Sinhalese speak Sinhala (official language); Tamils speak Tamil (equal with Sinhala as official language since July 29, 1987); English spoken in government and educated circles by about 10 percent of population.

Education and Literacy: Schooling organized in four levels: primary (six years), junior secondary (five years), senior secondary (two years), and tertiary (at least two years). Education compulsory to age thirteen, free in government schools, and fee paid in private institutions. Number of students enrolled (1986) about 3.75 million (government) and 101,000 (private). Government expenditure on education (1986) about 3.6 million rupees (see Glossary). Overall literacy (over age 10) about 87 percent.

Religion: Theravada Buddhist, 69 percent; Hindu, 15 percent; Christian, 8 percent; Muslim, 8 percent. Sinhalese generally Buddhist; Tamils Hindu; Burghers, Eurasians, and minority of Sinhalese and Tamils profess Christianity; Moors adherents of Islam.

Health and Welfare: Nationwide health care system, including maternity services provided by government, but facilities and personnel overtaxed, supplies and equipment lacking; medical infrastructure consists of more than 3,000 Western-trained physicians, 8,600 nurses, 338 central dispensaries, and 490 hospitals of all types. Smallpox eradicated; incidence of malaria declining; unsanitary conditions and lack of clean water major cause of gastroenteritis among adults and infants. Death rate declined from 6.6 to 6.1 per 1,000 in decade from mid-1970s to mid-1980s; infant mortality declined from 50 to 34 deaths per 1,000 in decade from early 1970s to early 1980s. Traditional medicine (*ayurveda*), supported by government, enjoys great credibility.

Economy

Gross Domestic Product (GDP): In mid-1980s, GDP rose incrementally at current and constant factor costs in spite of insurgency and domestic turmoil. Gross national product (GNP) increased from US$5.48 billion (US$349 per capita) in 1984 to US$5.71 billion (US$354 per capita) in 1986. GDP went from US$5.57 billion in 1984 to US$5.84 billion in 1986, with additional increase to US$6.08 billion (subject to revision) in 1987 and projected US$6.27 billion in 1988. Real (constant) growth rate dipped from 5.1 percent in 1984 to 4.3 percent in 1986, with a further estimated 1.5 percent decline for 1987. Reversal of trend expected in 1988, with increase to 3.5 percent growth.

Agriculture: Including forestry and fishing, agriculture accounted for slightly over 25 percent of GDP in 1982–86, but occupied nearly half of labor force during same period. Wet rice (paddy) main subsistence crop with two harvests a year; paddy hectareage and production have risen steadily since 1977; reached about 900,000 hectares under cultivation and 2.6 million tons harvested in 1986, making country about 75 percent self-sufficient in rice production. Principal commercial crops tea, rubber, and coconuts; tea production in the 1980s varied between 180 and 210 million kilograms annually; rubber production remained constant at about 140 million kilograms annually since 1983; coconut production rose by about 10 percent a year in 1980s, reaching a peak of slightly over 3 million nuts in 1986. Production of all crops dealt setback by drought in 1987, with recovery expected in 1988.

Industry: Contributes somewhat over 15 percent of GDP and occupies nearly 30 percent of labor force; major industrial output consumer goods, especially garments and textiles, and processed agriculture commodities. State plays major role in manufacturing sector, controlling some twenty large-scale enterprises and about fifty corporations; government committed to expanding role of private sector in developing nontraditional exports, import substitutes, and employment opportunities.

Energy: Firewood traditional source, accounts for 60 to 70 percent of energy consumption; main commercial/industrial sources hydroelectric and thermal power; installed capacity in 1986 slightly over a thousand megawatts. Accelerated Mahaweli Program, when completed, expected to provide extra 450 megawatts of power and render nation self-sufficient in energy production.

Services: Accounts for about 15.7 percent of labor force. Active tourism sector slumped badly because of widespread unrest in country after 1983.

Imports: Equivalent to US$1.95 billion in 1986. Major imported commodities include petroleum products, machinery, transportation equipment, food (including rice, wheat, flour, sugar), fertilizer, yarn, and textiles. Principal trading partners Japan, Saudi Arabia, and the United States. Imports from United States dominated by wheat, machinery, and equipment.

Exports: Equivalent to approximately US$1.22 billion in 1986; major exported goods ready-made clothing and processed agricultural commodities such as tea, rubber, coconuts, and spices. Dominant trading partner throughout 1980s the United States, which took US$350 million worth of goods in 1987, or fully 25 percent of all Sri Lankan exports.

Balance of Payments: Negative balance of payments throughout 1980s, but chronic trade deficit partially offset by foreign aid and remittances from abroad. Current account balance amounted to minus US$425 million for 1986, with minus US$357 million estimated for 1987. Total external debt for 1986 amounted to US$412 billion, with debt service ratio about 18.4 percent.

Exchange Rate: For five-year period ending in mid-1988, exchange rate of Sri Lankan rupee fluctuated, on average, less than ten percent annually against value of United States dollar. Most precipitous decline occurred from 1987 to 1988, when value of rupee fell from 26 (free rate) or 28.93 (official rate) to 32.58 (free rate) or 32.32 (official rate) per dollar.

Transportation and Communications

Railroads: Government owned; about 1,944 kilometers of track; network extends radially from Colombo to northern, eastern, and southern coastal cities; service to northern and eastern areas erratic because of domestic unrest.

Roads: Total approximately 75,000 kilometers; paved (bituminous) about 25,500 kilometers; 478,000 registered vehicles in mid-1980s.

Waterways: About 430 kilometers of rivers and canals navigable by shallow draft vessels.

Ports: Deep water ports at Colombo, Trincomalee, and Galle, latter two underutilized; government shipping corporation possessed eight freighters and two tankers in late 1980s.

Airfields: Fourteen, of which twelve usable in late 1980s, eleven having permanent surface runways, one (Bandaranaike International Airport at Katunayaka) with runway more than 2,500 meters.

Telecommunications: International service provided by satellite earth station and submarine cable; international telephone, telex, and direct dialing in operation; about 106,500 telephones nationwide; about 29 radio stations, 24 of which are AM, at least 5 are FM) in operation, with more than 2 million registered receivers in use; 2 television networks broadcast over 4 channels; 350,000 television sets nationwide.

Government and Politics

Government: Constitution of September 7, 1978, guarantees fundamental rights of thought, conscience, and worship and established unitary state with strong executive power. President, elected directly for six-year term, serves as chief of state and government and appoints cabinet of ministers; October 1982 presidential election won by incumbent Junius R. ("J.R.") Jayewardene of United National Party (UNP), who received 52.9 percent of vote. Legislature consists of 196-member unicameral Parliament having power to pass laws by simple majority and amend Constitution by two-thirds majority. Parliamentary members, chosen by universal suffrage from electoral constituencies corresponding generally to administrative districts, serve six-year terms. Below national level, popularly elected provincial councils established in seven of nine provinces in 1988. Until provincial councils fully operational, basic administrative subdivision remains district governed by council of elected and appointed members, presided over by district minister, who serves concurrently in Parliament. At lowest governmental echelon, administrative functions carried out by popularly elected urban, municipal, town, and village councils. In rural areas, village councils exercise governance over 90 percent of nation's territory.

Politics: UNP headed by President Jayewardene, in power since 1977, retained over two-thirds majority in Parliament and won provincial council elections in 1988. Sri Lanka Freedom Party (SLFP), left-of-center, alternated in power with UNP since independence, but boycotted 1988 provincial council elections, and surrendered place as principal opposition group to newly formed United Socialist Alliance (USA), which finished second in elections. USA consisted of four left-of-center parties: Communist Party of Sri Lanka (CPSL), Ceylon Equal Society Party (Lanka Sama Samaja Party—LSSP), New Equal Society Party (Nava Sama Samaja Party—NSSP), and Sri Lanka People's Party (SLPP—Sri Lanka Mahajana Pakshaya). Sri Lanka Muslim Congress (SLMC) only minor party to gain seats in provincial council elections. Tamil United Liberation Front (TULF) principal Tamil party, advocates separate Tamil state in Sri Lanka, but not represented in Parliament since 1983. People's Liberation Front (Janatha Vimukthi Peramuna—JVP), formally proscribed, in armed opposition to government.

Administrative Divisions: Nine provinces (Northern and Eastern provinces may be combined into a single province in 1989); twenty-four administrative districts.

Legal System: 1978 Constitution guarantees independence of judiciary. Legal system based on British common law, Roman-Dutch (Napoleonic) law, and customary practices of Sinhalese, Tamils, and Muslims. Supreme Court, highest court in nation, has chief justice and between six and ten associate justices appointed by president. Country divided into five judicial circuits, subdivided into districts with district courts and divisions with magistrates' courts. Lowest courts are conciliation boards with responsibility for minor criminal and civil cases.

International Memberships: Asian Development Bank, Colombo Plan, Commonwealth of Nations, Group of 77, Intelsat, Interpol, Inter-Parliamentary Union, Nonaligned Movement, South Asian Association for Regional Cooperation, United Nations and specialized agencies, World Federation of Trade Unions.

National Security

Armed Forces: Total strength about 48,000 personnel, including reservists on active duty. President serves as commander in chief and defense minister. Minister of national security reports to president, serves as deputy defense minister, presides over Joint Operations Command, which exercises overall responsibility for government counterinsurgency and counterterrorist effort. Chain of command extends downward to individual service commanders, deputy commanders, and chiefs of staff.

Army: Total strength including reservists on active duty, up to 40,000 personnel. Major tactical units five infantry brigade-sized task forces, each with three battalions. Other formations include one or two battalion-sized reconnaissance regiments, plus artillery, engineer, signals, and logistical units. In 1988 army reorganized territorially with individual battalions assigned to each of twenty-one sectors, corresponding generally to administrative districts; sectors grouped into two area commands: Division One for southern half of country, Division Two for northern half. Following Indo-Sri Lankan Accord of July 1987, army deployed against Tamil insurgents in Mannar and Vavuniya Districts, Northern Province, and against JVP terrorists in Southern Province. Military equipment includes small arms of Chinese, Singapore, Pakistani, and Western origin; armored cars and armored personnel carriers of British, South African, and domestic manufacture; mortars and light-to-medium-artillery pieces from Yugoslavia, Pakistan, and the Federal Republic of Germany (West Germany).

Navy: Total strength, including reservists on active duty, about 4,000 to 6,000 personnel. Service organized administratively into three naval area commands: Northern, Eastern, and Western (a fourth, Southern, to be established), with main naval base at Trincomalee, smaller installations at Karainagar, Tangalla, and Kalpitiya, major facility under construction at Galle. In 1988 principal naval mission patrol of "surveillance zone" in Palk Strait to prevent gun-running by Tamil insurgents between India and Sri Lanka; other naval tasks include enforcement of Sri Lankan Exclusive Economic Zone. Total inventory fifty-five vessels; major surface combatants six command ships (used as tenders for patrol vessels in "surveillance zone"); other ships include Cougar patrol craft and amphibious vessels from Britain, Dvora and Super Dvora craft from Israel, plus locally manufactured and older patrol boats from China and the Soviet Union; additional ships under construction in Republic of Korea (South Korea).

Air Force: Total strength, including reservists on active duty, about 3,700 personnel deployed at 3 large and 9 smaller airbases country-wide. Principal air force missions tactical air support for ground operations, military airlift, and medical evacuation. Organization and inventory include one counterinsurgency squadron with Italian SIAI Marchetti SF–260TP light trainer aircraft, one helicopter squadron with United States Bell models 212, 412, and Jet Ranger, and French SA–365 Dauphin-IIs rotary wing aircraft; one transport squadron with Chinese Yun-8 and Yun-12 turboprops, plus assorted older aircraft, including United States DC–3s (C–47s) and an Indian HS–748; and one trainer squadron of light aircraft, including United States Cessnas.

Paramilitary Forces: Sri Lankan National Police, total strength 21,000 to 28,000 personnel, organized territorially into three "ranges," subdivided into divisions, districts, and police stations; includes National Intelligence Bureau and Police Special Force (formerly Special Task Force), latter comprising 1,100 personnel organized into one oversize battalion of seven companies, with units deployed against JVP terrorists in Southern Province, or serving in rotation as presidential security guard.

Foreign Military Presence: Prior to Indo-Sri Lankan Accord of 1987, small number of Pakistani, Israeli, and retired British military advisers. Since August 1987 Indian Peacekeeping Force (IPKF), reported strength 70,000 personnel, organized into 15 brigades, plus supporting units, deployed against Tamil insurgents in Northern and Eastern provinces.

Defense Expenditures: Increased from less than 1 percent of GDP in early 1980s to over 5 percent in 1987 because of Tamil insurgency, but levelled off following Indo-Sri Lankan Accord. In 1987 expenditures, including supplemental appropriations, amounted to US$408 million or about 5.4 percent of GDP. Projected defense expenditures for 1988 expected to decline somewhat to US$340 million.

Internal Security: Insurgent movement known generically as Tamil Tigers, active since about 1975, fighting for independent state in Tamil areas of Sri Lanka; total estimated strength 5,000 combatants; most prominent insurgent group Liberation Tigers of Tamil Eelam (LTTE); other groups include People's Liberation Organization of Tamil Eelam (PLOT or PLOTE), Eelam Revolutionary Organization of Students (EROS), Tamil Eelam Liberation Organization (TELO), Eelam People's Revolutionary Liberation Front (EPRLF). Separate terrorist movement, known as JVP, composed of Sinhalese chauvinists, estimated strength several hundred, opposed to Indo-Sri Lankan Accord, active in Southern Province.

Figure 1. Administrative Divisions of Sri Lanka, 1988

Introduction

SRI LANKA WAS NOT IMMUNE to the spirit of the global and monumental change that swept the world in the late 1980s, promising to usher in a new international order in the 1990s. Indeed, at this writing events on the troubled island nation somehow seemed more under control than they had been in the immediate past. Yet Sri Lanka still had to cope with many of the same daunting and unresolved security problems that it faced in 1983, when a vicious separatist war broke out in the north—a situation later aggravated by an altogether different but equally debilitating insurrection in the south.

Sri Lanka's descent into violence was especially disturbing because for many years the nation was considered a model of democracy in the Third World. A nation with one of the world's lowest per capita incomes, Sri Lanka nevertheless had a nascent but thriving free-market economy that supported one of the most extensive and respected education systems among developing countries. Sadly, in 1990 the recollection of a peaceful and prosperous Sri Lanka seemed a distant memory.

Prospects for an enduring peace, however remote, lingered as the new decade began. On February 4, 1990, as Sri Lanka celebrated its forty-second Independence Day, the president, Ranasinghe Premadasa, who had assumed power a little over one year before, once again appealed directly to the island nation's more than 16 million people for an end to the long-standing communally based friction between the majority Sinhalese and the largest ethnic minority group, the Sri Lankan Tamils. He also pleaded for a cessation of the internecine struggle among competing groups within the Tamil community and of the open warfare by Sinhalese extremists against the government. The collective strife on the island nation, according to international human rights groups, had over the previous year alone taken as many as 20,000 lives and over the span of a decade killed thousands more. The economy was crippled, the democratic values of the country threatened, and the national memory scarred.

Soothsayers had characterized Premadasa's assumption of power in early 1989 as auspicious. Sri Lanka needed a person of stature and vision to guide the country in its healing process. Many thought Premadasa could fill that role. For the first time since independence, Sri Lanka had a leader who did not belong to the island's high-born Sinhalese Buddhist caste, the Goyigama. Premadasa came instead from more humble origins and was viewed by many Sri Lankans as more accessible than his predecessor, Junius Richard (J.R.) Jayewardene, under whom he had served as prime minister for ten years. One of Premadasa's first actions on assuming office in January 1989 was to lift the five-and-a-half-year state of emergency declared by his predecessor. Six months later, Premadasa was praised by both the Tamils and the Sinhalese for his unyielding opposition to the presence of the Indian Peacekeeping Force (IPKF), a military contingent sent into Sri Lanka in 1987 after an agreement between former Indian prime minister Rajiv Gandhi and Jayewardene. The IPKF, originally a small force tasked with performing a police action to disarm Tamil separatists in the north, became increasingly entangled in the ethnic struggle and guerrilla insurrection and had grown at one point to as many as 70,000 troops.

By mid-1989 Premadasa was demanding from a sullen India the quick withdrawal of the remaining 45,000 Indian soldiers then on the island. Considering the resentment most Sri Lankans—both Sinhalese and Tamil—had by then developed toward India, the entreaty was both popular and politically expedient. Yet, having to rely on the Sri Lankan military's questionable ability to control the island's mercurial political milieu was a calculated gamble. Still, in June 1989, hopes soared as delicate negotiations were initiated between the government and the most powerful of the Tamil separatist groups, the Liberation Tigers of Tamil Eelam (LTTE). But by then Premadasa was faced with more immediate challenges. A spate of assassinations in the south and a nationwide transportation strike were orchestrated by Sinhalese extremists who had been in the forefront of political agitation against the presence of Indian troops on the island and also against any concessions the government made to Tamil demands for increased autonomy. Premadasa was forced to take urgent action, and he reimposed a national state of emergency, giving his security forces new and draconian powers of enforcement. As bickering between the Sri Lankan and Indian governments over a timetable for the Indian troop withdrawal continued, the Sri Lankan government unleashed a brutal campaign against the Sinhalese extremists. Reports of "death squads" composed of army and police officers who in their zealous pursuit of the subversives also claimed the lives of many innocent victims attracted the attention and ire of Amnesty International and other international human rights groups.

In late March 1990, India withdrew its last troops from Sri Lanka, thereby ending its much maligned three-year period of foreign entanglement, which had inflamed rather than defused the island's communal and political passions. The pullout created a power vacuum in the island's Tamil-dominated Northeastern Province that was expected to be filled by the resurgent Tamil Tigers. The Tamil Tigers, represented by their own political party, the People's Front of the Liberation Tigers—cautiously recognized by the government—were expected to combine political as well as military pressure against the rival Tamil groups favored by the Indians. Without waiting for the completion of the Indian departure, the Tamil Tigers already were reasserting their control, waging a vigorous and thus far successful military offensive against the Eelam People's Revolutionary Liberation Front, which headed the provincial government, and several secondary Tamil politico-military groups and their allied militia—the India-armed and trained Tamil National Army. Politically, their prestige enhanced by a reputation honed by their prolonged and skillful combat against the Indians, and what they called their Tamil "quislings," the feared Tamil Tigers were in a good position to win the elections for the Northeastern Provincial Council to be held later in 1990.

In their dialog with the government, the Tamil Tigers no longer emphasized full secession and seemed instead to be more intent, in the absence of their Indian adversaries, on consolidating their military and political power over rival Tamil groups. The government, aware that the Tamil Tigers had not formally renounced the concept of a separate Tamil state, however, realized that the hiatus in fighting could end in renewed fighting and in what could ultimately be the "Lebanization" of the country.

What went so tragically wrong for the beautiful island sometimes referred to as Shangri-la? The answer is elusive and can only partly be explained by the duress experienced by a multifaceted traditional culture undergoing rapid change in an environment restrained by limited resources. A close reckoning also would have to be made of the island's troubled past—both ancient and recent.

Sri Lanka claims the world's second-oldest continuous written history—a history that chronicles the intermittent hostility between two peoples—the Indo-Aryan Sinhalese or "People of the Lion," who arrived from northern India around 500 B.C. to establish magnificent Buddhist kingdoms on the north-central plains, and the Tamils of Dravidian stock, who arrived a few centuries later from southern India. The Tamil symbol became the tiger, and during one brief juncture in the island's history during the tenth century, Sri Lanka was ruled as a province by the Tamil Chola dynasty in southern India. The ancient linkage of northern Sri Lanka with the Tamil kingdoms of southern India has not been forgotten by today's Sinhalese, who cite as a modern embodiment of the historical threat of Tamil migration, the proximity of India's southern Tamil Nadu state and its 55 million Tamils—a source of psychological and military support for Tamil separatists on the island.

In the sixteenth century, the island was colonized by the Portuguese, later to be followed by the Dutch, and finally, and most significantly, the British in the late eighteenth century. The British succeeded in uniting the island, which they called Ceylon. They established and then broadened a colonial education system centered in British liberalism and democratic values, which would eventually groom the generation of native leaders who had successfully lobbied for independence. The British favored the Tamils somewhat over the Sinhalese, enabling them to take better advantage of what educational and civil service opportunities were available. By the time independence was attained in 1948, a body of able Sri Lankans, pooled from both the Sinhalese and Tamil elites, was ready to take control from the British in a peaceful and well-orchestrated transfer of power.

In its early post-independence years, Sri Lanka was fortunate to be led by Don Stephen Senanayake. He was a Sinhalese who was leader of the United National Party (UNP), an umbrella party of disparate political groups formed during the pre-independence years and one of the two political parties that has since dominated Sri Lankan politics. Senanayake was a man scrupulously even-handed in his approach to ethnic representation, but his vision of communal harmony survived only for a short time after his death in 1952. He was succeeded briefly by two UNP successors, one of whom was his son Dudley. In 1956 control of the government went to the opposition Sri Lanka Freedom Party (SLFP) led by Solomon West Ridgeway Dias (S.W.R.D.) Bandaranaike, who became the island's fourth prime minister after winning an emotionally charged election.

The 1956 election marked the first instance of serious communal disharmony since independence and presaged the troubled years to come. Symbolically, the election coincided with the 2,500th anniversary of the death of the Buddha and also that of the arrival of Vijaya—the legendary founder of the Sinhalese people—on the island. Emotions became dangerously overwrought because Bandaranaike ran primarily on a "Sinhala Only" platform, which decreed that the language of the Sinhalese would be the only official language, with both English and Tamil branded as cultural imports. Bandaranaike also proclaimed that he would restore Buddhism to its historically elevated place in Sri Lankan society. The argument can be made that the 1956 election and its attendant emotionalism marked the beginning of the great division between what have become two completely separate and mutually hostile political systems in Sri Lanka, one Sinhalese and Buddhist, the other Tamil and Hindu. Post-election emotions escalated, and it was not long before tragedy followed. In 1958 an anti-Tamil rumor was all that was needed to trigger nationwide riots in which hundreds of people, most of whom were Tamils, died. The riots marked the first major episode of communal violence after independence and left a deep psychological rift between the two major ethnic groups.

In the years after the death of S.W.R.D. Bandaranaike in 1959, the SLFP has been headed by his widow Sirimavo, who led her left of center party to victory in the election of 1960 and again in 1970. Popularly regarded as a woman with a mandate to carry on her husband's legacy, she was esteemed by many Sinhalese who heeded her political guidance even when she was out of power. While in office, she vigorously enforced legislation such as the Official Language Act, which openly placed Sinhalese interests over Tamil, further dividing the body politic. During Bandaranaike's last tenure in power, from 1970 to 1977, the deteriorating security situation on the island intensified. In 1971 her new government sanctioned university admissions regulations that were openly prejudicial to Tamils. In the following year, she promulgated a new constitution that declared Sri Lanka a republic, but that was notorious for its lack of protection for minorities.

In 1972 a serious new threat to the stability of the island appeared. Established in the late 1960s, the People's Liberation Front (Janatha Vimukthi Peramuna—JVP), a violent movement alternatively described as Maoist and Trokskyite but one indisputably chauvinist in its championship of Sinhalese values, launched its first major offensive in 1972. The JVP attempted a blitzkrieg operation to take over the country within twenty-four hours; it was suppressed only after considerable fighting during a protracted state of emergency declared by the government. In the late 1980s, an invigorated JVP would arise and gather strength from the anti-Indian sentiment that followed the Indo-Sri Lankan Accord and the arrival of Indian troops in 1987.

In 1977 the UNP, led by J.R. Jayewardene, easily defeated Bandaranaike, whose Common Programme with its loosely administered socialist politics had proven so injurious to the economy. Declaring that his government would inaugurate an era of *dharmishta,* or righteous society, Jayewardene crafted a new constitution the following year, changing the previous Westminster-style parliamentary government to a new presidential system modeled after that of France. The 1978 Constitution, unlike its predecessor, made substantial concessions to Tamil sensitivities. The most blatant excesses of the Bandaranaike government were stopped, especially the discriminatory university admissions criteria aimed at Tamils and the refusal to give Tamil national language status. Yet these measures appeared to be a classical case of too little too late. The political disillusionment of Tamil youth, which had grown during the Bandaranaike years, continued unabated, and the separatist call for a Tamil Eelam, or "Precious Land," became increasingly accompanied by attacks on government targets.

Jayewardene, widely admired as one of the most learned leaders in South Asia, nevertheless was criticized for his inability—or reluctance—to recognize the disturbances in Sri Lanka as something more profound than merely a law and order problem. In 1979 with communal unrest growing steadily worse, his government passed the Prevention of Terrorism Act, at first a temporary, but later a permanent, piece of legislation that gave unbridled powers of search and arrest to the police and military. Government abuses soon followed, attracting the harsh scrutiny and condemnation of international human rights organizations. In time, Jayewardene was forced to broaden his assessment of the deteriorating security situation, and he initiated a series of negotiations on increased autonomy with the major Tamil political organization on the island, the Tamil United Liberation Front (TULF). While the TULF and the government pressed for a conference of all appropriate bodies—a peace forum to represent all the religious and ethnic groups in the country—the Tamil Tigers escalated their terrorist attacks, provoking a Sinhalese backlash against Tamils and precluding any successful accommodation resulting from the talks. Thereafter, the talks took place intermittently and at best with only partial representation between representatives of the heterogeneous Tamil community and the government.

Important opportunities for a constructive dialog on Tamil and Sinhalese concerns continued to be missed as negotiators, driven by events seemingly beyond their control, hardened their positions. Under steady pressure from Tamil extremists and in their abhorrence of the Prevention of Terrorism Act, the moderate Tamil political organizations, notably the TULF, decided to boycott the 1982 presidential election. When the government proposed the following year to amend the Constitution to ban all talk of separatism, all sixteen TULF members of parliament were expelled for refusing to recite a loyalty oath. The government lost its vital link to mediation. The fissures in Sri Lankan society also grew wider with each new episode of communal violence. Serious rioting again broke out in 1977 and 1981, but the magnitude of unrest and violence that exploded in the July 1983 riots could not have been anticipated. The riots unleashed an unprecedented wave of violence that engulfed the island and divided Sri Lankan society. The aftermath of that social conflagration was still felt in the early 1990s.

The 1983 riots were in response to the ambush and killing of thirteen Sinhalese soldiers by the Tamil Tigers on the outskirts of Jaffna, the capital of Sri Lanka's Tamil-dominated Northern Province. A five-day rampage ensued, with lynchings and summary executions occurring all over the island. As many as 1,000 people, mostly Tamils, were slaughtered. Carefully carried out attacks by Sinhalese rioters in possession of voter lists and addresses of Tamils suggested collusion by some members of Sri Lanka's military and security forces.

Shortly after the riots Jayewardene hurriedly convened an All Party Conference, which was envisioned as a series of ongoing talks with the aim of bringing Tamils and Sinhalese together to negotiate a political settlement of their communal confrontation. The conference, which was first convened in January 1984, resulted in a series of proposals. These proposals, however, were rejected by several of the major Tamil opposition parties, including the TULF. In July 1985, the government, now joined by the active participation of Prime Minister Rajiv Gandhi of India, reopened a dialog with the TULF and other smaller Tamil political groups in a series of proposals and counter-proposals. Tamil demands focused on the issues of the devolution of central legislative, administrative, and judicial authority. Progress in the talks soon proved illusory, however, because the moderate TULF had little credibility among the militants, especially the powerful Tamil Tigers, who were steadfast in their opposition to any settlement with the government short of the establishment of a Tamil Eelam.

Jayewardene notified India and the TULF in 1986 that he would significantly devolve state powers, a concession he was previously unwilling to make. Jayewardene's proposed plan offered all nine provinces substantial autonomy, with many of the central government powers pertaining to law and order, representation, and land settlement transferred to provincial councils. The proposed devolution of central powers at that time fell short of meeting Tamil demands for a merger of the Northern and Eastern provinces into a single Tamil-speaking unit. Predictably, the Jayewardene Plan was attacked by Bandaranaike, who also refused to participate in the 1986 All Party Conference through which Jayewardene had hoped to achieve a national consensus.

By early summer 1987 Jayewardene, sensing that Tamil Tiger guerrilla activities against the government were an insurmountable impediment to his efforts at a negotiated peace settlement, launched a military campaign to dislodge them from their stronghold in the north. The Sri Lankan military succeeded in wresting a good proportion of the Jaffna Peninsula from the Tamil Tigers, who then withdrew to the city of Jaffna relying on the consummate guerrilla tactic of using a sympathetic citizenry to insulate them from pursuing troops. When the troops continued to advance and threatened to enter the Tamil stronghold, India, pressured by its Tamil politicians, warned that it would militarily intervene to prevent them from doing so.

New Delhi accused Colombo of employing starvation tactics against the people of Jaffna in its anti-Tiger military operations and demanded to be allowed to send humanitarian relief. Insulted, Sri Lanka refused the demand. In response, India sent a small flotilla of fishing vessels, carrying supplies of food and medicine. Sri Lanka's tiny but tenacious navy turned it away, however, changing India's gesture into a public relations fiasco. Perhaps because of wounded pride, India sent cargo planes escorted by fighters into Sri Lanka's airspace dropping a few symbolic supplies over Jaffna. Sri Lanka, vociferously protesting that its territorial sovereignty had been violated, labeled India a regional bully. While Tamil separatists applauded India's move, most others in Sri Lanka were incensed. Relations between the two countries plummeted.

Good relations with India had been of great importance to Sri Lanka since independence, but the ethnic crisis between the Sinhalese and the Tamils, which culminated in the mid-1980s, poisoned relations between the two states. India had been particularly strident in its accusations of alleged atrocities by the Sri Lankan security forces against the Sri Lankan Tamils and once went so far as to declare that the Sri Lankan government's "genocide" was responsible for the flight of thousands of refugees to India. Sri Lanka accused India of encouraging Tamil separatism and providing Tamil guerrillas sanctuary and training facilities in the southern Indian state of Tamil Nadu since the early 1980s. Jayewardene specifically leveled his public outrage at Tamil Nadu, calling the Liberation Tigers of Tamil Eelam guerrillas a private army of the late M.G. Ramachandran, then the Tamil Nadu chief minister. Ranasinghe Premadasa, as Jayewardene's prime minister, did not distinguish Tamil Nadu's role from that of India, calling that country's alleged support of Sri Lanka's Tamil separatism the "terrorist equation."

Overcoming much bitterness, both Gandhi and Jayewardene eventually agreed that a confrontational approach would never address the complicated security and bilateral issues linking the two nations. On July 29, 1987, within two months of the airdrop incident, an agreement, henceforth referred to as the Indo-Sri Lankan Accord, was signed between the Indian and Sri Lankan leaders with the purpose of establishing peace and normalcy in Sri Lanka. The accord was timely and politically advantageous to both leaders. Jayewardene in Colombo was increasingly perceived as isolated from the events in the north, and his instrument of influence there, the Sri Lankan military, was depicted by the international media as an ill-trained and poorly disciplined force. He agreed to a plan of devolution that would give Sri Lankan Tamils more autonomy over a newly created Northeastern Province but would at the same time safeguard Sri Lanka's unitary status. Gandhi's government, reeling from an arms scandal, was able to trumpet a foreign relations victory as regional peacekeeper. Gandhi's strategy was to exercise India's military clout to weaken the separatist insurgency in Sri Lanka by collecting weapons from the same Tamil militant groups that it was accused of having previously trained and equipped. Furthermore, it was agreed that India would expel all Sri Lankan Tamil citizens resident in India who were found to be engaging in terrorist activities or advocating separatism in Sri Lanka. To enforce this new state of cooperation between the two nations, the Indian Navy and Indian Coast Guard would assist the Sri Lankan Navy in intercepting arms from Tamil militants based in India.

The Indo-Sri Lankan Accord had another, lesser known aspect, the importance of which Indian officials acknowledged afterwards, which bears on India's geopolitical perception of itself as a regional superpower. India, wary of competing influence in the Indian Ocean region, insisted that the accord be accompanied by documents which assured New Delhi veto power over what foreign nation could use the harbor facilities at Trincomalee in the northeast. Sri Lanka also was asked to cancel an earlier agreement with the United States that gave the Voice of America rights to expand its transmission installations on the island.

New Delhi was able to obtain the agreement of the TULF, as well as some of the lesser Tamil political groups, and for a brief time the acquiescence of the powerful LTTE, for a cease-fire. Within forty-eight hours of the signing of the agreement in Colombo, the cease-fire went into effect and the first troops of the IPKF arrived in northern Sri Lanka. Yet implementation of the accord proved problematic. Rioting Sinhalese mobs, inspired by anti-accord rhetoric voiced by Bandaranaike, disrupted the capital. At the farewell ceremony for Gandhi, following the signing of the accord, in a circumstance that proved more embarrassing than dangerous, a Sri Lankan honor guard clubbed the Indian leader with his rifle butt. Against this backdrop, it is not surprising that the accord held for less than three months.

By early September, violence was breaking out in Eastern Province where Sinhalese and Muslims were protesting the provisional merger of the Northern and Eastern provinces effected for the purpose of electing a single provincial council. The Sinhalese and Muslims felt that because the Northern Province was overwhelmingly Tamil, a merger of the two provinces would result in their minority status. Bandaranaike's SLFP skillfully capitalized on this atmosphere of panic, allying itself with influential Buddhist monks, who together mounted a well publicized campaign against the government's "betrayal" of the non-Tamil population of the Eastern Province.

In October 1987, the accord was repudiated outright by the LTTE following a bizarre episode in which seventeen Tamil Tigers were arrested for trying to smuggle in a cache of weapons from India. While in transit to Colombo, fifteen of the seventeen Tamil Tigers committed suicide by swallowing cyanide capsules. The LTTE, claiming that the prisoners had been forced to take such a desperate action while in custody, immediately made a number of retaliatory attacks on Sinhalese settlements in the east. The IPKF, ill suited to counter-guerrilla warfare, was accused by many Sinhalese of allowing the attacks to take place. Jayewardene angrily declared that if the Indians could not protect the citizenry, he would order the IPKF to withdraw from the province and put his own soldiers on the job. India denounced the Tamil Tigers for attempting to wreck the accord and declared its determination to maintain law and order. The IPKF then began what was the first of its many operations against the Tamil Tigers. The Jaffna operation was costly, taking the lives of over 200 Indian soldiers and bringing home to India the realization that it had underestimated the strength and persistence of the Tamil Tigers. Taking advantage of the distractions in the north, Sinhalese extremists of the JVP gained strength in the south, successfully carrying out several arms raids on military camps. The most spectacular attack the JVP attempted occurred in August 1987 during a government parliamentary group meeting, when a hand grenade exploded near the table where President Jayewardene and Prime Minister Premadasa were sitting.

In 1988 Jayewardene continued working toward the controversial merger of the Northern and Eastern provinces, where the Tamil separatists had long been active. The merger, initially a temporary measure, was a central part of the 1987 Indo-Sri Lankan Accord under which India sought to ensure that an elected provincial council in the Tamil majority areas enjoyed substantial power to administer Tamil affairs. Although the LTTE boycotted the provincial election and tried to disrupt it, as did the JVP, there was a surprisingly high voter turnout. Still, few Sinhalese voted, and without LTTE participation, the credibility of the provincial council was limited. Furthermore, many viewed the resulting provincial government, dominated by the Tigers' main rival group, the Eelam People's Revolutionary Liberation Front, as a creation of India.

As 1988 drew to a close, Jayewardene announced he would retire and not run in the presidential election scheduled for December. Premadasa, the UNP's candidate, ran against two others, the SLFP's Bandaranaike and a relative political unknown. As the presidential election approached, JVP subversives concentrated on crippling essential services such as buses and trains, fuel supplies, and banking. The UNP's presidential candidate, Premadasa, stated that this was a battle between the ballot and the bullet and that the bullet must not win. The election proved to be the bloodiest in Sri Lanka's history, but the ballot did in fact prevail, with voters defying threats from Tamil as well as Sinhalese extremists. Despite predictions that the voter turnout would not exceed 30 percent in contrast to the 80 percent turnout in the past presidential election, well over 50 percent of the nations's 9.4 million eligible voters showed up at the polls. Premadasa won by a large margin over his closest rival, Sirimavo Bandaranaike.

One of Premadasa's first problems when he took over on January 2, 1989, was what to do about the JVP, which was believed responsible for numerous assassinations the year before. In his victory speech, Premadasa appealed to the JVP to enter into talks with him. The Sinhalese extremists initially were willing to distinguish between him and the outgoing president, Jayewardene, whom they had earlier tried to assassinate. The JVP, which unleashed a steady barrage of anti-Indian propaganda against "Indian expansionism, invading Indian armies," was impressed by Premadasa's anti-Indian rhetoric and even went so far as to praise him as a patriotic leader. Encouraged, Premadasa used the occasion of Sri Lanka's Independence Day celebrations to make an impassioned appeal for an end to the killings on the island and proceeded a little more than a week later to hold the nation's first parliamentary elections in eleven years. The nation had endured another challenge to its democratic institutions despite the killing of substantial numbers of candidates of various parties and their supporters by the LTTE and JVP.

In May 1989, LTTE guerrillas decided to negotiate with the new government of Premadasa, holding the first direct peace talks between the Sri Lankan government and the Tamil Tiger separatist fighters since July 1985. The unexpected decision underscored the fundamental changes that had been taking place among Sri Lanka's Tamil political groups. Political differences among the groups had widened, with some former separatist groups now represented in the Northeastern Provincial Council and in the national Parliament. The LTTE, the remaining guerrilla army in the field, had been isolated and weakened by prolonged combat with Indian troops. Premadasa, stating that he wanted to settle the Tamil problem among Sri Lankans, circumvented Indian participation in the talks. On June 1, Premadasa abruptly called for the withdrawal by the end of July of 45,000 Indian soldiers still in Sri Lanka. Gandhi, for his part, was determined not to lose face by having his forces hurried out of Sri Lanka too quickly in an election year. Yet, India's participation in the struggle had been costly in human, military, and diplomatic terms. The Indian troops were viewed suspiciously by most Sri Lankans, and India's police action had made its neighbors in South Asia uneasy. The Indians, with more than 1,200 casualties, accepted that it was time to go—but at their own pace.

There were critics who believed that Premadasa, who in June 1989 was forced to reimpose a state of national emergency after having lifted it for the previous six months, was making unrealistic demands on India to withdraw quickly; they also believed that he was unwisely pandering to prevalent anti-Indian emotions in order to recover from an early period of unpopularity. Although the argument was made that the longer the IPKF stayed in Sri Lanka, the stronger the support would be for the JVP, it was questionable whether the Sri Lankan military, which admittedly had grown dramatically since 1983, could have successfully controlled the ferocity of both the Tamil Tigers and the JVP without Indian help. Yet, as one Sri Lankan politician admitted, the president was in the unenviable position of having the "IPKF holding his legs and the JVP at his throat."

The Tamil Tigers, despite their truce with the government, remained a ruthless and effective military force. It was not known in 1990 how long their gesture of conciliation would last. The JVP had lost its charismatic leader, Rohana Wijewera, in November 1989, when he was captured and subsequently killed by government security forces, and it had been brutally suppressed by the government in late 1989 and early 1990. The group, however, still was active and might ultimately pose the most dangerous long-term threat to Sri Lanka's national security.

Premadasa placed much faith in his poverty alleviation plan—his remedy for much of the unrest plaguing the island. But the plan as originally unveiled alarmed both foreign lenders and many Sri Lankan technocrats and would have greatly burdened the already huge government budget. After a period of mounting defense expenditures, systematic destruction of the economic infrastructure by subversives, a worldwide decline in demand for Sri Lanka's traditional raw products, and the partial eclipse of its once robust tourist industry, Premadasa's plan, while well intentioned, was perceived as economically unfeasible.

As Sri Lanka entered the 1990s, there were no clear answers as to whether its democratic institutions could survive another onslaught of anarchy, terror, and violence. As India withdrew its last troops from the island amid charges that it had failed to perform its primary task of disarming Tamil separatists, it, too, accused Sri Lanka of not having fully implemented the 1987 Indo-Sri Lankan Accord—charging that there had not been an adequate devolution of central power. Yet Premadasa has declared that "Sri Lanka's problems must be settled among Sri Lankans."

Certainly Sri Lanka's problems were increasingly complex and difficult to comprehend. Perhaps the culture of the island with its countervailing forces and fractured institutions can be glimpsed in the somber evocation of struggle captured in lines from "Elephant," a poem written by D.H. Lawrence following a visit to Sri Lanka:

In elephants and the east are two devils, in all men maybe.
The mystery of the dark mountain of blood, reeking in
   homage, in lust, in rage,
And passive with everlasting patience. . . .

May 1, 1990   Peter R. Blood

Chapter 1. Historical Setting

Reclining and standing Buddhas at Polonnaruwa

SRI LANKA'S HISTORICAL AND CULTURAL HERITAGE covers more than 2,000 years. Known as Lanka—the "resplendent land"—in the ancient Indian epic *Ramayana*, the island has numerous other references that testify to the island's natural beauty and wealth. Islamic folklore maintains that Adam and Eve were offered refuge on the island as solace for their expulsion from the Garden of Eden. Asian poets, noting the geographical location of the island and lauding its beauty, called it the "pearl upon the brow of India." A troubled nation in the 1980s, torn apart by communal violence, Sri Lanka has more recently been called India's "fallen tear."

Sri Lanka claims a democratic tradition matched by few other developing countries, and since its independence in 1948, successive governments have been freely elected. Sri Lanka's citizens enjoy a long life expectancy, advanced health standards, and one of the highest literacy rates in the world despite the fact that the country has one of the lowest per capita incomes.

In the years since independence, Sri Lanka has experienced severe communal clashes between its Buddhist Sinhalese majority—approximately 74 percent of the population—and the country's largest minority group, the Sri Lankan Tamils, who are Hindus and comprise nearly 13 percent of the population. The communal violence that attracted the harsh scrutiny of the international media in the late 1980s can best be understood in the context of the island's complex historical development—its ancient and intricate relationship to India's civilization and its more than four centuries under colonial rule by European powers.

The Sinhalese claim to have been the earliest colonizers of Sri Lanka, first settling in the dry north-central regions as early as 500 B.C. Between the third century B.C. and the twelfth century A.D., they developed a great civilization centered around the cities of Anuradhapura and later Polonnaruwa, which was noted for its genius in hydraulic engineering—the construction of water tanks (reservoirs) and irrigation canals, for example—and its guardianship of Buddhism. State patronage gave Buddhism a heightened political importance that enabled the religion to escape the fate it had experienced in India, where it was eventually absorbed by Hinduism.

The history of Buddhism in Sri Lanka, especially its extended period of glory, is for many Sinhalese a potent symbol that links

3

the past with the present. An enduring ideology defined by two distinct elements—*sinhaladipa* (unity of the island with the Sinhalese) and *dhammadipa* (island of Buddhism)—designates the Sinhalese as custodians of Sri Lankan society. This theme finds recurrent expression in the historical chronicles composed by Buddish monks over the centuries, from the mythological founding of the Sinhalese "lion" race around 300 B.C. to the capitulation of the Kingdom of Kandy, the last independent Sinhalese polity in the early nineteenth century.

The institutions of Buddhist-Sinhalese civilization in Sri Lanka came under attack during the colonial eras of the Portuguese, the Dutch and the British. During these centuries of colonialization, the state encouraged and supported Christianity—first Roman Catholicism, then Protestantism. Most Sinhalese regard the entire period of European dominance as an unfortunate era, but most historians—Sri Lankan or otherwise—concede that British rule was relatively benign and progressive compared to that of the Dutch and Portuguese. Influenced by the ascendant philosophy of liberal reformism, the British were determined to anglicize the island, and in 1802, Sri Lanka (then called Ceylon) became Britain's first crown colony. The British gradually permitted native participation in the governmental process; and under the Donoughmore Constitution of 1931 and then the Soulbury Constitution of 1946, the franchise was dramatically extended, preparing the island for independence two years later.

Under the statesmanship of Sri Lanka's first postindependence leader, Don Stephen (D.S.) Senanayake, the country managed to rise above the bitterly divisive communal and religious emotions that later complicated the political agenda. Senanayake envisioned his country as a pluralist, multiethnic, secular state, in which minorities would be able to participate fully in government affairs. His vision for his nation soon faltered, however, and communal rivalry and confrontation appeared within the first decade of independence. Sinhalese nationalists aspired to recover the dominance in society they had lost during European rule, while Sri Lankan Tamils wanted to protect their minority community from domination or assimilation by the Sinhalese majority. No compromise was forthcoming, and as early as 1951, Tamil leaders stated that "the Tamil-speaking people in Ceylon constitute a nation distinct from that of the Sinhalese by every fundamental test of nationhood."

Sinhalese nationalists did not have to wait long before they found an eloquent champion of their cause. Solomon West Ridgeway Dias (S.W.R.D.) Bandaranaike successfully challenged the nation's Westernized rulers who were alienated from Sinhalese culture; he became prime minister in 1956. A man particularly adept at harnessing Sinhalese communal passions, Bandaranaike vowed to make Sinhala the only language of administration and education and to restore Buddhism to its former glory. The violence unleashed by his policies directly threatened the unity of the nation, and communal riots rocked the country in 1956 and 1958. Bandaranaike became a victim of the passions he unleashed. In 1959 a Buddhist monk who felt that Bandaranaike had not pushed the Buddhist-Sinhalese cause far enough assassinated the Sri Lankan leader. Bandaranaike's widow, Sirimavo Ratwatte Dias (S.R.D.) Bandaranaike, ardently carried out many of his ideas. In 1960, she became the world's first woman prime minister.

Communal tensions continued to rise over the following years. In 1972 the nation became a republic under a new constitution, which was a testimony to the ideology of Sirimavo Bandaranaike, and Buddhism was accorded special status. These reforms and new laws discriminating against Tamils in university admissions were a symbolic threat the Tamil community felt it could not ignore, and a vicious cycle of violence erupted that has plagued successive governments. Tamil agitation for separation became associated with gruesome and highly visible terrorist acts by extremists, triggering large communal riots in 1977, 1981, and 1983. During these riots, Sinhalese mobs retaliated against isolated and vulnerable Tamil communities. By the mid-1980s, the Tamil militant underground had grown in strength and posed a serious security threat to the government, and its combatants struggled for a Tamil nation—"Tamil Eelam"—by an increasing recourse to terrorism. The fundamental, unresolved problems facing society were surfacing with a previously unseen force. Foreign and domestic observers expressed concern for democratic procedures in a society driven by divisive symbols and divided by ethnic loyalties.

Origins

Ancient Indian and Sri Lankan myths and chronicles have been studied intensively and interpreted widely for their insight into the human settlement and philosophical development of the island. Confirmation of the island's first colonizers—whether the Sinhalese or Sri Lankan Tamils—has been elusive, but evidence suggests that Sri Lanka has been, since earliest times, a multiethnic society. Sri Lankan historian K.M. de Silva believes that settlement and colonization by Indo-Aryan speakers may have preceded the arrival of Dravidian settlers by several centuries, but that early mixing rendered the two ethnic groups almost physically indistinct.

Ancient Legends and Chronicles

The first major legendary reference to the island is found in the great Indian epic, the *Ramayana* (Sacred Lake of the Deeds of Rama), thought to have been written around 500 B.C. The *Ramayana* tells of the conquest of Lanka in 3000 B.C. by Rama, an incarnation of the Hindu god Vishnu. Rama's quest to save his abducted wife, Sita, from Ravanna, the demon god of Lanka, and his demon hordes, is, according to some scholars, a poetic account of the early southward expansion of Brahmanic civilization.

Buddhist Chronicles

The most valuable source of knowledge for scholars probing the legends and historical heritage of Sri Lanka is still the *Mahavamsa* (Great Genealogy or Dynasty), a chronicle compiled in Pali, the language of Theravada Buddhism, in the sixth century. Buddhist monks composed the *Mahavamsa,* which was an adaptation of an earlier and cruder fourth century epic, the *Dipavamsa* (Island Genealogy or Dynasty). The latter account was compiled to glorify Buddhism and is not a comprehensive narrative of events. The *Mahavamsa,* however, relates the rise and fall of successive Buddhist kingdoms beginning with Vijaya, the legendary colonizer of Sri Lanka and primogenitor of the Sinhalese migrant group. In the *Mahavamsa,* Vijaya is described as having arrived on the island on the day of the Buddha's death (*parinibbana*) or, more precisely, his nirvana or *nibbana* (see Glossary), his release from the cycle of life and pain. The *Mahavamsa* also lavishes praise on the Sinhalese kings who repulsed attacks by Indian Tamils.

Vijaya is the central legendary figure in the *Mahavamsa.* He was the grandson of an Indian princess from Vanga in northern India who had been abducted by an amorous lion, Simha, and son of their incestuous and half-leonine offspring. Along with 700 of his followers, Vijaya arrived in Lanka and established himself as ruler with the help of Kuveni, a local demon-worshiping princess. Although Kuveni had betrayed her own people and had given birth to two of Vijaya's children, she was banished by the ruler, who then arranged a marriage with a princess from Madurai in southeastern India. Kuveni's offspring are the folkloric ancestors of the present day Veddahs, an aboriginal people now living in scattered areas of eastern Sri Lanka (see Ethnic Groups, ch. 2). Many scholars believe that the legend of Vijaya provides a glimpse into the early settlement of the island. Around the fifth century B.C., the first bands of Sri Lankan colonists are believed to have come from the coastal areas of northern India. The chronicles support evidence that the royal progeny of Vijaya often sought wives from the Pandyan and other Dravidian (Tamil) kingdoms of southern India. The chronicles also tell of an early and constant migration of artisan and mercantile Tamils to Sri Lanka.

From the fifth century A.D onward, periodic palace intrigues and religious heresies weakened Buddhist institutions leaving Sinhalese-Buddhist culture increasingly vulnerable to successive and debilitating Tamil invasions. A chronicle, a continuation of the *Mahavamsa,* describes this decline. The main body of this chronicle, which assumed the less than grandiloquent title *Culavamsa* (Lesser Genealogy or Dynasty), was attributed to the thirteenth century poet-monk, Dhammakitti. The *Culavamsa* was later expanded by another monk the following century and, concluded by a third monk in the late eighteenth century.

The Impact of Buddhism

Buddhism was introduced to Sri Lanka in the third century B.C. from India, where it had been established by Siddartha Gautama three centuries earlier (see Buddhism, ch. 2). The powerful Indian monarch, Asoka, nurtured the new comprehensive religio-philosophical system in the third century B.C. Asoka's conversion to Buddhism marks one of the turning points in religious history because at that time, Buddhism was elevated from a minor sect to an official religion enjoying all the advantages of royal patronage. Asoka's empire, which extended over most of India, supported one of the most vigorous missionary enterprises in history.

The Buddhist tradition of chronicling events has aided the verification of historical figures. One of the most important of these figures was King Devanampiya Tissa (250–c. 207 B.C.). According to the *Mahavamsa,* Asoka's son and emissary to Sri Lanka, Mahinda, introduced the monarch to Buddhism. Devanampiya Tissa became a powerful patron of Buddhism and established the monastery of Mahavihara, which became the historic center of Theravada Buddhism in Sri Lanka.

Subsequent events also contributed to Sri Lanka's prestige in the Buddhist world. It was on the island, for example, that the oral teachings of the Buddha—the Tripitaka—were committed to writing for the first time.

Devanampiya Tissa was said to have received Buddha's right collarbone and his revered alms bowl from Asoka and to have built the Thuparama Dagoba, or stupa (Buddhist shrine), to honor these highly revered relics. Another relic, Buddha's sacred tooth, had arrived in Sri Lanka in the fourth century A.D. The possession of the Tooth Relic came to be regarded as essential for the legitimization of Sinhalese royalty and remained so until its capture and probable destruction by the Portuguese in 1560. The sacred Tooth Relic (thought by many to be a substitute) that is venerated in the Temple of the Tooth in Kandy links legendary Sri Lanka with the modern era. The annual procession of Perahera held in honor of the sacred Tooth Relic serves as a powerful unifying force for the Sinhalese in the twentieth century. Asoka's daughter, Sanghamitta, is recorded as having brought to the island a branch of the sacred bo tree under which the Buddha attained enlightenment. According to legend, the tree that grew from this branch is near the ruins of the ancient city of Anuradhapura in the north of Sri Lanka. The tree is said to be the oldest living thing in the world and is an object of great veneration.

The connection between religion, culture, language, and education and their combined influence on national identity have been an age-old pervasive force for the Sinhalese Buddhists. Devanampiya Tissa employed Asoka's strategy of merging the political state with Buddhism, supporting Buddhist institutions from the state's coffers, and locating temples close to the royal palace for greater control. With such patronage, Buddhism was positioned to evolve as the highest ethical and philosophical expression of Sinhalese culture and civilization. Buddhism appealed directly to the masses, leading to the growth of a collective Sinhalese cultural consciousness.

In contrast to the theological exclusivity of Hindu Brahmanism, the Asokan missionary approach featured preaching and carried the principles of the Buddha directly to the common people. This proselytizing had even greater success in Sri Lanka than it had in India and could be said to be the island's first experiment in mass education.

Buddhism also had a great effect on the literary development of the island. The Indo-Aryan dialect spoken by the early Sinhalese was comprehensible to missionaries from India and facilitated early attempts at translating the scriptures. The Sinhalese literati studied Pali, the language of the Buddhist scriptures, thus influencing the development of Sinhala as a literary language.

The Classical Age, 200 B.C.-A.D. 1200
Early Settlements

The first extensive Sinhalese settlements were along rivers in the dry northern zone of the island. Because early agricultural activity—primarily the cultivation of wet rice—was dependent on unreliable

Seated Buddha statue near Polonnaruwa
Courtesy Embassy of Sri Lanka, Washington

9

monsoon rains, the Sinhalese constructed canals, channels, water-storage tanks, and reservoirs to provide an elaborate irrigation system to counter the risks posed by periodic drought. Such early attempts at engineering reveal the brilliant understanding these ancient people had of hydraulic principles and trigonometry. The discovery of the principle of the valve tower, or valve pit, for regulating the escape of water is credited to Sinhalese ingenuity more than 2,000 years ago. By the first century A.D., several large-scale irrigation works had been completed.

The mastery of hydraulic engineering and irrigated agriculture facilitated the concentration of large numbers of people in the northern dry zone, where early settlements appeared to be under the control of semi-independent rulers (see Land Use and Settlement Patterns, ch. 2). In time, the mechanisms for political control became more refined, and the city-state of Anuradhapura emerged and attempted to gain sovereignty over the entire island. The state-sponsored flowering of Buddhist art and architecture and the construction of complex and extensive hydraulic works exemplify what is known as Sri Lanka's classical age, which roughly parallels the period between the rise and fall of Anuradhapura (from ca. 200 B.C. to ca. A.D. 993).

The Sinhalese kingdom at Anuradhapura was in many ways typical of other ancient hydraulic societies because it lacked a rigid, authoritarian and heavily bureaucratic structure. Theorists have attributed Anuradhapura's decentralized character to its feudal basis, which was, however, a feudalism unlike that found in Europe. The institution of caste formed the basis of social stratification in ancient Sinhalese society and determined a person's social obligation, and position within the hierarchy.

The caste system in Sri Lanka developed its own characteristics. Although it shared an occupational role with its Indian prototype, caste in Sri Lanka developed neither the exclusive Brahmanical social hierarchy nor, to any significant degree, the concept of defilement by contact with impure persons or substances that was central to the Indian caste system. The claims of the Kshatriya (warrior caste) to royalty were a moderating influence on caste, but more profound was the influence of Buddhism, which lessened the severity of the institution. The monarch theoretically held absolute powers but was nevertheless expected to conform to the rules of dharma, or universal laws governing human existence and conduct (see Religion, ch. 2).

The king was traditionally entitled to land revenue equivalent to one-sixth of the produce in his domain. Furthermore, his subjects owed him a kind of caste-based compulsory labor (*rajakariya* in Sinhala) as a condition for holding land and were required to provide labor for road construction, irrigation projects, and other public works. During the later colonial period, the Europeans exploited the institution of *rajakariya,* which was destined to become an important moral and economic issue in the nineteenth century (see European Encroachment and Dominance, 1500–1948, this ch.).

Social divisions arose over the centuries between those engaged in agriculture and those engaged in nonagricultural occupations. The Govi (cultivators—see Glossary) belonged to the highest Sinhalese caste (Goyigama) and remained so in the late twentieth century. All Sri Lankan heads of state have, since independence, belonged to the Goyigama caste, as do about half of all Sinhalese. The importance of cultivation on the island is also reflected in the caste structure of the Hindu Tamils, among whom the Vellala (cultivator) is the highest caste.

Rise of Sinhalese and Tamil Ethnic Awareness

Because the *Mahavamsa* is essentially a chronicle of the early Sinhalese-Buddhist royalty on the island, it does not provide information on the island's early ethnic distributions. There is, for instance, only scant evidence as to when the first Tamil settlements were established. Tamil literary sources, however, speak of active trading centers in southern India as early as the third century B.C. and it is probable that these centers had at least some contact with settlements in northern Sri Lanka. There is some debate among historians as to whether settlement by Indo-Aryan speakers preceded settlement by Dravidian-speaking Tamils, but there is no dispute over the fact that Sri Lanka, from its earliest recorded history, was a multiethnic society. Evidence suggests that during the early centuries of Sri Lankan history there was considerable harmony between the Sinhalese and Tamils.

The peace and stability of the island were first significantly affected around 237 B.C. when two adventurers from southern India, Sena and Guttika, usurped the Sinhalese throne at Anuradhapura. Their combined twenty-two-year rule marked the first time Sri Lanka was ruled by Tamils. The two were subsequently murdered, and the Sinhalese royal dynasty was restored. In 145 B.C., a Tamil general named Elara, of the Chola dynasty (which ruled much of India from the ninth to twelfth centuries A.D.), took over the throne at Anuradhapura and ruled for forty-four years. A Sinhalese king, Dutthagamani (or Duttugemunu), waged a fifteen-year campaign against the Tamil monarch and finally deposed him.

Dutthagamani is the outstanding hero of the *Mahavamsa,* and his war against Elara is sometimes depicted in contemporary accounts as a major racial confrontation between Tamils and Sinhalese. A less biased and more factual interpretation, according to Sri Lankan historian K.M. de Silva, must take into consideration the large reserve of support Elara had among the Sinhalese. Furthermore, another Sri Lankan historian, Sinnappah Arasaratnam, argues that the war was a dynastic struggle that was purely political in nature. As a result of Dutthagamani's victory, Anuradhapura became the locus of power on the island. Arasaratnam suggests the conflict recorded in the *Mahavamsa* marked the beginning of Sinhalese nationalism and that Dutthagamani's victory is commonly interpreted as a confirmation that the island was a preserve for the Sinhalese and Buddhism. The historian maintains that the story is still capable of stirring the religio-communal passions of the Sinhalese.

The Tamil threat to the Sinhalese Buddhist kingdoms had become very real in the fifth and sixth centuries A.D. Three Hindu empires in southern India—the Pandya, Pallava, and Chola—were becoming more assertive. The Sinhalese perception of this threat intensified because in India, Buddhism—vulnerable to pressure and absorption by Hinduism—had already receded. Tamil ethnic and religious consciousness also matured during this period. In terms of culture, language, and religion, the Tamils had identified themselves as Dravidian, Tamil, and Hindu, respectively.

Another Sinhalese king praised in the *Mahavamsa* is Dhatusena (459–77), who, in the fifth century A.D., liberated Anuradhapura from a quarter-century of Pandyan rule. The king was also honored as a generous patron of Buddhism and as a builder of water storage tanks. Dhatusena was killed by his son, Kasyapa (477–95), who is regarded as a great villain in Sri Lankan history. In fear of retribution from his exiled brother, the parricide moved the capital from Anuradhapura to Sigiriya, a fortress and palace perched on a monolithic rock 180 meters high. Although the capital was returned to Anuradhapura after Kasyapa was dethroned, Sigiriya is an architectural and engineering feat displayed in an inaccessible redoubt. The rock fortress eventually fell to Kasyapa's brother, who received help from an army of Indian mercenaries.

In the seventh century A.D., Tamil influence became firmly embedded in the island's culture when Sinhalese Prince Manavamma seized the throne with Pallava assistance. The dynasty that Manavamma established was heavily indebted to Pallava patronage and continued for almost three centuries. During this time, Pallava influence extended to architecture and sculpture, both of which bear noticeable Hindu motifs.

By the middle of the ninth century, the Pandyans had risen to a position of ascendancy in southern India, invaded northern Sri Lanka, and sacked Anuradhapura. The Pandyans demanded an indemnity as a price for their withdrawal. Shortly after the Pandyan departure, however, the Sinhalese invaded Pandya in support of a rival prince, and the Indian city of Madurai was sacked in the process.

In the tenth century, the Sinhalese again sent an invading army to India, this time to aid the Pandyan king against the Cholas. The Pandyan king was defeated and fled to Sri Lanka, carrying with him the royal insignia. The Chola, initially under Rajaraja the Great (A.D. 985–1018), were impatient to recapture the royal insignia; they sacked Anuradhapura in A.D. 993 and annexed Rajarata—the heartland of the Sinhalese kingdom—to the Chola Empire. King Mahinda V, the last of the Sinhalese monarchs to rule from Anuradhapura, fled to Rohana, where he reigned until 1017, when the Chola took him prisoner. He subsequently died in India in 1029.

Under the rule of Rajaraja's son, Rajendra (1018–35), the Chola Empire grew stronger, to the extent that it posed a threat to states as far away as the empire of Sri Vijaya in modern Malaysia and Sumatra in Indonesia. For seventy-five years, Sri Lanka was ruled directly as a Chola province. During this period, Hinduism flourished, and Buddhism received a serious setback. After the destruction of Anuradhapura, the Chola set up their capital farther to the southeast, at Polonnaruwa, a strategically defensible location near the Mahaweli Ganga, a river that offered good protection against potential invaders from the southern Sinhalese kingdom of Ruhunu (see fig. 2). When the Sinhalese kings regained their dominance, they chose not to reestablish themselves at Anuradhapura because Polonnaruwa offered better geographical security from any future invasions from southern India. The area surrounding the new capital already had a well-developed irrigation system and a number of water storage tanks in the vicinity, including the great Minneriya Tank and its feeder canals built by King Mahasena (A.D. 274–301), the last of the Sinhalese monarchs mentioned in the *Mahavamsa*.

King Vijayabahu I drove the Chola out of Sri Lanka in A.D. 1070. Considered by many as the author of Sinhalese freedom, the king recaptured Anuradhapura but ruled from Polonnaruwa, slightly less than 100 kilometers to the southeast. During his forty-year reign, Vijayabahu I (A.D. 1070–1110) concentrated on rebuilding the Buddhist temples and monasteries that had been neglected during Chola rule. He left no clearly designated successor

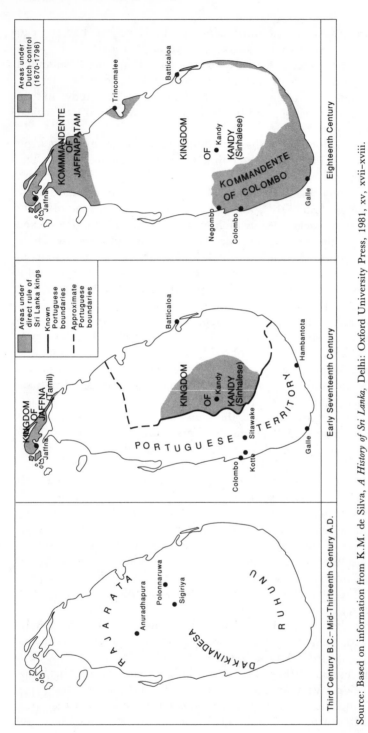

Source: Based on information from K.M. de Silva, *A History of Sri Lanka*, Delhi: Oxford University Press, 1981, xv, xvii–xviii.

Figure 2. The Early Kingdoms of Sri Lanka, Third Century B.C.–Eighteenth Century A.D.

to his throne, and a period of instability and civil war followed his rule until the rise of King Parakramabahu I, known as the Great (A.D. 1153–86).

Parakramabahu is the greatest hero of the *Culavamsa,* and under his patronage, the city of Polonnaruwa grew to rival Anuradhapura in architectural diversity and as a repository of Buddhist art. Parakramabahu was a great patron of Buddhism and a reformer as well. He reorganized the *sangha* (community of monks) and healed a longstanding schism between Mahavihara—the Theravada Buddhist monastery—and Abhayagiri—the Mahayana Buddhist monastery. Parakramabahu's reign coincided with the last great period of Sinhalese hydraulic engineering; many remarkable irrigation works were constructed during his rule, including his crowning achievement, the massive Parakrama Samudra (Sea of Parakrama or Parakrama Tank). Polonnaruwa became one of the magnificent capitals of the ancient world, and nineteenth-century British historian Sir Emerson Tenant even estimated that during Parakramabahu's rule, the population of Polonnaruwa reached 3 million—a figure, however, that is considered to be too high by twentieth-century historians.

Parakramabahu's reign was not only a time of Buddhist renaissance but also a period of religious expansionism abroad. Parakramabahu was powerful enough to send a punitive mission against the Burmese for their mistreatment of a Sri Lankan mission in 1164. The Sinhalese monarch also meddled extensively in Indian politics and invaded southern India in several unsuccessful expeditions to aid a Pandyan claimant to the throne.

Although a revered figure in Sinhalese annals, Parakramabahu is believed to have greatly strained the royal treasury and contributed to the fall of the Sinhalese kingdom. The post-Parakramabahu history of Polonnaruwa describes the destruction of the city twenty-nine years after his death and fifteen rulers later.

For the decade following Parakramabahu's death, however, a period of peace and stability ensued during the reign of King Nissankamalla (A.D. 1187–97). During Nissankamalla's rule, the Brahmanic legal system came to regulate the Sinhalese caste system. Henceforth, the highest caste stratum became identified with the cultivator caste, and land ownership conferred high status. Occupational caste became hereditary and regulated dietary and marriage codes. At the bottom of the caste strata was the Chandala, who corresponded roughly to the Indian untouchable. It was during this brief period that it became mandatory for the Sinhalese king to be a Buddhist.

Decline of the Sinhalese Kingdom, 1200-1500

Sinhalese Migration to the South

After Nissankamalla's death, a series of dynastic disputes hastened the breakup of the kingdom of Polonnaruwa. Domestic instability characterized the ensuing period, and incursions by Chola and Pandyan invaders created greater turbulence, culminating in a devastating campaign by the Kalinga, an eastern Indian dynasty. When Magha, the Kalinga king, died in 1255, another period of instability began, marking the beginning of the abandonment of Polonnaruwa and the Sinhalese migration to the southwest from the northern dry zone. The next three kings after Magha ruled from rock fortresses to the west of Polonnaruwa. The last king to rule from Polonnaruwa was Parakramabahu III (1278-93). The migration is one of the great unsolved puzzles of South Asian history and is of considerable interest to academics because of the parallel abandonment of dry-zone civilizations in modern Cambodia, northern Thailand, and Burma.

A Weakened State: Invasion, Disease, and Social Instability

The Sinhalese withdrawal from the north is sometimes attributed to the cumulative effect of invasions from southern India (a rationale that has been exploited against the Tamils in modern Sinhalese politics). This interpretation has obvious weaknesses because after each of the south Indian invasions of the preceding centuries, the Sinhalese returned to the dry zone from the hills and repaired and revived the ancient irrigation system. K.M. de Silva suggests that the cumulative effects of repeated invasions "ate into the vitals of a society already losing its vigour with age." A civilization based on a dry-zone irrigation complex presupposes a high degree of organization and a massive labor force to build and maintain the works. The decline of these public works mirrored the breakdown in the social order. Another factor that seems to have retarded the resettlement of the dry zone was the outbreak of malaria in the thirteenth century. The mosquito found ideal breeding grounds in the abandoned tanks and channels. (Malaria has often followed the destruction of irrigation works in other parts of Asia.) Indeed, all attempts at large-scale resettlement of the dry area in Sri Lanka were thwarted until the introduction of modern pesticides.

During the thirteenth century, the declining Sinhalese kingdom faced threats of invasion from India and the expanding Tamil kingdom of northern Sri Lanka. Taking advantage of Sinhalese weakness, the Tamils secured control of the valuable pearl fisheries around Jaffna Peninsula. During this time, the vast stretches of jungle that cover north-central Sri Lanka separated the Tamils and the Sinhalese. This geographical separation had important psychological and cultural implications. The Tamils in the north developed a more distinct and confident culture, backed by a resurgent Hinduism that looked to the traditions of southern India for its inspiration. Conversely, the Sinhalese were increasingly restricted to the southern and central area of the island and were fearful of the more numerous Tamils on the Indian mainland. The fact that the Hindu kingdom at Jaffna was expending most of its military resources resisting the advances of the expansionist Vijayanagara Empire (1336–1565) in India enhanced the Sinhalese ability to resist further Tamil encroachments. Some historians maintain that it was the arrival of the Portuguese in the sixteenth century that prevented the island from being overrun by south Indians.

Foreign rulers took advantage of the disturbed political state of the Sinhalese kingdom, and in the thirteenth century Chandrabhanu, a Buddhist king from Malaya, invaded the island twice. He attempted to seize the two most sacred relics of the Buddha in Sinhalese custody, the Tooth Relic and the Alms Bowl. In the early fifteenth century, the Ming dynasty Chinese interceded on behalf of King Parakramabahu VI (1412–67), an enlightened monarch who repulsed an invasion from the polity of Vijayanagara in southern India, reunited Sri Lanka, and earned renown as a patron of Buddhism and the arts. Parakramabahu VI was the last Sinhalese king to rule the entire island.

During this extended period of domestic instability and frequent foreign invasion, Sinhalese culture experienced fundamental change. Rice cultivation continued as the mainstay of agriculture but was no longer dependent on an elaborate irrigation network. In the wet zone, large-scale administrative cooperation was not as necessary as it had been before. Foreign trade was of increasing importance to the Sinhalese kings. In particular, cinnamon—in great demand by Europeans—became a prime export commodity. Because of the value of cinnamon, the city of Kotte on the west coast (near modern Colombo) became the nominal capital of the Sinhalese kingdom in the mid-fifteenth century. Still, the Sinhalese kingdom remained divided into numerous competing petty principalities.

European Encroachment and Dominance, 1500–1948

The Portuguese

By the late fifteenth century, Portugal, which had already established its dominance as a maritime power in the Atlantic, was exploring new waters. In 1497 Vasco da Gama sailed around the

Cape of Good Hope and discovered an ocean route connecting Europe with India, thus inaugurating a new era of maritime supremacy for Portugal. The Portuguese were consumed by two objectives in their empire-building efforts: to convert followers of non-Christian religions to Roman Catholicism and to capture the major share of the spice trade for the European market. To carry out their goals, the Portuguese did not seek territorial conquest, which would have been difficult given their small numbers. Instead, they tried to dominate strategic points through which trade passed. By virtue of their supremacy on the seas, their knowledge of firearms, and by what has been called their "desperate soldiering" on land, the Portuguese gained an influence in South Asia that was far out of proportion to their numerical strength.

At the onset of the European period in Sri Lanka in the sixteenth century, there were three native centers of political power: the two Sinhalese kingdoms of Kotte and Kandy and the Tamil kingdom at Jaffna. Kotte was the principal seat of Sinhalese power, and it claimed a largely imaginary overlordship not only over Kandy but also over the entire island. None of the three kingdoms, however, had the strength to assert itself over the other two and reunify the island.

In 1505 Don Lourenço de Almeida, son of the Portuguese viceroy in India, was sailing off the southwestern coast of Sri Lanka looking for Moorish ships to attack when stormy weather forced his fleet to dock at Galle. Word of these strangers who "eat hunks of white stone and drink blood (presumably wine) . . . and have guns with a noise louder than thunder . . ." spread quickly and reached King Parakramabahu VIII of Kotte (1484–1508), who offered gifts of cinnamon and elephants to the Portuguese to take back to their home port at Cochin on the Malabar Coast of southwestern India. The king also gave the Portuguese permission to build a residence in Colombo for trade purposes. Within a short time, however, Portuguese militaristic and monopolistic intentions became apparent. Their heavily fortified "trading post" at Colombo and open hostility toward the island's Muslim traders aroused Sinhalese suspicions.

Following the decline of the Chola as a maritime power in the twelfth century, Muslim trading communities in South Asia claimed a major share of commerce in the Indian Ocean and developed extensive east-west, as well as Indo-Sri Lankan, commercial trade routes. As the Portuguese expanded into the region, this flourishing Muslim trade became an irresistible target for European interlopers. The sixteenth-century Roman Catholic Church was intolerant of Islam and encouraged the Portuguese to take over the profitable shipping trade monopolized by the Moors. In addition, the Portuguese would later have another strong motive for hostility toward the Moors because the latter played an important role in the Kandyan economy, one that enabled the kingdom successfully to resist the Portuguese.

The Portuguese soon decided that the island, which they called Cilao, conveyed a strategic advantage that was necessary for protecting their coastal establishments in India and increasing Lisbon's potential for dominating Indian Ocean trade. These incentives proved irresistible, and, the Portuguese, with only a limited number of personnel, sought to extend their power over the island. They had not long to wait. Palace intrigue and then revolution in Kotte threatened the survival of the kingdom. The Portuguese skillfully exploited these developments. In 1521 Bhuvanekabahu, the ruler of Kotte, requested Portuguese aid against his brother, Mayadunne, the more able rival king who had established his independence from the Portuguese at Sitawake, a domain in the Kotte kingdom. Powerless on his own, King Bhuvanekabahu became a puppet of the Portuguese. But shortly before his death in 1551, the king successfully obtained Portuguese recognition of his grandson, Dharmapala, as his successor. Portugal pledged to protect Dharmapala from attack in return for privileges, including a continuous payment in cinnamon and permission to rebuild the fort at Colombo on a grander scale. When Bhuvanekabahu died, Dharmapala, still a child, was entrusted to the Franciscans for his education, and, in 1557, he converted to Roman Catholicism. His conversion broke the centuries-old connection between Buddhism and the state, and a great majority of Sinhalese immediately disqualified the young monarch from any claim to the throne. The rival king at Sitawake exploited the issue of the prince's conversion and accused Dharmapala of being a puppet of a foreign power.

Before long, rival King Mayadunne had annexed much of the Kotte kingdom and was threatening the security of the capital city itself. The Portuguese were obliged to defend Dharmapala (and their own credibility) because the ruler lacked a popular following. They were subsequently forced to abandon Kotte and retreat to Colombo, taking the despised puppet king with them. Mayadunne and, later, his son, Rajasinha, besieged Colombo many times. The latter was so successful that the Portuguese were once even forced to eat the flesh of their dead to avoid starvation. The Portuguese would probably have lost their holdings in Sri Lanka had they not had maritime superiority and been able to send reinforcements by sea from their base at Goa on the western coast of India.

The Kingdom of Sitawake put up the most vigorous opposition
to Western imperialism in the island's history. For the seventy-
three-year period of its existence, Sitawake (1521–94) rose to become the predominant power on the island, with only the Tamil
kingdom at Jaffna and the Portuguese fort at Colombo beyond its
control. When Rajasinha died in 1593, no effective successors were
left to consolidate his gains, and the kingdom collapsed as quickly
as it had arisen.

Dharmapala, despised by his countrymen and totally compromised by the Portuguese, was deprived of all his royal duties
and became completely manipulated by the Portuguese advisers
surrounding him. In 1580 the Franciscans persuaded him to make
out a deed donating his dominions to the king of Portugal. When
Dharmapala died in 1597, the Portuguese emissary, the captain-
general, took formal possession of the kingdom.

Portuguese missionaries had also been busily involving themselves in the affairs of the Tamil kingdom at Jaffna, converting
almost the entire island of Mannar to Roman Catholicism by 1544.
The reaction of Sangily, king of Jaffna, however, was to lead an
expedition to Mannar and decapitate the resident priest and about
600 of his congregation. The king of Portugal took this as a personal affront and sent several expeditions against Jaffna. The Portuguese, having disposed of the Tamil king who fled south, installed
one of the Tamil princes on the throne, obliging him to pay an
annual tribute. In 1619 Lisbon annexed the Kingdom of Jaffna.

After the annexation of Jaffna, only the central highland Kingdom of Kandy—the last remnant of Buddhist Sinhalese power—
remained independent of Portuguese control. The kingdom acquired a new significance as custodian of Sinhalese nationalism.
The Portuguese attempted the same strategy they had used successfully at Kotte and Jaffna and set up a puppet on the throne.
They were able to put a queen on the Kandyan throne and even
to have her baptized. But despite considerable Portuguese help,
she was not able to retain power. The Portuguese spent the next
half century trying in vain to expand their control over the Kingdom of Kandy. In one expedition in 1630, the Kandyans ambushed
and massacred the whole Portuguese force, including the captain-
general. The Kandyans fomented rebellion and consistently frustrated Portuguese attempts to expand into the interior.

The areas the Portuguese claimed to control in Sri Lanka were
part of what they majestically called the Estado da India and were
governed in name by the viceroy in Goa, who represented the king.
But in actuality, from headquarters in Colombo, the captain-
general, a subordinate of the viceroy, directly ruled Sri Lanka with

Gadaladeniya Temple, fourteenth century
Courtesy Embassy of Sri Lanka, Washington

all the affectations of royalty once reserved for the Sinhalese kings.

The Portuguese did not try to alter the existing basic structure of native administration. Although Portuguese governors were put in charge of each province, the customary hierarchy, determined by caste and land ownership, remained unchanged. Traditional Sinhalese institutions were maintained and placed at the service of the new rulers. Portuguese administrators offered land grants to Europeans and Sinhalese in place of salaries, and the traditional compulsory labor obligation was used for construction and military purposes.

The Portuguese tried vigorously, if not fanatically, to force religious and, to a lesser extent, educational, change in Sri Lanka. They discriminated against other religions with a vengeance, destroyed Buddhist and Hindu temples, and gave the temple lands to Roman Catholic religious orders. Buddhist monks fled to Kandy, which became a refuge for people disaffected with colonial rule. One of the most durable legacies of the Portuguese was the conversion of a large number of Sinhalese and Tamils to Roman Catholicism. Although small pockets of Nestorian Christianity had existed in Sri Lanka, the Portuguese were the first to propagate Christianity on a mass scale.

Sixteenth-century Portuguese Catholicism was intolerant. But perhaps because it caught Buddhism at its nadir, it nevertheless

21

became rooted firmly enough on the island to survive the subsequent persecutions of the Protestant Dutch Reformists. The Roman Catholic Church was especially effective in fishing communities—both Sinhalese and Tamil—and contributed to the upward mobility of the castes associated with this occupation. Portuguese emphasis on proselytization spurred the development and standardization of educational institutions. In order to convert the masses, mission schools were opened, with instruction in Portuguese and Sinhalese or Tamil. Many Sinhalese converts assumed Portuguese names. The rise of many families influential in the twentieth century dates from this period. For a while, Portuguese became not only the language of the upper classes of Sri Lanka but also the lingua franca of prominence in the Asian maritime world.

The Dutch

The Dutch became involved in the politics of the Indian Ocean in the beginning of the seventeenth century. Headquartered at Batavia in modern Indonesia, the Dutch moved to wrest control of the highly profitable spice trade from the Portuguese. The Dutch began negotiations with King Rajasinha II of Kandy in 1638. A treaty assured the king assistance in his war against the Portuguese in exchange for a monopoly of the island's major trade goods, particularly cinnamon. Rajasinha also promised to pay the Dutch's war-related expenses. The Portuguese fiercely resisted the Dutch and the Kandyans and were expelled only gradually from their strongholds. The Dutch captured the eastern ports of Trincomalee and Batticaloa in 1639 and restored them to the Sinhalese. But when the southwestern and western ports of Galle and Negombo fell in 1640, the Dutch refused to turn them over to the king of Kandy. The Dutch claimed that Rajasinha had not reimbursed them for their vastly inflated claims for military expenditures. This pretext allowed the Dutch to control the island's richest cinnamon lands. The Dutch ultimately presented the king of Kandy with such a large bill for help against the Portuguese that the king could never hope to repay it. After extensive fighting, the Portuguese surrendered Colombo in 1656 and Jaffna, their last stronghold, in 1658. Superior economic resources and greater naval power enabled the Dutch to dominate the Indian Ocean. They attacked Portuguese positions throughout South Asia and in the end allowed their adversaries to keep only their settlement at Goa.

The king of Kandy soon realized that he had replaced one foe with another and proceeded to incite rebellion in the lowlands where the Dutch held sway. He even attempted to ally the British in Madras in his struggle to oust the Dutch. These efforts ended with a serious rebellion against his rule in 1664. The Dutch profited from this period of instability and extended the territory under their control. They took over the remaining harbors and completely cordoned off Kandy, thereby making the highland kingdom landlocked and preventing it from allying itself with another foreign power (see fig. 2). This strategy, combined with a concerted Dutch display of force, subdued the Kandyan kings. Henceforth, Kandy was unable to offer significant resistance except in its internal frontier regions. The Dutch and the Kingdom of Kandy eventually settled down to an uneasy modus vivendi, partly because the Dutch became less aggressive. Despite underlying hostility between Kandy and the Dutch, open warfare between them occurred only once—in 1762—when the Dutch, exasperated by Kandy's provocation of riots in the lowlands, launched a punitive expedition. The expedition met with disaster, but a better-planned second expedition in 1765 forced the Kandyans to sign a treaty that gave the Dutch sovereignty over the lowlands. The Dutch, however, maintained their pretension that they administered the territories under their control as agents of the Kandyan ruler.

After taking political control of the island, the Dutch proceeded to monopolize trade. This monopoly was at first limited to cinnamon and elephants but later extended to other goods. Control was vested in the Dutch East India Company, a joint-stock corporation, which had been established for the purpose of carrying out trade with the islands of Indonesia but was later called upon to exercise sovereign responsibilities in many parts of Asia.

The Dutch tried with little success to supplant Roman Catholicism with Protestantism. They rewarded native conversion to the Dutch Reformed Church with promises of upward mobility, but Catholicism was too deeply rooted. (In the 1980s, the majority of Sri Lankan Christians remained Roman Catholics.) The Dutch were far more tolerant of the indigenous religions than the Portuguese; they prohibited open Buddhist and Hindu religious observance in urban areas, but did not interfere with these practices in rural areas. The Dutch banned Roman Catholic practices, however. They regarded Portuguese power and Catholicism as mutually interdependent and strove to safeguard against the reemergence of the former by persecuting the latter. They harassed Catholics and constructed Protestant chapels on confiscated church property.

The Dutch contributed significantly to the evolution of the judicial, and, to a lesser extent, administrative systems on the island. They codified indigenous law and customs that did not conflict directly with Dutch-Roman jurisprudence. The outstanding

example was Dutch codification of the Tamil legal code of Jaffna—
the Thesavalamai. To a small degree, the Dutch altered the traditional land grant and tenure system, but they usually followed the
Portuguese pattern of minimal interference with indigenous social
and cultural institutions. The provincial governors of the territories of Jaffnapatam, Colombo, and Trincomalee were Dutch. These
rulers also supervised various local officials, most of whom were
the traditional *mudaliyar* (headmen).

The Dutch, like the Portuguese before them, tried to entice their
fellow countrymen to settle in Sri Lanka, but attempts to lure members of the upper class, especially women, were not very successful. Lower-ranking military recruits, however, responded to the
incentive of free land, and their marriages to local women added
another group to the island's already small but established population of Eurasians—the Portuguese Burghers. The Dutch Burghers
formed a separate and privileged ethnic group on the island in the
twentieth century.

During the Dutch period, social differences between lowland and
highland Sinhalese hardened, forming two culturally and politically distinct groups. Western customs and laws increasingly influenced the lowland Sinhalese, who generally enjoyed a higher
standard of living and greater literacy. Despite their relative economic and political decline, the highland Sinhalese were nonetheless proud to have retained their political independence from the
Europeans and thus considered themselves superior to the lowland
Sinhalese.

The British

Early Contacts

In 1592 an English privateer attacked the Portuguese off the
southwestern port of Galle. This action was England's first recorded
contact with Sri Lanka. A decade later, Ralph Fitch, traveling from
India, became the first known English visitor to Sri Lanka. The
English did not record their first in-depth impressions of the island
until the mid-seventeenth century, when Robert Knox, a sailor,
was captured when his ship docked for repairs near Trincomalee.
The Kandyans kept him prisoner between 1660 and 1680. After
his escape, Knox wrote a popular book entitled *An Historical Relation of the Island of Ceylon* in which he described his years among
his "decadent" captors.

By the mid-eighteenth century, it was apparent that the Mughal
Empire (1526–1757) in India faced imminent collapse, and the
major European powers were positioning themselves to fill the power

vacuum in the subcontinent. Dutch holdings on Sri Lanka were challenged in time by the British, who had an interest in the excellent harbor at Trincomalee. The British interest in procuring an all-weather port was whetted when they almost lost the Indian port of Madras to the French in 1758. The Dutch refused to grant the British permission to dock ships at Trincomalee (after The Netherlands's decision to support the French in the American War of Independence), goading the British into action. After skirmishing with both the Dutch and French, the British took Trincomalee in 1796 and proceeded to expel the Dutch from the island.

The British Replace the Dutch

In 1766 the Dutch had forced the Kandyans to sign a treaty, which the Kandyans later considered so harsh that they immediately began searching for foreign assistance in expelling their foes. They approached the British in 1762, 1782, and 1795. The first Kandyan missions failed, but in 1795, British emissaries offered a draft treaty that would extend military aid in return for control of the seacoast and a monopoly of the cinnamon trade. The Kandyan king unsuccessfully sought better terms, and the British managed to oust the Dutch without significant help in 1796.

The Kandyans' search for foreign assistance against the Dutch was a mistake because they simply replaced a relatively weak master with a powerful one. Britain was emerging as the unchallenged leader in the new age of the Industrial Revolution, a time of technological invention, economic innovations, and imperialist expansion. The nations that had launched the first phase of European imperialism in Asia—the Portuguese and the Dutch—had already exhausted themselves.

While peace negotiations were under way in Europe in 1796, the British assumed Sri Lanka would eventually be restored to the Dutch. By 1797 however, London had decided to retain the island as a British possession. The government compelled the British East India Company to share in the administration of the island and guaranteed the company a monopoly of trade, especially the moderately profitable—but no longer robust—cinnamon trade. The governor of the island was responsible for law and order, but financial and commercial matters were under the control of the director of the East India Company. This system of "dual control" lasted from 1798 to 1802. After the Dutch formally ceded the island to the British in the 1801 Peace of Amiens, Sri Lanka became Britain's first crown colony. Following Lord Nelson's naval victory over the French at Trafalgar in 1805, British superiority on the seas was unchallenged and provided new security for the British colonies in Asia.

Once the British had established themselves in Sri Lanka, they aggressively expanded their territorial possessions by a combination of annexation and intervention, a policy that paralleled the approach pursued by Lord Wellesley in India in the early nineteenth century. This strategy directly threatened the continued existence of the Kingdom of Kandy. Unrest at the Kandyan court between a ruling dynasty of alien, southern Indian antecedents and powerful, indigenous Sinhalese chieftains provided opportunities for British interference. The intrigue of the king's chief minister precipitated the first Kandyan war (1803). With the minister's knowledge, a British force marched on Kandy, but the force was ill prepared for such an ambitious venture and its leaders were misinformed of the extent of the king's unpopularity. The British expedition was at first successful, but on the return march, it was plagued by disease, and the garrison left behind was decimated. During the next decade, no concerted attempt was made to take Kandy. But in 1815 the British had another opportunity. The king had antagonized local Sinhalese chiefs and further alienated the Sinhalese people by actions against Buddhist monks and temple property. In 1815 the Kandyan rebels invited the British to intervene. The governor quickly responded by sending a well-prepared force to Kandy; the king fled with hardly a shot fired.

Kandyan headmen and the British signed a treaty known as the Kandyan Convention in March 1815. The treaty decreed that the Kandyan provinces be brought under British sovereignty and that all the traditional privileges of the chiefs be maintained. The Kingdom of Kandy was also to be governed according to its customary Buddhist laws and institutions but would be under the administration of a British "resident" at Kandy, who would, in all but name, take the place of the monarch.

In general, the old system was allowed to continue, but its future was bleak because of the great incongruity between the principles on which the British administration was based and the principles of the Kandyan hierarchy. Because the changes under the treaty tended to diminish the power and influence of the chiefs, the British introduced the new procedures with great caution. The monks, in particular, resented the virtual disappearance of the monarchy, which was their traditional source of support. They also resented the monarchy's replacement by a foreign and impartial government. Troubled by the corresponding decline in their status, the monks began to stir up political and religious discontent among the Kandyans almost immediately following the British

Kandyan dancer,
Temple of the Tooth
Courtesy Doranne Jacobson

annexation. The popular and widespread rebellion that followed was suppressed with great severity. When hostilities ended in 1818, the British issued a proclamation that brought the Kandyan provinces under closer control. British agents usurped the powers and privileges of the chiefs and became the arbitrators of provincial authority. Finally, the British reduced the institutional privileges accorded Buddhism, in effect placing the religion on an equal footing with other religions. With the final British consolidation over Kandy, the country fell under the control of a single power—for the first time since the twelfth-century rule of Parakramabahu I and Nissankamalla.

Modernization and Reform

According to Sri Lankan historian Zeylanicus, each of the three epochs of European rule on the island lasted roughly 150 years, but rather than being assessed separately, these epochs should be thought of collectively as a "mighty cantilever of time with the Pax Britannica as the central pillar." Many British institutions have survived and currently have a direct and lasting influence on cultural and political events. Historian E.F.C. Ludowyck concurs, stating that whatever the Portuguese and Dutch did, the British improved upon. He attributed this accomplishment to British grounding in liberalism, a belief in the emancipation of slaves, the absence of religious persecution, and conscious attempts to maintain good relations between the rulers and the ruled.

27

When the British first conquered the maritime provinces of Sri Lanka, the indigenous population of the island was estimated at only 800,000. When the British left a century and a half later, the population had grown to more than 7 million. Over a relatively short period, the island had developed an economy capable of supporting the burgeoning population. Roads, railways, schools, hospitals, hydroelectric projects, and large well-operated agricultural plantations provided the infrastructure for a viable national economy.

In the early years of British colonization, Sri Lanka was not considered a great economic asset but was viewed instead almost exclusively in terms of its strategic value. By the 1820s, however, this perception was changing. As governor, Sir Edward Barnes was responsible for consolidating British military control over the Kandyan provinces through a program of vigorous road construction. He also began experimenting with a variety of commercial crops, such as coffee. These experiments provided the foundation of the plantation system that was launched a decade later. In administrative matters, the British were initially careful not to change the existing social order too quickly and were not inclined to mingle socially. A sharp distinction was made between the rulers and the ruled, but in time the distinction became less defined. The governor, who held all executive and legislative power, had an advisory council made up of colonial officials with top posts filled by members of a civil service recruited in Britain. The governor was under the director of the Colonial Office in London but was given whatever discretionary powers he needed to balance the colony's budget and to make sure that the colony brought in enough revenue to cover its military and administrative expenses.

By the early 1830s, the British had almost finished consolidating their position in Sri Lanka and began to take more of an interest in securing the island's political stability and economic profitability. A new wave of thought, influenced by the reformist political ideology articulated by Jeremy Bentham and James Mill, promised to change fundamentally Britain's relationship to its colonies. Known as utilitarianism, and later as philosophical radicalism, it promoted the idea of democracy and individual liberty. This philosophy sponsored the idea of the trusteeship, i.e., that new territories would be considered trusts and would receive all the benefits of British liberalism. These philosophical abstractions were put into practical use with the recommendations of a commission led by W.M.G. Colebrooke and C.H. Cameron. Their *Colebrooke Report* (1831–32) was an important document in the history of the island. G.C. Mendis, considered by many to be the doyen of modern Sri

Lankan history, considers the Colebrooke-Cameron reforms to be the dividing line between the past and present in Sri Lanka.

The Colebrooke-Cameron Reforms

In 1829 the British Colonial Office sent a Royal Commission of Eastern Inquiry—the Colebrooke-Cameron Commission—to assess the administration of the island. The legal and economic proposals made by the commission in 1833 were innovative and radical. The proposed reforms opposed mercantilism, state monopolies, discriminatory administrative regulations, and, in general, any interference in the economy. Many of the proposals were adopted and helped set a pattern of administrative, economic, judicial, and educational development that continued into the next century.

The commission worked to end the protested administrative division of the country along ethnic and cultural lines into low-country Sinhalese, Kandyan Sinhalese, and Tamil areas. The commission proposed instead that the country be put under one uniform administrative system, which was to be divided into five provinces. Colebrooke believed that in the past, separate administrative systems had encouraged social and cultural divisions, and that the first step toward the creation of a modern nation was the administrative unification of the country. Cameron applied the same principle to the judicial system, which he proposed be unified into one system and be extended to all classes of people, offering everyone equal rights in the eyes of the law. His recommendations were adopted and enforced under the Charter of Justice in 1833.

The commissioners also favored the decentralization of executive power in the government. They stripped away many of the autocratic powers vested in the governor, replacing his advisory council with an Executive Council, which included both official and unofficial nominees. The Executive Council appointed the members of the Legislative Council, which functioned as a forum for discussion of legislative matters. The Legislative Council placed special emphasis on Sri Lankan membership, and in 1833 three of the fifteen members were Sri Lankans. The governor nominated them to represent low-country Sinhalese, Burghers, and Tamils, respectively. The commissioners also voted to change the exclusively British character of the administrative services and recommended that the civil service include local citizens. These proposed constitutional reforms were revolutionary—far more liberal than the legal systems of any other European colony.

The opening of the Ceylon Civil Service to Sri Lankans required that a new emphasis be placed on English education. In time, the opening contributed to the creation of a Westernized elite, whose members would spearhead the drive for independence in the twentieth century. The Colebrooke-Cameron Commission emphasized the standardization of educational curriculum and advocated the substitution of English for local languages. Local English schools were established, and the missionary schools that had previously taught in the vernacular also adopted English.

Economic Innovations

The Colebrooke-Cameron reforms had an immediate impact on the economic development of the island. Many features of the economic structure the reforms helped put into place still exist. The commission advocated a laissez-faire economy. To encourage free trade, the government monopolies over cinnamon cultivation and trade were abolished. Traditional institutions, such as land tenure by *accommodessan* (the granting of land for cultivation, as opposed to its outright sale), was abolished, as was the *rajakariya* system. *Rajakariya* was opposed not only on moral grounds but also because it slowed the growth of private enterprise, impeded the creation of a land market, and interfered with the free movement of labor.

In the mid-1830s, the British began to experiment with a variety of plantation crops in Sri Lanka, using many of the technological innovations developed earlier from their experience in Jamaica. Within fifteen years, one of these crops, coffee, became so successful that it transformed the island's economy from reliance upon subsistence crops to plantation agriculture. The first coffee plantation was opened in the Kandyan hill region in 1827, but it was not until the mid-1830s that a number of favorable factors combined to make the widespread cultivation of the crop a highly profitable enterprise. Governor Edward Barnes (1824–31) foresaw the possibilities of coffee cultivation and introduced various incentives for its cultivation, particularly the lifting of coffee export duties and exemption from the land produce tax. When slavery was abolished in the West Indies and coffee production there declined, Sri Lankan coffee exports soared, filling the gap in the world market. The problem of limited availability of land for coffee estates was solved when the British government sold lands that it had acquired from the Kandyan kings.

The coffee plantation system faced a serious labor shortage. Among the Sinhalese, a peasant cultivator of paddy land held a much higher status than a landless laborer. In addition, the low wages paid to hired workers failed to attract the Kandyan peasant, and the peak season for harvesting plantation coffee usually coincided with the peasant's own harvest. Moreover, population pressure and underemployment were not acute until the twentieth century. To compensate for this scarcity of native workers, an inexpensive and almost inexhaustible supply of labor was found among the Tamils in southern India. They were recruited for the coffee-harvesting season and migrated to and from Sri Lanka, often amid great hardships. The immigration of these Indian Tamils began as a trickle in the 1830s and became a regular flow a decade later, when the government of India removed all restrictions on the migration of labor to Sri Lanka.

British civilian and military officials resident in Kandy provided initial capital for coffee cultivation, provoking contemporary observations in the 1840s that they behaved more like coffee planters than government employees. This private capitalization led to serious abuses, however, culminating in an 1840 ordinance that made it virtually impossible for a Kandyan peasant to prove that his land was not truly crown land and thus subject to expropriation and resale to coffee interests. In this period, more than 80,000 hectares of Kandyan land were appropriated and sold as crown lands.

Between 1830 and 1850, coffee held the preeminent place in the economy and became a catalyst for the island's modernization. The greater availability of capital and the increase in export trade brought the rudiments of capitalist organization to the country. The Ceylon Bank opened in 1841 to finance the rapid expansion of coffee plantations. Since the main center of coffee production was in the Kandyan provinces, the expansion of coffee and the network of roads and railroads ended the isolation of the old Kandyan kingdom. The coffee plantation system had served as the economic foundation for the unification of the island while reinforcing the administrative and judicial reforms of the Colebrooke-Cameron Commission.

The plantation system dominated the economy in Sri Lanka to such an extent that one observer described the government as an "appendage of the estates (plantations)." Worldwide depression in 1846 temporarily checked the rapid development of the plantation system. Falling coffee prices caused financial disruption, aggravating the friction that had been developing between the static traditional feudal economy and modernized commercial agriculture. In order to make up for lost revenue, the government imposed a series of new taxes on firearms, dogs, shops, boats, carriages, and bullock carts. All of these taxes affected Sinhalese farmers. Other measures that further alienated the Kandyans included a land tax and a road ordinance in 1848 that reintroduced a form of *rajakariya* by requiring six days' free labor on roads or the payment of a cash equivalent. But the measure that most

31

antagonized the Kandyans (especially those associated with the Buddhist *sangha*) was the alienation of temple lands for coffee plantations.

British troops so severely repressed a rebellion that broke out among the Kandyans in 1848 that the House of Commons in London commissioned an investigation to look into the matter. The governor and his chief secretary were subsequently dismissed, and all new taxes, except the road ordinance, were repealed. The government adopted a new policy toward Buddhism after the rebellion, recognizing the importance of Buddhist monks as leaders of Kandyan public opinion.

The plantation era transformed the island's economy. This was most evident in the growth of the export sector at the expense of the traditional agricultural sector. The colonial predilection for growing commercial instead of subsistence crops later was considered by Sri Lankan nationalists to be one of the unfortunate legacies of European domination. Late nineteenth-century official documents that recorded famines and chronic rural poverty support the nationalists' argument. Other issues, notably the British policy of selling state land to planters for conversion into plantations, are equally controversial, even though some members of the indigenous population participated in all stages of plantation agriculture. Sri Lankans, for example, controlled over one-third of the area under coffee cultivation and most of the land in coconut production. They also owned significant interests in rubber.

In 1869 a devastating leaf disease—*hemleia vastratrix* struck the coffee plantations and spread quickly throughout the plantation district, destroying the coffee industry within fifteen years. Planters desperately searched for a substitute crop. One crop that showed promise was *chinchona* (quinine). After an initial appearance of success, however, the market price of the crop fell and never fully recovered. Cinnamon, which had suffered a setback in the beginning of the century, was revived at this time, but only to become an important minor crop.

Among all of the crops experimented with during the decline of coffee, only tea showed any real promise of success. A decline in the demand for Chinese tea in Britain opened up possibilities for Indian tea, especially the fine variety indigenous to Assam. Climatic conditions for the cultivation of tea were excellent in Sri Lanka, especially in the hill country. By the end of the century, tea production on the island had risen enormously. Because of the inelasticity of the market, however, British outlets soon became saturated. Attempts to develop other markets, especially in the

United States, were largely unsuccessful, and a glut emerged after World War II.

The tea estates needed a completely different type of labor force than had been required during the coffee era. Tea was harvested throughout the year and required a permanent labor force. Waves of Indian Tamil immigrants settled on the estates and eventually became a large and permanent underclass that endured abominable working conditions and squalid housing. The census of 1911 recorded the number of Indian laborers in Sri Lanka at about 500,000—about 12 percent of the island's total population. In the 1980s, the Indian Tamils made up almost 6 percent of the island's population (see Population, ch. 2).

The Tamil laborers emigrated to Sri Lanka from India not as individuals but as part of family units or groups of interrelated families. Thus, they tended to maintain their native cultural patterns on the estates where they settled. Although the Indian Tamils spoke the same language as the Sri Lankan Tamils, were Hindus, and traced their cultural origins to southern India, they considered themselves to be culturally distinct from the Sri Lankan Tamils. Their distinctiveness as a group and their cultural differences from the Sinhalese and the Sri Lankan Tamils were recognized in the constitutional reforms of 1924, when two members of the Indian Tamil community were nominated to the Legislative Council.

As the nineteenth century drew to a close, experimentation in crop diversification, on a moderate level in the years before the collapse of the coffee market, became of greater importance. Responding to international market trends, planters attempted to diversify the crops they produced to insulate their revenues from world price fluctuations. Not all their experiments were successful. The first sugar plantation was established in 1837, but sugar cultivation was not well-suited to the island and has never been very successful. Cocoa was also tried for a time and has continued as one of the lesser exports. Rubber, which was introduced in 1837, became a major export during the slump in the tea export market in the 1900s. The rubber export trade exceeded that of tea during World War I. But after suffering severe losses during the depression of the 1930s, rubber exports never again regained their preeminent position.

Rise of the Sri Lankan Middle Class

By the nineteenth century, a new society was emerging—a product of East and West. It was a society with strict rules separating the rulers from the ruled, and most social association between the British and Sri Lankans was taboo. The British community was largely a microcosm of English society with all its class divisions. At the top of the social pyramid were the British officials of the Ceylon Civil Service. Elaborate social conventions regulated the conduct of the service's members and served to distinguish them as an exclusive caste. This situation, however, changed slowly in the latter part of the nineteenth century and quite rapidly in the next century.

In Sri Lanka as in India, the British created an educated class to provide administrative and professional services in the colony. By the late nineteenth century, most members of this emerging class were associated directly or indirectly with the government. Increased Sri Lankan participation in government affairs demanded the creation of a legal profession; the need for state health services required a corps of medical professionals; and the spread of education provided an impetus to develop the teaching profession. In addition, the expansion of commercial plantations created a legion of new trades and occupations: landowners, planters, transport agents, contractors, and businessmen. Certain Sinhalese caste groups, such as the fishermen (Karava) and cinnamon peelers (Salagama), benefited from the emerging new economic order, to the detriment of the traditional ruling cultivators (Goyigama).

The development of a capitalist economy forced the traditional elite—the chiefs and headmen among the low-country Sinhalese and the Kandyan aristocracy—to compete with new groups for the favors of the British. These upwardly mobile, primarily urban, professionals formed a new class that transcended divisions of race and caste. This class, particularly its uppermost strata, was steeped in Western culture and ideology. This anglicized elite generally had conservative political leanings, was loyal to the government, and resembled the British so much in outlook and social customs that its members were sometimes called brown sahibs. At the apex of this new class was a handful of Sri Lankans who had been able to join the exclusive ranks of the civil service in the nineteenth century. The first Sri Lankan entered by competitive examination in 1840. At that time, entrance examinations were held only in London and required an English education, so only a few members of the native middle class could aspire to such an elitist career. Consequently, in spite of the liberal policies that Colebrooke and Cameron recommended, the British held virtually all high posts in the colonial administration.

Buddhist Revivalism

Beginning around the middle of the nineteenth century, the Buddhist clergy attempted to reform the *sangha* (religious community), particularly as a reaction against Christian missionary activities. In the 1870s, Buddhist activists enlisted the help of an American, Colonel Henry Steele Olcott. An ardent abolitionist in the years leading up to the American Civil War, Olcott cofounded and later became president of the Theosophical Movement, which was organized on a worldwide basis to promote goodwill and to champion the rights of the underprivileged. Shortly after his arrival in Sri Lanka, Olcott organized a Buddhist campaign against British officials and British missionaries. His Buddhist Theosophical Society of Ceylon went on to establish three institutions of higher learning: Ananda College, Mahinda College, and Dharmaraja College. Olcott's society founded these and some 200 lower schools to impart Buddhist education with a strong nationalist bias. Olcott and his society took a special interest in the historical past of the Sinhalese Buddhist kingdoms on the island and managed to persuade the British governor to make Vesak, the chief Buddhist festival, a public holiday.

Constitutional Reform

The rediscovery of old Buddhist texts rekindled a popular interest in Sri Lanka's ancient civilization. The study of the past became an important aspect of the new drive for education. Archaeologists began work at Anuradhapura and at Polonnaruwa, and their finds contributed to the resurgent national pride. In the 1880s, a Buddhist-inspired temperance movement was also initiated to fight drunkenness, and the Ceylon Social Reform Society was founded in 1905 to combat other temptations associated with Westernization. Encouraged by the free reign of expression that the government extended to these reformists, a growing number of communal and regional political associations began to press for constitutional reform in the closing years of the nineteenth century. The colonial government was petitioned for permission to have Sri Lankan representation in the Executive Council and expanded regional representation in the Legislative Council. In response, the colonial government permitted a modest experiment in 1910, allowing a small electorate of Sri Lankans to send one of their members to the Legislative Council. Other seats held by Sri Lankans retained the old practice of communal representation.

World War I

World War I had only a minimal military impact on Sri Lanka, which entered the war as part of the British Empire. The closest fighting took place in the Bay of Bengal, where an Australian warship sank a German cruiser. But the war had an important influence on the growth of nationalism. The Allies' wartime propaganda extolled the virtues of freedom and self-determination of nations, and the message was heard and duly noted by Sri Lankan nationalists. There was, however, an event, only indirectly related to the war, that served as the immediate spark for the growth of nationalism. In 1915 communal rioting broke out between the Sinhalese and Muslims on the west coast. The British panicked, misconstruing the disturbances as part of an antigovernment conspiracy; they blamed the majority ethnic group and indiscriminately arrested many Sinhalese, including D.S. Senanayake—the future first prime minister of Sri Lanka—who had actually tried to use his influence to curb the riots. The British put down the unrest with excessive zeal and brutality, which shocked British and Sri Lankan observers alike. Some sympathetic accounts of the unrest take into consideration that the judgment of the governor of the time, Sir Robert Chalmers (1913–16), may have been clouded by the loss of his two sons on the Western Front in Europe. At any rate, his actions insured that 1915 was a turning point in the nationalist movement. From then on, activists mobilized for coordinated action against the British.

The nationalist movement in India served as a model to nationalists in Sri Lanka. In 1917 the Indian National Congress and the Muslim League mended their differences and issued a joint declaration for the "progressive realization" of responsible government in India. Nationalists in Sri Lanka learned from their Indian counterparts that they had to become more national and less partisan in their push for constitutional reform. In 1919 the major Sinhalese and Tamil political organizations united to form the Ceylon National Congress. One of the first actions of the congress was to submit a proposal for a new constitution that would increase local control over the Executive Council and the budget. These demands were not met, but they led to the promulgation of a new constitution in 1920. Amendments to the constitution in 1924 increased Sri Lankan representation. Although the nationalists' demand for representation in the Executive Council was not granted, the Legislative Council was expanded to include a majority of elected Sri Lankan unofficial members, bringing the island closer to representative government. Yet the franchise remained restrictive and included only about 4 percent of the island's population.

The Donoughmore Commission

In 1927 a royal commission under the Earl of Donoughmore visited Sri Lanka to ascertain why representative government as chartered by the 1924 constitution had not succeeded and to suggest constitutional changes necessary for the island's eventual self-rule. The commission declared that the constitution had authorized a government characterized by the "divorce of power from responsibility," which at times seemed "rather like holy matrimony at its worst." The 1924 constitution, considered by the commission to be "an unqualified failure," failed to provide a strong, credible executive body of representatives. To remedy these shortcomings, the commission proposed universal adult franchise and an experimental system of government to be run by executive committees. The resulting Donoughmore Constitution, promulgated in 1931 to accommodate these new proposals in government, was a unique document that provided Sri Lankans with training for self-government. The document, however, reserved the highest level of responsibility for the British governor, whose assent was necessary for all legislation. The legislative branch of the government— the State Council—functioned in both an executive and legislative capacity. Seven committees performed executive duties. Each committee consisted of designated members of the State Council and was chaired by an elected Sri Lankan, who was addressed as minister. Three British officers of ministerial rank, along with the seven Sri Lankan ministers, formed a board of ministers. The British ministers collectively handled responsibility for defense, external affairs, finance, and judicial matters.

The Donoughmore Constitution ushered in a period of experimentation in participatory democracy but contemporary political scientists have criticized it for not having provided an atmosphere conducive to the growth of a healthy party system. The system of executive committees did not lead to the development of national political parties. Instead, a number of splinter political groups evolved around influential personalities who usually followed a vision too limited or an agenda too communally partisan to have an impact on national politics.

Among the Sinhalese, a form of nationalism arose that sought once again to restore Buddhism to its former glory. The Great Council of the Sinhalese (Sinhala Maha Sabha), which was founded by S.W.R.D. Bandaranaike in 1937, was the strongest proponent of this resurgent ideology. Other groups followed suit, also organizing on communal grounds. These groups included the Burgher Political Association in 1938, the Ceylon Indian Congress in 1939, and the All Ceylon Tamil Congress in 1944.

Growth of Leftist Parties

During the Donoughmore period of political experimentation, several leftist parties were formed. Unlike most other Sri Lankan parties, these leftist parties were noncommunal in membership. Working-class activism, especially trade unionism, became an important political factor during the sustained economic slump between the world wars. The first important leftist party was the Labour Party, founded in 1931 by A.E. Goonesimha. Three Marxist-oriented parties—the Ceylon Equal Society Party (Lanka Sama Samaja Party—LSSP), the Bolshevik-Leninist Party, and the Communist Party of Sri Lanka (CPSL)—represented the far left. All three were divided on both ideological and personal grounds. The Soviet Union's expulsion of Leon Trotsky from the Communist Party after Lenin's death in 1924 and Stalin's subsequent decision to enter World War II on the Allied side exacerbated these differences, dividing the Communists into Trotskyites and Stalinists. The LSSP, formed in 1935 and the oldest of the Sri Lankan Marxist parties, took a stance independent of the Soviet Union, becoming affiliated with the Trotskyite Fourth International, which was a rival of the Comintern. Most LSSP leaders were arrested during World War II for their opposition to what they considered to be an "imperial war." Although in more recent years, the LSSP has been considered a politically spent force, gaining, for example less than 1 percent of the vote in the 1982 presidential elections, it has nevertheless been touted as the world's only successful Trotskyite party.

The CPSL, which began as a Stalinist faction of the LSSP that was later expelled, formed its own party in 1943, remaining faithful to the dictates of the Communist Party of the Soviet Union. The Bolshevik-Leninist Party was formed in 1945 as another breakaway group of the LSSP. The leftist parties represented the numerically small urban working class. Partly because these parties operated through the medium of trade unionism, they lacked the wider mass appeal needed at the national level to provide an effective extraparliamentary challenge to the central government. Nonetheless, because the leftists occasionally formed temporary political coalitions before national elections, they posed more than just a mere "parliamentary nuisance factor."

World War II and the Transition to Independence

When Singapore fell to the Japanese in February 1942, Sri Lanka became a central base for British operations in Southeast Asia, and the port at Trincomalee recaptured its historically strategic importance. Because Sri Lanka was an indispensable strategic bastion for the British Royal Navy, it was an irresistible military target for the Japanese. For a time, it seemed that Japan planned a sweeping westward offensive across the Indian Ocean to take Sri Lanka,

Colombo Harbor with its breakwater
Courtesy Embassy of Sri Lanka, Washington

sever the Allies' lifeline to Persian Gulf oil, and link up with the Axis powers in Egypt. Admiral Isoroku Yamamoto, mastermind of the raid on Pearl Harbor, ordered Vice Admiral Chuichi Nagumo to command a large armada to seek and destroy the British Eastern Fleet in the Indian Ocean. The two nations' fleets played a game of hide-and-seek, but never met. Some military historians assert that if they had met, the smaller British fleet would have met with disaster. The British instead fought several desperate air battles over Colombo and Trincomalee and lost about thirty-six aircraft and several ships.

Yamamoto's grand strategy failed to isolate and destroy any major units of the British fleet. But if the Japanese had persisted with their offensive, the island, with its limited British naval defenses, probably would have fallen. The Japanese carrier force, however, suffered such high aircraft losses over Sri Lanka—more than 100 warplanes—that it returned to Japan for refitting rather than press the attack. By returning to Japan, the force lost its opportunity for unchallenged supremacy of the Indian Ocean. The focus of the war in this theater then shifted away from the island.

On the whole, Sri Lanka benefited from its role in World War II. The plantation sector was busy meeting the urgent demands of the Allies for essential products, especially rubber, enabling the country to save a surplus in hard currency. Because Sri Lanka was the seat of the Southeast Asia Command, a broad infrastructure of health services and modern amenities was built to accommodate the large number of troops posted into all parts of the country. The inherited infrastructure improved the standard of living in postwar, independent Sri Lanka.

Unlike India, where nationalists demanded a guarantee of independence as recompense for their support in the war effort, Sri Lanka committed itself wholeheartedly to the Allied war effort. Although the island was put under military jurisdiction during the war, the British and the Sri Lankans maintained cooperative relations. Sri Lankan pressure for political reform continued during the war, however, and increased as the Japanese threat receded and the war neared its end. The British eventually promised full participatory government after the war.

In July 1944, Lord Soulbury was appointed head of a commission charged with the task of examining a new constitutional draft that the Sri Lankan ministers had proposed. The commission made recommendations that led to a new constitution. As the end of the war approached, the constitution was amended to incorporate a provision giving Sri Lanka dominion status.

British constitutional principles served as a model for the Soulbury Constitution of independent Sri Lanka, which combined a parliamentary system with a bicameral legislature. Members of the first House of Representatives were directly elected by popular vote. Members of the Senate, or upper house, were elected partly by members of the House and partly by the governor general, who was primarily a figurehead. The British monarch appointed the governor general on the advice of the most powerful person in the Sri Lankan government—the prime minister (see Historical Perspective, 1802–1978, ch. 4).

Independence

The British negotiated the island's dominion status with the leader of the State Council, D.S. Senanayake, during World War II. Senanayake was also minister of agriculture and vice chairman of the Board of Ministers. The negotiations ended with the Ceylon Independence Act of 1947, which formalized the transfer of power. Senanayake was the founder and leader of the United National Party (UNP), a partnership of many disparate groups formed during the Donoughmore period, including the Ceylon National Congress, the Sinhala Maha Sabha, and the Muslim League. The UNP easily won the 1947 elections, challenged only by a collection of small, primarily leftist parties. On February 4, 1948, when the new constitution went into effect (making Sri Lanka a dominion), the UNP embarked on a ten-year period of rule.

Divisions in the Body Politic

The prospects for an economically robust, fully participatory, and manageable democracy looked good during the first years of independence. In contrast to India, which had gained independence a year earlier, there was no massive violence and little social unrest. In Sri Lanka there was also a good measure of governmental continuity. Still, important unresolved ethnic problems soon had to be addressed. The most immediate of these problems was the ''Indian question,'' which concerned the political status of Tamil immigrants who worked on the highland tea plantations. The Soulbury Commission had left this sensitive question to be resolved by the incoming government.

After independence, debate about the status of the Indian Tamils continued. But three pieces of legislation—the Ceylon Citizenship Act of 1948, the Indian and Pakistani Residents Act No. 3 of 1948, and the Ceylon Parliamentary Elections Amendment Act No. 48 of 1949—all but disenfranchised this minority group. The Ceylon Indian Congress vigorously but unsuccessfully opposed the legislation. The acrimonious debate over the laws of 1948 and 1949 revealed serious fissures in the body politic. There was a cleavage along ethnic lines between the Sinhalese and the Tamils, and also a widening rift between Sri Lankan Tamils and Indian Tamils.

In 1949 a faction of the Ceylon Tamil Congress (the major Tamil party in Sri Lanka at the time) broke away to form the (Tamil) Federal Party under the leadership of S.J.V. Chelvanayakam. The creation of the Federal Party was a momentous postindependence development because it set the agenda for Tamil exclusivity in Sri Lankan politics. Soon after its founding, the Federal Party replaced the more conciliatory Tamil Congress as the major party among Sri Lankan Tamils and advocated an aggressive stance vis-à-vis the Sinhalese.

United National Party "Majority" Rule, 1948–56

The largest political party in independent Sri Lanka, the United National Party (UNP), emerged as an umbrella party from the colonial era. It was similar in some respects to the Indian National Congress. Like its Indian counterpart, the UNP represented a union of a number of groups espousing different personalities and ideologies. Known later as the ''uncle-nephew party'' because of the kinship ties among the party's top leadership, the UNP served as the standard-bearer of conservative forces. In late 1947, when the party won the country's first general election, the UNP attempted to establish an anticommunist, intercommunal parliamentary form of government. Prominent nationalists, such as D.S. Senanayake and S.W.R.D. Bandaranaike (the country's first and fourth prime ministers, respectively), led the UNP. The party's internal differences gradually worsened, however. The first and most serious break came in July 1951, when Bandaranaike's left-of-center bloc seceded to form the Sri Lanka Freedom Party (SLFP), the first major non-Marxist political movement to oppose the UNP.

Despite the benevolent guidance of Senanayake, the UNP could not defuse the nascent dissension between the Sinhalese and the Tamils. Some of Senanayake's policies, particularly his awarding of land grants to Sinhalese settlers for the resettlement of the northern dry zone, precipitated renewed competition between the two ethnic groups.

When Senanayake died in a horseback-riding accident in March 1952, not only the UNP, but also the entire nation suffered from the loss of the only man who could pose as a credible symbol for the country's unity. In the election that was held immediately after Senanayake's death, the UNP, led by his son Dudley, and the SLFP, led by Bandaranaike, vied for Sinhalese votes, while the Tamil Congress and Federal Party competed for the Tamil vote. The UNP won the election, and the SLFP emerged as major opposition party. The SLFP managed to win only nine out of forty-eight seats in Parliament. The Tamil Congress, having supported the UNP, lost much of its following to the Federal Party, which continued to advocate an autonomous homeland within a Sri Lankan federation. Ethnic tensions, although mounting, remained manageable.

After D. S. Senanayake's death, the nation's economic problems became apparent. The terms of world trade were turning against Sri Lanka. The population was growing faster than production in most sectors. A World Bank (see Glossary) study completed in 1952 noted that social and welfare services were consuming 35 percent of the budget. The report recommended that the government rice subsidy—which accounted for the major portion of the expenditure—be reduced. Prime Minister Senanayake followed the advice, but the move proved to be his political undoing. A massive, sometimes violent civil disobedience movement was launched to protest the reduction of the rice subsidy and provoked the resignation of Senanayake. In October 1953, his cousin, Sir John Kotelawala, became prime minister and remained in office until the UNP defeat in the 1956 election.

The UNP government under Kotelawala disagreed with India's interpretation of political solidarity in the developing world. This divergence became painfully clear to India at the Colombo Conference of 1954 and the Bandung Conference in Indonesia in 1955. Kotelawala's strident condemnation of communism, as well as the more fashionable condemnation of Western imperialism, especially irritated India's Prime Minister Jawaharlal Nehru. Kotelawala was also anxious to have Ceylon join the Southeast Asia Treaty Organization (SEATO), but he encountered strong domestic opposition to the plan. The Soviet Union was especially sensitive to what it considered the government's pro-Western attitude and repeatedly vetoed Sri Lanka's application to join the United Nations (UN). Sri Lanka was finally admitted in 1955 as part of an East-West agreement.

The UNP continued a defense agreement with the British that spared Sri Lanka the cost of maintaining a large military establishment. National defense consumed less than 4 percent of the government budget in the postindependence years, and hence the military was not in a position to interfere with politics.

Emergence of the Sri Lanka Freedom Party

Following its defeat in 1952, the SLFP marshaled its forces in preparation for the next national election. The 1956 election was destined to become a turning point in the modern history of Sri Lanka and is seen by many observers as a social revolution resulting in the eclipse of the Westernized elite. S.W.R.D. Bandaranaike campaigned as the "defender of a besieged Sinhalese culture" and demanded radical changes in the system. Bandaranaike came from a family of Westernized Sinhalese and was educated at Oxford, but early in his political career, he rejected many of the Western elements of his background and embraced the Buddhist faith and adopted native garb (regarded at the time as an affectation among members of his class). Bandaranaike brought to the election a deep knowledge of the passions that communal politics could provoke. His Sinhala Maha Sabha, founded in 1937 as a movement within the Ceylon National Congress, was the only wing of the congress at that time that sought to infuse a Sinhala consciousness into Sri Lankan nationalism. The Sinhala Maha Sabha formed the backbone of Bandaranaike's SLFP and helped spread his 1956 election warning that Buddhism was in danger. Accusations of a "conspiracy" between the UNP and the Roman Catholic Church helped raise emotions feverishly. As one commentator put it, "Bandaranaike built up a popular following based on the Sinhalese dislike of Christian influence, essentially stoking the fires of communal and religious bigotry.''

Bandaranaike and his supporters used the UNP's pro-Western stance as a potent propaganda weapon against the party. He claimed that the independence granted in 1948 was "fake" and that real independence could only be attained by severing all links with the Commonwealth of Nations. In economic matters, Bandaranaike planned to nationalize plantations, banks, and insurance companies. He advocated the control over trade and industry vested in Sinhalese hands. With such a radical platform, Bandaranaike managed to unite many disparate groups into his People's United Front (Mahajana Eksath Peramuna—MEP), a political coalition under the leadership of his SLFP formed to defeat the UNP. In addition, he was able to forge a no-contest pact with two Marxist parties, the LSSP and the CPSL.

The central and most explosive issue of the 1956 election was a linguistic one. After independence, it was commonly accepted that Sinhala and Tamil would replace English as the language of administration, but Bandaranaike announced that only Sinhala would be given official status if his coalition won the election. Bandaranaike introduced a dangerous emotionalism into the election with his "Sinhala only" platform, which labeled both Tamil and English as cultural imports.

The 2,500th anniversary of the death of the Buddha (which also marked the legendary landing of Vijaya and his followers on the island) coincided with the 1956 election, electrifying the political atmosphere. The UNP was susceptible to the emotional power of these issues. In what was later seen as a shameless last-minute reversal, the party also espoused the "Sinhala only" program. This political about-face came too late to help the UNP, for the party lost the election, winning only eight seats in parliament. The People's United Front won the majority share of fifty-one seats.

Tamil Politics

Some political commentators hold that it was in the wake of the 1956 elections that two completely separate and basically hostile political systems emerged in Sri Lanka: one for the Sinhalese and another for the Tamils. The trend toward Tamil exclusivity, however, despite periods of accommodation with Sinhalese political parties, had begun developing before independence. The first political organization to be formed specifically to protect the welfare of an ethnic minority was the All Ceylon Tamil Congress (ACTC), which G.G. Ponnambalam founded in 1944. The Tamil Congress attempted to secure adequate constitutional safeguards before the country attained its independence. These attempts reflected Tamil anxieties that British domination would simply give way to domination by the Sinhalese majority.

After independence, a dissident Tamil group in the ACTC emerged under the leadership of S.J.V. Chelvanayakam. The new group disagreed with Ponnambalam's policy of collaboration with the intercommunal, but Sinhalese-dominated, UNP. In 1949 the dissidents broke away from the ACTC and formed the rival Federal Party, which proposed establishing an autonomous Tamil linguistic state within a federal union of Sri Lanka. The Federal Party regarded this alternative as the only practical way to preserve Tamil identity.

In 1956 the Federal Party emerged as the dominant Tamil political group as a result of its convincing victory over the conservative Tamil Congress. The Federal Party had a distinct advantage because the Tamil Congress had suffered considerably from the stigma of its association with the UNP (which had abandoned its policy of making both Sinhala and Tamil national languages in an attempt to obtain the support of the numerically greater Sinhalese vote).

The Federal Party continued to consolidate its strength and became an important player in national politics. In 1965 the party became a component of the UNP-led coalition government by committing its bloc of parliamentary seats to the UNP, which at that time needed the Federal Party's support to form a stable parliamentary majority. In 1968 however, the Federal Party withdrew from the UNP government because its leaders were convinced that the party could no longer derive any tangible benefits from further association with the UNP. In 1970 the Federal Party campaigned independently, unlike the Tamil Congress, whose leaders called on the Tamils to join a united front with the Sinhalese.

Sri Lanka Freedom Party Rule, 1956–65

Legislation and Communal Agitation

Some of the first actions taken by the new SLFP government reflected a disturbing insensitivity to minority concerns. Shortly after its victory, the new government presented parliament with the Official Language Act, which declared Sinhala the one official language. The act was passed and immediately caused a reaction among Tamils, who perceived their language, culture, and economic position to be under attack.

The passage of the Official Language Act precipitated a current of antagonism between the Tamils and the Sinhalese. The Sri

Lankan Tamils, represented by the Federal Party, launched a *satyagraha* (nonviolent protest) that resulted in a pact between S.W.R.D. Bandaranaike and S.J.V. Chelvanayakam. The agreement provided a wide measure of Tamil autonomy in Northern and Eastern provinces. It also provided for the use of the Tamil language in administrative matters. The Bandaranaike-Chelvanayakam Pact also promised that "early consideration" would be extended to Indian "plantation" Tamils on the question of Sri Lankan citizenship. But the pact was not carried out because of a peaceful protest by Buddhist clergy, who, with support from the UNP, denounced the pact as a "betrayal of Sinhalese-Buddhist people."

In May 1958, a rumor that a Tamil had killed a Sinhalese sparked off nationwide communal riots. Hundreds of people, mostly Tamils, died. This disturbance was the first major episode of communal violence on the island since independence. The riots left a deep psychological scar between the two major ethnic groups. The government declared a state of emergency and forcibly relocated more than 25,000 Tamil refugees from Sinhalese areas to Tamil areas in the north.

Populist Economic Policies

The Bandaranaike government actively expanded the public sector and broadened domestic welfare programs, including pension plans, medical care, nutrition programs, and food and fuel subsidies. This social agenda threatened to drain the nation's treasury. Other popular but economically unfeasible schemes promoted by the Bandaranaike government included restrictions on foreign investment, the nationalization of critical industries, and land reform measures that nationalized plantations and redistributed land to peasants.

When a Buddhist extremist assassinated Bandaranaike in September 1959, the nation faced a period of grave instability. The institution of parliamentary multiparty politics proved strong enough to endure, however, and orderly, constitutional actions resolved the leadership succession. The office of prime minister passed to the minister of education, Wijeyananda Dahanayake, who pledged to carry on the socialist policies of his predecessor. But policy differences and personality clashes within the ruling circle forced the new leader to dissolve Parliament in December 1959. The short-lived Dahanayake government, unable to hold Bandaranaike's coalition government together, was defeated by the UNP in the March 1960 general elections. The UNP won 33 percent of the seats in the lower house, giving the party a plurality but not a majority.

United National Party Interlude

The new prime minister, Dudley Senanayake, honored his election pledge to avoid compromise with the leftist parties and formed an all-UNP government with support from minor right-of-center parties. His overall parliamentary majority, however, was below the minimum seats required to defeat an opposition motion of no-confidence in the UNP cabinet. Less than a month after its formation, the UNP government fell. A new election was scheduled for July 1960.

Return of the Sri Lanka Freedom Party

The UNP fell because it lacked the support of any other major party in Parliament. The leftists tried to bring it down, and the Tamils withheld their support because the UNP had earlier hedged on the issue of the use of the Tamil language. Most important, the UNP had earned the reputation among Sinhalese voters of being a party inimical to Sinhalese nationalism.

Meanwhile the SLFP had grown stronger because of its unwavering support for making Sinhala the only official language. The SLFP found in the former prime minister's widow, Sirimavo Ratwatte Dias (S.R.D.) Bandaranaike, a candidate who was more capable of arousing Sinhalese emotions than Dahanayake had been in the March elections.

In the July 1960 general election, Bandaranaike was profiled as a woman who had nobly agreed to carry on the mandate of her assassinated husband. She received the support of many of the same small parties on the right and left that had temporarily joined together to form the People's United Front coalition (which had brought her husband victory in 1956). She won the election with an absolute majority in Parliament and became Sri Lanka's seventh, and the world's first woman, prime minister. The new government was in many ways the torchbearer for the ideas of S.W.R.D. Bandaranaike, but under his widow's direction, the SLFP carried out these ideas with such zeal and force that Sinhalese-Tamil relations sharply deteriorated. One of Sirimavo Bandaranaike's first official actions was to enforce the policy of Sinhala as the only officially recognized language of government. Her aggressive enforcement of this policy sparked immediate Tamil resistance, which resulted in civil disobedience in restive Northern and Eastern provinces. Bandaranaike reacted by declaring a state of emergency and curtailing Tamil political activity.

Bandaranaike also antagonized other significant minority groups, particularly the Christians. In response to a recommendation by an unofficial Buddhist commission, her government took over the management of state-assisted denominational schools. The move deprived many Christian missionary schools of support. Roman Catholic activists spearheaded demonstrations, which forced the government to reconsider some of its measures. Still, relations between the prime minister and the Christian denominations remained unstable.

Bandaranaike moved vigorously early in her administration to nationalize significant sectors of the economy, targeting industries that were under foreign control. The 1961 creation of the State Petroleum Corporation adversely affected the major petroleum companies—Shell, Esso, and Caltex. The new corporation was guaranteed 25 percent of the country's total petroleum business. Under Bandaranaike's instruction, state corporations began to import oil from new sources, effectively altering for the first time the pattern of trade that had been followed since British rule. Sri Lanka signed oil import agreements with the Soviet Union, Romania, Egypt, and other countries not traditionally involved in Sri Lankan trade. The government also put important sectors of the local economy, particularly the insurance industry, under state control. Most alarming to Bandaranaike's conservative opponents, however, were her repeated unsuccessful attempts to nationalize the largest newspaper syndicate and establish a press council to monitor the news media.

In foreign relations, Bandaranaike was faithful to her late husband's policy of "dynamic neutralism," which aimed to steer a nonaligned diplomatic stance between the superpowers. Sri Lanka exercised its new foreign policy in 1962 by organizing a conference of neutralist nations to mediate an end to the Sino-Indian border war of 1962. Although the conference failed to end the war, it highlighted Sri Lanka's new role as a peacebroker and enhanced its international status.

The UNP opposition was apprehensive of Bandaranaike's leftward drift and was especially concerned about the SLFP alliance with the Trotskyite LSSP in 1964. The UNP approached the March 1965 election as a senior partner in a broad front of "democratic forces" dedicated to fight the "totalitarianism of the left." It enjoyed significant support from the Federal Party (representing Sri Lankan Tamils) and the Ceylon Workers' Congress (representing Indian Tamils).

The United National Party Regains Power, 1965-70

The UNP "national government" emerged victorious in the March 1965 elections, capturing more than 39 percent of parliamentary seats, compared to SLFP's 30.2 percent. One of the first actions of the new government, led by Senanayake, was to declare that the nation's economy was virtually bankrupt. Senanayake also announced his intention to improve relations with the United States. (In 1963 the United States had suspended aid to Sri Lanka because of Bandaranaike's nationalization of foreign oil concerns.)

The government tried to develop a mixed economy with an emphasis on the private sector. Between 1965 and 1970, private sector investment was double that of the public sector, thereby reversing the trend set in the previous administration. Despite the UNP's emphasis on the private sector, the economy generally failed to show a major improvement. This failure was partly caused by a nearly 50 percent increase in the cost of rice imports after a worldwide shortage in 1965 and a concurrent steep decline in the price of Sri Lanka's export commodities. In 1966 the UNP government was forced to declare a state of emergency to ward off food riots. Senanayake reduced the subsidized weekly rice ration by half. The reduction remained in effect throughout the remainder of the "national government" period and contributed greatly to UNP's defeat in the 1970 general elections.

The UNP paid more attention to Buddhist sensitivities than it had in the past, and in an effort to widen the party's popularity, it replaced the Christian sabbath with the Buddhist *poya* full-moon holiday. This action satisfied Buddhist activists but alienated the small but powerful Roman Catholic lobby. The UNP also tried to earn favor with the Tamils by enacting the Tamil Regulations in 1966, which were designed to make Tamil a language officially "parallel" to Sinhala in Tamil-speaking regions. Sinhalese activists immediately expressed hostility toward the Tamil Regulations. Civil violence ensued, and the government was forced to proclaim a state of emergency that lasted for most of the year.

United Front Rule and Emerging Violence, 1970–77

In order to prepare for the 1970 general election, Sirimavo Bandaranaike formed a coalition in 1968 with the LSSP and CPSL to oppose the UNP. The new three-party United Front (Samagi Peramuna) announced that it would work toward a "people's government" under the leadership of Bandaranaike and that it would follow a so-called Common Programme, which promised radical structural changes, including land reform, increased rice subsidies, and nationalization of local and foreign banks.

The United Front resurrected communal emotionalism as a timely and potent campaign weapon. It attacked the UNP for its alliance with the two main Tamil political groups, the Federal Party and the Ceylon Workers' Congress. At the same time, the United Front also announced that it would adopt a new constitution to make Sri Lanka a republic and that it would restore "Buddhism to its rightful place." The United Front won 118 of the 135 seats it contested, with the SLFP, the biggest-single party, winning 90 seats, the LSSP 19 seats, and the CPSL 6 seats. The UNP won a meager seventeen seats.

The United Front government moved quickly to implement key features of its Common Programme. The philosophy of the coalition government was seen most transparently from its foreign and economic policies. The United Front issued declarations that it followed a nonaligned path; opposed imperialism, colonialism, and racism; and supported national liberation movements. The government quickly extended diplomatic relations to the German Democratic Republic (East Germany), the Democratic Republic of Vietnam (then North Vietnam), the Democratic People's Republic of Korea (North Korea), and the Provisional Revolutionary Government of South Vietnam. It also pledged to suspend recognition of Israel. In economic matters, the United Front vowed to put private enterprise in a subsidiary role.

Prime Minister Bandaranaike tolerated the radical left at first and then lost control of it. Sensing mounting unrest, the government declared a state of emergency in March 1971. In April, the People's Liberation Front (Janatha Vimukthi Peramuna—JVP), a Maoist and primarily rural Sinhalese youth movement claiming a membership of more than 10,000, began a "blitzkrieg" operation to take over the government "within 24 hours." The JVP followed a program—known as the Five Lectures—that included an agenda to deal with "Indian expansionism," the island's unstable economic situation, and the inability of the traditionalist leftist leadership to assert power or attract widespread support (an allusion to the LSSP and the CPSL). The JVP threatened to take power by extraparliamentary means. Fierce fighting erupted in the north-central, south-central, and southern rural districts of the island, causing an official estimate of 1,200 dead. Unofficial tallies of the number of dead were much higher. The JVP came perilously close to overthrowing the government but the military finally suppressed the movement and imprisoned JVP's top leadership and about 16,000 suspected insurgents.

In May 1972, the United Front followed through on its 1970 campaign promise to promulgate a new constitution to make Sri Lanka a republic. Under the new constitution, the legislative, executive, and judicial branches of government were vested in the

National State Assembly. Many important and vocal sectors of society opposed this concentration of power. The 1972 constitution disturbed the UNP, which feared an authoritarian government might emerge because of the new document. The UNP was especially alarmed that a Trotskyite, Dr. Colvin de Silva (Bandaranaike's minister of constitutional affairs), had drafted the constitution.

The distinct lack of protection for the rights of minorities in the new constitution dismayed many sectors of the population. The Tamils were especially disturbed because the 1972 constitution contained no elements of federalism. Instead, a newly conferred status for Buddhism replaced the provisions for minorities provided by Article 29 in the 1948 constitution. The constitution also sanctioned measures that discriminated against Tamil youth in university admissions. Tamil youth were particularly irked by the "standardization" policy that Bandaranaike's government introduced in 1973. The policy made university admissions criteria lower for Sinhalese than for Tamils. The Tamil community—the Federal Party, the Tamil Congress, and other Tamil organizations—reacted collectively against the new atmosphere the new constitution produced, and in May 1972, they founded the Tamil United Front (which became the Tamil United Liberation Front—TULF—in 1976).

By the mid-1970s, the antagonism between the right and left was destroying the United Front coalition. The growing political influence of the right wing led by Sirimavo Bandaranaike's son, Anura, precipitated the expulsion of the LSSP from the United Front in September 1975. The withdrawal of the CPSL in 1977 further weakened the coalition.

The United National Party Returns to Power

After Dudley Senanayake died in 1973, a struggle for the leadership of the UNP ensued between his nephew, Rukman Senanayake, and Junius Richard (J.R.) Jayewardene, a more distant relative. Jayewardene had been involved in politics for years, having been elected to the State Council, the parliament's colonial predecessor, as early as 1943. A leader of the UNP since independence, Jayewardene had deferred to the Senanayake family. But in 1970, when the UNP suffered a resounding defeat to the United Front, Jayewardene became more assertive. His party manifesto—*The UNP in Opposition, 1970*—contended that the majority of Sri Lankans perceived the party as the party of the "haves, the affluent, and the employers." He also contended that the people had come to perceive the SLFP as the party of the "have nots, the needy,

and the unemployed.'' Jayewardene moved forcefully to refurbish
UNP's image and announced that the party would inaugurate an
era of a just and righteous (*dharmishta*) society. After becoming president of the party, Jayewardene began to restructure the UNP and
make the party more attractive, especially to young people. By the
time of the general election of 1977, Jayewardene had developed
an extensive grass roots party organization.

Election of 1977 and More Violence

After molding the UNP around his personality and having successfully built up the party's infrastructure, Jayewardene easily became prime minister. The UNP won an unprecedented landslide
victory in the 1977 elections, winning 140 of 168 seats. The SLFP
was reduced to eight seats. The Sri Lankan Tamils, however, gave
little support to Jayewardene or any other non-Tamil politician.
The Sri Lankan Tamils entered the parliamentary election fray
under the banner of TULF, which had elevated its earlier demand
for regional self-rule to a demand for an independent state, or Eelam
(see Glossary). TULF became the largest opposition party in Parliament and captured all fourteen seats in the heavily Tamil Northern Province and four east coast seats. TULF won in every
constituency with a Tamil majority on the island, except one. In
Jaffna District, TULF candidates won all eleven seats, although
forty-seven other candidates contested the seats. TULF originally
included the largest Indian (plantation) Tamil political organization, the Ceylon Workers' Congress, but after the 1977 election,
the leader of the Ceylon Workers' Congress accepted a cabinet post
in the UNP government. The Sri Lankan Tamil demand for Tamil
Eelam had never been of central concern to the Indian Tamils,
who lived mostly outside the territory being claimed for the Tamil
state.

The opportunities for peace that the 1977 UNP electoral victory provided were soon lost. Just before the 1977 elections, Chelvanayakam, the charismatic leader of TULF, died, leaving the party
without strong leadership. A Tamil separatist underground (which
had split into six or more rival and sometimes violently hostile
groups that were divided by ideology, caste, and personal antagonisms) was filling the vacuum left by the weakened TULF and
was gaining the allegiance of an increasing number of disenchanted
Tamil youths. These groups were known collectively as the Tamil
Tigers. The strongest of these separatists were the Liberation Tigers
of Tamil Eelam (LTTE), founded in 1972 by Velupillai Prabhakaran. The LTTE was responsible for some of the earliest and most
gruesome acts of Tamil terrorism (see the Tamil Insurgency, ch. 5).

The LTTE first gained notoriety by its 1975 assassination of the mayor of Jaffna, a supporter of the SLFP. During the 1977 elections, many Tamil youths began to engage in extraparliamentary and sometimes violent measures in their bid for a mandate for a separate state. These measures precipitated a Sinhalese backlash. An apparently false rumor that Sinhalese policemen had died at the hands of Tamil terrorists, combined with other rumors of alleged anti-Sinhalese statements made by Tamil politicians, sparked brutal communal rioting that engulfed the island within two weeks of the new government's inauguration. The rioting marked the first major outbreak of communal violence in the nineteen years since the riots of 1958. Casualties were many, especially among Tamils, both the Sri Lankan Tamils of Jaffna and the Indian Tamil plantation workers. The Tamil Refugee Rehabilitation Organization estimated the death toll at 300 persons.

Constitution of 1978

After coming to power, Jayewardene directed the rewriting of the constitution. The document that was produced, the new Constitution of 1978, drastically altered the nature of governance in Sri Lanka. It replaced the previous Westminster-style, parliamentary government with a new presidential system modeled after France, with a powerful chief executive. The president was to be elected by direct suffrage for a six-year term and was empowered to appoint, with parliamentary approval, the prime minister and to preside over cabinet meetings. Jayewardene became the first president under the new Constitution and assumed direct control of the government machinery and party.

The new regime ushered in an era that did not auger well for the SLFP. Jayewardene's UNP government accused former prime minister Bandaranaike of abusing her power while in office from 1970 to 1977. In October 1980, Bandaranaike's privilege to engage in politics was removed for a period of seven years, and the SLFP was forced to seek a new leader. After a long and divisive battle, the party chose her son, Anura. Anura Bandaranaike was soon thrust into the role of the keeper of his father's legacy, but he inherited a political party torn apart by factionalism and reduced to a minimal role in the Parliament.

The 1978 Constitution included substantial concessions to Tamil sensitivities. Although TULF did not participate in framing the Constitution, it continued to sit in Parliament in the hope of negotiating a settlement to the Tamil problem. TULF also agreed to Jayewardene's proposal of an all-party conference to resolve the island's ethnic problems. Jayewardene's UNP offered other concessions in a bid to secure peace. Sinhala remained the official language and the language of administration throughout Sri Lanka, but Tamil was given a new "national language" status. Tamil was to be used in a number of administrative and educational circumstances. Jayewardene also eliminated a major Tamil grievance by abrogating the "standardization" policy of the United Front government, which had made university admission criteria for Tamils more difficult. In addition, he offered many top-level positions, including that of minister of justice, to Tamil civil servants.

While TULF, in conjunction with the UNP, pressed for the all-party conference, the Tamil Tigers escalated their terrorist attacks, which provoked Sinhalese backlash against Tamils and generally precluded any successful accommodation. In reaction to the assassination of a Jaffna police inspector, the Jayewardene government declared an emergency and dispatched troops, who were given an unrealistic six months to eradicate the terrorist threat.

The government passed the Prevention of Terrorism (Temporary Provisions) Act in 1979. The act was enacted as a temporary measure, but it later became permanent legislation. The International Commission of Jurists, Amnesty International, and other human rights organizations condemned the act as being incompatible with democratic traditions. Despite the act, the number of terrorist acts increased. Guerrillas began to hit targets of high symbolic value such as post offices and police outposts, provoking government counterattacks. As an increasing number of civilians were caught in the fighting, Tamil support widened for the "boys," as the guerrillas began to be called. Other large, well-armed groups began to compete with LTTE. The better-known included the People's Liberation Organization of Tamil Eelam, Tamil Eelam Liberation Army, and the Tamil Eelam Liberation Organization. Each of these groups had forces measured in the hundreds if not thousands. The government claimed that many of the terrorists were operating from training camps in India's Tamil Nadu State. The Indian government repeatedly denied this claim. With the level of violence mounting, the possibility of negotiation became increasingly distant.

The Riots of 1981

In June 1981, local elections were held in the north to elect members of the newly established district development councils. TULF had decided to participate and work in the councils. In doing so, TULF continued to work toward autonomy for the Tamil areas. Extremists within the separatist movement, however, adamantly opposed working within the existing political framework. They viewed participation in the elections as compromising the objective of a separate state. Shortly before the elections, the leading candidate of the UNP was assassinated as he left a political rally. The sporadic communal violence that persisted over the following three months foreshadowed the devastating communal riots of 1983. When elections were held a few days later, concomitant charges of voting irregularities and mishandling of ballots created the nation's first election scandal since the introduction of universal suffrage fifty years earlier.

Presidential Election of 1982

TULF decided to boycott the 1982 presidential elections, partly in reaction to the harsh Prevention of Terrorism Act and partly in response to pressures exerted by Tamil extremists. Only 46 percent of the voters in Jaffna District turned out. In Sinhalese districts, 85 percent of voters turned out. Increasing violence by Tamil youths in the north and east of the island accompanied the call for a Tamil Eelam. The rising level of violence in 1983 led the government to pass a sixth amendment to the Constitution, which specifically banned talk of separatism. All sixteen TULF members of parliament were expelled for refusing to recite a loyalty oath, thus removing a critical channel for mediation.

The Riots of July 1983

In July 1983, the most savage communal riots in Sri Lanka's history erupted. Conservative government estimates put the death toll at 400— mostly Tamils. At least 150,000 Tamil fled the island. The riots began in retaliation for an ambush of an army patrol in the north that left thirteen Sinhalese soldiers dead. The army was reputed to have killed sixty Tamil civilians in Jaffna, but most of the violence occurred in Colombo, where Sinhalese mobs looked for Tamil shops to destroy. More than any previous ethnic riot on the island, the 1983 riots were marked by their highly organized mob violence. Sinhalese rioters in Colombo used voter lists containing home addresses to make precise attacks on the Tamil community. From Colombo, the anti-Tamil violence fanned out to the entire island. The psychological effects of this violence on Sri Lanka's complex and divided society were still being assessed in the late 1980s. Nevertheless, in the aftermath of the communal rioting, a self-evident truth was that the island's history, and the complexity of its society, had a portentous message for the present: Sinhalese and Tamil Sri Lankans were fated by history and geography to coexist in close proximity. This coexistence could be discordant or amicable, and examples of both could be drawn from

Sri Lanka's history. It was a message, however, whose meaning was forgotten as the ethnic communities were drawn increasingly into a vortex of rancor and violence that made the restoration of harmony a persistently elusive goal for the Sri Lankan government.

* * *

Informative general histories of Sri Lanka include K.M. de Silva's *A History of Sri Lanka,* E.F.C. Ludowyk's *A Short History of Ceylon,* Zeylanicus's *Ceylon,* S. Arasaratnam's *Ceylon,* and Chandra Richard de Silva's *Sri Lanka: A History.* Source books on medieval history are Wilhelm Geiger's translations of the Pali chronicles, the *Mahavamsa* and *Culavamsa,* and the comprehensive *The Early History of Ceylon* by G.C. Mendis. Highly informative for the study of modern political events and ethnic disturbances are S.J. Tambiah's *Sri Lanka: Ethnic Fratricide and the Dismantling of Democracy,* A. Jeyaratnam Wilson's *Politics in Sri Lanka,* and *Government and Politics in South Asia* by Craig Baxter, Yogendra K. Malik, Charles H. Kennedy, and Robert C. Oberst. (For further information and complete citations, see Bibliography.)

Chapter 2. The Society and Its Environment

Woman bringing "ambula" (noon meal) to the field

SRI LANKA LIES practically in the center of the Indian Ocean and thus has climatic and cultural links with three continents. Monsoon winds, driving against Sri Lanka's peaks, support lush vegetation on the southern half of the island, but the northern half is a dry zone. The winds affect human culture as well, having brought wave after wave of immigrants and merchants following the southerly trade routes. Outsiders found a wide range of ecological niches on the coast, on the plains, or in the mountains, and they built a remarkably variegated civilization. Merchants long have sought Sri Lanka as the source of pearls, jewels, spices, and tea. Visitors for centuries have marvelled at the beauty and great diversity of the island.

The South Asian landmass to the north has strongly influenced Sri Lankan culture in the past and continues to do so. From an outlander's perspective, some of the main aspects of Sri Lankan society—language, caste, family structure—are regional variants of Indian civilization. From the perspective of the islander, however, the Indian influence is but the largest part of a continuing barrage of stimuli coming to Sri Lanka from all sides. The people of the island have absorbed these influences and built their own civilization.

The Sinhalese (see Glossary), a distinct ethnic group speaking the Sinhala (see Glossary) language and practicing a variant of Theravada Buddhism (see Glossary), comprise the majority—74 percent—of the population, and their values dominate public life. There are, however, substantial minority groups. The Tamils, speaking the Tamil language and generally practicing Hinduism, comprise almost 18 percent of the population. Muslims, many of whom speak Tamil as their main language, make up 7 percent of the populace. Each of the main ethnic groups is subdivided into several major categories, depending on variables of religion or geography. There also are sizable Christian minorities among the Sinhalese and Tamil. People living in the central highland region of the country generally adhere more closely to their traditional ethnic customs than lowland dwellers.

Caste creates other social divisions. The Goyigama (see Glossary) caste of the Sinhalese—traditionally associated with land cultivation—is dominant in population and public influence, but in the lowlands other castes based on commercial activities are influential. The Tamil Vellala caste resembles the Goyigama in its dominance and traditional connection with agriculture, but it is completely separate from the Sinhalese caste hierarchy. Within their separate caste hierarchies, Sinhalese and Tamil communities are fragmented through customs that separate higher from lower orders. These include elaborate rules of etiquette and a nearly complete absence of intercaste marriages. Differences in wealth arising from the modern economic system have created, however, wide class cleavages that cut across boundaries of caste, religion, and language. Because of all these divisions, Sri Lankan society is complex, with numerous points of potential conflict.

The population of Sri Lanka has grown considerably since independence in 1948, and in the 1980s was increasing by approximately 200,000 people or 1.37 percent each year. Because of this population pressure, the government has faced a major development problem as it has attempted to reconcile the divergent interests of caste, class, and ethnic groups while trying to ensure adequate food, education, health services, and career opportunities for the rapidly expanding population. Politicians and officials have attempted to meet these needs through a form of welfare socialism, providing a level of support services that is comparatively high for a developing nation. Building on colonial foundations, Sri Lanka has created a comprehensive education system, including universities, that has produced one of the best-educated populations in Asia. A free state-run health system provides basic care that has raised average life expectancy to the highest level in South Asia. Ambitious housing and sanitation plans, although incomplete, promised basic amenities to all citizens by the year 2000. In 1988 the government addressed the nutritional deficiencies of the poor through a subsidized food stamp program and free nutrition programs for children and mothers.

The crucial problem facing Sri Lanka's plural society is whether it can evolve a form of socialism that will address the needs of all groups, or whether frustrated aspirations will engender further conflict. In the field of education, for example, excellent accomplishments in elementary schooling have emerged alongside bitter competition for coveted places in the university system; this competition has fueled ethnic hatred between the Sinhalese and Tamil communities. In a land with limited resources, the benefits of social welfare programs highlight the inadequacies of progress for some regional or ethnic groups. In these circumstances, caste, ethnic, or religious differences become boundaries between warring parties, and a person's language or place of worship becomes a sign of political affiliation. The social organization of Sri Lanka is thus an important component of the politics and economy in the developing nation.

The Physical Environment

Geology

More than 90 percent of Sri Lanka's surface lies on Precambrian strata, some of it dating back 2 billion years. The metamorphic rock surface was created by the transformation of ancient sediments under intense heat and pressure during mountain-building processes. The theory of plate tectonics suggests that these rocks and related rocks forming most of south India were part of a single southern landmass called Gondwanaland. Beginning about 200 million years ago, forces within the earth's mantle began to separate the lands of the Southern Hemisphere, and a crustal plate supporting both India and Sri Lanka moved toward the northeast. About 45 million years ago, the Indian plate collided with the Asian landmass, raising the Himalayas in northern India, and continuing to advance slowly to the present time. Sri Lanka experiences few earthquakes or major volcanic events because it rides on the center of the plate.

The island contains relatively limited strata of sedimentation surrounding its ancient hills. Aside from recent deposits along river valleys, only two small fragments of Jurassic (140 to 190 million years ago) sediment occur in Puttalam District, while a more extensive belt of Miocene (5 to 20 million years ago) limestone is found along the northwest coast, overlain in many areas by Pleistocene (1 million years ago) deposits (see fig. 1). The northwest coast is part of the deep Cauvery (Kaveri) River Basin of southeast India, which has been collecting sediments from the highlands of India and Sri Lanka since the breakup of Gondwanaland.

Topography

Extensive faulting and erosion over time have produced a wide range of topographic features, making Sri Lanka one of the most scenic places in the world. Three zones are distinguishable by elevation: the Central Highlands, the plains, and the coastal belt (see fig. 3).

The south-central part of Sri Lanka—the rugged Central Highlands—is the heart of the country. The core of this area is a high plateau, running north-south for approximately sixty-five kilometers. This area includes some of Sri Lanka's highest mountains. (Pidurutalagala is the highest at 2,524 meters.) At the plateau's southern end, mountain ranges stretch 50 kilometers to

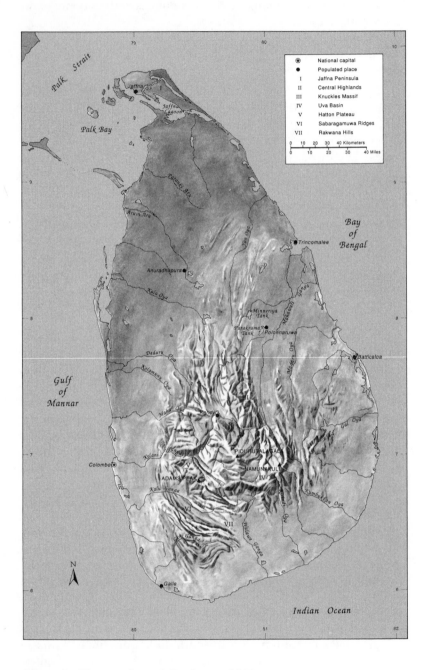

Figure 3. Topography and Drainage, 1988

the west toward Adams Peak (2,243 meters) and 50 kilometers to the east toward Namunakuli (2,036 meters). Flanking the high central ridges are two lower plateaus. On the west is the Hatton Plateau, a deeply dissected series of ridges sloping downward toward the north. On the east, the Uva Basin consists of rolling hills covered with grasses, traversed by some deep valleys and gorges. To the north, separated from the main body of mountains and plateaus by broad valleys, lies the Knuckles Massif: steep escarpments, deep gorges, and peaks rising to more than 1,800 meters. South of Adams Peak lie the parallel ridges of the Rakwana Hills, with several peaks over 1,400 meters. The land descends from the Central Highlands to a series of escarpments and ledges at 400 to 500 meters above sea level before sloping down toward the coastal plains.

Most of the island's surface consists of plains between 30 and 200 meters above sea level. In the southwest, ridges and valleys rise gradually to merge with the Central Highlands, giving a dissected appearance to the plain. Extensive erosion in this area has worn down the ridges and deposited rich soil for agriculture downstream. In the southeast, a red, lateritic soil covers relatively level ground that is studded with bare, monolithic hills. The transition from the plain to the Central Highlands is abrupt in the southeast, and the mountains appear to rise up like a wall. In the east and the north, the plain is flat, dissected by long, narrow ridges of granite running from the Central Highlands.

A coastal belt about thirty meters above sea level surrounds the island. Much of the coast consists of scenic sandy beaches indented by coastal lagoons. In the Jaffna Peninsula, limestone beds are exposed to the waves as low-lying cliffs in a few places. In the northeast and the southwest, where the coast cuts across the stratification of the crystalline rocks, rocky cliffs, bays, and offshore islands can be found; these conditions have created one of the world's best natural harbors at Trincomalee on the northeast coast, and a smaller rock harbor at Galle on the southwestern coast.

Sri Lanka's rivers rise in the Central Highlands and flow in a radial pattern toward the sea. Most of these rivers are short. There are sixteen principal rivers longer than 100 kilometers in length, with twelve of them carrying about 75 percent of the mean river discharge in the entire country. The longest rivers are the Mahaweli Ganga (335 kilometers) and the Aruvi Aru (170 kilometers). In the highlands, river courses are frequently broken by discontinuities in the terrain, and where they encounter escarpments, numerous waterfalls and rapids have eroded a passage. Once they reach the plain, the rivers slow down and the waters meander across flood plains and deltas. The upper reaches of the rivers are wild and usually unnavigable, and the lower reaches are prone to seasonal flooding. Human intervention has altered the flows of some rivers in order to create hydroelectric, irrigation, and transportation projects. In the north, east, and southeast, the rivers feed numerous artificial lakes or reservoirs (tanks) that store water during the dry season. During the 1970s and 1980s, large-scale projects dammed the Mahaweli Ganga and neighboring streams to create large lakes along their courses (see Agriculture, ch. 3). Several hundred kilometers of canals, most of which were built by the Dutch in the eighteenth century, link inland waterways in the southwestern part of Sri Lanka.

Climate

Sri Lanka's position between 5° and 10° north latitude endows the country with a warm climate, moderated by ocean winds and considerable moisture. The mean temperature ranges from a low of 15.8°C in Nuwara Eliya in the Central Highlands (where frost may occur for several days in the winter) to a high of 29°C in Trincomalee on the northeast coast (where temperatures may reach 37°C). The average yearly temperature for the country as a whole ranges from 26°C to 28°C. Day and night temperatures may vary by 4° to 7°. January is the coolest month, causing people, especially those in the highlands, to wear coats and sweaters. May, the hottest period, precedes the summer monsoon rains.

The rainfall pattern is influenced by the monsoon winds of the Indian Ocean and Bay of Bengal and is marked by four seasons. The first is from mid-May to October, when winds originate in the southwest, bringing moisture from the Indian Ocean. When these winds encounter the slopes of the Central Highlands, they unload heavy rains on the mountain slopes and the southwestern sector of the island. Some of the windward slopes receive up to 250 centimeters of rain per month, but the leeward slopes in the east and northeast receive little rain. The second season occurs in October and November, the intermonsoonal months. During this season, periodic squalls occur and sometimes tropical cyclones bring overcast skies and rains to the southwest, northeast, and eastern parts of the island. During the third season, December to March, monsoon winds come from the northeast, bringing moisture from the Bay of Bengal. The northeastern slopes of the mountains may be inundated with up to 125 centimeters of rain during these months. Another intermonsoonal period occurs from March until mid-May, with light, variable winds and evening thundershowers.

Humidity is typically higher in the southwest and mountainous areas and depends on the seasonal patterns of rainfall. At Colombo, for example, daytime humidity stays above 70 percent all year, rising to almost 90 percent during the monsoon season in June. Anuradhapura experiences a daytime low of 60 percent during the intermonsoonal month of March, but a high of 79 percent during the November and December rains. In the highlands, Kandy's daytime humidity usually ranges between 70 and 79 percent.

Ecological Zones

The pattern of life in Sri Lanka depends directly on the availability of rainwater. The mountains and the southwestern part of the country, known as the "wet zone," receive ample rainfall (an annual average of 250 centimeters). Most of the southeast, east, and northern parts of the country comprise the "dry zone," which receives between 120 and 190 centimeters of rain annually. Much of the rain in these areas falls from October to January; during the rest of the year there is very little precipitation, and all living creatures must conserve precious moisture. The arid northwest and southeast coasts receive the least amount of rain—60 to 120 centimeters per year—concentrated within the short period of the winter monsoon (see fig. 4).

The natural vegetation of the dry zone is adapted to the annual change from flood to drought. The typical ground cover is scrub forest, interspersed with tough bushes and cactuses in the driest areas. Plants grow very fast from November to February when rainfall is heavy, but stop growing during the hot season from March to August. Various adaptations to the dry conditions have developed. To conserve water, trees have thick bark; most have tiny leaves, and some drop their leaves during this season. Also, the topmost branches of the tallest trees often interlace, forming a canopy against the hot sun and a barrier to the dry wind. When water is absent, the plains of the dry zone are dominated by browns and grays. When water becomes available, either during the wet season or through proximity to rivers and lakes, the vegetation explodes into shades of green with a wide variety of beautiful flowers. Varieties of flowering acacias are well adapted to the arid conditions and flourish on the Jaffna Peninsula. Among the trees of the dry-land forests are some valuable species, such as satinwood, ebony, ironwood, and mahogany.

In the wet zone, the dominant vegetation of the lowlands is a tropical evergreen forest, with tall trees, broad foliage, and a dense undergrowth of vines and creepers. Subtropical evergreen forests resembling those of temperate climates flourish in the higher altitudes. Montane vegetation at the highest altitudes tends to be stunted and windswept.

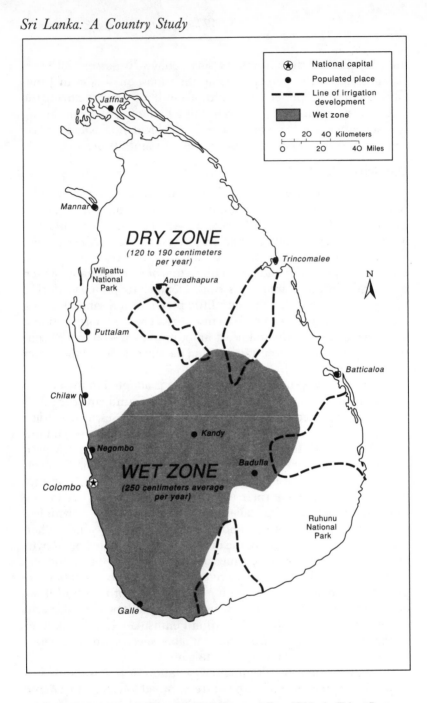

Source: Based on information from *Agro-Bio-Environmental Chart of Sri Lanka,* Tokyo, Resources
Council, Science and Technology Agency, 1977.

Figure 4. Precipitation and Irrigation

Forests at one time covered nearly the entire island, but by the late twentieth century lands classified as forests and forest reserves covered only one-fifth of the land. The southwestern interior contains the only large remnants of the original forests of the wet zone. The government has attempted to preserve sanctuaries for natural vegetation and animal life, however. Ruhunu National Park in the southeast protects herds of elephant, deer, and peacocks, and Wilpattu National Park in the northwest preserves the habitats of many water birds, such as storks, pelicans, ibis, and spoonbills. During the Mahaweli Ganga Program of the 1970s and 1980s in northern Sri Lanka, the government set aside four areas of land totalling 190,000 hectares as national parks.

Land Use and Settlement Patterns

The dominant pattern of human settlement during the last 2,500 years has consisted of village farming communities. Even in the 1980s, the majority of people lived in small villages and worked at agricultural pursuits. Traditional farming techniques and lifestyles revolve around two types of farming—"wet" and "dry"—depending upon the availability of water (see Agriculture, ch. 3).

The typical settlement pattern in the rice-growing areas is a compact group of houses or neighborhood surrounding one or several religious centers that serve as the focus for communal activities. Sometimes the houses may be situated along a major road and include a few shops, or the village may include several outlying hamlets. The life-sustaining rice fields begin where the houses end and stretch into the distance. Some irrigated fields may include other cash crops, such as sugarcane, or groves of coconut trees. Palmyra trees grow on the borders of fields or along roads and paths. Individual houses also may have vegetable gardens in their compounds. During the rainy seasons and thereafter, when the fields are covered by growing crops, the village environment is intensely verdant.

The nature of agricultural pursuits in Sri Lanka has changed over the centuries and has usually depended upon the availability of arable land and water resources. In earlier times, when villagers had access to plentiful forests that separated settlements from each other, slash-and-burn agriculture was a standard technique. As expanding population and commercial pressures reduced the amount of available forestland, however, slash-and-burn cultivation steadily declined in favor of permanent cultivation by private owners. Until the thirteenth century, the village farming communities were mainly on the northern plains around Anuradhapura and then Polonnaruwa, but they later shifted to the southwest (see Decline of the Sinhalese Kingdom, 1200–1500, ch. 1). In the 1980s, wide expanses of the northern and eastern plains were sparsely populated, with scattered villages each huddled around an artificial lake. The Jaffna Peninsula, although a dry area, is densely populated and intensively cultivated. The southwest contains most of the people, and villages are densely clustered with little unused land (see Population, this ch.). In the Central Highlands around Kandy, villagers faced with limited flat land have developed intricately terraced hillsides where they grow rice. In the 1970s and 1980s, the wet cultivation area was expanding rapidly, as the government implemented large-scale irrigation projects to restore the dry zone to agricultural productivity. In the 1980s, the area drained by the Mahaweli Ganga changed from a sparsely inhabited region to a wet rice area similar to the southwest. Through such projects, the government of Sri Lanka has planned to recreate in the dry zone the lush, irrigated landscape associated with the ancient Sinhalese civilization.

Beginning in the sixteenth century and culminating during the British rule of the nineteenth and twentieth centuries, the plantation economy came to dominate large sections of the highlands. Plantation farming resulted in a drastic reduction in the natural forest cover and the substitution of domesticated crops, such as rubber, tea, or cinnamon. It also brought about a changed life-style, as the last hunting-and-gathering societies retreated into smaller areas and laborers moved into the highlands to work on plantations. Through the late twentieth century, workers on large plantations lived in villages of small houses or in "line rooms" containing ten to twelve units. The numerous plantations of small landholders frequently included attached hamlets of workers in addition to the independent houses of the plantation owners.

The coastal belt surrounding the island contains a different settlement pattern that has evolved from older fishing villages. Separate fishing settlements expanded laterally along the coast, linked by a coastal highway and a railway. The mobility of the coastal population during colonial times and after independence led to an increase in the size and number of villages, as well as to the development of growing urban centers with outside contacts. In the 1980s, it was possible to drive for many kilometers along the southwest coast without finding a break in the string of villages and bazaar centers merging into each other and into towns.

People

Population

During the early nineteenth century, the population of Sri Lanka was small and concentrated in the southwestern part of the island and in the Jaffna Peninsula in the north. The first official census,

The Society and Its Environment

conducted by the British in 1871, recorded a total population of
2.8 million. Between then and the 1980s, the population increased
sixfold. Population growth until around 1900 was given impetus
by considerable immigration from southern India, as the British
brought in hundreds of thousands of Tamils to work the plantation economy. These immigrants accounted for an estimated 40
to 70 percent of the population increase during the nineteenth century. Another significant factor in the growth of population after
1900 was a decline in mortality rates (see Health, this ch.). The
period of fastest growth was the decade after independence, when
the annual rate of increase was 2.8 percent. The official total in
the 1981 census was 14,846,750, and some projections suggested
a total of 18 million by 1991 and between 20 and 21 million by
2001. Furthermore, if the 1980s trends continue, the population
will double in forty years (see table 2, Appendix).

Although the increase in the number of people remained a major
problem for Sri Lanka, there were indications in the 1980s that the
country had moved beyond a period of uncontrolled population expansion into a pattern similar to that of more industrialized nations.
The crude fertility rate declined from 5.3 in 1953—at the height
of the postindependence baby boom—to 3.3 in 1981. Emigration,
which outpaced immigration after 1953, also contributed to the
decline in population growth. Between 1971 and 1981, for example,
313,000 Tamil workers from the plantation areas emigrated to south
India. Increased employment opportunities in the Arab nations also
attracted a substantial annual flow of workers from Sri Lanka (a
total of 57,000 in 1981 alone). The lowering of the population growth
rate was accompanied by changes in the age distribution, with the
older age-groups increasing, and by the concentration of people in
urban areas. Those phenomena also accompanied lower population
growth in Europe and the United States.

Population is not uniformly spread but is concentrated within
the wet zone and urban centers on the coast and the Jaffna Peninsula. The country's mean population density—based on 1981 census
data—was 230 persons per square kilometer, but in Colombo District density was 2,605 persons per square kilometer. In contrast,
the dry zone districts of Vavuniya, Mannar, Mullaittivu, and
Moneragala had fewer than fifty-five persons per square kilometer.
One reason for the unequal settlement pattern was the rainfall distribution, which made it possible for the wet zones to support larger
village farming populations. Another reason was the slow but steady
concentration of people in urban centers during the twentieth century. The ratio of Sri Lankans living in cities increased from 11
percent in 1871 to 15 percent in 1946 and 21.5 percent in 1981
(see fig. 5).

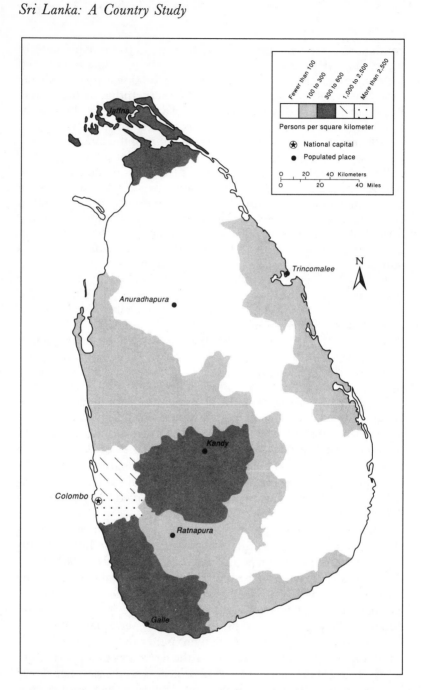

Source: Based on information from the Central Bank of Sri Lanka, Statistics Department, *Economic and Social Statistics of Sri Lanka,* Colombo, 1985.

Figure 5. Distribution of Population, 1985

By 1985 a slowly declining crude birth rate hinted at a gradual aging of the population and changed requirements for social services (see table 3, Appendix). For the time being, however, there was considerable pressure for jobs, education, and welfare facilities from the large number of people who were raising families or pursuing careers. In the remaining decades of the century and beyond there was likely to be greater pressure for housing and health care for an aging population.

Urbanization has affected almost every area of the country since independence. Local market centers have grown into towns, and retail or service stores have cropped up even in small agricultural villages. The greatest growth in urban population, however, has occurred around a few large centers. In 1981 the urbanized population was 32.2 percent in Trincomalee District and 32.6 percent in Jaffna District, in contrast to the rural Moneragala District where only 2.2 percent of the people lived in towns. Colombo District, with 74.4 percent urban population, experienced the largest changes. Between 1881 and 1981, the city of Colombo increased its size from 25 to 37 square kilometers and its population from 110,502 to 587,647.

Since independence was granted in 1948, there have been four main trends in migration. First, every year more people move from rural areas to the cities. Second, the cities have changed from concentrated centers to sprawling suburbs. During the 1970s, the city of Colombo actually lost population, mostly to neighboring cities in Colombo District. Part of the suburban growth has resulted from a planned strategy to reduce urban congestion. For example, a new parliamentary complex opened in Sri Jayewardenepura in the suburb of Kotte east of Colombo in 1982 (although Colombo is still considered the national capital). Much of the growth, however, has been the unplanned proliferation of slums inhabited by poor and unskilled masses and lacking public utilities or services. Third, government irrigation projects attracted many farmers from the wet zone to the pioneer settlements in the dry zone. During the decade ending in 1981, the highest rates of population increase occurred in the districts of Anuradhapura and Polonnaruwa, where the Mahaweli Ganga Program attracted immigrant farmers. Fourth, Sinhalese-Tamil ethnic struggles displaced many people during the 1970s and 1980s. During a Tamil repatriation program in the 1970s, large numbers of Tamil plantation workers left for India or moved out of the hill areas toward the north and the east. After the intensification of communal fighting in 1983, an estimated 100,000 Tamil refugees fled to India, where they lived in refugee camps in Tamil Nadu State, and thousands more were relocated

71

through refugee agencies in Sri Lanka (see The Tamil Insurgency, ch. 5). During the counterinsurgency operations of the Sri Lankan and Indian armies in 1987 and 1988, many residents of the Jaffna Peninsula fled their homes for temporary shelter in refugee camps (see The Armed Forces, ch. 5).

As in South Asia as a whole—and in contrast to global patterns—Sri Lankan males outnumbered females in the mid-1980s. In Sri Lanka, for every 100 female births registered there were 104 males. In the past, the gender ratio of the general population was even more unequal—113 men to 100 women in 1941. In part, this imbalance is attributed to the emigration of plantation workers, many of whom were men. Much of the change, however, may be due to a growing sensitivity to the health of women. Since 1963, the average female life expectancy has increased by seven years, while male life expectancy has risen by three years.

Ethnic Groups

The people of Sri Lanka are divided into ethnic groups whose conflicts have dominated public life since the nineteenth century. The two main characteristics that mark a person's ethnic heritage are language and religion, which intersect to create four major ethnic groups—the Sinhalese, the Tamils, the Muslims, and the Burghers (see fig. 6). Ethnic divisions are not based on race or physical appearance; some Sri Lankans claim to determine the ethnicity of a person by his facial characteristics or color, but in reality such premises are not provable. There is nothing in the languages or religious systems in Sri Lanka that officially promotes the social segregation of their adherents, but historical circumstances have favored one or more of the groups at different times, leading to hostility and competition for political and economic power.

Sinhalese

The Sinhalese are the largest ethnic group in the country, officially comprising 11 million people or 74 percent of the population in 1981. They are distinguished primarily by their language, Sinhala, which is a member of the Indo-European linguistic group that includes Hindi and other north Indian tongues as well as most of the languages of Europe. It is likely that groups from north India introduced an early form of Sinhala when they migrated to the island around 500 B.C., bringing with them the agricultural economy that has remained dominant to the twentieth century. From early times, however, Sinhala has included a large number of loan words and constructs from Tamil, and modern speech includes many expressions from European languages, especially English.

The Sinhalese claim to be descendants of Prince Vijaya and his band of immigrants from northern India, but it is probable that the original group of Sinhalese immigrants intermarried with indigenous inhabitants (see Ancient Legends and Chronicles, ch. 1). The Sinhalese gradually absorbed a wide variety of castes or tribal groups from the island and from southern India during the last 2,500 years.

The Buddhist religion reinforces the solidarity of the Sinhalese as an ethnic community. In 1988 approximately 93 percent of the Sinhala speakers were Buddhists, and 99.5 percent of the Buddhists in Sri Lanka spoke Sinhala. The most popular Sinhalese folklore, literature, and rituals teach children from an early age the uniqueness of Buddhism in Sri Lanka, the long relationship between Buddhism and the culture and politics of the island, and the importance of preserving this fragile cultural inheritance. Buddhist monks are accorded great respect and participate in services at the notable events in people's lives. To become a monk is a highly valued career goal for many young men. The neighboring Buddhist monastery or shrine is the center of cultural life for Sinhalese villagers (see Buddhism, this ch.).

Their shared language and religion unite all ethnic Sinhalese, but there is a clear difference between the "Kandyan" and the "low-country" Sinhalese. Because the Kingdom of Kandy in the highlands remained independent until 1818, conservative cultural and social forms remained in force there. English education was less respected, and traditional Buddhist education remained a vital force in the preservation of Sinhalese culture. The former Kandyan nobility retained their social prestige, and caste divisions linked to occupational roles changed slowly. The plains and the coast of Sri Lanka, on the other hand, experienced great change under 400 years of European rule. Substantial numbers of coastal people, especially among the Karava (see Glossary) caste, converted to Christianity through determined missionary efforts of the Portuguese, Dutch, and British; 66 percent of the Roman Catholics and 43 percent of the Protestants in the early 1980s were Sinhalese. Social mobility based on economic opportunity or service to the colonial governments allowed entire caste or kin groups to move up in the social hierarchy. The old conceptions of noble or servile status declined, and a new elite developed on the basis of its members' knowledge of European languages and civil administration. The Dutch legal system changed traditional family law. A wider, more cosmopolitan outlook differentiated the low-country Sinhalese from the more "old fashioned" inhabitants of highlands (see Caste, this ch.).

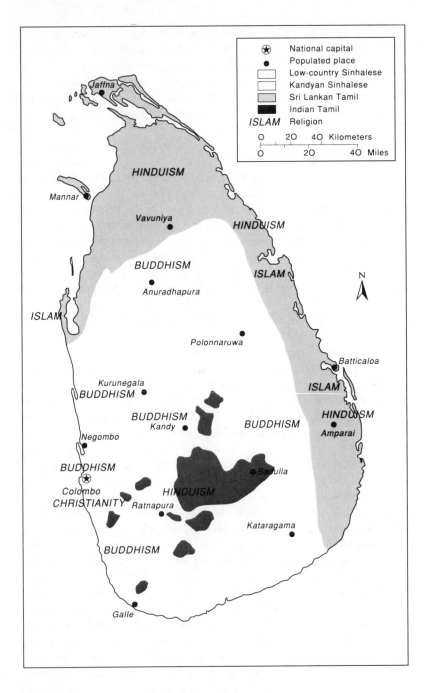

Figure 6. Ethnolinguistic Groups and Religions, 1988

Tamils

The people collectively known as the Tamils (see Glossary), comprising 2,700,000 persons or approximately 18 percent of the population in 1981, use the Tamil language as their native tongue. Tamil is one of the Dravidian (see Glossary) languages found almost exclusively in peninsular India. It existed in South Asia before the arrival of people speaking Indo-European languages in about 1500 B.C. Tamil literature of a high quality has survived for at least 2,000 years in southern India, and although the Tamil language absorbed many words from northern Indian languages, in the late twentieth century it retained many forms of a purely Dravidian speech—a fact that is of considerable pride to its speakers. Tamil is spoken by at least 40 million people in the Indian state of Tamil Nadu (the "land of the Tamils"), and by millions more in neighboring states of southern India and among Tamil emigrants throughout the world.

There was a constant stream of migration from southern India to Sri Lanka from prehistoric times. Once the Sinhalese controlled Sri Lanka, however, they viewed their own language and culture as native to the island, and in their eyes Tamil-speaking immigrants constituted a foreign ethnic community. Some of these immigrants appear to have abandoned Tamil for Sinhala and become part of the Sinhalese caste system. Most however, continued to speak Tamil and looked toward southern India as their cultural homeland. Their connections with Tamil Nadu received periodic reinforcement during struggles between the kings of Sri Lanka and southern India that peaked in the wars with the Chola (see Rise of Sinhalese and Tamil Ethnic Awareness, ch. 1). It is probable that the ancestors of many Tamil speakers entered the country as a result of the Chola conquest, for some personal names and some constructions used in Sri Lankan Tamil are reminiscent of the Chola period.

The Tamil speakers in Sri Lanka are divided into two groups that have quite different origins and relationships to the country. The Sri Lankan Tamils trace their immigration to the distant past and are effectively a native minority. In 1981 they numbered 1,886,872, or 12.7 percent of the population. The Indian Tamils are either immigrants or the descendants of immigrants who came under British sponsorship to Sri Lanka to work on plantations in the central highlands. In 1981 they numbered 818,656, or 5.5 percent of the population. Because they lived on plantation settlements, separate from other groups, including the Sri Lankan Tamils, the Indian Tamils have not become an integral part of society and indeed have been viewed by the Sinhalese as foreigners. The population of Indian Tamils has been shrinking through programs repatriating them to Tamil Nadu (see Independence, ch. 1).

Ethnic Tamils are united to each other by their common religious beliefs, and the Tamil language and culture. Some 80 percent of the Sri Lankan Tamils and 90 percent of the Indian Tamils are Hindus. They have little contact with Buddhism, and they worship the Hindu pantheon of gods. Their religious myths, stories of saints, literature, and rituals are distinct from the cultural sources of the Sinhalese (see Hinduism, this ch.). The caste groups of the Tamils are also different from those of the Sinhalese, and they have their rationale in religious ideologies that the Sinhalese do not share. Religion and caste do, however, create divisions within the Tamil community. Most of the Indian Tamils are members of low Indian castes that are not respected by the upper- and middle-level castes of the Sri Lankan Tamils (see Caste, this ch.). Furthermore, a minority of the Tamils—4.3 percent of the Sri Lankan Tamils and 7.6 percent of the Indian Tamils—are converts to Christianity, with their own places of worship and separate cultural lives. In this way, the large Tamil minority in Sri Lanka is effectively separated from the mainstream Sinhalese culture and is fragmented into two major groups with their own Christian minorities.

Muslims

Muslims, who make up approximately 7 percent of the population, comprise a group of minorities practicing the religion of Islam. As in the case of the other ethnic groups, the Muslims have their own separate sites of worship, religious and cultural heroes, social circles, and even languages. The Muslim community is divided into three main sections—the Sri Lankan Moors, the Indian Moors, and the Malays, each with its own history and traditions.

The Sri Lankan Moors make up 93 percent of the Muslim population and 7 percent of the total population of the country (1,046,926 people in 1981). They trace their ancestry to Arab traders who moved to southern India and Sri Lanka some time between the eighth and fifteenth centuries, adopted the Tamil language that was the common language of Indian Ocean trade, and settled permanently in Sri Lanka. The Sri Lankan Moors lived primarily in coastal trading and agricultural communities, preserving their Islamic cultural heritage while adopting many southern Asian customs. During the period of Portuguese colonization, the Moors suffered from persecution, and many moved to the Central Highlands, where their descendants remain. The language of the Sri Lankan Moors is Tamil, or a type of "Arabic Tamil" that contains a large number of Arabic words. On the east coast, their family lines are traced through women, as in kinship systems of the southwest Indian state of Kerala, but they govern themselves through Islamic law (see Family; Islam, this ch.).

The Indian Moors are Muslims who trace their origins to immigrants searching for business opportunities during the colonial period. Some of these people came to the country as far back as Portuguese times; others arrived during the British period from various parts of India. The Memon, originally from Sind (in modern Pakistan), first arrived in 1870; in the 1980s they numbered only about 3,000. The Bohra and the Khoja came from northwestern India (Gujarat State) after 1880; in the 1980s they collectively numbered fewer than 2,000. These groups tended to retain their own places of worship and the languages of their ancestral homelands.

The Malays originated in Southeast Asia. Their ancestors came to the country when both Sri Lanka and Indonesia were colonies of the Dutch. Most of the early Malay immigrants were soldiers, posted by the Dutch colonial administration to Sri Lanka, who decided to settle on the island. Other immigrants were convicts or members of noble houses from Indonesia who were exiled to Sri Lanka and who never left. The main source of a continuing Malay identity is their common Malay language (*bahasa melayu*), which includes numerous words absorbed from Sinhalese and Tamil, and is spoken at home. In the 1980s, the Malays comprised about 5 percent of the Muslim population in Sri Lanka.

Burghers

The term Burgher was applied during the period of Dutch rule to European nationals living in Sri Lanka. By extension it came to signify any permanent resident of the country who could trace ancestry back to Europe. Eventually it included both Dutch Burghers and Portuguese Burghers. Always proud of their racial origins, the Burghers further distanced themselves from the mass of Sri Lankan citizens by immersing themselves in European culture, speaking the language of the current European colonial government, and dominating the best colonial educational and administrative positions. They have generally remained Christians and live in urban locations. Since independence, however, the Burgher community has lost influence and in turn has been shrinking in size because of emigration. In 1981 the Burghers made up .3 percent (39,374 people) of the population.

Veddah

The Veddah (see Glossary) are the last descendants of the ancient inhabitants of Sri Lanka, predating the arrival of the Sinhalese.

They have long been viewed in the popular imagination as a link to the original hunting-and-gathering societies that gradually disappeared as the Sinhalese spread over the island. In the 1980s, Veddah lived in the eastern highlands, where some had been relocated as a result of the Mahaweli Ganga Program. They have not preserved their own language, and they resemble their poorer Sinhalese neighbors, living in small rural settlements. The Veddah have become more of a caste than a separate ethnic group, and they are generally accepted as equal in rank to the dominant Goyigama caste of the Sinhalese (see Caste, this ch.).

Ethnic Group Relations

The different ethnic groups are not evenly spread throughout the island, but live in concentrated areas, depending upon where they settled historically (see fig. 6). The Indian Tamils are heavily concentrated in the highland districts, especially in Nuwara Eliya, where they constitute almost half the population. This settlement pattern reflects their strong relationship with the plantation economy for which they provided much of the unskilled labor. The Sri Lankan Tamils, on the other hand, make up more than 95 percent of the population in the Jaffna Peninsula, more than 70 percent of the population in Batticaloa District, and substantial minorities in other northern and eastern districts. This pattern reflects the historical dominance of Tamil kingdoms in the northern half of the island. The Muslims are not in the majority anywhere, although they make up large minorities in Mannar District on the northwest coast and in the east coast districts; their strongest presence is in Amparai District, where they comprise 42 percent of the population. The Sinhalese exist in substantial numbers everywhere except in the Jaffna and Batticaloa districts, and in some southern districts they comprise almost the entire population. Colombo District approaches the closest to an ethnic melting pot, with a Sinhalese majority and substantial Tamil and Muslim minorities. Colombo is also home to most of the Burghers (72 percent) and Malays (65 percent).

In many cases, the different ethnic communities live in separate villages or sections of villages, and in towns or cities they inhabit different neighborhoods. The fact that primary education is in either Tamil or Sinhala effectively segregates the children of the different communities at an early age. Business establishments run by, or catering to a specific ethnic group, tend to broadcast their ethnicity by signs either in Sinhala or Tamil, each of which possesses its own distinctive script. Sports teams tend to include members of only one community, while Buddhist and Hindu religious services

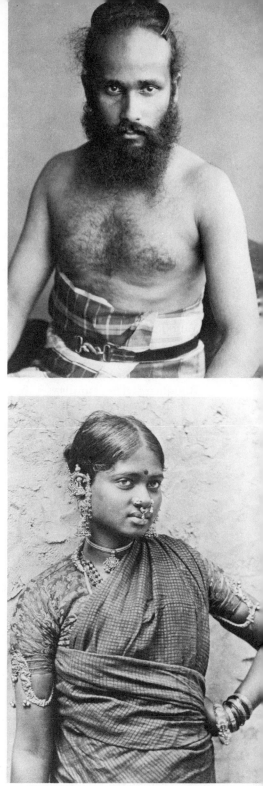

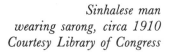

Sinhalese man
wearing sarong, circa 1910
Courtesy Library of Congress

Tamil nautch
(dancing girl), circa 1910
Courtesy Library of Congress

are automatically limited to one ethnic group. Relatively few persons are fluent in both Tamil and Sinhala, and accents betray which native community a person belongs to very quickly. Countering the intense pressures favoring segregation, however, are official government policies that treat all citizens equally and numerous personal networks within neighborhoods and among individuals that link members of different ethnic groups and foster friendships.

Ethnic segregation is reinforced by fears that ethnic majorities will try to dominate positions of influence and repress the religious, linguistic, or cultural systems of minorities. The Sinhalese are the overwhelming majority of residents within Sri Lanka, but they feel intimidated by the large Tamil population in nearby India; the combined Tamil populations of India and Sri Lanka outnumber the Sinhalese at least four to one. The recent memories of Tamil prominence in colonial and postcolonial administration, combined with a modern renaissance in Tamil consciousness in south India, are constant reminders of the potential power of the Tamil community. The Sinhalese feel quite isolated as the only group in the world speaking their language and professing their variant of Theravada Buddhism. The Tamils, on the other hand, are a minority within Sri Lanka. They cannot be sure of Indian support, and they experience increasing restrictions on social mobility as the Sinhalese majority increases its hold on the government. Anti-Tamil riots and military actions in the 1980s alienated a large sector of the Tamil community. In the middle are the Muslims, who speak Tamil but whose religious and cultural systems are alien to both other ethnic groups. Muslim leaders increasingly seek to safeguard the cultural heritage of their own community by adopting a public stance of ethnic confrontation.

Social Organization

Caste

Nature of Caste

When the Portuguese began to trade extensively with South Asia, they quickly noticed a fundamental difference between South Asian societies and those of other world areas. In India and Sri Lanka, societies are broken up into a large number of groups who do not intermarry, who are ranked in relation to each other, and whose interactions are governed by a multitude of ritualized behaviors. The Portuguese called these groups *casta,* from which the English term *caste* is derived. In South Asia, they are described by the term *jati,* or birth. According to traditional culture, every person is born into a particular group that defines his or her unchangeable position within society.

One of the most basic concepts underlying caste is purity. On one level this idea translates into a concern for personal hygiene, but the concept ultimately refers to a psychic or spiritual purity that lies beyond the physical body. A religious interpretation associated with Indian thought asserts that personal salvation or enlightenment is the ultimate goal of life, and that the individual goes through many lives and experiences before attaining sufficient knowledge to transcend the material world. Those beings who have gone farther on this road to enlightenment have purified their consciousness and regulate their lives in order to prevent more gross experiences from interfering with their progress toward salvation. Those groups of people whose life-styles are the purest are farthest along on the spiritual road and are most deserving of respect. These ideas about purity offer a rationale for dividing society into a large number of groups, ranked according to the purity of their life-styles or occupations. The persons in each group must be careful to preserve the relative purity of their own group and to avoid close contact with persons of lower purity; otherwise, they may sully or "pollute" themselves or the members of purer groups.

The idea of psychic purity blends with a series of traditional notions about pure or polluting substances and about behaviors and rituals, resulting in a rich system that explains caste segregation and modes of caste interaction. It is possible for people to transmit their qualities to others by touching them or by giving them objects. In extreme cases, even the shadow of a very low-caste individual can pollute an individual of the highest, priestly castes. If the physical contact is intimate or if people have manipulated certain objects for a long time, the intensity of the transmitted qualities increases. Simple objects such as tools, for example, may change hands between persons of different caste without problem. Food, however, which actually enters and becomes part of a person's body, is a more serious matter. Cooked food, involving processing and longer periods of contact, is more problematic than uncooked food. There is thus a series of prohibitions on the sharing of food between members of different castes. Members of higher castes may avoid taking food from members of lower castes, although lower-caste persons may not mind taking food from members of the higher orders. The most intimate contact is sexual because it involves the joining of two bodies and the transmission of the very substances that determine caste for life. Sexual contact between persons of different castes is discouraged, and intercaste marriage is rare. When intercaste sexual affairs do occur, they are almost always between men of higher caste and women of lower caste, for it is less polluting to send forth substances than to receive them. In the distant past, women who had sexual contact with men of lower castes were killed, and they would still be ostracized today in some villages. When polluting contacts occur between members of different castes, personal purity may be restored by performing cleansing rituals. In general, these concepts of purity prevent partaking of meals together and intermarriage between different castes, regulate intercaste relations through a wide variety of ritual behaviors, and preserve deep-seated social cleavages throughout Sri Lanka.

There has been a strong tendency to link the position of different castes in the social hierarchy to their occupations. Groups who wash clothes or who process waste, thus coming in contact with undesirable substances from many persons, are typically given low status. In both Hindu and Buddhist thought, the destruction of life is very ignoble, because it extinguishes other beings struggling for consciousness and salvation. This idea has rationalized views of fishermen or leather workers, who kill animals, as low and impure groups. In many cases, however, the labeling of an occupational group as a caste with a particular status has depended on historical developments rather than theories of purity. As the village farming economy spread over time, many tribal societies probably changed from hunters and gatherers to low-status service castes, ranked below the landowning farmers. Many poor agricultural laborers in Sri Lanka remain members of low castes as well. Other immigrant groups came to Sri Lanka, fit into particular occupational niches, and became known as castes with ranks linked to their primary occupations. Castes with members who accumulated wealth and power have tended to rise gradually in their relative positions, and it is not uncommon for members of rising caste groups to adopt vegetarianism or patronize religious institutions in an attempt to raise their public ritual status.

Caste among the Sinhalese

The dominant caste among the Sinhalese population is the Goyigama. Although the government keeps no official statistics on caste, it appears that the Goyigama comprise at least half the Sinhalese population. The traditional occupation of this caste is agriculture, and most members are still peasant farmers in villages almost everywhere in Sri Lanka. In traditional Sinhalese society, they monopolized the highest positions at royal courts and among the landowning elite. In the democratic society of the twentieth century, their members still dominate the political scene. In most villages they might be no richer than their non-Goyigama neighbors, but the richest landlord groups tend to be Goyigama, while the poorest agricultural laborers tend to include few Goyigama.

In the Central Highlands, some traditions of the Kingdom of Kandy survived after its collapse in 1818, preserved in unique forms of the caste system until the postindependence period. The most important feature of the old system was *rajakariya,* or the "king's work," which linked each caste to a specific occupation and demanded services for the court and religious institutions. The connection of caste and job is still stronger in the Central Highlands, and at events such as the Kandy Perahera, an annual festival honoring gods and the Buddha, the various castes still perform traditional functions. The Goyigama in the highlands differ from those of the low country because they preserve divisions within the caste that derive from the official ranking of noble and commoner families in the old kingdom. Honorific titles hearkening back to ancestral homes, manors (*vasagama*), or noble houses (*gedara*) still marked the pedigrees of the old aristocracy in the 1980s, and marriages between members of these families and common Goyigama were rare. In the low country, these subcastes within the Goyigama have faded away, and high status is marked by European titles and degrees rather than the older, feudal titles.

There are still major differences between the caste structures of the highlands and those of the low country, although some service groups are common to both. The southwest coast is home to three major castes whose ancestors may have immigrated but who have become important actors in the Sinhalese social system: the Karava (fishermen), the Durava (toddy tappers—see Glossary), and the Salagama (cinnamon peelers). Originally of marginal or low status, these groups exploited their traditional occupations and their coastal positions to accumulate wealth and influence during the colonial period. By the late twentieth century, members of these castes had moved to all parts of the country, occupied high business and academic positions, and were generally accorded a caste rank equal to or slightly below the Goyigama. The highland interior is home to the Vahumpura, or traditional makers of jaggery (a sugar made from palm sap), who have spread throughout the country in a wide variety of occupations, especially agriculture. In the Kandy District of the highlands live the Batgam (or Padu), a low caste of agricultural laborers, and the Kinnara, who were traditionally segregated from other groups because of their menial status. Living in all areas are service groups, such as the Hena (Rada), traditional washermen who still dominate the laundry trade; the Berava, traditional temple drummers who work as cultivators in many villages; and the Navandanna (Acari), traditional artisans. In rural environments, the village blacksmith or washerman may still belong to the old occupational caste groups, but accelerating social mobility and the growing obsolescence of the old services are slowly eroding the link between caste and occupation.

Caste among the Tamils

The caste system of the Sri Lankan Tamils resembles the system of the Sinhalese, but the individual Tamil castes differ from the Sinhalese castes. The dominant Tamil caste, constituting well over 50 percent of the Tamil population, are the Vellala. Like the Goyigama, members are primarily cultivators. In the past, the Vellala formed the elite in the Jaffna kingdom and were the larger landlords; during the colonial period, they took advantage of new avenues for mobility and made up a large section of the educated, administrative middle class. In the 1980s, the Vellala still comprised a large portion of the Tamil urban middle class, although many well-off families retained interests in agricultural land. Below the Vellala, but still high in the Tamil caste system, are the Karaiya (see Glossary), whose original occupation was fishing. Like the Sinhalese Karava, they branched out into commercial ventures, raising their economic and ritual position during the nineteenth century. The Chetti, a group of merchant castes, also have a high ritual position. In the middle of the caste hierarchy is a group of numerically small artisan castes, and at the bottom of the system are more numerous laboring castes, including the Palla, associated with agricultural work.

The caste system of the Tamils is more closely tied to religious bases than the caste system of the Sinhalese. Caste among the Sri Lankan Tamils derives from the Brahman-dominated system of southern India. The Brahmans, a priestly caste, trace their origins to the dawn of Indian civilization (ca. 1500 B.C.), and occupy positions of the highest respect and purity because they typically preserve sacred texts and enact sacred rituals. Many conservative Brahmans view the caste system and their high position within it as divinely ordained human institutions (see Hinduism, this ch.). Because they control avenues to salvation by officiating at temples and performing rituals in homes, their viewpoint has a large following among traditionally minded Hindus. The standards of purity set forth by the Brahmanical view are so high that some caste groups, such as the Paraiyar (whose name came into English as "pariah"), have been "untouchable," barred from participation in the social functions or religious rituals of other Hindus. Untouchability also has been an excuse for extreme exploitation of lower-caste workers.

Although Brahmans in Sri Lanka have always been a very small minority, the conservative Brahmanical world-view has remained

Elephants bathing in a jungle river
Courtesy Embassy of Sri Lanka, Washington

strong among the Vellala and other high castes. Major changes have occurred, however, in the twentieth century. Ideas of equality among all people, officially promoted by the government, have combined with higher levels of education among the Tamil elites to soften the old prejudices against the lowest castes. Organizations of low-caste workers have engaged in successful militant struggles to open up employment, education, and Hindu temples for all groups, including former untouchables.

The Indian Tamils are predominantly members of low castes from southern India, whose traditional occupations were agricultural labor and service for middle and high castes. Their low ritual status has reinforced their isolation from the Sinhalese and from the Sri Lankan Tamils.

Caste Interactions in Daily Life

The divisions between the castes are reaffirmed on a daily basis, especially in rural areas, by many forms of language and etiquette. Each caste uses different personal names and many use slightly different forms of speech, so it is often possible for people to determine someone's caste as soon as the person begins speaking. Persons of lower rank behave politely by addressing their superiors with honorable formulas and by removing their headgear. A standard furnishing in upper caste rural houses is a low stool (*kolamba*), provided so that members of lower castes may take a lower seat while visiting. Villages are divided into separate streets or neighborhoods according to caste, and the lowest orders may live in separate hamlets. In times past, low-caste persons of both sexes were prohibited from covering their upper bodies, riding in cars, or building large homes. These most offensive forms of discrimination were eliminated by the twentieth century after extensive agitation.

Outside the home, most social interactions take place without reference to caste. In villages, business offices, and factories, members of different groups work together, talking and joking freely, without feeling uncomfortable about their caste inequalities. The modern urban environment makes excessive concern about caste niceties impossible; all kinds of people squeeze onto buses with few worries about intimate personal contact. Employment, health, and educational opportunities are officially open to all, without prejudice based on caste. In urban slums, the general breakdown of social organization among the destitute allows a wide range of intercaste relationships. Despite the near invisibility of caste in public life, caste-based factions exist in all modern institutions, including political parties, and when it comes to marriage—the true test of adherence to ritual purity—the overwhelming majority of unions occur between members of the same caste.

Family

Among all ethnic and caste groups, the most important social unit is the nuclear family—husband, wife, and unmarried children. Even when economic need causes several families (Sinhala, *ge;* Tamil, *kudumbam*) or generations to live together, each wife will maintain her own cooking place and prepare food for her own husband as a sign of the individuality of the nuclear family. Among all sections of the population, however, relatives of both the wife and the husband form an important social network that supports the nuclear family and encompasses the majority of its important social relations. The kindred (*pavula*, in Sinhala) of an individual often constitute the people with whom it is possible to eat or marry. Because of these customs, local Sinhalese society is highly fragmented, not only at the level of ethnic group or caste, but also at the level of the kindred.

The kinship systems of Sri Lanka share with most of South Asia and the Middle East the institution of preferred cross-cousin marriage. This means that the most acceptable person for a young man to marry is the daughter of his father's sister. The most suitable partner for a young woman is the son of her mother's brother.

Parallel cousins—the son of the father's brother or the daughter of the mother's sister—tend to be improper marriage partners. There is a close and special relationship between children and their aunts or uncles, who may become their fathers-or mothers-in-law. Special kinship terminology exists in both Tamil and Sinhalese for relatives in preferred or prohibited marriage categories. In many villages, people spend their entire childhood with a clear knowledge of their future marriage plans and in close proximity to their future spouses. The ties between cross-cousins are so close in theory that persons marrying partners other than their cross-cousins may include a special ritual in their marriage ceremonies during which they receive permission from their cousins to marry an outsider. The system of cross-cousin marriage is ideally suited to maintaining the closed ritual purity of an extended kinship group and retaining control over property within a small circle of relatives.

The vast majority of marriages in Sri Lanka are monogamous, that is, they involve one woman and one man. Unions between one man and more than one woman (polygyny) are neither illegal nor unknown, however, and wealthy men can take several wives if they can afford to support the families. Unions involving one woman and more than one man (polyandry) are also legal and possible.

In the Kandyan region, descent and inheritance are traced through both spouses: both husband and wife possess their own property and may bequeath it in equal shares to their descendants. In the low country, where Dutch Roman Law is in effect, marriages create joint property between husband and wife, which on their death is divided among their heirs. On the east coast, Tamil Muslim families trace descent and inheritance through the mother, and men will typically reside with their in-laws. There is a preference for living near the husband's family in most areas of the country, although a family with no sons may prefer that a son-in-law live nearby and manage their lands. Among all the variations of inheritance and descent, the husband is typically the manager of the nuclear family's property and represents his family in most public duties and functions.

In the rural areas of Sri Lanka, traditional marriages did not require a wedding ceremony or legal registration of the union. The man and the woman simply started living together, with the consent of their parents (who were usually related to one another). This type of customary marriage still survives, although it has been declining in recent years. In 1946 about 30 percent of marriages in Sri Lanka were not registered, but in 1981 that figure had declined to 10 percent. Most such unions were concentrated along the north and east coasts and in the Central Highlands. Legal divorce is easy to obtain, and divorces of customary marriages occur through mutual consent of the partners in consultation with their extended families. Most marriages, however, are quite stable because of the considerable social pressure and support exerted by kindred of both the husband and the wife. In 1981 the divorce rate per 10,000 persons amounted to only 30.5.

Most Sri Lankan families have small means and do not spend large sums on wedding parties. Among wealthier families in both the countryside and the cities, marriages occur more often between families that were not previously related, and more elaborate ceremonies take place. In such cases the bride may receive a substantial dowry, determined beforehand during long negotiations between her family and her future in-laws. Preceding these well-publicized affairs are detailed discussions with matchmakers and astrologers who pick the most auspicious times for the marriage. Except for some of the well-educated urban elite, the parents arrange all marriages, although their children may meet future spouses and veto a particularly unattractive marriage. The average age at marriage has been increasing in recent years because of longer periods required for education and establishing a stable career. In 1981 the average age of grooms was twenty-seven or twenty-eight, and the average age of brides was twenty-four. Betrothals arranged by parents could begin much earlier, and in rural areas marriages between persons in their early teens still occurred. Whatever the arrangements, however, marriage and the propagation of children were the desired state for all groups, and by age thirty-nine, 86 percent of both sexes had married at least once.

All ethnic groups in Sri Lanka preserve clear distinctions in the roles of the sexes. Women are responsible for cooking, raising children, and taking care of housework. In families relying on agriculture, women are in charge of weeding and help with the harvest, and among poor families women also perform full-time work for the more well-to-do. The man's job is to protect women and children and provide them with material support, and in this role men dominate all aspects of business and public life. At the center of the system are children, who mix freely until puberty and receive a great deal of affection from both sexes. As they enter their teens, children begin to adopt the adult roles that will keep them in separate worlds: girls help with household chores and boys work outside the home. Among the middle- and upper-income groups, however, education of children may last into their early twenties, and women may mix with males or even take on jobs that were in the past reserved for men. There has been a tendency to view the educational qualifications of women as a means for obtaining favorable

marriage alliances, and many middle-class women withdraw from the workplace after marriage.

Religion

Buddhism

The Life and Message of the Buddha

The founder of Buddhism was a man named Siddartha Gautama, a prince of the Sakya clan in what is now Nepal during the sixth century B.C. Popular stories of his life include many miraculous events: before his birth his mother experienced visions that foretold his future greatness; when he was born, he could immediately walk and talk; wise men who encountered the child predicted that he would become either a great sage or a great emperor. Behind these legends is the tale of a young man reared in luxury, who began to question the meaning of life. At the age of thirty, he abandoned his home (including his beautiful wife and child) and wandered throughout northeast India as a beggar, searching for truth.

Gautama studied under several religious teachers and became adept at techniques of meditation and self-imposed austerity. Finally, he sat down under a bo (pipal) tree and resolved not to move from that spot until he had achieved perfect enlightenment. He entered into deeper and deeper concentration, until he finally

reached an understanding of the nature of existence and the purpose of life. He thus became the one who knows, the Buddha (from
the verb *budh,* to know or understand). At first he debated whether
other beings would be able to comprehend the knowledge that he
had gained, but compassion moved him to bring his message to
the world and lead others to enlightment. He spent the next fifty
years traveling throughout northeast India, discussing his knowledge
with all sorts of people. By the end of his life, his message and example had attracted large numbers of converts, from kings to beg-
gars, from rich men to robbers. At his death around 483 B.C.,
he left behind a dedicated group of disciples who carried on his work.

The Buddha summed up his message in Four Noble Truths that
still form the core of Buddhist belief. The first truth is that life is
suffering (*dukkha*). The material world, thoughts, emotions, and
ideas are all transitory and do not express or contain any eternal
truths. All beings repeatedly experience pain and loss as they pass
through innumerable lives, never able to emerge from a conditioned
existence (samsara) created through their own consciousness. The
second truth describes the cause of suffering as attachment to the
world and the products of one's own consciousness. This attachment, or craving for existence, causes beings to create mental views
of the world and believe they are correct, to form relationships with
other beings, to struggle and desire. Such efforts are in vain because none of these strategies allows them to escape from their limited, suffering world. The third truth says that the way to break
the limiting trap of samsara is to stop attachment. Once one has
concentrated awareness so intensely that all material and spiritual
phenomena appear empty, without real substance, then existence
becomes liberated and suffering ceases. The fourth truth is the Noble
Eightfold Path of behavior, which roots out attachment and the
conditioned view of the world and leads toward the state of enlightenment (*nibbana*—nirvana, see Glossary) gained by the Buddha. The true follower of the Buddha rejects the world, becomes
a full-time searcher after truth, and practices meditation that concentrates awareness.

The Buddhist Community

In the absence of the Buddha, the custodian of his message is
the assembly (*sangha*—see Glossary) of monks who carry on his
work. The members of the Buddhist assembly practice the discipline
(*vinaya*) set forth by the Buddha as a system of rules for a monastic
order. The discipline calls for strict control over the senses and dedicated meditation by the individual monk (*bhikku*—see Glossary).
Following the Buddha's example, the monk should spend the

morning begging for food from the lay community, then abstain from meals after noon. He should shave his head, wear orange (or yellow) robes, and own only his clothes and a begging bowl. He should avoid all sexual contact or any other forms of sensual pleasure. The *bhikku* should rest in one place for an extended period only during the rainy season, when groups of mendicants may stay together in communal houses (*vihara*). Elaborate rules evolved for admitting novices to the monastic community and conferring ordination on *bhikku* who passed through a period of initiation and training. The strict organization of the monastic order created a solid basis for the preservation of the Buddha's message and a readily adaptable institution that was transplanted in a variety of social environments throughout Asia.

Buddhism in Sri Lanka has its roots deep in one of the earliest variants of Buddhism that survives in the world today. The Sinhalese call their beliefs Theravada, or "the doctrine of the elders." Their tradition, frequently described as Hinayana (meaning "lesser vehicle"), preserves a clear understanding of the Buddha as a man who achieved enlightenment and developed monks (*arhat*) as accomplished followers of his teachings. This tradition differs from the more widespread Mahayana ("great vehicle"), which often treats the Buddha as a superhuman being and fills the universe with a pantheon of enlightened figures (bodhisattvas) who help others achieve enlightenment. In Sri Lanka, people do not officially worship the Buddha, but show reverence to his memory. The most striking expressions of public reverence are *dagoba* or *thupa* (stupa), large mounds built over sites where relics of the Buddha or a great monk are buried. The *dagoba* in Sri Lanka preserve a spherical shape and a style of architectural embellishment that link them directly to the monuments originally erected over the Buddha's remains in ancient India. The traditions of the Sinhalese indicate that their oldest *dagoba* are at least 2,000 years old, from a period when genuine relics of the Buddha came to Sri Lanka. The conservative nature of Sinhalese Buddhism is strengthened through the preservation and living tradition of ancient scriptures in the Pali (see Glossary) language. A dialect related to Sanskrit, the classical language of India, Pali is probably close to the popular language in northeastern India during the Buddha's time. The monks of Sri Lanka have kept alive an unbroken Pali transmission of monastic rules, stories of the Buddha's life, and philosophical treatises that may constitute the oldest body of written Buddhist traditions.

For people who do not become monks, the most effective method of progressing on the road to enlightenment is to accumulate merit

Sri Lanka: A Country Study

(*pin*) through moral actions. One who performs duties faithfully in this world, who supports the monastic order, and who is compassionate to other living beings may hope to achieve a higher birth in a future life, and from that position accumulate sufficient merit and knowledge to achieve enlightenment. Meritorious activities include social service, reverence of the Buddha at shrines or at *dagoba,* and pilgrimage to sacred places. Gifts to monks rank among the most beneficial merit-making activities. Lay devotees invite monks to major events, such as a death in the family or the dedication of a building, and publicly give them food and provisions. In return, the monks perform *pirit,* the solemn recitation of Pali Buddhist scriptures. Although the average person may not understand a word of the ancient language, simply hearing the words and bestowing presents on the monks accumulates merit for the family or even for deceased family members. Some wealthy donors may hold gift-giving ceremonies simply for the public accumulation of merit. The monks thus perform important roles for the laity at times of crisis or accomplishment, and they serve as a focus for public philanthropy.

Popular Sinhalese Religion

There is no central religious authority in Theravada Buddhism, and the monastic community has divided into a number of orders with different styles of discipline or recruitment. The broad outlines of the modern orders originated in the eighteenth century. By that time, monastic personnel came entirely from the upper levels of the Goyigama caste, and enjoyed easy lives as recipients of income from monastic estates worked by lower castes. The official line of monastic ordination had been broken, since monks at that time no longer knew the Pali tradition. In 1753 the Kandyan king fulfilled his duty as a protector of Buddhism by arranging for Theravada monks from Thailand to ordain Sinhalese novices. These initiates set up a reformed sect known as the Siyam Nikaya (the Siamese order), which invigorated the study and propagation of the ancient Sinhalese heritage. The order remained a purely Goyigama enclave. By the nineteenth century, members of rising low-country castes were unhappy with Goyigama monopoly over the *sangha,* and rich merchants arranged for Karava youths to receive ordination from Thai monks. These initiates formed a new sect called the Amarapura Nikaya, that subsequently split along caste lines. Disputes over doctrinal matters and the role of meditation led to the establishment of another order, the Ramanna Nikaya, in the late nineteenth century. In the 1980s, the Sinhalese *sangha* of 20,000 monks fell into three major orders, subdivided

92

Like father, like son: two generations of Buddhist monks
Courtesy Paige W. Thompson

into "families": the Siyam Nikaya contained six divisions; the Amarapura Nikaya, twenty-three; and the Ramanna Nikaya, two. Each family maintained its own line of ordination traced back to great teachers and ultimately to the Buddha. Caste determined membership in many of the sects.

The members of the Buddhist monastic community preserve the doctrinal purity of early Buddhism, but the lay community accepts a large body of other beliefs and religious rituals that are tolerated by the monks and integrated into Sinhalese religion. Many of the features of this popular religion come from Hinduism and from very old traditions of gods and demons. Sinhalese Buddhism is thus a syncretic fusion of various religious elements into a unique cultural system.

There is a thin boundary between reverence for the Buddha's memory and worship of the Buddha as a god, and the unsophisticated layperson often crosses this line by worshiping him as a transcendent divine being. The relics of the Buddha, for example, have miraculous powers; the literature and folklore of the Sinhalese are full of tales recounting the amazing events surrounding relics. During the construction of a Buddha image, the painting of the eyes is an especially important moment when the image becomes "alive" with power. At the Temple of the Tooth in Kandy, where the Buddha's Tooth Relic is enshrined, rituals include elements from Hindu

93

temple worship, such as feeding and clothing of the Buddha (see Hinduism, this ch.). In general, devotees believe that the Buddha's enlightenment makes him an all-powerful being, able to control time and space and all other supernatural beings.

The Buddha is so pure and powerful that he does not intervene personally in the affairs of the world. That is the job of a pantheon of gods (*deva*) and demons (*yakka*) who control material and spiritual events. The Buddha never denied the existence of the gods or demons, but said that attention to these matters simply detracts from concentration on the path to enlightenment. The Sinhalese believe that the all-powerful Buddha has given a warrant (*varan*) to a variety of spiritual entities that allows them to regulate reality within set boundaries (*sima*). For help in matters of everyday life, the Sinhalese petition these spiritual entities rather than the Buddha. Near many *dagoba,* or shrines of the Buddha, there are separate shrines (*devale*) for powerful deities. After reverencing the Buddha, devotees present prayers and petitions to the gods for help with daily life. The shrines for the gods have their own priests (*kapurala*), who practice special rituals of purification that allow them to present offerings of food, flowers, or clothing to the gods. Propitiation of demons occurs far away from Buddhist shrines and involves special rituals featuring the assistance of exorcists.

The popularity of different deities changes over time, as people come to see particular deities as more effective in solving their problems. The principal gods include Vishnu (also a Hindu god, identified by Buddhists as a bodhisattva, or "enlightened being," who helps others attain enlightenment), Natha, Vibhisana, Saman (the god of Adams Peak and its vicinity), and the goddess Pattini (originally an ordinary woman whose devotion to her husband, immortalized in poetry, elevated her to divine rank). During the twentieth century, the god Vibhisana has declined in popularity while the god Kataragama, named after his hometown in Moneragala District, has become extremely powerful. The annual Kataragama festival brings tens of thousands of worshipers to his small town, including Hindus who worship him as a manifestation of the god Murugan and Muslims who worship at the mosque there. This common devotion to sacred sites and sacred persons is one of the most important features of popular religion in Sri Lanka.

Another example of this religious syncretism is the cult of Sri Lanka's leading oracle, Gale Bandara Deviyo, who originally was a Muslim prince slain by the Sinhalese to prevent his accession to the throne. He is revered by Buddhists and Muslims alike at his shrine in the town of Kurunegala (in Kurunegala District). As transportation and communication facilities have expanded in modern Sri Lanka, there has been a big expansion of major pilgrimage sites that are jointly patronized by Sinhalese, Tamils, and Muslims, thus providing a commonality that may lead to closer cultural cooperation among competing ethnic groups.

Buddhism and Politics

Buddhism plays an eminent political role in Sri Lanka and serves as a unifying force for the Sinhalese majority . Although the monks must renounce worldliness, they of necessity maintain close relationships with the lay community, whose members must supply them with food, shelter, and clothing. During the past century, as Sinhalese nationalism fueled lay devotion to Buddhism, there was a proliferation of lay support organizations, such as the All-Ceylon Buddhist Congress, the Colombo Buddhist Theosophical Society, the All-Ceylon Buddhist Women's Association, and the Young Men's Buddhist Association. The state has similarly retained close ties with the *sangha*. Since the time of Asoka, the first great Indian emperor (third century B.C.), the head of state has been seen by Buddhist thinkers as the official protector of Buddhism, the "turner of the wheel of the law" (see Historical Perspective, 1802–1978, ch. 4). One of the recurring problems in the history of Sri Lanka has been a definition of the state as the official supporter of Buddhism, which in turn has been the religion of the ethnic Sinhalese. To be successful among the Sinhalese, a government must provide visible signs of its allegiance to the *sangha* by building or maintaining *dagoba,* judging disputes among the orders of monks, and fostering education in the Pali Buddhist tradition.

Individual monks and entire sects have involved themselves in party politics, but seldom do all families and orders unite behind a coherent policy. When they do unite, they are a potent political force. In 1956, for example, a rare union of monastic opinion gave crucial support to the election of the Sinhalese political leader Solomon West Ridgeway Diaz (S.W.R.D.) Bandaranaike (see Sri Lanka Freedom Party Rule, 1956–65, ch. 1). As of 1988, the *sangha* controlled extensive estates in the interior of Sri Lanka and retained an independent power base that, combined with high status in the eyes of the Sinhalese population, gave the Buddhist orders influence as molders of public opinion. Monks remained prominent at rallies and demonstrations promoting ethnic Sinhalese issues.

Hinduism

Whereas Buddhism claims a historical founder, a basic doctrine, and a formal monastic structure, Hinduism embraces a vast and varied body of religious belief, practice, and organization. In its widest sense, Hinduism encompasses all the religious and cultural systems originating in South Asia, and many Hindus actually accept the Buddha as an important sectarian teacher or as a rebel against or reformer of ancient Hindu culture. The medieval Arabs first used the term *Hindu* to describe the entire cultural complex east of the Sindhu, or Indus, River (in contemporary Pakistan). Hindu beliefs and practices in different regions claim descent from common textual sources, while retaining their regional individuality. In Sri Lanka, Hinduism is closely related to the distinctive cultural systems of neighboring Tamil Nadu.

Classical Hinduism includes as a central tenet of belief the concept of nonviolence (ahimsa), a concept that was of great importance to the Buddha and to such reformers as Mahatma Gandhi some 2,500 years later. Veneration of pure life, especially of the cow, has come to be intimately associated with orthodox Hinduism of all sects. The cow is regarded as, among other things, the sacred embodiment of motherhood and fruitfulness. The deliberate killing of a cow is scarcely less terrible than the killing of a Brahman. For the miscreant it results in immediate and irrevocable outcasting; even the accidental killing of a cow requires elaborate purification ceremonies.

The earliest and most sacred sources of Hinduism are the Vedas, a compilation of hymns originating in northern India around 1,500 B.C. They are the oldest surviving body of literature in South Asia, created by the culture of the Arya (the ''noble'' or ''pure'' ones) in northwest India. Composed in an archaic form of the Sanskrit language, the Vedas were sung by a caste of priests (Brahmans) during sacrifices for the ancient gods. Families of Brahmans have passed down the oral recitation of these hymns for thousands of years, and Brahman claims to high status ultimately rest on their association with Vedic hymns. The vast majority of Hindus know almost nothing of Sanskrit or the Vedas, but even in the late twentieth century Brahmans frequently officiate at important ceremonies such as weddings, reciting ancient hymns and making offerings into sacred flames.

By the time of the Buddha, intellectual speculations gave rise to philosophical concepts that still influence all of South Asia. These speculations became books called Upanishads, originally written as commentaries on the Vedas but later viewed as sacred works in their own right. The Upanishads discuss *brahman,* an impersonal, eternal force that embodies all good and all knowledge. The individual ''soul,'' or atman, partakes of the same qualities as *brahman* but remains immersed in ignorance. Action (karma—see

Glossary) is the cause of its ignorance; reason continually searches
for meaning in the material world and in its own mental creations,
instead of concentrating on *brahman,* the one true reality. The
individual soul, immersed in action, migrates from life to life, until
it achieves identity with *brahman* and is released. There is a close
relationship between the Buddha's understanding of suffering and
enlightenment, and the ideas of atman, karma, and *brahman* that
became basic to Hindu philosophy. The Buddha, however, claimed
that even the idea of the soul was a mental construct of no value,
whereas Hindu thought has generally preserved a belief in the soul.

As India became a major center of civilization with extensive
political and economic systems, Hinduism became associated with
new visions of the gods and worship in temples. Tamil Nadu was
a major center of this transformation. By about A.D. 1000, the
Tamils had reworked Brahmanical culture into a southern Indian
type of devotional (*bhakti*) religion. This religion claimed to be based
on the Vedas and the philosophy of the Upanishads, but its roots
lay just as deep in strong attachments to local deities and a desire
for salvation (*moksha*) through their intercession.

Several gods predominate in the many myths, legends, and styles
of worship. One of the main Hindu gods is Vishnu, often represented as a divine king accompanied by his beautiful wife, Lakshmi,
the bestower of wealth and good fortune. Besides presiding as a
divine monarch, Vishnu periodically descends to earth, assuming
a physical form to help beings attain salvation. Vishnu has ten main
incarnations, two of which—Rama and Krishna—are particularly
popular. Rama was a great hero, whose exploits in rescuing his
wife from the demon king of Lanka are recounted in the epic
Ramayana. Vishnu's most popular incarnation is Krishna, who com-
bines in a single divine figure the mythic episodes of a warrior prince
and a rustic cowherd god. As warrior, Krishna figures prominently
in what is perhaps the single most important Hindu text, the
Bhagavad Gita, where he stresses the importance of doing one's
duty and devotion to god. As divine cowherd, Krishna served as
an inspiration for a vast body of religious poetry in Sanskrit and
the regional South Asian languages. From the eighth to the twelfth
centuries, Tamil devotees of Vishnu (*alvars*) composed poetry in
praise of the god. These Tamil poems, collected in anthologies,
are still recited during worship and festivals for Vishnu.

The second major Hindu deity, and by far the most important
god among the Tamils in Sri Lanka, is Siva. He differs considerably from Vishnu. In many stories he reigns as a king, but often
he appears as a religious ascetic, smeared with ashes, sitting on
a tiger skin in the jungle, with a snake around his neck. He is the

97

lord of animals. Although he is an ascetic, he is also a sexual figure, married to the beautiful Parvati (the daughter of the mountain), and his image is often a single rock shaped like a phallus (*lingam*). He is often a distant figure whose power is destructive, but paradoxically he is a henpecked husband who has to deal with family squabbles involving his sons. His devotees enjoy retelling his myths, but worshipers visualize him as a cosmic creator who will save his creatures when they have abandoned themselves totally to his love. One of the most powerful expressions of his creative role is the image of Nataraja, "Lord of the Dance," who gracefully manifests the rhythm of the universe. Great Tamil devotees (*nayanmar*) of the early middle ages created a large collection of poems dedicated to Siva and his holiest shrines. These collections are still revered among the Tamils as sacred scriptures on the same plane as the Vedas.

Female deities are very important among the Hindu Tamils. At temples for Siva or Vishnu there are separate shrines for the god and for his consort, and in many cases the shrine for the goddess (*amman*) receives much more attention from worshipers. Hindu philosophy interprets the goddess as the Shakti, or cosmic energy, of the god in the world and therefore the most immediate creative or destructive force, to be thanked or placated. Many of the manifestations of the goddess are capricious or violent, and she is often seen as a warrior who destroys demons on her own or whom Siva himself has to defeat in combat. As Mariamman, she used to bring smallpox, and she is still held responsible for diseases of the hot season.

In addition to the main gods, there are a number of subordinate divine beings, who are often the most popular deities. Ganesha, or Pillaiyar or Ganapati, the elephant-headed son of Siva and Parvati, is the patron of good fortune and is worshiped at the beginning of a religious service or a new venture, such as a business deal or even a short trip. Murugan, his brother, is a handsome young warrior who carries a spear and rides a peacock. He is worshiped near hills or mountains, and his devotees are known for fierce vows and austerity that may include self-mutilation. Every village has its own protective deities, often symbolized as warriors, who may have their own local stories and saints.

Worship of the gods is known as *puja*. Worship can occur mentally or in front of the most rudimentary representations, such as stones or trees. Most people assemble pictures or small statues of their favorite deities and create small shrines in their homes for daily services, and they make trips to local shrines to worship before larger and more ornate statues. Public temples (*kovil*) consist of a central shrine containing images of the gods, with a surrounding courtyard and an enclosing wall entered through ornately carved towers (*gopuram*). During worship, the images become the gods after special rituals are performed. Worshipers then offer them presents of food, clothing, and flowers as they would honored guests. The gifts are sanctified through contact with the gods, and worshipers may eat the sacred food or smear themselves with sacred ash in order to absorb the god's grace. In public temples, only consecrated priests (*pujari*) are allowed into the sanctum housing the god's image, and worshipers hand offerings to the priests for presentation to the god. Most of the time, worship of the gods is not congregational, but involves offerings by individuals or small family groups at home or through temple priests. During major festivals, however, hundreds or thousands of people may come together in noisy, packed crowds to worship at temples or to witness processions of the gods through public streets.

Islam

The religion of Islam began, like Buddhism, with the experience of a single man, but the religious environment of early Islam was the Judeo-Christian world of Arabia. Many of the basic premises and beliefs of Islam are thus quite different than those of Buddhism or Hinduism and more closely resemble the systems of Judaism or Christianity. During the last 1,000 years, however, Islam has played a major part in the cultures of South and Southeast Asia, including Sri Lanka. Islam in Sri Lanka has preserved the doctrines derived from Arabia, while adapting to the social environment of South Asia.

During the early seventh century A.D., Muhammad experienced a series of messages from God in the city of Mecca, a trading center in western Arabia. He became a prophet, one of the line of biblical prophets including Abraham, Moses, and Jesus Christ (in Arabic, Ibrahim, Musa, and Isa), and he conveyed to the people of Mecca the last and greatest of the revelations given by God to the world. The message was simple and powerful: "submission" (Islam) to the mercy of a single, all-powerful God (Allah). God exists for eternity, but out of love he created the world and mankind, endowing both men and women with immortal souls. Human beings have only one life, and when it ends their souls go to either heaven or hell according to their behavior on earth. Correct behavior is known through the revelation of prophets inspired by God, and Muhammad is the last of these prophets. To believe in Islam, to become "one who submits" (a Muslim), one must accept the will of the one true God and the message of Muhammad, which is encapsulated in the *shahada*: "There is no God but God, and

Muhammad is His Prophet.'' His message is immortalized in the Quran, a series of revelations conveyed by the angel Gabriel, and in the hadith, the sayings and example of the prophet Muhammad.

Muhammad described some of the most important actions necessary for a believer who wished to submit to God's love and will. In addition to commandments against lying, stealing, killing, and other crimes, the moral code includes prayer five times daily, fasting, giving alms to the poor, pilgrimage to Mecca if financially possible, abstention from gambling and wine, and dietary restrictions similar to those of Judaism. The Prophet linked behavior to salvation so closely that bodies of Islamic law (sharia) grew up in order to interpret all human activity according to the spirit of the Quran. In practice, to be a Muslim requires not simply a belief in God and in Muhammad's status as the final prophet, but acceptance of the rules of Islamic law and following them in one's own life. Islam thus encompasses a rich theology and moral system, and it also includes a distinctive body of laws and customs that distinguish Muslims from followers of other faiths. Islam is theoretically a democratic union of all believers without priests, but in practice scholars (*ulama*) learned in Islamic law interpret the Quran according to local conditions, legal officials (*qazi*) regulate Muslim life according to Islamic law, and local prayer leaders coordinate group recitation of prayers in mosques (*masjid,* or *palli*).

By the fifteenth century, Arab traders dominated the trade routes through the Indian Ocean and Southeast Asia. Some of them settled down along the coasts of India and Sri Lanka, married local women, and spoke Arabized Tamil rather than pure Arabic. Their families followed Islam and preserved the basic doctrines and Islamic law, while also adopting some local social customs (such as matrilineal and matrilocal families) that were not part of early Islamic society in the Arabian Peninsula. When the Portuguese took control in the sixteenth century, they persecuted the Muslim traders of the southwest coast, and many Muslims had to relocate in the Central Highlands or on the east coast (see European Encroachment and Dominance, 1500–1948, ch. 1). They retained their separate religious identity, but also adopted some aspects of popular religion. For example, pilgrimage sites, such as Kataragama, may be the same for Muslims as for Hindus or Buddhists, although Muslims will worship at mosques rather than reverence the Buddha or worship Hindu gods (see Buddhism, this ch.).

The growth in ethnic consciousness during the last two centuries has affected the Muslim community of Sri Lanka. Muslim revivalism has included an interest in the Arabic roots of the community, increased emphasis on the study of Arabic as the basis for understanding the Quran, and an emphasis on separate schools for Muslim children. Whether there should be an independent Islamic law for Muslims, preserving the distinct moral culture passed down from Muhammad, is a continuing issue. On a number of occasions, agitation has developed over attempts by the Sri Lankan government to regulate Muslim marriage and inheritance. In order to prevent further alienation of the Muslim community, in the 1980s the government handled its dealings with Muslims through a Muslim Religious and Cultural Affairs Department.

Christianity

According to Christian traditions, the Apostle Thomas was active in Sri Lanka as well as southern India during the first century A.D. Small Christian communities existed on the coasts of Sri Lanka during the succeeding centuries, flourishing on the edges of the Indian Ocean trade routes as Islam did in later times. Christianity made significant inroads only after the fifteenth century, as aggressive Portuguese missionary efforts led to many conversions, especially among the Karava and other low-country castes. When the Dutch took control of Sri Lanka, they encouraged their own missionaries of the Dutch Reformed Church. Under their patronage, 21 percent of the population in the low country was officially Christian by 1722. The British, in turn, allowed Anglican and other Protestant missionaries to proselytize.

The relative number of Christians in Sri Lanka has declined steadily since the end of colonial rule. In 1900 a reported 378,859 people, or 10.6 percent of the population, were officially Christians. Although in 1980, the number of Christians had increased to 1,283,600, the percentage of Christians in the total population had declined to approximately 8 percent. This decline occurred primarily because the non-Christian population expanded at a faster rate. Emigration abroad, conversions of some Christians to Buddhism and fewer conversions to Christianity among Buddhists, Hindus, or Muslims also were reasons for the decline. In the 1980s, Christians still were concentrated heavily in the low country in the southwest. They comprised 30 percent of the population in Colombo.

Some 88 percent of the Christians were Roman Catholics who traced their religious heritage directly to the Portuguese. The Roman Catholic Church has a well-established organization that encompasses the entire island. In 1985 there were 9 dioceses comprising 313 parishes, 682 priests, and 15 bishops (including two archbishops and a cardinal). The remainder of Christians were almost evenly split between the Anglican Church of Ceylon (with

101

two dioceses) and other Protestant faiths. The Dutch Reformed Church, now the Presbytery of Ceylon, consisted mostly of Burghers, and its numbers were shrinking because of emigration. Other Christian communities—Congregationalists, Methodists, and Baptists—were small in number. Since the 1970s, there has been a movement of all Protestant Churches to join together in a united Church of Sri Lanka. The Sinhalese community, however, has strenuously opposed this movement.

Social Services

Education

Traditional and Colonial Systems

The education system of Sri Lanka until colonial times primarily was designed for a small elite in a society with relatively low technology. The vast majority of the population was illiterate or semiliterate. Among the Sinhalese, learning was the job of Buddhist monks. At the village level, literate monks would teach privileged students in the *pansal,* or temple school. The curriculum there, still taught to young children, included the Sinhala alphabet and memorization of elementary Buddhist literature—the *Nam potha* (Book of Names) of Buddhist shrines, the *Magul lakuna* (Book of Auspicious Symbols on the Buddha's body), and classic stories of the Buddha's life. The pursuit of higher education typically was reserved for men who became monks and took place at universities (*pirivena*) dedicated almost exclusively to memorization and commentary on the Pali scriptures. Among the Tamil population, village schools, which were located near temples, were run by literate Brahmans or educated Vellalas (see Glossary). Technical training was highly developed for students of the arts (such as architecture or sculpture); for engineers, who applied geometry to problems of irrigation; and for craftsmen in various trades. This training, however, was generally the preserve of closed corporations, castes, or families. Knowledge was often passed down from fathers to sons.

Although colonization brought European-style education to Sri Lanka, especially to prepare students for positions in the colonial administrations, few women went to school and most people remained uneducated. During the sixteenth century, Portuguese missionaries established up to 100 schools designed to foster a Roman Catholic culture among the growing Christian community in the low country. When the Dutch took over in 1656, they set up a well-organized system of primary schools to support the missionary efforts of the Dutch Reformed Church. By 1760 they had 130

Sinhalese twins near
Hikkaduwa
Courtesy
Paige W. Thompson

schools with an attendance of nearly 65,000 students. The British takeover led to the closing of many Dutch schools and a short-term contraction of European-style education in the low country. By the mid-nineteenth century, government-funded schools and Christian schools were again expanding; in 1870, however, their combined student bodies had fewer than 20,000 students. Because they were educated in English, the graduates of the European-style schools, a large portion of them Christians from the low country in the southwest, went on to fill lower and middle-level positions in the colonial administration. Apart from the European-style schools, education continued through the traditional system in Tamil and Sinhala.

In 1870 a series of events revolutionized the education system in Sri Lanka. The government began to expand the number of state-run schools and instituted a program of grants for private schools that met official standards. Medical and law colleges were established in Colombo. There was a big increase in the number of students (which totalled more than 200,000 by 1900), but the lopsided development that had characterized the early nineteenth century became even more apparent by the early twentieth century. Private schools taught in English, which offered the best road for advancement, were dominated by Christian organizations, remained concentrated in the southwest, and attracted a disproportionate number of Christian and Tamil students. Although institutions that

103

used Tamil and Sinhala continued to function as elementary schools, secondary institutions that taught exclusively in English attracted an elite male clientele destined for administrative positions. The education of women lagged behind; by 1921 the female literacy rate among the Christians was 50 percent, among the Buddhists 17 percent, among the Hindus 10 percent, and among the Muslims only 6 percent.

The colonial pattern began to change in the 1930s, after legislative reforms placed the Ministry of Education under the control of elected representatives. The government directly controlled an ever-larger proportion of schools (about 60 percent by 1947) and teacher-training colleges. As part of a policy to promote universal literacy, education became free in government schools, elementary and technical schools were set up in rural areas, and vernacular education received official encouragement. In 1942 with the establishment of the University of Ceylon, free education was available from kindergarten through the university level. When independence came in 1948, Sri Lanka had a well-developed education infrastructure. Although still hampered by gross ethnic, geographic, and gender inequalities, it formed the basis for a modern system.

The Modern Education System

Since independence in 1948, the government has made education one of its highest priorities, a policy that has yielded excellent results (see table 4, Appendix). Within a period of less than 40 years, the number of schools in Sri Lanka increased by over 50 percent, the number of students increased more than 300 percent, and the number of teachers increased by more than 400 percent. Growth has been especially rapid in secondary schools, which in 1985 taught 1.2 million students, or one-third of the student population. Teachers made up the largest government work force outside the plantation industry. The literate population has grown correspondingly, and by the mid-1980s over 90 percent of the population was officially literate (87 percent for those above ten years of age), with near universal literacy among the younger population. This is by far the most impressive progress in South Asia and places Sri Lanka close to the leaders in education among developing nations.

The government has taken an ever larger role in education. Because private institutions no longer receive grants from the government, they are forced to charge fees while competing with free state-run schools. The percentage of students in the state system has grown constantly, and by the 1980s, 99 percent of female students and 93 percent of male students at the primary school level were being trained in government-run schools. The government did not have a monopoly over education because Buddhist *pansala* and *pirivena,* Muslim schools, and Christian schools still thrived (the Roman Catholic Church alone operated several hundred institutions from kindergarten to secondary level, teaching over 80,000 children). The education system of the state, however, had an overwhelming influence on the majority of the population, especially the Sinhalese.

The state has tried to change the language of instruction in its primary and secondary schools from English to Tamil or Sinhala. By the 1960s, the vernacular languages were the primary medium in all government secondary schools. In the 1980s, English remained, however, an important key to advancement in technical and professional careers, and there was still competition among well-to-do families to place members in private English-language programs in urban areas. Ethnic minorities long associated with European-style education still formed a large percentage of the English-speaking elite. In the 1980s, for example, almost 80 percent of the Burghers knew English, while among the Sinhalese the English-speakers comprised only 12 percent.

Children from age five to ten attend primary school; from age eleven to fifteen they attend junior secondary school (terminating in Ordinary Level Examination); and from age sixteen to seventeen they attend senior secondary school (terminating in the Advanced Level Examination). Those who qualify can go on to the university system, which is totally state-run. In the late 1980s, there were 8 universities and 1 university college with over 18,000 students in 28 faculties, plus 2,000 graduate and certificate students. The university system included the University of Peradeniya, about six kilometers from Kandy, formed between 1940 and 1960; the universities of Vidyalankara and Vidyodaya, formed in the 1950s and 1960s from restructured *pirivena;* the College of Advanced Technology in Katubedda, Colombo District, formed in the 1960s; the Colombo campus of the University of Ceylon, created in 1967; the University of Ruhunu (1979); and Batticaloa University College (1981). There was also the Buddhist and Pali University of Sri Lanka, established in Colombo in 1982.

Among the major problems still facing the educational system in the late 1980s were a serious dropout rate in the primary grades and a continuing bias toward urban environments at the expense of the countryside. The median level of educational attainment in Sri Lanka was somewhere between grades 5 and 9, and almost 40 percent of the students dropped out of school after 9 years. The reasons were not hard to discern in a primarily agricultural society, where many young people were more urgently needed in the fields or at home than in school once they had achieved an operational level of literacy and arithmetic skills. Many urban youth from low-income backgrounds also dropped out at an early age. This pattern provided two-thirds of the students with an education through grade 5 but less than 10 percent of the population with a high school diploma and less than 1 percent with a college degree. Despite government efforts in the 1980s to expand opportunities for youth from rural areas and more sparsely inhabited districts, the pressures for early dropout were more pressing in precisely those areas where illiteracy was most prevalent. In Colombo, for example, the overall literacy rate was 94 percent in 1988, while in Amparai District it was only 75 percent. Rural schools were more widely scattered, with poor facilities and inadequate equipment, especially in the sciences. Teachers preferred not to work in the countryside, and many rural schools did not even go up to the level of twelfth grade.

The most dynamic field in education during the 1970s and 1980s was technical training. In the late 1980s, the Ministry of Higher Education operated a network of twenty-seven technical colleges and affiliated institutes throughout the country. Courses led to national diplomas in accountancy, commerce, technology, agriculture, business studies, economics, and manufacture. Other government institutions, including the Railway, Survey, and Irrigation Departments, ran their own specialized training institutes. The Ministry of Labour had three vocational and craft training institutes. The number of students in all state-run technical institutes by the mid-1980s was 22,000. In addition, the government operated schools of agriculture in four locations, as well as practical farm schools in each district. A continuing problem in all fields of technical education was extreme gender differentiation in job training; women tended to enroll in home economics and teaching courses rather than in scientific disciplines.

Education and Ethnic Conflict

During the first fifteen years after independence, students sought a university degree primarily to qualify for service in government, which remained by far the major employer of administrative skills. Liberal arts, leading to the bachelor of arts degree, was the preferred area of study as a preparation for administrative positions. Because the university exams were conducted in English—the language of the elite—the potential pool of university applicants was relatively small, and only 30 percent of all applicants were admitted. By the mid-1960s, the examinations were conducted in Sinhala and Tamil, opening the universities to a larger body of applicants, many of

Sinhalese boy with flowers
Courtesy
Paige W. Thompson

whom were trained in the vernacular languages in state-run secondary schools. At the same time, university expansion slowed down because of lack of funds, and it became impossible to admit the increasing numbers of qualified candidates; by 1965 only 20 percent of applicants were admitted, and by 1969 only 11 percent. Those students who did manage to enter the university followed the traditional road to a bachelor's degree, until neither the government nor private enterprises could absorb the glut of graduates. In this way, the direction of educational expansion by the late 1960s led to two major problems surrounding the university system: the growing difficulty of admissions and the growing irrelevance of a liberal arts education to employment. The big losers were members of the Sinhalese community, who were finally able to obtain high school or university degrees, but who found further advancement difficult. Frustrated aspirations lay behind the participation of many students in the abortive uprising by the People's Liberation Front (Janatha Vimukthi Peramuna—JVP) in 1971 (see Independence, ch. 1).

During the colonial period and the two decades after independence, the Sri Lankan Tamil community—both Hindu and Christian—outstripped the Sinhalese community in the relative percentage of students in secondary schools and university bachelor of arts degree programs. As the government increasingly fell into the hands of the Sinhalese, however, possibilities for government

107

service declined for Tamil students. Tamil secondary schools then used their strength in science curriculums to prepare their students in science and medicine, and by the 1960s Tamils dominated the university student bodies in those fields. Thus, at precisely the time when Sinhalese bachelor of arts candidates found their careers thwarted by changes in the job market, Tamil science students were embarking on lucrative professional careers. Sinhalese agitation aimed at decreasing the numbers of Tamil students in science and medical faculties became a major political issue.

Overt political favoritism did not eliminate the dominance of well-trained Tamil students until 1974, when the government instituted a district quota system of science admissions. When each district in the country had a number of reserved slots for its students, the Sinhalese community benefited because it dominated a majority of districts. Tamil admissions ratios remained higher than the percentage of Tamils in the population, but declined precipitously from previous levels. In the 1980s, 60 percent of university admissions were allocated according to district quotas, with the remaining 40 percent awarded on the basis of individual merit. This system guaranteed opportunity for all ethnic groups in rough approximation to their population throughout the country.

Although the admissions controversy and the quota system resulted in a more equitable distribution of opportunities for Sri Lankans in general, they damaged the prospects of many excellent Tamil students coming out of secondary schools. The education policies of the government were perceived by educated members of the Tamil community as blatant discrimination. Many Tamil youths reacted to the blockage of their educational prospects by supporting the Tamil United Liberation Front and other secessionist cells (see The Political Party System, ch. 4; The Tamil Insurgency, ch. 5). Large-scale improvements in education had, paradoxically, contributed to ethnic conflict.

Health

Sri Lanka has one of the most effective health systems among developing nations. The crude death rate in the early 1980s was 6 per 1,000, down from 13 per 1,000 in 1948 and an estimated 19 per 1,000 in 1871. The infant mortality rate registered a similar decline, from 50 deaths per 1,000 births in 1970 to 34 deaths per 1,000 births in the early 1980s. These figures placed Sri Lanka statistically among the top five Asian countries. Improvements in health were largely responsible for raising the average life span in the 1980s to sixty-eight years.

Traditional medicine (*ayurveda*—see Glossary) is an important part of the health system in Sri Lanka. The basis of traditional medicine is the theory of "three humors" (*tridhatu*), corresponding to elements of the universe that make up the human body: air appears as wind, fire as bile, and water as phlegm. Imbalances among the humors (the "three ills," or *tridosha*) cause various diseases. The chief causes of the imbalances are excesses of heat or cold. Treatment of disease requires an infusion of hot or cold substances in order to reestablish a balance in the body. The definition of "hot" or "cold" rests on culturally defined norms and lists in ancient textbooks. For example, milk products and rice cooked in milk are cool substances, while certain meats are hot, regardless of temperature. Treatment may also involve a variety of herbal remedies made according to lore handed down from ancient times. Archaeological work at ancient monastic sites has revealed the antiquity of the traditional medical system; for example, excavations have revealed large tubs used to immerse the bodies of sick persons in healing solutions. Literate monks, skilled in *ayurveda*, were important sources of medical knowledge in former times. Village-level traditional physicians also remained active until the mid-twentieth century. In the late 1980s, as part of a free state medical system, government agencies operated health clinics specializing in *ayurveda*, employed over 12,000 *ayurvedic* physicians, and supported several training and research institutes in traditional medicine.

Western-style medical practices have been responsible for most of the improvements in health in Sri Lanka during the twentieth century. Health care facilities and staff and public health programs geared to combat infectious disease are the most crucial areas where development has taken place. The state maintains a system of free hospitals, dispensaries, and maternity services. In 1985 there were more than 3,000 doctors trained in Western medicine, about 8,600 nurses, 490 hospitals, and 338 central dispensaries. Maternity services were especially effective in reaching into rural areas; less than 3 percent of deliveries took place without the assistance of at least a paramedic or a trained midwife, and 63 percent of deliveries occurred in health institutions—higher rates than in any other South Asian nation. As is the case for all services in Sri Lanka, the most complete hospital facilities and highest concentration of physicians were in urban areas, while many rural and estate areas were served by dispensaries and paramedics. The emergency transport of patients, especially in the countryside, was still at a rudimentary level. Some progress has been made in controlling infectious diseases. Smallpox has been eliminated, and the state has been cooperating with United Nations agencies in programs to eradicate malaria. In 1985 Sri Lanka spent 258 rupees (for value of rupee—see Glossary) per person to fight the disease. Although the number of malaria cases and fatalities has declined, in 1985 more than 100,000 persons contracted the disease.

Sri Lanka had little exposure to Acquired Immune Deficiency Syndrome (AIDS) during the 1980s. As late as 1986, no Sri Lankan citizens had contracted the disease at home, but by early 1988 six cases had been diagnosed, including those of foreigners and of Sri Lankan citizens who had traveled abroad. Government regulations in the late 1980s required immediate expulsion of any foreigner diagnosed as an AIDS carrier, and by 1988 the government had deported at least one foreign AIDS victim. Government ministers have participated in international forums dealing with the problem, and the government formed a National Committee on AIDS Prevention in 1988.

Mortality rates in the late 1980s highlighted the gap that remained between the urban and rural sectors and the long way good medical care still had to go to reach the whole population. Over 40 percent of the deaths in urban areas were traced to heart or circulatory diseases, a trend that resembled the pattern in developed nations. Cancer, on the other hand, accounted for only about 6 percent of deaths, a pattern that did not resemble that of developed nations. Instead, intestinal infections, tuberculosis, and parasitic diseases accounted for 20 percent of urban deaths and over 12 percent of rural deaths annually. The leading causes of death in rural environments were listed as ''ill-defined conditions'' or ''senility,'' reflecting the rather poor diagnostic capabilities of rural health personnel. Observers agreed that considerable work needed to be done to reduce infectious diseases throughout the country and to improve skilled medical outreach to rural communities.

Living Conditions

In the late 1980s, vast differences remained in the wealth and life-styles of citizens in Sri Lanka. In urban areas, such as Colombo, entire neighborhoods consisted of beautiful houses owned by well-off administrators and businessmen. This elite enjoyed facilities and opportunities on a par with those of middle- and upper-middle-class residents of Europe or North America. In the countryside, families that controlled more extensive farms lived a rustic but healthy life, with excellent access to food, shelter, clothing, and opportunities for education and employment. In contrast, at lower levels in the class pyramid, the vast majority of the population experienced a much lower standard of living and range of opportunities. A sizable minority in both the cities and rural villages led a marginal existence, with inadequate food and facilities and poor chances for upward mobility.

Intervention by successive governments has had marginal success in decreasing the differences between income groups. In the rural sector, legislation has mandated a ceiling on private land-ownership and has nationalized plantations, but these programs have provided extra land to relatively few people (see Agriculture, ch. 3). Although resettlement programs have benefitted hundreds of thousands of people, they have not kept pace with population growth. In rural environments, most people remained peasants with smallholdings, agricultural laborers working for small wages on the lands of others, or landless plantation workers. Migration to the cities often did not lead to a great improvement in people's lifestyles because most immigrants had little education and few skills. As a result, urban slums have proliferated; by the 1980s almost half the people in greater Colombo were living in slums and shanties. Because economic growth has not kept pace with these population changes, double-digit unemployment continued with the poorest sections of the urban and rural population suffering the most. A hard-core mass of poor and underemployed people, totalling between 20 and 25 percent of the population, remained the biggest challenge for the government.

Cramped and insufficient housing detracted from the quality of life in Sri Lanka. In the 1980s, most housing units in Sri Lanka were small: 33 percent had only one room, 33 percent two rooms, and 20 percent three rooms. More than five persons lived in the average housing unit, with an overcrowding rate (three or more persons per room) of 40 percent. In urban areas, permanent structures with brick walls, tiled roofs, and cement floors constituted 70 percent of houses, but in the countryside permanent houses made up only 24 percent of the units. The rural figures included a large number of village dwellings built of such materials as thatch, mud, and timber, designed according to traditional styles with inner courtyards, or verandas, and providing ample room for living and sleeping in the generally warm climate. The rates of overcrowding were declining in the 1980s, as the government sponsored intensive programs for increasing access to permanent housing.

Many of the infectious diseases that caused high mortality in Sri Lanka were water-borne, and improvements in water facilities occupied a high priority in government welfare programs of the 1980s and planning for the 1990s. In urban areas, about half the drinking water was piped and half came from wells, while in the countryside 85 percent of the water came from wells and 10 percent from unprotected, open sources. Almost one-third of the well water was also unprotected against backflows that could cause leakage of sewage. Only about one out of three houses had toilets. With help from United Nations Children's Fund (UNICEF), United States Agency for International Development (AID), Britain, the Federal Republic of Germany (West Germany), and the Netherlands, the government of Sri Lanka set a goal of clean, piped water and sewage facilities for the entire urban population and for at least half the rural population by 1990. Observers doubted, however, that this goal could be reached in the northern and eastern districts torn by ethnic conflict.

Food was another major issue. Beginning in the 1940s, the government ran a food subsidy program that paid farmers a minimum price for their crops and also operated a rationing system that allowed people to obtain rice at a guaranteed low price. The importance of this program to the people was dramatically demonstrated in 1953, when the state's attempt to reduce subsidies led to food riots and the fall of the government (see United National Party "Majority" Rule, 1948–56, ch. 1). Since 1979 when the subsidy program was abolished, the government has operated a food stamp scheme that allows people in lower-income brackets to obtain free rice, wheat flour, sugar, milk powder, condensed milk, dried fish, and kerosene for cooking. This program has reached almost half the population, accounting for approximately 7 percent of the state budget. The government also operated supplementary feeding programs, including a School Biscuit Programme designed to reach malnourished children and a Thriposha Programme to provide for 600,000 needy infants, preschool children, and pregnant mothers. (*Thriposha* is a precooked, protein-fortified cereal food supplement.)

Despite government intervention in the food market, malnutrition continued to be a problem among the poor, the bottom 60 percent of the population who earned less than 30 percent of the national income. As in so many other sectors, the problem remained worse in rural areas, although urban slums possessed their own share of misery. In Colombo city and district, 1 or 2 percent of preschool children experienced severe symptoms of malnutrition, while the rate was 3 or 4 percent in Puttalam District. Mild forms of malnourishment, resulting in some stunted growth, affected around 33 percent of the young children in Colombo but up to 50 percent in rural Vavuniya or Puttalam districts. Malnutrition also affected adults: one out of three agricultural laborers consumed less than 80 percent of recommended calories daily. This problem became worse after the inflation of the early 1980s that reduced the real value of food stamps by up to 50 percent (see Finance,

Coastal village south of Colombo
Courtesy Paige W. Thompson

113

Sri Lanka: A Country Study

ch. 3). Observers doubted that poverty and malnutrition would be alleviated during the 1980s or early 1990s, while the country experienced economic uncertainty and the government was forced to spend more on security matters (see The Defense Budget, ch. 5).

* * *

An excellent short survey of Sri Lanka's geology, topography, and climate is found in *Sri Lanka: A Survey,* edited by K.M. de Silva. A more detailed study is J.W. Herath's *Mineral Resources of Sri Lanka.*

The authoritative source for population statistics is *Population and Housing, 1981: General Report* published by the Sri Lanka Ministry of Plan Implementation. Beginning with basic population data, the Central Bank of Sri Lanka's *Economic and Social Statistics of Sri Lanka* also includes useful data on health, education, and welfare. Basic texts for ethnic, caste, and family topics are *Caste in Modern Ceylon* by Bruce Ryan and *Under the Bo Tree* by Nur Yalman. Michael Robert's more recent *Caste Conflict and Elite Formation* concentrates on the dominant low-country castes. *Muslims of Sri Lanka,* edited by M.A.M. Shukri, is a collection of essays dealing with the history and culture of the different groups within the Muslim community.

Heinz Bechert, Hans Dieter-Evers, Richard Gombrich, and Gananath Obeyesekere are major figures in the study of Sinhalese religion. Bechert and Gombrich have edited *The World of Buddhism,* with contributors discussing all world areas; the sections on Indian and Sinhalese Buddhism are excellent introductions. Gombrich's *Precept and Practice* is a scholarly investigation of popular Sinhalese religion and its relationship to Buddhist doctrines. For the basic ideas of Hinduism, Thomas J. Hopkins's *The Hindu Religious Tradition* is useful. Kamil Zvelebil's *The Smile of Murugan* and *Hymns of the Tamil Saivite Saints* by F. Kingsbury and G.E. Phillips provide more detailed information on Tamil Hindu traditions. Expositions of the basic doctrines of Islam are found in H.A.R. Gibb's *Mohammedanism* and Fazlur Rahman's *Islam.*

Education in Colonial Ceylon by Ranjit Ruberu describes the precolonial and colonial education systems. Chandra Richard de Silva and Daya de Silva give a detailed description of the postindependence education system in *Education in Sri Lanka.* The relationship between education and ethnic conflict are discussed in chapters by K.M. de Silva and Chandra Richard de Silva in *From Independence to Statehood: Managing Ethnic Conflict in Five African and Asian States.* Health and welfare conditions, and government

114

programs addressing them, are summarized in Piyasiri Wickramasekara's long article in *Strategies for Alleviating Poverty in Rural Asia.* A more detailed study of rural conditions is Rachel Kurian's *Women Workers in the Sri Lanka Plantation Sector.* (For further information and complete citations, see Bibliography.)

Chapter 3. The Economy

Economic activity in Sri Lanka: rubber tapper, tea picker, rice cultivator, and handicraft worker

THE DOMINANT SECTOR of the Sri Lankan economy historically has been wet rice (paddy) cultivation. Its importance in ancient times is demonstrated by the extensive irrigation works constructed in the north-central region of the island in the first millennium A.D. In the thirteenth century, the civilization based on these reservoirs began to decline, and population shifted to the wet zone of the southern and southwestern areas, where irrigation was less necessary to grow rice. Cinnamon and other spices which were valuable in the European market became important export commodities in the sixteenth century, when Europeans, first the Portuguese and then the Dutch, established control over the coastal areas of the island.

Commercial agriculture came to dominate the economy during the British period (1796–1948). Extensive coffee plantations were established in the mid-nineteenth century. Coffee failed when a leaf disease ravaged it in the 1870s and 1880s, but it was quickly replaced by the important commercial crops of tea, rubber, and coconut. Although wet rice cultivation remained important, Sri Lanka had to import more than one-half of the rice it needed during the late nineteenth and early twentieth centuries because of the land and labor devoted to the commercial crops. At independence in 1948, almost all of the islands' foreign exchange earnings were derived from commercial agriculture.

The fundamental economic problem since the 1950s has been the declining terms of trade. The proceeds from the traditional agricultural exports of tea, rubber, and coconut have had less and less value in the international marketplace. Beginning in the early 1960s, governments responded by intervening directly in the largely free-market economy inherited from the colonial period. Imports and exports were tightly regulated, and the state sector was expanded, especially in manufacturing and transportation. This trend accelerated between 1970 and 1977, when a coalition headed by the Sri Lanka Freedom Party nationalized the larger plantations and imposed direct controls over internal trade.

The United National Party (UNP) contested the 1977 general election with a platform calling for less regulation of the economy. After its electoral victory, the new UNP government made some effort to dismantle the state sector in agriculture and manufacturing. At the same time, it encouraged private enterprise, welcomed foreign investment and slackened import controls. It also shifted spending away from subsidies and social welfare to investment in the nation's infrastructure, most notably a massive irrigation project, the Mahaweli Ganga Program, which was expected to make Sri Lanka self-sufficient in rice and generate enough hydroelectric power to fill the nation's requirements. These policies resulted in higher rates of economic growth in the late 1970s and early 1980s, but at the cost of a mounting external debt. Foreign aid from the United States, Western Europe, Japan, and international organizations kept the economy afloat.

Sri Lanka's economy became more diverse in the 1970s and 1980s, and in 1986 textiles surpassed tea for the first time as the country's single largest export. Nonetheless, the performance of the traditional agricultural exports remained essential to the country's economic health. Other important sources of foreign exchange included remittances from Sri Lankans working overseas, foreign aid, and tourism.

Nature of the Economy

Sri Lanka's economic prospects in early 1988 were linked at least in part to the political and security situation. If political violence could be brought under control, the government had commitments from foreign investors and donors to finance a reconstruction program that would ensure economic growth in the short term. If the violence were to continue, the diversion of resources into defense and the negative impact on tourism and foreign investment appeared likely to result in economic stagnation.

Structure of the Economy

Agriculture, both subsistence and commercial, has played a dominant role in Sri Lanka's economy for many centuries. The Portuguese and Dutch, who ruled the coastal regions of the island from the sixteenth through the eighteenth centuries, were primarily interested in profiting from cinnamon and other spices (see European Encroachment and Dominance, 1500–1948; The Dutch, ch. 1). Trade with India, Sri Lanka's nearest neighbor, was also important during this period. Sri Lanka exported pearls, areca nuts, shells, elephants, and coconuts, and in return received rice and textiles.

The island's economy began to assume its modern form in the 1830s and 1840s, when coffee plantations were established in the Central Highlands. Coffee soon became the dominant force in the economy, its proceeds paying for increasingly large imports of food, especially rice. When coffee fell victim to a leaf disease in the 1870s, it was quickly replaced by tea, which soon covered more land than had coffee at its height. Coconut plantations also expanded rapidly in the late nineteenth century, followed by rubber, another cash crop introduced in the 1890s. Stimulated by demand generated by the development of the automobile industry in Western Europe and North America, rubber soon passed coconuts in importance. These three products—tea, coconuts, and rubber—provided the export earnings that enabled Sri Lanka to import food, textiles, and other consumer goods in the first half of the twentieth century. At independence in 1948, they generated over 90 percent of export proceeds.

Wet rice was grown extensively as a subsistence crop throughout the colonial period. In the nineteenth century, most of it was consumed in the villages where it was grown, but in the final decades of British rule the internal market in rice expanded. Nonetheless, more than half of the rice consumed was imported, and the island depended on the proceeds of plantation crops for its food supply.

The economy gradually became more diverse after the late 1950s, partly as a result of government policies that encouraged this trend. The main reason successive administrations tried to reduce the country's dependence on tea, rubber, and coconuts was the long-term decline in their value relative to the cost of imports. Even when Sri Lanka increased the production of its major cash crops, the amount of imports that could be bought with their proceeds declined.

Much of the diversification of the economy, especially in the 1960s and the early 1970s, took the form of import substitution, producing for the local market goods that the island could no longer afford to import. Sri Lanka also had some success in diversifying exports after 1970. The proportion of exports linked to the three traditional cash crops fell from over 90 percent in the late 1960s to 71 percent in 1974 and 42 percent in 1986. Textiles, which made up only 0.7 percent of exports in 1974, accounted for over 28 percent in 1986 (see table 5, Appendix A).

In 1986 agriculture, forestry, and fishing made up 27.7 percent of the gross national product (GNP—see Glossary), down from 39.4 percent in 1975 (see table 6, Appendix A). In 1986 wholesale and retail trade accounted for 19.9 percent of GNP, and manufacturing for 15.6 percent. Transport, storage, and communications stood at 11.2 percent of GNP, and construction at 7.7 percent. The relative importance of the various sectors of the economy was fairly stable during the 1980s.

Role of Government

The role of government in the economy during the final decades of British colonial rule was considerable. The plantation economy

121

required extensive infrastructure; the colonial state developed and owned railroad, electrical, postal, telegraphic, telephone, and water supply services. Quasi-state financial institutions served the colony's commercial needs, and during World War II the government set up production units for plywood, quinine, drugs, leather, coir, paper, ceramics, acetic acid, glass, and steel. Welfare policies also began during colonial rule, including a network for free and subsidized rice and flour established in 1942. Free education, relief for the poor, and subsidized medical care were introduced in the late British period. Moreover, after 1935 the government took an active role in the planning and subsidizing of colonization schemes. This policy was designed to remove landless peasants from heavily populated areas to newly irrigated tracts in the dry zone.

Economic policy since independence is divided into two periods. During the first, which lasted from 1948 to 1977, government intervention was often seen as the solution to economic problems. The expansion of government participation in the economy was fairly steady, resulting in a tightly regulated system. This trend was especially marked during the period of S.R.D. Bandaranaike's second government, from 1970 to 1977, when the state came to dominate international trade and payments; the plantation, financial, and industrial manufacturing sectors; and the major trade unions outside the plantation sector. It also played a major role in the domestic wholesale and retail trade.

The trend toward greater government involvement was largely a response to the deteriorating terms of trade. The plantation economy had financed social programs such as subsidized food in the late colonial period, but when the value of exports declined after 1957, the economy's capacity to support these programs was strained. When the foreign exchange reserves of the early 1950s dwindled, import-substituting industrialization was seen as a solution. Because the private sector viewed industrial development as risky, the government took up the slack. When balance of payment deficits became chronic, some nationalizations were justified by the need to stem the drain of foreign exchange. Similar concerns led to the tighter regulation of private business and the establishment of state-owned trading corporations. When there were shortages of necessities, governments expanded state control over their distribution in order to make them available at low prices.

The 1977 elections were largely a referendum on the perceived failures of the closed economy. The UNP, which supported a deregulated, open economy, won decisively. The new government rejected the economic policies that had evolved over the previous twenty years. Some observers believed that the economy had been

Villagers and cart in rural Sri Lanka, circa 1910
Courtesy Library of Congress

shackled by excessive regulation, an excess of consumption expenditure over investment, and wasteful state enterprises. Under the UNP, market forces were to play a greater role in allocating resources, and state enterprises were to compete with the private sector (see The United National Party Returns to Power, ch. 1).

The main elements of the new policy were investment incentives for foreign and domestic capital, a shift in the composition of public spending from subsidies to infrastructure investment, and a liberalized international trade policy designed to encourage export-led growth. Employment creation was a central objective, both through encouragement of domestic and foreign capital investment, and through an ambitious public works program, including the Accelerated Mahaweli Program, which aimed to bring new land under irrigation and substantially increase hydroelectric generating capacity (see Government Policies, this ch.). Two other policies that sought to create employment were the establishment of investment promotion zones (free trade zones) and extensive government investment in housing.

The role of government during the decade after 1977 remained significant; the public investment program, for instance, was implemented on a greater scale than anything attempted previously, and in early 1988 the state remained heavily involved in many areas of economic activity. But while the government increased its efforts to develop the nation's infrastructure, it reduced its role in regulation, commerce, and production. Its initiatives received the enthusiastic support of the international development community. As a result, Sri Lanka received generous amounts of foreign aid to finance its post-1977 development program. This foreign assistance was integral to the government's economic strategy. Because budget deficits were large even before 1977, external financial resources were necessary to pay for the increased spending on infrastructure and to make up for the revenue lost as a result of the tax incentives given business. Similarly, relaxing import controls put pressure on the balance of payments, which could be relieved only with the help of foreign aid.

Development Planning

During the early years of independence, successive governments placed little emphasis on development planning, in part because the immediate economic problems appeared to be manageable. The National Planning Council was established in 1956 as part of the Ministry of Finance. Between 1957 and 1959, the council and the Central Bank of Sri Lanka invited a number of foreign economists to visit Sri Lanka and offer the government both their diagnoses of the country's economic problems and their prescriptions for the planning and implementation of recommended remedies. These studies provided many of the rationales for economic policies and planning in the 1960s.

In 1959 the National Planning Council issued a Ten-Year Plan, the most ambitious analysis of the economy and projection of planning that had yet been officially published. This plan sought to increase the role of industry in the economy. Unfortunately, its forecasts were based on faulty projections of population and labor force growth rates. Moreover, attempts to implement it collided with the exchange and price crunch of 1961 and 1962, and the plan became increasingly out of touch with the changing economic situation.

A new Ministry of Planning and Economic Affairs (no longer in existence) was established in 1965. The ministry decided not to draft another single long-term plan involving a five- or ten-year period. Instead, it drew up a number of separate, detailed, well-integrated, five-year plans involving different ministries. The government targeted agriculture, especially wet rice, as the area in which growth could best be achieved.

The UNP government that came to power in 1970 shifted toward a more formal and comprehensive state direction of the economy. The Five-Year Plan for 1972–76 had two principal aspects. First, it sought to remove disparities in incomes and living standards. Second, the plan sought to promote economic growth and to reduce unemployment. It envisioned rapid growth in agriculture, not only in the traditional crops of wet rice, tea, rubber, and coconut, but in such minor crops as sunflower, manioc, cotton, cashew, pineapple, and cocoa. Like the Ten-Year Plan of 1959, this plan proved to be based on overly optimistic assumptions, and it soon ceased to exercise influence on the government's economic policy. In 1975 it was replaced by a Two-Year Plan that placed even greater emphasis on agricultural growth and less on industrial development.

After 1977 the government continued to accept the principle of state direction of economic activity, but in contrast to the 1970–77 period the government encouraged the private sector to participate in the economy. Its first Five-Year Plan (1978–83) included an ambitious public investment program to be financed largely by overseas grants and loans. Its immediate objective was to reduce unemployment, which had risen during the tenure of the previous government.

A series of five-year rolling investment plans was set in motion by the Ministry of Finance and Planning in the 1980s. The plan for the 1986–90 period envisaged investment of Rs268 billion (for value of the rupee—see Glossary) with the emphasis on infrastructure projects such as roads, irrigation, ports, airports, telecommunications, and plantations. Of this total, 50 percent was to be spent by the state sector. Foreign sources were to supply Rs69 billion. The target annual average growth for the gross domestic product (GDP—see Glossary) was 4.5 percent, a decrease from the 5.2 percent envisaged by the plan for the 1985–89 period and the 6 percent actually achieved between 1977 and 1984.

The Economy in the Late 1980s

Growth in GDP was estimated at 3 percent in 1987, down from 4.3 percent in 1986, and the lowest level in a decade (see table 7, Appendix A). By 1987 it was clear that the ongoing civil unrest was causing serious economic difficulties, mainly because rapidly increasing defense outlays forced the government to cut back capital expenditure and to run a large budgetary deficit. Concern over the decline in foreign investment and extensive damage to infrastructure mounted as sectors such as tourism, transportation, and wet rice farming suffered production losses directly related to the decline in security.

By early 1988, the ethnic conflict had resulted in extensive property damage. Infrastructure damage in Northern and Eastern provinces was estimated at Rs7.5 billion in August 1987 and was

125

expected to be revised upwards to include the widespread destruction in the Jaffna Peninsula (see fig. 1). In the predominantly Sinhalese areas, riots against the 1987 Indo-Sri Lankan Accord caused damage to government property estimated at Rs4.8 billion (see Foreign Relations, ch. 4).

In early 1988, future economic prospects were closely linked to the security situation (see Primary Threats to National Security, ch. 5). Late the previous year, the government succeeded in obtaining commitments from foreign nations and international organizations to finance an extensive reconstruction program for the 1988–90 period (see Foreign Aid, this ch.). If there were a pronounced ebb in the political violence plaguing the island nation, it would be probable that the official target of Rs80 billion foreign aid over this three-year period would be reached. Aid on this scale, which would be a substantial increase on the already generous levels received, would not only enable the rebuilding of infrastructure destroyed by the violence but also fuel growth and allow the large trade and budget deficits to continue. Accordingly, the 1988 budget foresaw a sharp decline in defense spending and an increase in capital expenditure. These economic plans, however, depended on a peaceful solution to the country's political problems. If political violence escalated in subsequent years, not only would the government have to shift its spending back to defense, but some of the expected foreign aid probably would be suspended.

Agriculture

Agriculture—including forestry and fishing—accounted for over 46 percent of exports, over 40 percent of the labor force, and around 28 percent of the GNP in 1986. The dominant crops were paddy, tea, rubber, and coconut. In the late 1980s, the government-sponsored Accelerated Mahaweli Program irrigation project opened a large amount of new land for paddy cultivation in the dry zone of the eastern part of the island (see fig. 7). In contrast, the amount of land devoted to tea, coconut, and rubber remained stable in the forty years after independence. Land reforms implemented in the 1970s affected mainly these three crops. Little land was distributed to small farmers; instead it was assumed by various government agencies. As a result, most tea and a substantial proportion of rubber production was placed under direct state control.

Changing Patterns

Since the beginning of the twentieth century, agriculture has been dominated by the four principal crops: rice, tea, rubber, and coconut. Most tea and rubber were exported, whereas almost all rice was for internal use. The coconut crop was sold on both domestic and international markets. The importance of other crops increased in the 1970s and 1980s, but no single crop emerged to challenge the four traditional mainstays.

Tea, rubber, and to a lesser extent, coconut are grown on plantations established in the nineteenth and early twentieth centuries. Before the plantations existed, villagers carried out three main types of cultivation. The valley bottoms and lowlands were occupied by rice paddies. These paddies were surrounded by a belt of residential gardens permanently cultivated with fruit trees and vegetables. The gardens in turn were surrounded by forests, parts of which were temporarily cleared for slash-and-burn cultivation, known as *chena* (see Glossary). Various grains and vegetables were grown on *chena* lands. The forests were also used for hunting, grazing for village cattle, gathering wild fruit, and timber. In some villages, especially in the dry zone, there was little rice cultivation, and people depended on the gardens and forests for their livelihood (see Land Use and Settlement Patterns, ch. 2).

Under legislation passed in 1840, the title of most forestland was vested in the government. In order to stimulate the production of export crops, the colonial administration sold large tracts to persons who wished to develop plantations. At first most buyers were British, but by the end of the nineteenth century many middleclass Sri Lankans had also acquired crown land and converted it to plantation use. The early coffee and tea plantations were often situated at high elevations, some distance from the nearest Sinhalese villages, but as time went on more estates were developed on land contiguous to villages. The precise impact of the plantations on village society remains controversial, but it is widely believed in Sri Lanka that the standard of living of villagers suffered as they lost use of the forestland.

Although the large coffee, tea, and rubber plantations relied mainly on Tamil migrants from southern India for their permanent labor supply, Sinhalese villagers were employed in the initial clearing of the forests, and some performed casual daily labor on the plantations in seasons when there was little work in the villages. The coconut plantations, being spatially closer to villages, employed considerable Sinhalese labor.

By the early twentieth century, there was no longer much land suitable for the expansion of cultivation in the wet zone, and in the 1930s the focus of agricultural development shifted from the wet zone to the dry zone and from plantation crops to rice. There was ample uncultivated land in the dry zone of the north-central region, but three major obstacles had to be overcome—the prevalence of malaria,

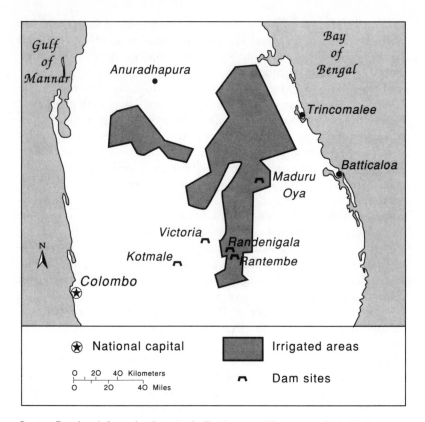

Source: Based on information from Asoka Bandarage, ''Women and Capitalist Development in Sri Lanka, 1977–87,'' *Bulletin of Concerned Asian Scholars,* 20, April–June 1988, 58; and Abhaya Attanayake, et al., *Mahaweli Saga: Challenge and Response,* Colombo, 1985, 55.

Figure 7. Accelerated Mahaweli Program, 1988

the lack of a reliable supply of water to carry out rice cultivation, and the absence of farmers to cultivate the soil. The first of these problems was solved by the success of the antimalarial campaigns of the 1940s. The others were tackled by government policies that sought to restore and build irrigation works and resettle peasants from the wet zone in the newly irrigated areas. In the 1980s, the pace of this program was quickened by the Accelerated Mahaweli Program (see Government Policies, this ch.).

The most important change in agriculture in the forty years after independence was the increase in rice production. This increase resulted from better yields and the enlarged amount of land under cultivation. In contrast, with the exception of rubber in the 1950s and 1960s, the principal export crops showed only modest gains in productivity, and the amount of land devoted to tea and rubber fell. After around 1970, there was growth in the production of other crops, including onions, chilies, sugar, soybeans, cinnamon, cardamom, pepper, cloves, and nutmeg.

Fishing, a traditional industry in coastal waters, accounted for 2.1 percent of GNP in 1986. Government efforts to offer incentives for modernization had little impact. The civil disturbances of the 1980s badly affected the industry. Before 1983 the northern region produced nearly 25 percent of the fish catch and around 55 percent of cured fish, but in the mid-1980s fishing was not possible there for long periods. The value of the fish catch off the northern coast fell from Rs495 million in 1981 to Rs52 million in 1986. Production off the southern and western coasts and from inland fisheries grew during this period, but not enough to prevent a decline in the island's total catch. In 1987 the government announced plans to provide funds for investment in fishing in the North and East, but implementation was likely to depend on improved security in these areas.

Land Use

Although there have been periodic agricultural censuses, they were limited in purpose and did not provide an overall picture of land use. In 1961, however, a survey of the use of the island's physical resources was compiled based on a 1956 aerial photographic survey of the entire country. The survey indicated that, of the country's total area of nearly 66 million hectares, 29 percent was under permanent cultivation, just over 15 percent under *chena* cultivation, 44 percent under forest cover, and about 6 percent under various types of grasses. Nearly 33,000 hectares consisted of swamp and marshlands, and about 63,000 hectares, or 1 percent, unused land. Just over 3 percent of the island's surface was covered by water. Of the total area, approximately 23 percent was in the wet zone, about 63 percent in the dry zone, and the balance lay in an area that the survey labeled ''intermediate,'' as it had characteristics of both zones.

Of the land under permanent cultivation in 1961, which included cropland, land under plantation, and homestead gardens, the survey indicated that some 75 percent was in the wet and intermediate zones and about 25 percent was in the dry zone. *Chena* cultivation, on the other hand, was predominantly in the dry zone, as were the grass, scrub, and forestlands. Although forest covered almost half the country, only about 0.2 percent and 3.1 percent of the forests were characterized as of high and intermediate yield, respectively. The study further indicated that approximately 70 percent of the land in the wet zone was under permanent cultivation, whereas in the dry zone under 12 percent was being cultivated on a permanent basis.

Since 1961 irrigation has enabled a much greater proportion of land in the dry zone to be cultivated and in 1978 it was estimated that nearly one-third of the country's dry-zone area was under permanent cultivation (see fig. 8). This proportion increased in the 1980s, when lands irrigated by the Accelerated Mahaweli Program were added to the total. As a result, the proportion of forestland declined and was estimated at just under 40 percent in 1987.

Although the forests had few high-yield timber stands, many areas suffered from deforestation because of the heavy demand for firewood in the 1980s. In 1987 it was estimated that 94 percent of households used firewood for cooking. Scarcities of firewood led to price increases well above the general level of inflation in the 1980s.

Government Policies

Government support for farmers takes several forms, including the provision of credit for producers, the setting of minimum prices for agricultural produce, the building of irrigation works, and the encouragement of internal migration to newly irrigated areas. Since the late colonial period, the government has played a growing role in the provision of credit to smallholders on favorable terms. Until 1986 the main instrument of this policy was the subvention of cooperative societies. Agricultural credit took three forms: short-term loans to farmers for the purchase of seeds and fertilizers; medium-term loans, intended for the purchase of machinery; and long-term loans for capital expenditure on storage, transport, and rice-milling apparatus. The long-term loans were not available for individual farmers, but were used by the cooperative societies to acquire infrastructural facilities.

The actual performance of credit provision through cooperatives generally fell short of expectations. Institutional credit did not displace the older sources of credit, such as the village moneylender, friends, and relatives. The inability to repay loans, procedural difficulties, and the existence of unpaid loans already taken from the cooperatives were some reasons given by farmers for preferring noninstitutional credit sources. Another problem with the credit furnished by cooperatives was the high rate of default. This rate may have been attributable partly to real difficulties in repayment, but it also was the result of a widely held impression that government loans were a form of social welfare and that it was not necessary to repay them.

The New Comprehensive Rural Credit Scheme implemented in 1986 sought to increase the flow of credit to smallholders. The Central Bank guaranteed up to 50 percent of each loan in the event of losses incurred by banks lending under the program, and eligible farmers received a line of credit for three years. Loans were automatically rescheduled at concessional rates when crops were damaged by events beyond the farmer's control. In 1986 cultivation loans under this program amounted to nearly Rs257 million, about 74 percent for paddy and the rest for other food crops.

Another important policy was the Guaranteed Price Scheme, which came into effect in 1942. Under this program the government agreed to purchase rice and some other produce at set prices. The intention was to support the farmer's standard of living. For a period in the early 1970s, when the island was threatened by food shortages, the government ordered peasants to market all of their rice through this scheme and at times set the price at a level lower than that of the free market. This policy had the effect of reducing the incentive to grow rice. The program lost some of its impetus in the 1980s. In 1986 the government set the price below the free-market rate for most of the year. As a result of the policy, purchases under the program accounted for only about 6 percent of the rice crop, mostly from districts where private traders were unwilling to operate because of the poor security situation.

Since the 1930s, governments have promoted irrigation works and colonization projects in the dry zone in an attempt to increase rice production and reduce land pressure and unemployment in the more densely settled wet zone. The lack of infrastructure and the prevalence of malaria hampered these programs in the early years. After the near eradication of malaria, increased government investment in infrastructure and enhanced financial support for migrants made the new lands more desirable. Between 1946 and 1971, the proportion of the population living in the dry zone increased from 12 to 19 percent (see Population, ch. 2).

At the end of 1968, about 352,000 hectares were under irrigation for rice cultivation; some 178,000 hectares under major storage reservoirs and barrages, and approximately 174,000 hectares in minor irrigation projects. In the 1970s and 1980s, governments pursued major irrigation programs, most notably the Mahaweli Ganga Program, which was lent added impetus and became the Accelerated Mahaweli Program in 1978. The increasing size of the Mahaweli project dwarfed its earlier endeavors. According to the plan, approximately 593,000 hectares of previously arid land would be brought under irrigation by 1992. In 1986 some 76,000 hectares of new land were under cultivation as a result of this project.

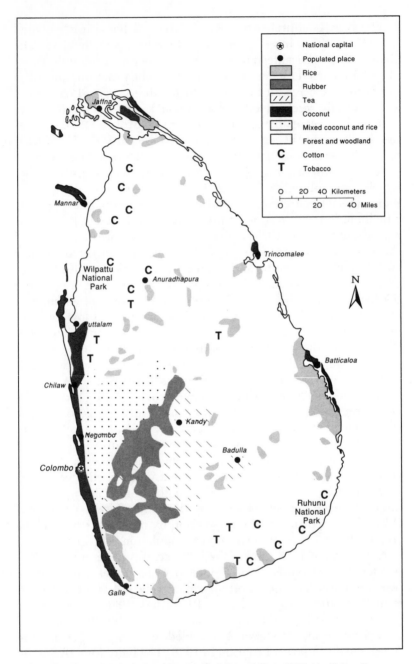

Source: Based on information from *Agro-Bio-Environmental Chart of Sri Lanka*, Tokyo: Resources
Council, Science and Technology Agency, 1977.

Figure 8. Agriculture and Land Use, 1988

Other long-standing government policies designed to help farmers included subsidies for fertilizer, seed paddy, and other inputs. Government efforts also partly contributed to the adoption of improved cultivation practices and high-yielding seed varieties in paddy farming in the 1960s.

Land Tenure

Modern land tenure policy dates from the Land Development Ordinance of 1935, which forbade the transfer of crown lands for purposes of cultivation except to enlarge the landholdings of near-landless or landless peasants. The intent of this ordinance was to help small farmers whose livelihood was seen to be at risk from the exploitation of rich peasants and urban landowners.

In 1958 the Paddy Lands Bill was enacted, mainly to benefit the tenant farmers of some 160,000 hectares of paddy land. The bill purported to assist tenants to purchase the land they worked, to protect them against eviction, and to establish a rent ceiling at around 25 percent of the crop. It also established cultivation committees, composed of rice farmers, to assume general responsibility for rice cultivation in their respective areas, including the direction and control of minor irrigation projects. Shortcomings in the law and official indifference in enforcing the act hampered its effectiveness, and many observers termed it a failure. In some regions tenants who tried to pay the lower, official rents were successfully evicted by landlords, and the old rents, often about 50 percent of the produce, remained in force. In the 1980s, however, the rent ceiling of 25 percent was effective in most districts.

The Land Reform Law of 1972 imposed a ceiling of twenty hectares on privately owned land and sought to distribute lands in excess of the ceiling for the benefit of landless peasants. Because both land owned by public companies and paddy lands under ten hectares in extent were exempted from the ceiling, a considerable area that would otherwise have been available for distribution did not come under the purview of the legislation. Between 1972 and 1974, the Land Reform Commission took over nearly 228,000 hectares, one-third of which was forest and most of the rest planted with tea, rubber, or coconut. Few rice paddies were affected because nearly 95 percent of them were below the ceiling limit. Very little of the land acquired by the government was transferred to individuals. Most was turned over to various government agencies or to cooperative organizations, such as the Up-Country Co-operative Estates Development Board.

The Land Reform Law of 1972 applied only to holdings of individuals. It left untouched the plantations owned by joint-stock companies, many of them British. In 1975 the Land Reform (Amendment) Law brought these estates under state control. Over 169,000 hectares comprising 395 estates were taken over under this legislation. Most of this land was planted with tea and rubber. As a result, about two-thirds of land cultivated with tea was placed in the state sector. The respective proportions for rubber and coconut were 32 and 10 percent. The government paid some compensation to the owners of land taken over under both the 1972 and 1975 laws. In early 1988, the state-owned plantations were managed by one of two types of entities, the Janatha Estates Development Board, or the Sri Lanka State Plantation Corporation.

Cropping Pattern

Rice cultivation has increased markedly since independence, although in the late 1980s yields remained well below those of the major rice-producing countries. Much of the improvement came in the late 1970s and 1980s. Rice remained a smallholder's crop, and production techniques varied according to region. In some villages, it was still sown by hand, with harvesting and threshing often engaging the entire family, plus all available friends and relatives.

Because no completely perennial sources of water exist, there was uncertainty regarding the adequacy of the supply each year. In the wet zone, flooding and waterlogging was experienced in the 1980s, whereas in the dry zone even the irrigated areas were subject to the possibility of insufficient water. In the mid- and up-country wet zone areas, most fields were sown twice a year in the 1980s; in the dry zone most holdings were sown only once; and in the low-country wet zone the amount of flooding or waterlogging determined whether to plant once or twice. The *maha* (greater monsoon—see Glossary) crops are sown between August and October and harvested five or six months later; the *yala* (lesser monsoon—see Glossary) crops sown between April and May and harvested about four or five months later.

Despite some increases in productivity, rice output was disappointing in the 1960s and early 1970s. Greater incentives to farmers after 1977 contributed to increases in production. Both the area under cultivation and the yield increased steadily between 1980 and 1985, when annual output reached 2.7 million tons, compared to an annual output of around 1.4 million tons in the early 1970s. In 1986 unfavorable weather and security difficulties led to a slight decline in production. A severe drought affected the crop in 1987, when output was estimated at only 2.1 million tons.

Tea is Sri Lanka's largest export crop. Only China and India produce more tea. The plants, originally imported from Assam in

Gemstone prospector near Ratnapura
Courtesy Paige W. Thompson

India, are grown in the wet zone at low, middle, and high altitudes, and produce a high-grade black tea. The higher altitudes produce the best tea, and terracing is used to eke out the limited area of upper altitude land. Tea cultivation is meticulous and time consuming, requiring the constant and skilled attention of two or three workers per hectare. Because of this requirement, tea is most

135

efficiently grown on estates, based on large capital investment and having a highly organized and disciplined management and labor supply.

Because working and living on estates was not attractive to Sinhalese peasants, the labor supply for the tea industry from its inception was provided by Indian Tamil immigrants who lived on the estates. Since independence the number of Sinhalese workers has increased, but in the late 1980s Tamils still dominated this sector (see Ethnic Groups, ch. 2).

The performance of the tea industry was disappointing in the 1970s and early 1980s, because of poor producer prices and low productivity. Tea production was 211 million kilograms in 1986, down from 220 million kilograms in 1969. The fundamental problem of the tea estates was the advanced age of the tea bushes. In 1987 their average age was around sixty years and only 15 percent of the total area under tea had been replanted with high-yielding varieties. Replanting had been neglected in the 1960s and 1970s partly because low tea prices and high export duties meant that profit margins were not high enough to make it a profitable enterprise. Between 1972 and 1974, the growing risk of nationalization also discouraged investment.

Rubber continues to be an important export crop in the late 1980s. It thrives under plantation conditions in the wet zone, although a significant proportion of the crop is produced by smallholders. Although rubber yields improved greatly in the first twenty years after independence, both the output and area planted with rubber declined in the 1980s. Output fell from 156 million kilograms in 1978 to 125 million kilograms in 1982. Improved prices caused production levels to recover to about 138 million kilograms in 1986.

Despite the importance of rubber, a large number of rubber plantations suffer from old age and neglect. The government offered incentives to encourage replanting and improve maintenance procedures. Nevertheless, the area replanted in 1986 was 12 percent less than in 1985. This drop in replanting resulted from a shortage of seeds and the reluctance of farmers to retire land from production at a time of relatively attractive prices. In early 1988, however, the short- and medium-term outlook for world rubber prices was considered good.

Most of the coconut production was sold in the domestic market, which consumed about 1.4 billion nuts in the mid-1980s. Most of the rest of the crop, usually between 2 billion and 3 billion nuts, was exported as copra, coconut oil, and desiccated coconut. Local uses for coconut include timber for construction, leaves for thatch and siding, coir for rope and rough textiles, and toddy and arrack for alcoholic beverages.

Coconut output fluctuates depending on weather conditions, fertilizer application, and producer prices. In the 1980s, smallholders dominated its production, which was concentrated in Colombo and Kurunegala districts and around the city of Chilaw in Puttalam District. Because of a drought in 1983, production suffered a setback during 1984 and fell to 1.9 billion nuts, its lowest level since 1977. The recovery during 1985 was impressive, leading to the record production of almost 3 billion nuts. This level was itself surpassed in 1986, when production rose a further 3 percent. But the average export price fell by 45 percent in 1985 and by 56 percent in 1986. In 1986 the farm gate price probably fell below the cost of production, and in early 1988 it appeared that fluctuations in the world price of coconut products would remain a problem for the foreseeable future. The 1987 drought was expected to reduce coconut production by at least 20 percent in both 1987 and 1988. Like tea and rubber, the coconut sector suffered from inadequate replanting. Consequently, a large proportion of the trees were old and past optimum productivity levels.

The importance of crops other than tea, rubber, and coconut increased after 1970, and in 1986 they accounted for around 51 percent of agricultural output. There was a substantial increase in minor food crops, including soybeans, chilies, and onions, all of which are grown as subsidiary crops on land irrigated by the Mahaweli project. In the 1960s and earlier, vegetables were imported from India in large quantities, but in the 1980s the island's import requirements were much smaller. Spices, including cloves, nutmeg, cardamom, and pepper, also registered large gains in the 1970s and 1980s. A large proportion of the spice output was being exported in the 1980s. Other crops of importance included corn, millet, sweet potatoes, cassava, dry beans, sesame seed, and tobacco. A wide variety of tropical fruits, including mangoes, pineapples, plantains, and papayas, also were grown; most were consumed in the domestic market. Sugar output increased in the early 1980s, although in 1986 it still accounted for only 11 percent of the domestic consumption. The expansion in sugar took place despite the problems of the state-run sugar mills and their associated sugar lands in Eastern Province, which have been disrupted by civil strife. Two new mills in Western Province accounted for the increase in production, and in early 1988 the outlook for further expansion was good.

Industry

Industry, including manufacturing, mining, energy, transportation, and construction, accounted for around 38 percent of GNP

137

in 1986. The most important products included refined oil, textiles, gems, and processed agricultural products. Construction and tourism both grew rapidly in the late 1970s and early 1980s, but contracted after the onset of ethnic violence in 1983. State-owned corporations accounted for over 50 percent of total industrial output. An investment promotion zone was established in 1979 with the goal of attracting foreign capital; textile factories accounted for a large proportion of investment there in its early years. The island's electricity supply was mainly fueled by hydropower (see Energy, this ch.).

Changing Patterns

Sri Lanka developed little industry under British rule, relying instead on the proceeds from agricultural exports to buy manufactured goods from other countries. Most industry during the colonial period involved processing the principal export commodities: tea, rubber, and coconut. Although these sectors remained important, in the 1980s there was a much greater variety of industrial establishments, including a steel mill, an oil refinery, and textile factories.

Industrial diversification began in the 1960s with the production of consumer goods for the domestic market. This trend was a consequence of government measures aimed at saving foreign exchange, which made it difficult to import many items that had previously been obtained from overseas. Heavy industries were established in the late 1960s, mostly in the state sector. During the 1970–77 period the state assumed an even greater role in manufacturing, but after the economic reforms of 1977 the government attempted to improve prospects for the private sector. The fastest growing individual sector in the 1980s was textiles, which made up approximately 29 percent of industrial production in 1986. The textiles, clothing, and leather products sector became the largest foreign exchange earner in 1986. Over 80 percent of the manufacturing capacity was concentrated in Western Province, particularly in and around Colombo.

Industrial Policies

The enactment of the State Industrial Corporations Act of 1957 provided for the reconstitution of existing state enterprises as well as the establishment of new corporations to promote the development of large-scale and basic industries. The period 1958 to 1963 witnessed the first phase in the rapid growth of state industrial corporations. By 1963 fourteen such corporations were engaged in such fields as textiles, cement, sugar, paper, chemicals, edible oils and fats, ceramics, mineral sands, plywood, and leather. By 1974 there

A rubber tapper's child
Courtesy
Paige W. Thompson

were twenty-five state corporations, including such major undertakings as a steel mill and an oil refinery.

Despite the 1977 policy shift in favor of the private sector, in early 1988 government-controlled enterprises continued to play a major role in industry. State-owned corporations accounted for nearly 60 percent of total industrial output. The most important public company was the Ceylon Petroleum Corporation, which accounted for about 55 percent of all public-sector production.

From the beginning, many industrial corporations in the state sector were troubled by such problems as management inefficiency, technical deficiencies in planning, overstaffing, and defective pricing policies. These difficulties contributed in many undertakings to poor economic results. Moreover, public sector enterprises were associated with objectives that reflected both growth and welfare considerations for the economy as a whole. They became the chief instruments furthering state ownership and social control in the economy, and they were expected to promote capital formation and long-term development. At times they were also looked upon chiefly as major sources of employment and enterprises providing goods and services to the public at relatively low prices. As a result, a number of the state industrial corporations have lost money. In 1987 the debts of state-owned corporations were Rs19 billion, of which Rs15 billion were owed to foreign sources and Rs4 billion to the two state-owned banks.

The liberalization of the economy in 1977 was largely prompted by the perceived inefficiency of the public sector, not by any ideological commitment to free enterprise. As a result, the government let private enterprise compete with the state corporations but took few steps to dismantle the state sector. Instead, it attempted to improve its efficiency. One major state venture, the National Milk Board, was dissolved in 1986, however. It had been established in 1953, but had never succeeded in developing the milk industry. In 1987 it was reported that consideration was being given to transferring to private control several state-run industrial enterprises. These included the four government textile mills, the State Distilleries Corporation, the National Paper Corporation, the Mineral Sands Corporation, Paranthan Chemicals, Sri Lanka Tyre, and Union Motors. In early 1988, however, doubts remained about the extent of the government's commitment to this program. Although the plan to sell the textile mills was expected to be implemented within two years, some of the government's economic advisers reportedly were urging the government to proceed cautiously in its privatization policy, in view of the limited capital markets, the concentration of private wealth, and the weak regulatory framework.

Manufacturing

The share of manufacturing in the economy declined from 21 to 15 percent of GDP between 1977 and 1986. This fall is somewhat misleading because it resulted in large part from the rapid growth in the service sector and the decline in output of the state-owned Ceylon Petroleum Corporation. The latter accounted for as much as one-third of the value of manufactured goods in some years and thus strongly affected aggregate manufacturing statistics. These statistics fluctuated along with changes in the value of the output of the oil refinery, which in turn varied with oil price levels and the extent of plant closings for maintenance. Some manufacturing sectors grew rapidly during this period.

Manufacturing was dominated for most of the twentieth century by the processing of agricultural produce for both the export and domestic markets. The most important industries were engaged in preparing and packaging for outside markets the principal export commodities—tea, rubber, and coconuts—for which Sri Lanka is noted. Such preparation generally involved low technology, comparatively modest capital investment on machinery, and uncomplicated, sequential procedures. Tea leaves, for example, follow a four-part process of withering, rolling (to extract bitter juices), fermentation, and heating (or roasting), before being packed in chests for export.

The processing of coconut and of rubber also were important industries, although their ratio in proportion to all manufacturing fell in the 1970s and early 1980s. The processing of the latter two commercial crops generally involved refining the basic commodities into a range of semi-finished products to be used in manufacturing finished goods at home or abroad. Coconuts, for example, are transformed into copra, desiccated coconut, coconut oil, fiber, *poonac* (a meal extract), and toddy. Copra and desiccated coconut are used as oils or as ingredients in food such as margarine; coconut oil is used to make soap; coconut fibers such as coir are used to make yarn, rope, or fishnets, while *poonac* is used as food for livestock. The coconut palm flower is also used in the production of alcoholic beverages.

Rubber is also processed in various ways, including latex or scrap crepe and ribbed or smoked sheet, which together account for much of Sri Lanka's export of this commodity. Processing methods for rubber are outdated, however, and Western consumer countries have protested against the hardness, high moisture content, and inconsistent quality of the Sri Lankan product.

Manufacturing received a boost in the early 1960s when import controls, which were the result of shortages in foreign exchange, made it difficult for consumers to obtain or afford foreign products. The result was a protected and profitable ready-made home market. This situation led to an expansion of both private-and public-sector manufacturing, with the private sector concentrating on consumer goods. These new enterprises, however, depended heavily on imported raw materials, and when the country's balance of payments difficulties became even more serious in the early 1970s, industry suffered from the lack of foreign exchange. In 1974 it was estimated that only 40 percent of the capacity of the industrial sector was used. After the 1977 liberalization, raw materials were more freely available, and in 1986 capacity utilization was estimated at 78 percent.

In 1978 the government established the Greater Colombo Economic Commission primarily to serve as the authority for the free trade zones to be set up near the capital. The first investment promotion zone consisted of a large tract that was established in 1979 at Katunayaka, near the Bandaranaike International Airport. A second zone was inaugurated in 1986 at Biyagama, in Colombo District. Foreign companies that built factories in the zones received generous tax concessions. The commission succeeded in attracting some foreign investment, especially from Hong Kong and other

Asian countries. At the end of 1985, a total of 119 enterprises had signed agreements with the commission, but only 7 were signed in 1986, when there were 72 units in production. The total number of people employed was nearly 42,000. Gross export earnings from the investment promotion zones in 1986 were around Rs5.5 billion, up 43 percent from 1985. Foreign investments outside the free trade zones were coordinated by the Foreign Investment Advisory Committee.

The principal change in manufacturing in the 1980s was the rapid growth of the textile sector, from 10.5 percent of output in 1980 to 29.2 percent in 1986 (see table 8, Appendix A). In the mid-1980s, the government was attempting to diversify foreign investment away from textiles. Most textile factories were located in the investment promotion zones (see fig. 9).

During the July 1983 riots, 152 factories were destroyed, but there was little long-term effect. Some observers expressed the view that the equipment destroyed was inefficient, and that modernization was long overdue.

Construction

Total expenditure for construction was estimated at 7.7 percent of GDP in 1986. The sector was given a boost by the ambitious public investment program of the government that came to power in 1977. Between 1977 and 1980, construction expanded at an annual rate of 20 percent in real terms. It stagnated in the 1980s as the number of new projects dwindled and the early ones were completed.

The largest construction project of the post-1977 period was the Mahaweli irrigation program. Conceived in the 1960s as the Mahaweli Ganga Program, the project originally was expected to bring approximately 364,000 additional hectares of land under irrigation and to provide an extra 540 megawatts of hydroelectric power to the national grid. Completion of the program was to require thirty years. Construction of the first two dams was completed in 1977 and opened about 53,000 hectares of new land to irrigation in a general area south of the old capital of Anuradhapura in the dry zone. When the United National Party swept into power in 1977, the project was given renewed impetus and renamed the Accelerated Mahaweli Program. Construction work was undertaken at five new sites between 1979 and 1982, with the intent of increasing the hectares under irrigation and generating an extra 450 megawatts of hydroelectric power for the national grid. By the end of 1987, new dams and reservoirs had been completed at Kotmale, Randenigala, Maduru Oya, and Victoria. The operational power stations at Randenigala and Victoria together generated 330 megawatts of power, with an additional 147 megawatts expected when the Kotmale station came on line. All construction related to the Accelerated Mahaweli Program was scheduled for completion by 1989. The total cost of the entire project was estimated at US$1.4 to 2 billion.

The Urban Development Authority was established in 1978 to promote integrated planning and development of important urban locations. Its responsibilities have included the new parliamentary buildings and the reconstruction of St. John's fish market in Colombo. Total expenditure of the Urban Development Authority was Rs529 million in 1986, well under its annual budget in the early 1980s. The Million Houses Program was established in 1984 to coordinate both public and private housing construction. In early 1988 the government's policy was to subsidize private housing rather than undertake extensive public housing programs.

Mining

Mining is carried out in both the public and private sectors. The most valuable products are precious and semiprecious stones, including sapphires, rubies, cats' eyes, topaz, garnets, and moonstones. Official exchange earnings from gems were negligible in the first two decades after independence because most of the output was smuggled out of the country. The setting up of a publicly owned State Gem Corporation in 1971 and export incentives for those exporting through legal channels brought a marked improvement. In 1986 legal exports were valued at Rs755 million, but many observers believed that a considerable quantity was still being exported illegally. In the late 1980s, Japan remained the most important market for Sri Lanka's gems. The Moors traditionally have played an important role in the industry (see Ethnic Groups, ch. 2).

Graphite also is of commercial significance. Almost the entire output is exported as crude graphite (plumbago). Ilmenite, a mineral sand used in the manufacture of paint and the fortification of metals, also is exported. Salt is produced by evaporation for the domestic market. Thorium deposits have been reported in Sabaragamuwa Province and in the beach sands of the northeast and southwest coasts. Exploration also has disclosed the presence of apatite (source of phosphate), dolomite (fertilizer component) and small pockets of economically extractable iron ore.

Energy

Over 70 percent of the island's total energy consumption was satisfied by firewood, agricultural residues, and animal waste,

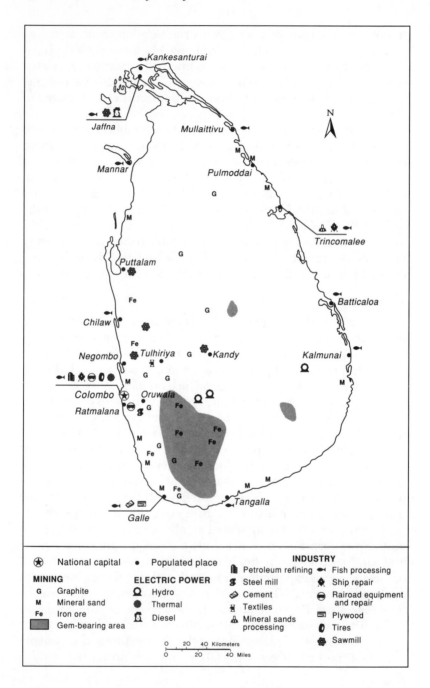

Figure 9. Industry, Mining, and Power, 1988

mostly for household use. The country had no coal or petroleum deposits, and the only other indigenous energy source was hydropower.

In 1927 the Department of Government Electrical Undertakings, now called the Ceylon Electricity Board, took over the transmission of electricity throughout the country. Hydroelectric power came into use in 1951 with the commissioning of the Laksapana project in Central Province. Demand for power increased from approximately 20 megawatts in 1951 to nearly 73 megawatts in 1963, about 90 percent of which was met from hydroelectric sources. In the 1970s, the island increasingly came to rely on imported oil for the generation of electricity, but new hydroelectric capacity from the Mahaweli project in the 1980s reduced the importance of oil. In 1986 total installed capacity was 1,010 megawatts, of which 74 percent was from hydropower.

In early 1988, it appeared that the Mahaweli project would solve Sri Lanka's electricity supply problem for the foreseeable future. This integrated power generation and irrigation project started contributing to power supplies in 1984 when the first two phases of the Victoria Dam were completed, adding 140 megawatts to installed power capacity. In April 1985, the final stage of the Victoria Dam increased capacity by 70 megawatts. A slightly greater capacity was expected to result in the late 1980s.

United States and British-owned oil companies in Sri Lanka were nationalized in 1963, and since then the importing, refining, and distributing of all oil products has been the responsibility of the Ceylon Petroleum Corporation, the state oil company. Its oil refinery started production in 1969. The main products in 1986 were fuel oil (559,497 tons), heavy diesel (60,995 tons), auto diesel (406,569 tons), kerosene (153,692 tons), and gasoline (123,089 tons).

Transportation

In 1987 the road network extended 74,954 kilometers, of which 25,504 were maintained by the Ministry of Highways and the remainder by local governments (see fig. 10). During 1984 the government embarked on a five-year road maintenance program at an estimated cost of Rs5 billion, to be financed by loans from the World Bank (see Glossary) and the Asian Development Bank, together with a grant from Japan. The total number of registered motor vehicles in 1986 was about 478,000.

Road haulage is handled by private companies; some businesses also have their own trucking operations. After 1978 container transport became an important mode of freight haulage for exports

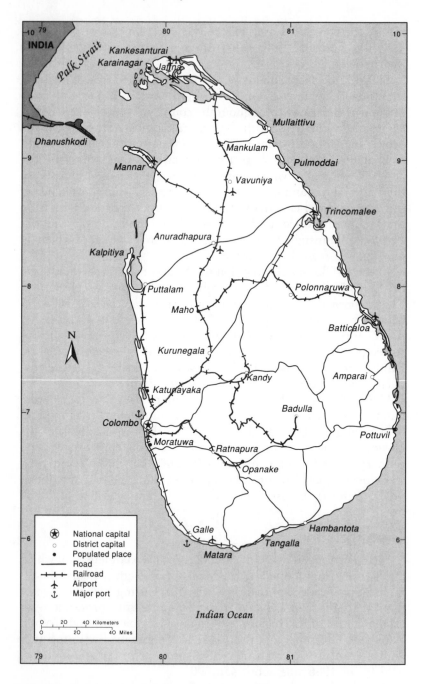

Figure 10. Transportation System, 1988

produced in the investment promotion zones. Intercity haulage is carried out by trucks. Bullock carts remained important in rural and suburban areas in the 1980s.

The Ceylon Transport Board had the sole responsibility for providing public passenger road transport from 1957 to 1978. Fares were heavily subsidized, but overcrowding was severe. In 1978 private buses were again allowed to operate, and the Sri Lanka Transport Board and nine regional transport boards replaced the Ceylon Transport Board. The Sri Lanka Transport Board had responsibility for overall transport policy, budgeting, and production planning, whereas the regional boards were responsible for the operation of regular regional and interregional bus services. In 1986 the revenue-cost ratio of the regional boards was 89 percent. Private road transport expanded rapidly in the late 1970s and early 1980s, but as in the state sector, there was some contraction in the mid-1980s as a result of the declining security in the northern and eastern parts of the country. In 1986 the private sector accounted for about half of the passenger-kilometers. Many buses in both the state and private sectors were in poor condition.

The island's first railroad line, from Colombo to Kandy, was opened in 1867, and in the 1980s Sri Lanka Railways had 1,944 kilometers of railroad track. In early 1988, service in Northern and Eastern provinces had been irregular for several years. The network's passenger-kilometers amounted to 1.9 billion in 1986, about 38 percent less than its total in 1982. Freight services, on the other hand, remained fairly steady in the mid-1980s. The railroads have been operated at a loss since independence.

Three ports can accommodate deep water vessels: Colombo, Trincomalee, and Galle. Colombo was by far the most important. In 1985 it handled nearly 3 million tons of cargo compared with about 600,000 jointly handled by the other two ports. In 1986 the Ceylon Petroleum Corporation began a project to build a single-point buoy mooring 9.6 kilometers offshore from Colombo port. When completed, this project will greatly reduce the costs of discharging crude oil to the refinery near Colombo.

In 1971 Sri Lanka launched its own merchant fleet. The state-owned Sri Lanka Shipping Corporation purchased its first vessel, a 14,000-ton freighter, in March 1971. By 1981 the corporation owned eight ships, including a 20,000 deadweight ton tanker. In 1987 the firm began to replace its aging fleet.

Colombo is a stopping place on international air routes between Europe and the Asia-Pacific region. The first stage of a redevelopment plan for the Bandaranaike International Airport at Katunayaka was completed in October 1986 with the opening of a new runway, built at a cost of Rs517 million. Some foreign airlines reduced or suspended services in the mid-1980s because of declining traffic due to the security situation.

Air Lanka, the nation's flag carrier, was established in 1980, and in early 1988 it connected Sri Lanka with Europe, the Middle East, and South and Southeast Asia. It was 60 percent government owned. In 1987 a presidential commission set up to inquire into the airline's financial affairs accused former members of the airline's board of subordinating the company's development to their private gain. Taking into account the realizable value of its assets and other costs associated with a forced sale, estimated cumulative losses up to the end of the fiscal year 1986 were Rs7.7 billion, or about Rs1.3 billion for each year of operation. In early 1988, a foreign airline was reportedly being sought to manage Air Lanka and turn it into a viable enterprise.

Telecommunications

In 1988 Sri Lanka's domestic and international telecommunications services were operated by the Posts and Telecommunications Department, of the Ministry of Posts and Telecommunications. Communications with most countries were available through telephone and telex services; an international direct dialing service was introduced in 1980 and by 1987 was in operation in most parts of the country. Advances in the telecommunications field, however, had not kept pace with the growth in the economic sector occurring since the 1970s. In the 1980s, the quality and availability of telecommunications services in Sri Lanka was average compared to other Asian countries, but poor compared to other parts of the world. With approximately 106,500 telephones in use in 1986, the telephone network was extremely overloaded, the exchanges nearing or exceeding capacity levels. Line congestion and long waiting lists for telephone connections were common. Telephone lines were concentrated in urban areas, with over 60 percent located in the Colombo area, which houses only 5 percent of Sri Lanka's population. Direct dialing was available within Colombo and to some major towns, but operator assistance was necessary for other connections, which often led to long delays.

The Sri Lanka Broadcasting Corporation operated radio services, and the Sri Lanka Rupavahini Corporation and the Independent Television Network operated television services in the 1980s. In 1987 almost 700 hours of weekly radio programming were broadcast domestically in Sinhala, Tamil, and English. Programs were transmitted internationally via a shortwave station at Ekala, and domestically through twenty-four medium-wave stations and FM

The Economy

stations located in five cities throughout Sri Lanka (see table 9, Appendix A). Over 2 million radio sets were in use in the mid-1980s. Foreign service broadcasts to Asia, Europe, Africa, and the Middle East were transmitted from Ekala in eight languages (English, Hindi, Kannada, Malayalam, Nepali, Sinhala, Tamil, and Telugu). Independent foreign broadcasts transmitting programs from Sri Lanka included the Deutsche Welle station at Trincomalee, and Voice of America radio station at Colombo, and the religious stations of Trans-World Radio and Adventist Radio.

Television transmissions began in 1979 and by 1986 there were some 350,000 receivers in place. Programs were broadcast over three channels in Sinhala, English, and Tamil for four hours daily via the main transmitter at Pidurutalagala, Nuwara Eliya District, and two relay stations at Kokkaville in northern Batticaloa District and Kandy. The Independent Television Network broadcast over one channel from the station at Wickramasinghapura.

International telecommunication services were provided mainly by the Padukka satellite station and the South East Asia-Middle East-Western Europe submarine cable system. The earth station, commissioned in 1975, continued to provide international telephone and television services via the Indian Ocean Region INTELSAT satellite. The submarine cable station located at Colombo was commissioned in 1984. It extended from Singapore to France via six countries (Indonesia, Sri Lanka, Djibouti, Saudi Arabia, Egypt, and Italy) and provided Sri Lanka with international telephone communications.

Sri Lanka was planning to invest Rs2.5 billion in telecommunications in the late 1980s. The advances were slated in the telephone network and other telecommunications services.

Labor

The formally employed population of Sri Lanka in the late 1980s was shifting gradually from agriculture to manufacturing, trade, and service employment. Nevertheless, over 40 percent of the work force remained agricultural in early 1988; most of these workers were smallholders, tenants, and plantation workers. The labor force growing most rapidly in the early and mid-1980s was in the service sector.

Characteristics and Occupational Distribution

A precise breakdown of the labor force and movement within it was not possible in the late 1980s because the official statistics were not reliable. Early censuses, taken when the island was a British colony, compiled long lists of occupations with little

149

Sri Lanka: A Country Study

comparability from one census to the next. The postindependence censuses also suffer from inconsistencies. They show a decline in the proportion of the work force engaged in agriculture, hunting, forestry, and fishing from 52 percent in 1953 to just over 45 percent in 1981. The proportion of the work force engaged in manufacturing remained steady over the same period, at 10 percent. The largest increase was in services, including commerce, banking, and finance. The proportion of workers in this category rose from 11.2 percent in 1953 to 15.7 percent in 1981. There was also an increase in construction, from 1.9 percent to just over 3 percent. Transport, storage, and communications increased from 3.5 percent to 4.8 percent over the same period. All such figures should be regarded as tentative and subject to revision.

Demographic and educational changes after independence altered the composition of the work force as much as economic development. Rapid population growth brought additional workers into the job market every year and lowered the average worker's age. The growth of the economy was too limited to provide opportunities for the new workers. Similarly, the extension of education qualified many thousands of youths for jobs that did not exist. This fact has been particularly true for women, who in the 1980s made up about 25 percent of the labor force despite equal access to education.

Government Labor Policies

During the nineteenth century, labor legislation dealt with the large plantations, and more general labor laws were passed only in the closing years of colonial rule. In 1941 the government enacted the Wages Boards Ordinance, the first comprehensive piece of legislation regarding the payment of wages, the regulation of working hours, and sick and annual leave; the ordinance also empowered the government to establish wages boards for any trade. The boards are composed of an equal number of representatives of workers and employers and three appointees proposed by the commissioner of labor.

Ordinances of 1942 and 1946 required all factories to be registered and established minimum standards for health and safety. The laws also gave the commissioner the right to send inspectors to the factories and to judge whether a plant was meeting minimum standards. The Shops and Offices Employees Act of 1954 extended the provisions of the factories legislation to small shops.

The Maternity Benefits Ordinance, as amended in 1957, entitled a woman who worked in a factory, mine, or estate to full compensation for a period of two weeks before her confinement and for six weeks afterward. The employee must have worked for the employer 150 days before her confinement to be eligible to receive the benefits.

The Employees Provident Fund, established in 1958, provided a national retirement program for the private sector. The Provident Fund required an employer to contribute 6 percent of total earnings and an employee to contribute 4 percent of earnings exclusive of overtime pay. Participation in this plan grew quickly, and in the 1980s most salaried workers in the formal sectors of the economy were members. Government employees had their own pension plans.

Although legislation protecting the health and welfare of workers was extensive, enforcement was inconsistent. The government departments charged with enforcement were chronically underfunded in the late 1980s. Moreover, many labor regulations were suspended in the investment promotion zones. Most labor legislation also did not apply to rice farming and other economic activities carried out informally.

Working Conditions

Working conditions varied greatly according to the type and size of employment activity in the 1980s. The Factories Ordinance of 1942 established guidelines for industrial safety and sanitation and made each factory liable to government inspection. Because this ordinance and other similar legislation has not been enforced consistently, workers frequently protested their working conditions. In the 1980s, strikes and boycotts often took place because of inadequate meals at factories that had their own lunchrooms or because of the lack of other facilities.

The Factories Ordinance prohibited work for women between 9:00 P.M. and 6:00 A.M. In the years after independence, a further series of laws restricted the employment of women and children to designated time periods and places. A 1957 law, for example limited working time for women to nine hours. Other laws prohibited women and children from working underground, in mines, for example.

Unemployment has been a problem since the 1960s, especially for young people, but the statistics available in 1988 were not very reliable. Observers estimated that unemployment increased from around 12 percent of the labor force in the early 1960s to 24 percent in the mid-1970s. Unemployment fell back to around 12 percent in the first few years after the economic liberalization that began in November 1977, but it was again on the increase in the mid-1980s. According to official data, in 1987 the labor force consisted of around 6.2 million persons, of whom 5.4 million, or 87 percent,

Victoria Dam approaches completion, Accelerated Mahaweli Program
Courtesy Embassy of Sri Lanka, Washington

were gainfully employed, but these figures understated unemployment, which the Ministry of Finance estimated at 18 percent in late 1987. All of these figures excluded persons said to be underemployed or partially employed, conditions that were prevalent in the rice-farming sector and in some of the urban-based service activities. The extent of labor underutilization, was believed to be much greater than indicated by the statistics for unemployment.

In the mid-1980s, sectors, such as tourism, that were sensitive to the security situation suffered job losses (see Tourism, this ch.). Migration to the Middle East, which also provided jobs in the early 1980s, was also on the decline, although still of substantial importance. In 1987 observers estimated that 100,000 Sri Lankans worked and lived in the Middle East—particularly in the small oil-rich states of the Arabian Peninsula, where wages for comparable work were much higher than in Sri Lanka.

A representative index showing changes in the general level of wages was not available in the late 1980s. Wages were low compared with those paid in developed countries, even in the unionized sectors, and incomes were unevenly distributed. Some indication of wage movements can be gained from the indices of minimum wage rates. These more than doubled between 1978 and 1986, but inflation probably kept their value little changed in real terms. The only price index, the Colombo Consumer Price Index, was based on data gathered in Colombo and was widely believed to understate inflationary increases, especially for the lower wage earners. It recorded an increase of 8 percent in 1986. Although this rate was considerably higher than the 1.5 percent increase recorded in 1985, it was low compared to the two-digit rates that prevailed during the 1978–84 period.

Low wages in the formal sector were partially offset by overtime payments, increments, bonuses, and other incentive programs, which often added considerable supplements to salaries. A five-day work week was standard in the 1980s. Sri Lanka had a large number of public holidays; twenty-four were celebrated in 1985. These included twelve full moon days, which are of religious significance to Buddhists.

Labor Relations

The labor movement was large and politically active in the 1980s, although it suffered a loss of influence after 1977. Urban strikes began in the 1890s and increased in number after World War I. The first major labor organization, the Ceylon Labour Union, was formed in 1922. In the 1930s, the legislature passed a series of laws, including the Trade Union Ordinance of 1935, to regulate the

The Economy

unions. This law made it mandatory for trade unions to register with the government and to keep political and labor funds separate. After World War II, the unions represented a large proportion of the labor force, especially in Colombo and on the large plantations. The leadership of nearly all trade unions has come from the English-educated elite.

Union membership in 1988 was subject to fluctuations because of competition among unions affiliated with different political parties and because of personal rivalries among union leaders, as well as a fairly rapid turnover of unions. The unions have traditionally been strong in the state sector, especially rail and road transport, the ports, and the government clerical service. In 1983 observers estimated that about 1.8 million workers, or just under one-third of the gainfully employed labor force, were union members. Membership was fragmented into over 1,000 unions. Many of the unorganized workers were small farmers and rural laborers.

Before 1977 many unions were affiliated with the Marxist parties, especially the Trotskyite Lanka Sama Samaja (Ceylon Equal Society Party), but in the late 1970s and early 1980s the influence of the Jatika Sevaka Sangamaya (National Employees' Union), which was affiliated with the ruling UNP, increased greatly, and it became the single largest trade union. This organization was especially strong in the state sector, and it had a reputation for intimidation, violence, and discrimination against Tamils. Another important trade union was the Ceylon Workers' Congress, which represented a large proportion of the Indian Tamil estate workers. After 1977 it was politically allied with the government, but it nonetheless used the political turmoil after 1983 to bargain for better working conditions.

Labor disputes were arbitrated through a variety of state agencies, but these agencies have not prevented frequent and costly strikes. Plantation strikes have been most common, involving as many as 477,000 workers (in 1949) and as many as 1.12 million lost workdays (in 1966). In the remainder of the private sector, the most turbulent period was in 1962 and 1963, when over 1.28 million workdays were lost by strikes. In 1970 new highs were reached, with 143 strikes and the loss of 1.31 million workdays. In the mid-1970s, when many trade unions pledged not to strike in return for substantial concessions, the number of nonplantation strikes fell dramatically, although plantation strikes increased. Since 1977 the unions in the nonplantation sectors have been in apparent decline, in part because of changes in the nature of the work force. Most employees of the new textile factories in the free trade zone were young, unmarried women doing shift work, who did not expect to be employed there for more than a few years and who were little interested in joining a union. Similarly, employees in the import and tourist industries, sectors that grew in the years after 1977, had not been successfully organized.

Trade

Sri Lanka's economy continues to be heavily dependent on foreign trade. Historically, the island has exported cash crops in order to import food to feed its population. Although the production of rice, the staple food crop, increased rapidly in the late 1970s and 1980s, in early 1988 the island remained short of self-sufficiency in food. Trade policy since independence has been dominated by the deteriorating terms of trade. Between the 1950s and the 1980s, the amount of imports that could be bought with a given amount of the traditional exports has declined. Governments responded in the 1960s and 1970s with strict controls over imports, foreign exchange, and some aspects of internal trade. When the economy was liberalized in 1977, many of these regulations were swept away. One result has been a large increase in the foreign trade deficit and the external debt.

Internal Trade

An overall measure of the size and shape of the internal market was provided by the Central Bank of Sri Lanka's breakdown of national income according to expenditures by the several sectors of the economy. In 1986 gross domestic expenditure was estimated at Rs200.3 billion. About Rs139.4 billion represented private consumption; Rs18.5 billion was for government consumption; and Rs42.3 billion went into fixed capital investment, of which almost Rs33 billion was in the state sector. The aggregate of private sector expenditures constituted just over 74 percent of total outlays.

No detailed information was available concerning consumer outlays in the late 1980s. Earlier surveys indicated that many families devoted about 50 percent of their total expenditure to food. Some government policies in the 1960s and the early 1970s kept inequalities of consumption relatively low. These measures included the subsidizing and rationing of essential goods, restrictions on imports of luxury goods, and heavy income taxes. The easing of many of these policies after the economy was liberalized in 1977 resulted in higher food prices and a flood of imported luxury items. According to the Consumer Finance and Socio-Economic Survey carried out by the Central Bank in 1978 and 1979, the poorest 10 percent of the population controlled 1.2 percent of total personal income, while the richest 10 percent had 39 percent of personal income.

Traditionally, the state has played an important role in retail trade. The government-controlled Co-operative Wholesale Establishment, which was created during World War II to handle the import and distribution of foodstuffs, had monopolies over the sale of imported sugar, canned fish, cement, hardware, and other products at various times in the 1960s and early 1970s. The monopolies were broken up after 1977, when government policy shifted toward promoting competition. In 1986 however, there still were 8,644 cooperatives serving as retail outlets. As in the past, they relied heavily on the distribution of basic consumer items such as rice, flour, and sugar under the food stamps scheme (see Budgetary Process, Revenues, and Expenditures, this ch.). They also helped overcome shortages of essential goods in areas where security difficulties made private business unwilling to operate. In 1986 their turnover was about Rs1.1 billion.

The ten state trading corporations in existence in early 1988 were expected to be commercially competitive with the private sector. Most were organized around specific commodities, such as building materials, fertilizer, paddy, textiles, gems, and drugs. Their total turnover was around Rs5.6 billion in 1986, down from Rs6.3 billion in 1985.

Importers and wholesalers had their own warehouses, most of them in Colombo, but some in the provinces. For the most part, wholesalers did not actively engage in trying to sell their wares, but left it to retailers to take the initiative. Markup margins varied widely. Inasmuch as traders were not generally in a position to obtain credit from institutional sources, sales tended to be on a cash basis, although the larger wholesalers did extend limited amounts of credit.

External Trade

Sri Lanka's balance of trade has been in a chronic state of deficit since 1957; the only year between 1957 and 1987 when there was a surplus was 1977 (see table 10, Appendix A). Although the ability to pay for imports has generally declined because of the long-term relative fall in the prices of tea, rubber, and coconut, the demand for imports has been fueled by population growth and rising expectations. The resulting shortage of foreign exchange has been the greatest problem in the economy during the period since independence. For most of the 1960s and 1970s, the government imposed strict import and exchange controls in an attempt to control these deficits. After 1977 the deficits were allowed to grow and

157

Sri Lanka: A Country Study

were financed by increased foreign support and heavy borrowing.

Few nations have experienced so drastic and long-term a deterioration in terms of trade as did Sri Lanka from the mid-1950s to the mid-1970s. As a result, the volume of imports fell, at first through severe restriction of luxury items, such as automobiles and spirits. But the structure of the economy limited the amount by which imports could be cut. Levels of food, medicines, spare parts, and fertilizer could not easily be reduced without damaging the economy or the population's welfare. The gap was met by borrowing, and debt service obligations further reduced import capacity. Although the volume of exports was nearly 18 percent more in 1975 than in 1960, the proceeds from these exports had a purchasing power worth only 37 percent of the smaller volume of exports in 1960.

Although the general trend in the terms of trade was against Sri Lanka between 1955 and 1988, there were occasional exceptions. The terms of trade showed a 35 percent improvement in 1976 over 1975, and 31 percent in 1977 over 1976, when tea prices experienced an unprecedented rise of 80 percent. From 1979 to 1982, however, the terms of trade again turned sharply against Sri Lanka, reaching record lows in 1981 and 1982. Between 1983 and 1987, the terms of trade hovered near the level for 1981, with the exception of 1984, when an increase in the price of tea produced a temporarily more favorable position.

After the liberalization of the economy in 1977, the trade deficit widened enormously as the import bill soared under the influence of the government's development program. Exports, however, remained largely static. The trade deficit thus expanded year by year and reached nearly Rs20.5 billion in 1982, equal to 22.4 percent of GDP. In 1983, as a result of good agricultural production, the deficit was held to the same level as in 1982. The following year, 1984, the deficit was cut to Rs10.2 billion as a result of exceptionally high tea prices. This gain was not sustained in 1985, when the trade deficit rose to Rs17.8 billion. In 1986, despite a static level of imports attributable primarily to the decline of world oil prices, the trade deficit again widened, to around Rs20.5 billion. Sharply reduced earnings from tea were only partly offset by improved exports of manufactured goods, especially textiles. Preliminary figures for 1987 showed a record trade deficit.

Sri Lanka's major export earnings were derived from a small number of commodities (see table 5, Appendix A). In 1986 textiles overtook tea for the first time as the leading export. Textile exports were worth around Rs9.6 billion, compared to under Rs9.3

158

A dam of the Accelerated Mahaweli Program
Courtesy Embassy of Sri Lanka, Washington

billion for tea. Rubber exports, which have declined since the 1970s, were worth Rs2.6 billion in 1986. Coconut products accounted for Rs2.4 billion, fuel oil products for Rs2.3 billion, and gems for over Rs1.6 billion. Other exports, including agricultural produce, graphite, and manufactured goods, were valued at around Rs7.8 billion. This breakdown reflects a substantial diversification of exports away from tea and rubber in the 1970s and 1980s, but in early 1988 the fluctuations in the world prices of these commodities continued to be an important factor not only in the island's export earnings but in the health of the economy as a whole.

Oil accounted for about 25 percent of the value of imports in the early and mid-1980s, but dropped to 11.5 percent in 1986 when its price fell sharply and additional hydroelectric power became available from the Accelerated Mahaweli project. Some of the output of Sri Lanka's single oil refinery was then reexported. Other significant imports included machinery and equipment, chemicals, motor vehicles, clothing, paper, and sugar. Rice imports declined in the late 1970s and early 1980s; by 1985 Sri Lanka was close to self-sufficiency in years with good weather. In 1986 rice accounted for only 1.9 percent of imports.

The United States was the most important foreign market, accounting in 1986 for approximately 26 percent of the island's exports, mostly in the form of textiles and tea. The Federal Republic of Germany (West Germany), Britain, and Japan also were important markets in the 1980s, although no single country other than the United States took more than 8 percent of exports in 1986. The leading source of imports was Japan, which accounted for over 17 percent in 1986. The United Arab Emirates, Saudi Arabia, the United States, Britain, China, and West Germany also were important sources of imports. In the 1960s and 1970s, about 50 percent of rubber exports went to China in return for rice on favorable terms, but after around 1980 Sri Lanka no longer needed to import large quantities of rice. Higher oil prices led to an increasing proportion of imports coming from the Middle East; this was paid for in part with increased exports of tea to this region.

Although the island's balance of payments position was closely related to the balance of trade, foreign aid and remittances from Sri Lankans employed overseas made the balance of payments more favorable than the balance of trade. As a result, Sri Lanka occasionally ran a small balance of payments surplus in the 1960s and 1970s, and again in 1984, when the economy benefited from high tea prices. In 1986 Sri Lanka had a balance of payments deficit of US$406 million, down from US$556 million in 1985. The main factor was the trade deficit of US$750.2 million. Private transfers, mostly remittances, amounted to US$294.5 million, about half of which were from the Middle East. Official transfers, including aid from governments and international organizations, accounted for US$181.2 million. Sri Lanka's services account ran a deficit. Exports of services, including earnings from tourism, were US$378.1 million, while imports in this sector, including interest payments on foreign loans, amounted to US$509.6 million.

Foreign Exchange System

In 1948 Sri Lanka had an essentially open-door policy on imports and an optimistic outlook for its foreign trade relations, but deterioration in the value of the country's export earnings led in 1953 to the Exchange Control Act, which placed some restrictions on the movement of foreign currency. In 1961, in response to balance of payments problems, a rigorous system of exchange controls was introduced. Licenses that acted as exchange permits were issued by the controller of imports and exports. All imports and exports were subject to these regulations, and foreign exchange entering the country, whether by way of exports, invisibles, or the movements of capital, had to be surrendered to the exchange control authorities. Only imports of goods classified as essential were permitted. The list of such items became smaller during the 1960s because of the increasing scarcity of foreign exchange and the availability of new items through local production. In the early 1970s, only imports of the barest minimum of foodstuffs, drugs, textiles, raw materials, and capital goods were allowed.

From 1970 to 1977, Sri Lanka had a dual exchange rate system in addition to exchange and import controls. Under the system, imports of indispensable items—such as food and drugs—were allowed at the official rate, while all other imports were subject to a higher rate. Foreign exchange earned from tea, rubber, and coconut was converted into rupees at the official exchange rate, while earnings from all other exports were given the benefit of the higher rate.

In November 1977, the exchange rate system was liberalized as part of the new government's economic reforms. The dual rate system was abolished, and the rupee was set free to float in response to international developments and the balance of payments position. The immediate effect of this measure was a devaluation of around 50 percent; after this time, the rupee continued to fall gradually against the major international currencies. In December 1987, US$1 equalled Rs32.32 compared with Rs19.3 six years earlier.

External Debt

The balance of payments deficits after the late 1950s led to a large foreign debt, most of which was accumulated after 1978. Rapid increases in the external debt, by comparison with the domestic debt, presented a double burden. Additions to the domestic debt involved only the problem of finding, through taxation, savings, or other means, the necessary additional local currency to meet the additional charges on the interest and amortization payments on the new debt. Increases in the foreign debt, however, required not only the same local currency to meet the enlarged budget item but also additional foreign currencies with which to transfer abroad the increased interest and amortization payments. This situation forced either a reduction in imports or still further borrowing abroad.

Governments addressed the balance of payments deficits in the 1960s by imposing direct controls that restricted imports. Even so they were unable to avoid increases in the foreign debt, which rose from around US$62 million in 1960 to US$231 million in 1969 and US$380 million in 1974. After the 1977 liberalization of the economy, import restrictions were loosened and foreign credit became much more readily available. The total external debt, including short-term loans and trade credits, was estimated to be just under US$4 billion at the end of 1986. Medium-and long-term debt of the government represented about 75 percent of this amount.

Another 7 percent was owed by government corporations. Debt service payments on all foreign loans were US$410 million in 1986, up from US$342 million in 1985. Total debt service payments as a ratio of export earnings from goods and services increased from 21 percent in 1985 to 26.7 percent in 1986.

Finance

After the early years of independence, the government consistently ran a budgetary deficit, which in the 1980s amounted to 15 percent of GDP. Foreign aid, which increased substantially after 1977, financed over 50 percent of the deficit in the 1980s and was essential for the health of the economy. Historically, a relatively high proportion of government expenditure was on social welfare programs, including health, education, and subsidized food, but after 1977 the importance of these programs, although still substantial by regional standards, declined. Banking and credit were dominated by government-controlled institutions, but the importance of the private sector in financial services was increasing.

Budgetary Process, Revenues, and Expenditures

The budget is announced annually in the budgetary speech of the finance minister, which is normally made in November. This speech reviews the economic situation of the current fiscal year, which corresponds to the calendar year, previews the government's expenditure program for the next year, and sets forth any proposed changes in taxation. Sometimes adverse public reaction, or pressure from members of parliament within the ruling party, forces changes in the measures announced in the finance minister's speech, but once formally introduced in parliament, the budget proposals are normally passed intact. All money bills must be introduced by a minister acting on behalf of the government. Opposition members may propose amendments to reduce expenditure under a specific head, but the success of such a motion would be a major defeat for the government and would probably cause its resignation. No amendments concerning taxes or to increase expenditure are allowed. Supplementary provisions are often presented by the government during the year. The government's finances are monitored by an auditor-general appointed by the president.

The colonial administration was heavily dependent on indirect taxes, especially import and export duties. Some changes in the structure of the revenue system were set in motion by the report of the Taxation Inquiry Commission, which was published in 1968. At that time, the tax system proper (exclusive of such items as fees, charges, and sales) of the central government consisted of various separate revenue sources: personal income taxes, corporate income taxes, wealth (luxury) tax, business turnover tax, import and export duties, resale of automobiles tax, and the levy on the transfer of property to nonnationals. The system was characterized by high taxes on major exports, by a miscellaneous collection of import taxes, and by high rates of income taxation. The income tax on corporations was 50 percent, and the top marginal rate on individuals was 80 percent, with rapid rates of progression. The wealth tax on individuals was also high.

The Taxation Inquiry Commission concluded that, for steady revenue flow, dependence should be placed on a broad-based set of consumption taxes, with differential rates to minimize the regressive tendency inherent in the consumption tax. This was recommended on a strictly pragmatic basis because both incomes and exports were already being taxed almost to their limit. There was thus no alternative to more and higher import duties and excises to secure the necessary additional revenue. Because the commission believed that taxable imports would in the future be replaced by domestically produced substitutes, it argued that consumption taxes would increasingly have to bear the brunt of the search for new revenue. The commission also advised the government to raise the exemptions, lower the top rates, and ease the progression rate on income, wealth, and gift taxes; to raise the excise taxes on tobacco, arrack, beer, and domestically consumed tea; and to increase the coverage and reduce the exemptions of the turnover tax. Most of these recommendations were implemented soon after the publication of this report.

In 1975 sales and turnover taxes raised almost 30 percent of the government's revenue, and income taxes and tariffs each raised about 15 percent. A little over a decade later, in 1986, the importance of the sales taxes and tariffs had increased, but income taxes raised a smaller proportion of the revenue than earlier (see table 11, Appendix A). In 1986 the general sales and turnover tax raised 15.4 percent of revenue, and selective sales taxes, which were primarily imposed on tobacco and liquor, raised 10.7 percent. Import duties accounted for 24.1 percent and export duties for only 3.8 percent. Income taxes raised 11.5 percent of state funds in 1986, over two-thirds of which came from corporate sources. Studies carried out in the 1970s, both before and after the liberalization of the economy, indicated that the tax system as a whole operated in a progressive manner. Almost 25 percent of the government's revenue in 1986 came from nontax sources, mainly interest, profits, dividends, and other receipts from government-owned enterprises.

In 1988 the maximum rate of personal income tax was 40 percent and the ceiling on both income and wealth tax was 50 percent of a person's income. The 1988 budget reflected a cut in the highest level of import duty from 100 to 60 percent. A large proportion of revenue from business came from the established forms of economic activity because new industries, such as tourism and the free trade zone factories, had preferential tax treatment.

No postindependence government has attempted to change, as a matter of policy, the proportion of the nation's GDP that it takes in revenue. This proportion generally hovered at just over 20 percent between 1950 and 1983. Annual variations derived more from external factors than from changes in government policy. Revenue from export duties on tea, rubber, and coconut, for instance, varies according to the price of these commodities on the international market. In 1984 when the price of tea rose temporarily, the government increased the export duty in order to gain a share of the windfall profits, and total revenue rose to 24.5 percent of GDP. In 1987 government revenue was only slightly below this level because of tax increases brought about by increased fiscal pressures, largely the product of higher defense allocations and the heavy foreign debt.

Government expenditure has consistently exceeded revenue, often by a considerable margin. From 1960 to 1977, expenditure was about 28 percent of GDP. After 1977 it increased, mainly as a result of investment in infrastructure. Between 1978 and 1987, the government spent around 38 percent of GDP. Of the nearly Rs70 billion spent in 1986, about half was classified as recurrent expenditure, and half as capital expenditure.

Governments have used expenditure as a tool of social policy. In comparison with other Third World countries, Sri Lanka has a long tradition of public spending on health, education, and other social services. These programs have contributed at least in part to the nation's very high levels of literacy and life expectancy relative to its per capita income (see Social Services, ch. 2). In the period between 1960 and 1977, about 9.5 percent of GDP, or one-third of the government's budget, was devoted to such programs.

After the liberalization of the economy in 1977, there were reductions in some social programs. In June 1978 the long-established system of rice rationing, which provided free and subsidized rice to nearly the entire population, was replaced by a food stamp program that covered only about 50 percent of the population. The value of the stamps was not indexed in order to keep place with inflation, and as a result the program's cost fell from 14 percent of government expenditure in 1979 to 7 percent in 1981 and 2.6

Offshore fishermen on their perches near Galle
Courtesy Embassy of Sri Lanka, Washington

percent in 1986. Although there was a drop in the standard of living for the very poor, in early 1988 the food stamp program continued to provide a safety net more effective than programs existing in other parts of South Asia. Overall, social services, education, and welfare accounted for just under 15 percent of government spending in 1986.

Foreign Aid

Foreign aid was essential in preventing acute foreign exchange shortages after 1977. It accounted for around 9 percent of GDP from 1978 to 1986. Aid has been of two types: outright grants and loans on concessionary terms. The annual level of grants grew from US$21.9 million in 1978 to US$178 million in 1986. Most of this money was tied to specific projects, such as the Accelerated Mahaweli Program. Both grant aid and concessionary loans come from Western Europe, the United States, Japan, and international organizations. Project loans amounted to US$351.2 million in 1986, and nonproject loans were US$77.1 million.

Most foreign aid to Sri Lanka was pledged at the meetings of the Aid Sri Lanka Consortium, which was organized by the World Bank on behalf of the major donor countries. The Sri Lankan government sent the World Bank an annual request outlining its needs. The member donors then met to consider these requests and coordinate their aid policies. The World Bank and most aid donors strongly supported the liberalization of the economy during the decade after 1977; indeed, at times they have urged the government to carry its free market policies further.

A special meeting of the consortium in December 1987 pledged US$493 million above its normal aid commitments toward a three-year reconstruction program. Much of this money was targeted for specific projects in Northern and Eastern provinces. Observers believed that if there were a peaceful solution to the nation's political problems, total foreign aid would reach US$2.7 billion in the years 1988 to 1990.

Fiscal Administration

In the 1960–77 period, budget deficits averaged about 8 percent of GDP. After 1977 increases in expenditures were not matched by corresponding increases in revenues, and the result was a rapid increase in the public debt. The budget deficit averaged 15 percent of GDP from 1978 to 1986. It temporarily dropped to 10.3 percent of GDP in 1984 when high tea prices caused increased revenue, but in both 1985 and 1986 it was close to 16 percent. The 1986 deficit of Rs28.1 billion was financed by Rs3.8 billion in foreign grants, Rs12.1 billion in foreign loans, and Rs11.5 billion domestic borrowing from banking and other sources. Foreign loans and grants financed about 50 percent of the budget deficits in the 1980s.

The public debt was about Rs150 billion at the end of 1986, and the total interest payments by the government in 1986 were Rs9.3

billion, or 5.2 percent of GDP. About 45 percent of the public debt was owed to domestic sources. Medium- and long-term debts accounted for 56 percent of the domestic debt, and short-term loans made up the balance. In 1986 rupee securities sold to the pension funds and the National Savings Bank accounts were the principal instrument of the domestic medium- and long-term debt. Domestic short-term financing was raised primarily through treasury bills. The majority of the foreign debt was negotiated at concessional terms (see External Debt, this ch.). In 1986 a total of Rs12 billion in new foreign loans was contracted, of which Rs9.9 billion were for specific projects. Repayments of earlier loans amounted to just over Rs3 billion. The accumulated foreign debt tended to increase annually in rupee terms in the 1980s because of the steady depreciation of the rupee in relation to the currencies of the lending nations.

Monetary Process

The Central Bank of Sri Lanka, which started operations in 1950, stood at the apex of the country's financial framework in 1988. The bank administered the exchange control system, implemented monetary policy, and regulated the money supply through such means as open market transactions, interest rate changes, and changes in the minimum reserve requirements of the commercial banks.

The private sector relied almost entirely on the banks for credit. In early 1988, the commercial banking system consisted of twenty-six banks: six Sri Lankan banks and twenty-two foreign banks. Two of the Sri Lankan banks—the Bank of Ceylon and the People's Bank—were state banks. These institutions dominated commercial banking, holding nearly 80 percent of total deposits. The profitability of these banks, like that of many other state enterprises, had been hindered by politicians using them to secure employment for their supporters. Recovering loans due from public corporations has also been a problem for these banks.

The four private Sri Lankan banks in 1988 were the Hatton National Bank, the Commercial Bank of Ceylon, the Investment and Credit Bank, and the Agro-Commercial Bank. The last two of these banks began operations in 1987, the first local banks founded after the liberalization of the economy in 1977.

Until 1979 the presence of foreign banks consisted of three British banks (Grindlays Bank, Chartered Bank, and the Bank of Hong Kong and Shanghai), three Indian banks (State Bank of India, Indian Bank, and Indian Overseas Bank), and one Pakistani bank (Habib Bank). In 1979, for the first time in many years, foreign banks were allowed to open branches, and many American and

European institutions took advantage of this policy. Newcomers included the Bank of Credit and Commerce International, Banque Indosuez, Citibank, American Express, Overseas Trust Bank, Bank of Oman, Bank of America, European Asian Bank, Algemene Bank Nederland, Chase Manhattan, Amsterdam Rotterdam Bank, Bank of the Middle East, and Bankers' Trust Company. The initial capital requirement, which had been set at Rs10 million in 1979, was increased in 1982 to Rs50 million. The Bank of America ended its activities in Sri Lanka at the end of 1986.

Although the arrival of foreign banks increased the level of competition and led to new facilities, the overall impact on the credit supply remained marginal in early 1988. Credit to the rural sector and small firms was still tight and was channeled mainly by the two state banks.

Interest rate policy in the 1980s encouraged high rates in order to combat inflation and encourage a higher flow of savings to bridge the gap between new investment and total domestic savings. At the end of 1986, treasury bills paid 11 percent and interbank loans cost between 12 percent and 12.75 percent. Loans and bank overdrafts were charged between 12 and 30 percent.

The Central Bank announced a deposit insurance program for small depositors in June 1987, but none of the commercial banks had joined at the end of the year. Only deposits of private individuals up to a value of Rs100,000 could be insured. Government, interbank, and local government deposits were not eligible. Banks that joined would pay four Sri Lankan cents for every Rs100 to the Central Bank. The Central Bank hopes that the confidence created by the program will offset the extra costs to the banks.

In late 1987, the Central Bank offered the commercial banks a number of incentives to join the insurance scheme, including lowering their reserve requirement to a flat rate of 10 percent. In 1987 the ratio was 18 percent on checking account deposits, 14 percent on fixed-term deposits, and 10 percent on other deposits.

The stock market, which was established in December 1985, was a minor source of capital. At the end of 1986, it quoted 173 companies having a total market capitalization of around Rs14 billion. Share transactions averaged Rs2.5 million a week. In 1987 legislation established a securities council to regulate the stock exchange. The proposed council was to be empowered to grant licenses to stockbrokers, set up a fund to compensate investors who suffered losses resulting from the failure of a licensed dealer to meet contractual obligations, and suspend or cancel the trading of securities for the protection of investors. The intent of this legislation was

Coastal fishing fleet north of Colombo
Courtesy Embassy of Sri Lanka, Washington

to create confidence in the stock market in the hope that it would attract more investors.

Tourism

In 1966 the government established the Ceylon Tourist Board, vesting in it the responsibility for invigorating the tourist industry. The board, operating as an autonomous corporation, was charged with promotional as well as organizational responsibilities. Most provisions for tourists were in the private sector, but the board had facilities in areas where private ones were considered inadequate.

Tourism expanded rapidly after 1966. The main attractions are the beach resorts of the southwestern coastal region, but many tourists also visit the ancient cities of the dry zone, the historic city of Kandy, and the mountainous region dominated by tea plantations. Between 1976 and 1982, the number of tourist arrivals increased at an annual rate of almost 24 percent, reaching a peak of 407,230 before declining to 337,342 arrivals in 1983 as a result of the Tamil insurgency. More than half the arrivals were from Western Europe.

Serious civil disturbances starting in July 1983 and the subsequent violence badly affected tourism. Total arrivals were 230,106 in 1986, down 43 percent from 1982. To ease the plight of the

169

industry, the government provided various concessions to hotels, such as the rescheduling of loans and the reduction of the turnover tax from 10 percent to 5 percent. The Ceylon Tourist Board also undertook a crash promotion program in an attempt to restore the island's image in world tourist markets. Tourist arrivals in the first six months of 1987, however, showed a decline of 23 percent compared with the same period the previous year. In early 1988, the outlook was for further contraction.

In 1988 it remained unclear whether the policies of economic liberalization Sri Lanka has pursued since 1977 would succeed in their principal goals of employment, wealth creation, and economic diversification. Although increased rice production, the growth of textile manufacturing, and an improved infrastructure were successes that could be attributed to the post-1977 policies, these gains came at the cost of a mounting foreign and domestic debt and declining living standards for the poor. In the mid-1980s, the declining security situation began to have an increasingly negative impact on the economy, and in early 1988 economic prospects for the 1990s appeared to be linked at least in part to a resolution of the ethnic conflict.

* * *

The most current and easily accessible sources on the Sri Lankan economy are two publications of the Economist Intelligence Unit in London: *Country Profile: Sri Lanka,* an annual survey of the economy; and *Country Report: Sri Lanka,* a quarterly publication that includes the latest economic information. For agriculture, the annual *South Asia: Situation and Outlook Report,* published by the Economic Research Service of the U. S. Department of Agriculture, is also useful and makes use of detailed information found in two annual publications of the Central Bank of Sri Lanka, the *Annual Report of the Central Bank of Sri Lanka* and the *Review of the Economy.*

No book-length general survey of the Sri Lankan economy appeared in the decade after the change of economic direction in 1977, and the earlier works, although valuable for historical background, are out of date. The various essays in *Sri Lanka: A Survey* edited by K. M. de Silva portray the course of the economy from independence to the mid-1970s. A critical analysis of the post-1977 economic policies is Ronald Herring's "Economic Liberalization Policies in Sri Lanka: International Pressures, Constraints and Supports." A more favorable evaluation of these policies is by Surjit S. Bhalla and Paul Glewwe, "Growth and Equity in Developing Countries: A Reinterpretation of the Sri Lankan Experience."

This reference should be read in conjunction with the rebuttals by Paul Isenman and Graham Pyatt in *World Bank Economic Review*. (For further information and complete citations, see Bibliography).

Chapter 4. Government and Politics

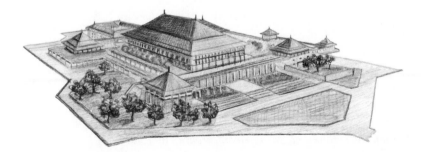

Parliament building at Sri Jayewardenepura, in Kotte

IN THE YEARS following Sri Lanka's attainment of independence on February 4, 1948, the country's political system appeared to be the very model of a parliamentary democracy. The country stood virtually alone among its South and Southeast Asian neighbors in possessing a viable two-party system in which the conservative United National Party (UNP) and the left-of-center Sri Lanka Freedom Party (SLFP) alternated with each other in power after fairly contested elections. Respect for legal institutions and the independence of the judiciary were well established. Sri Lanka's military, never sizable, refrained from intervening in politics, and the country's leadership pursued generally moderate policies in its relations with other states. Although per capita income was low compared to that of India and other South Asian countries, over the decades successive governments invested heavily in health, educational, and other social service facilities. As a result, standards of health and literacy were high and seemed to provide a firm foundation for democracy and political stability.

Sri Lanka was, however, heir to cultural and historical traditions at variance with its constitutionally defined parliamentary political institutions. Family and caste played major roles in determining the leadership of the major parties and the ebb and flow of political patronage. But ethnicity and religion were the most important and politically relevant determinants in this traditionally diverse society. After 1948 and especially after passage of the Official Language Act, popularly known as the "Sinhala Only" bill, in 1956, the Sri Lankan Tamil community, which was largely Hindu, came to feel that its political interests were being ignored and belittled by the mainstream political parties led by Buddhist Sinhalese. The feeling of grievance festered during the 1970s in the wave of preferential policies that favored Sinhalese applicants for university positions and government jobs. Abandonment of the idea of a secular state—the 1972 constitution guaranteed "the foremost place" for the Buddhist religion of the Sinhalese—further aroused Tamil alienation. Conversely, the Sinhalese, who regarded the Tamils as an economically and educationally privileged group, were determined to secure what they considered "majority rights," including freedom from alleged economic exploitation by Tamils. They also feared that the Sri Lankan Tamils could be a "fifth column" for the much larger Tamil population in neighboring India. From the Buddhist Sinhalese perspective, it was they, living in a "sea" of Hindu Tamils, who were the true minority, not the Sri Lankan Tamils.

In a sense, the effectiveness of democratic institutions in conveying the viewpoints of middle class and working-class Sinhalese, electorally a majority of voters, promoted ethnic polarization. Politicians such as S.W.R.D. and Sirimavo Bandaranaike effectively used appeals to Sinhalese chauvinism to unseat their UNP opponents. Neither the UNP nor the SLFP parties dared make concessions to the Tamils for fear of alienating the majority Sinhalese. Thus the UNP government of Junius Richard (J.R.) Jayewardene, which came to power in July 1977, was as determined as the earlier SLFP governments not to yield to Tamil demands for language parity and regional autonomy. By the early 1980s, armed groups of young Tamil extremists, committed to establishing an independent Tamil Eelam, or state, were well established in Tamil-majority areas in the northern and eastern parts of the country or operating out of bases in India's Tamil Nadu State.

In July 1977, Jayewardene won an unprecedented majority in the national legislature, gaining 140 out of 168 seats. In 1978 a new Constitution, the third in Sri Lanka's postindependence history, was promulgated providing for a strong presidency. Jayewardene became the first chief executive under the new system. Some observers interpreted controversial amendments to the Constitution, such as the extension of the life of Parliament for another six years, passed in December 1982, as an illegitimate manipulation of the legal political process designed to give the UNP a virtually uncontested monopoly of political power. In terms of the ethnic crisis, an August 1983 amendment outlawing the advocacy of separatism, which resulted in the expulsion of members of the Tamil United Liberation Front (TULF) from Parliament, was most fateful. Against a background of escalating communal violence, it deprived Sri Lankan Tamils of political representation.

July 1983 was a turning point in the worsening ethnic crisis. Anti-Tamil riots in Colombo and other cities, prompted by the killing of thirteen Sinhalese soldiers by Tamil Tiger guerrillas in the north, resulted in hundreds and perhaps as many as 2,000 deaths. The government was unprepared for the scale of violence and faced accusations of sublime unconcern for the Tamils' welfare, while foreign observers told of the active connivance of government figures in mob violence. The inability or unwillingness of President Jayewardene and the UNP to forge a workable settlement of ethnic issues brought India, which had immense interests of its own in the matter, directly into the crisis. According to the Indian press, under the government of Prime Minister Indira Gandhi India unofficially

permitted the establishment of training camps for the Sri Lankan
Tamil insurgents in the state of Tamil Nadu. With the assumption of power by Gandhi's son and successor, Rajiv Gandhi, New
Delhi adopted a more even-handed approach and sought to mediate the escalating crisis in Sri Lanka by bringing government and
Tamil insurgent negotiators together for talks. Eventually, the New
Delhi government went further and came down squarely on the
side of Colombo with the signing of the Indo-Sri Lankan Accord
of July 29, 1987. The pact committed New Delhi to the deployment of a peacekeeping force on the island, as asked by the Sri
Lankan government, and made the Indian government the principal guarantor of a solution to the ethnic crisis.

The accord was designed to meet Sri Lankan Tamil demands
for self-determination through the merging of the Northern and
Eastern provinces and the devolution of substantial executive, legislative, and judicial powers. Tamil was made an official language,
on a par with Sinhala. A cease-fire was arranged, and the Liberation Tigers of Tamil Eelam (LTTE) and other guerrilla groups
surrendered some but not all of their arms. Many doubted that
the accord, which the guerrillas had not played a role in formulat-
ing and the LTTE opposed, would bring lasting peace. By
mid-1988, the Indian Army, in a series of hard-fought engagements
that had caused it several hundred casualties, generally cleared the
Jaffna Peninsula in Northern Province of Tamil guerrillas. The
Indian Peacekeeping Force established a semipermanent garrison,
and a measure of tranquility returned to the area. In Eastern
Province, the Indian Peacekeeping Force had less success in sup-
pressing the insurgents and the situation remained precarious.
Bands of Tamil guerrillas remained at large, surfacing apparently
at will to initiate violent incidents that led to an unremitting loss
of life among innocent civilians, Sinhalese and Tamil, as well as
among military personnel of both the Sri Lankan and Indian armed
forces. In the predominantly Sinhalese, southern fringe of the island, the Jayewardene government faced escalating violence at the
hands of Sinhalese militants who opposed the Indo-Sri Lankan Accord as a sellout to the Tamil extremists.

Politics and Society
Race, Religion, and Politics

Like other nations in the South Asia region, Sri Lanka has a
diverse population. Various communities profess four of the world's
major religions: Buddhism, Hinduism, Islam, and Christianity.
The major ethnic groups include not only the Sinhalese and the

Sri Lanka: A Country Study

Sri Lankan Tamils, who compose 74 and 12.6 percent of the population, respectively, but also Indian Tamils (5.5 percent of the population) who view themselves as separate from the Sri Lankan Tamils, as well as "Moors" or Muslims (7.1 percent), "Burghers" and other people of mixed European and Sri Lankan descent (0.4 percent), Malays (0.4 percent), and tiny percentages of others including the aboriginal Veddahs, who are considered to be the island's original inhabitants (see People, ch. 2).

The society also possesses a caste system similar to that of India's. Caste in Sri Lanka is politically important for two reasons. First, members of the national political elite tend to be members of the higher status castes. Since independence the overwhelming majority of the prime ministers and the one president have been members of the Sinhalese Goyigama (cultivator) caste. Also, voters tend to support people of their own caste, though caste identification rarely becomes a campaign issue because electoral districts tend to be homogeneous in terms of caste and the major parties generally put up candidates of that caste.

Among Sinhalese, there is also a historically significant distinction between people who live in the coastal and lowland areas and those who live in the mountainous central part of the island, the area that constituted the Kingdom of Kandy before its conquest by the British in the early nineteenth century. During the British colonial period and to a lesser extent in independent Sri Lanka, the two groups, which possess somewhat different cultures and ways of life, frequently perceived their interests to be divergent. During the 1920s, for example, the Kandyan National Assembly advocated a federal state in which the Kandyan community would be guaranteed regional autonomy (see European Encroachment and Dominance, 1500–1948, ch. 1).

Apart from religion, ethnicity, and caste, there are social differences that emerged as a result of British colonialism. Despite a history of popular support for Marxist parties, especially the Trotskyite Ceylon Equal Society Party (Lanka Sama Samaja Party—LSSP), economically based classes in the European sense are poorly developed in Sri Lanka. Nevertheless, well-defined elite groups, including families with planter, merchant, and professional backgrounds, continued to be important in the late 1980s despite the redistributive policies of recent governments. Marks of their special status included not only wealth but education in the island's most prestigious schools or overseas, fluency in English, and a higher degree of Westernization than among other Sri Lankans. In a 1985 survey of government party parliamentarians since 1970, political scientist Robert Oberst discovered not only that there was a disproportionate number of graduates of a handful of elite schools among UNP and SLFP legislators, but also that elite secondary school graduates were more likely to assume ministerial posts and play a central role in the passage of bills than nonelite school graduates. Nonelite graduates tended to be backbenchers with limited influence.

In a society as diverse as Sri Lanka's, social divisions have had a direct and weighty impact on politics. In the late 1980s, the ethnically, linguistically, and religiously based antagonism of the Sinhalese and Sri Lankan Tamils overshadowed all other social divisions: the civil war that resulted, especially since mid-1983, seemed to bode a permanent division of the country. Yet in the routine operation of day-to-day politics, allegiances based on family, caste, or region also continued to be of major importance.

As in India, matters of religion, ethnicity, region, and language have become public rather than private issues. Persons have typically viewed personal advancement not only in terms of individual initiative but also in terms of the fortunes of their ethnic, caste, or religious community. In India, however, there are so many different groups, spread out over the country like a vast mosaic, that no single group has been strong enough to seriously destabilize the national-level political system. Dissident movements, such as the Sikh militants in the northwestern Indian state of Punjab have tended to be limited to a single region. India's ruling party, Congress (I), preserved national unity by forming electoral coalitions with disparate groups such as high-caste Hindus, Muslims, and untouchables and balancing them off against other groups loyal to opposition parties.

In Sri Lanka, however, both the nature of diversity and the attitude of the government have been different. Within the island's much smaller geographical area, politics have become polarized because the politically prominent groups are few in number and clearly defined in terms of language, custom, religion, and geographical region. Successive governments moreover, have never attempted to adopt an impartial role in relation to ethnic rivalries.

Concrete economic and social equity·issues have played a major role in the ethnic antagonisms of Sinhalese and the Sri Lankan Tamils since independence. Ethnic rivalry, however, draws upon older and deeper roots. Each community views itself as possessing a unique and superior culture, based on religion, language, and race. The integrity of this culture is perceived to be threatened by the encroachments of the other group. Both Sinhalese and Tamils, occupying relatively well-defined geographical areas (the Sri Lankan Tamils in the Northern Province and parts of the Eastern Province, but with vulnerable enclaves in large cities; and the Sinhalese in the central and southern parts of the island), regard themselves as besieged minorities. The Sinhalese perceive themselves as the only group of "Aryans" and Buddhists in an overwhelmingly Dravidian and Hindu region (including the populous state of Tamil Nadu and other parts of southern India), while the Tamils see themselves as an endangered minority on the island itself. During the 1980s, this state of mutual paranoia, sharpened the ethnic boundaries of both groups and intensified economic and social conflicts.

The Sinhalese: Racial Uniqueness and Politicized Buddhism

Many Sinhalese view themselves as a "chosen people." The *Mahavamsa,* an epic piece of "mythohistory" composed by Buddhist monks around the fifth century A.D., traces the origins of the Sinhalese to the regions of northern and eastern India inhabited in ancient times by Aryan peoples. Evidence to back this claim includes not only their language, which is related to the languages of northern India including Sanskrit, but the supposedly "fairer" complexions of the Sinhalese compared to their Dravidian neighbors. The *Mahavamsa* depicts the history of Sri Lanka as a bitter struggle between the Sinhalese and darker-skinned Dravidian intruders from the mainland (see Origins, ch. 1). In the eyes of Sinhalese chauvinists, this struggle for survival continues to the present day.

Religion has defined Sinhalese identity over the centuries far more than race. Buddhism was brought to Sri Lanka around the third century B.C. by missionaries sent by Indian emperor Asoka and was fervently adopted by the Sinhalese king, Devanampiya Tissa (250-c.210 B.C.). The Theravada school of Buddhism was established after a great council of monks and scholars was held on Sri Lanka in 88–77 B.C. to codify the Pali scriptures. The faith was later transmitted by Sri Lankan monks to Southeast Asian countries such as Burma, Thailand, and Cambodia. Sinhalese Buddhists regard Theravada (or Hinayana) Buddhism as the purest form of their religion, unencumbered by the superstitions and false beliefs that allegedly contaminate the Mahayana sects of Buddhism found in East Asia (see Religion, ch. 2).

Anthropologist S. J. Tambiah, himself a Sri Lankan Tamil whose family includes both Hindus and converts to Christianity, argues that in both traditional and contemporary Sinhalese Buddhism the religion's original message of universalism, compassion, and non-violence was eclipsed by a narrower appeal to nationalism and race: "the Sinhalese chronicles. . . in postulating the unity of nation and religion constitute a profound transformation of the Asokan message of dharma (rule by righteousness and nonviolence) in a multireligious society of Buddhists, Jains, adherents of Brahmanical values, and others.'' This was clearly evident, he argues, in the *Mahavamsa*, which describes King Dutthagamani's heroic defense of Buddhism against invaders from southern India in the second century B.C. as a holy war. Tambiah, a specialist in Southeast Asian Buddhism, asserts that Buddhism in contemporary Sri Lanka has lost its ethical and philosophical bearings (''the substantive contents which make Buddhism a great religion and a source of a rich civilization'') and has become either a set of ritualized devotions, undertaken by believers to obtain worldly good fortune, or an aggressive political movement that attracts the poorest classes of Sinhalese.

Politicized Buddhism in its modern form emerged in the opening years of the twentieth century when adherents of the religion, deploring the social evils of alcoholism, organized a temperance movement and criticized the colonial government for keeping taverns open as a source of tax revenue. The campaign was, implicitly, anti-Western and anti-Christian. With the passing of the colonial order, Buddhist activism was increasingly preoccupied with Sinhalese ''majority rights,'' including the ''Sinhala Only'' language policy backed by SLFP leader S.W.R.D. Bandaranaike (who was assassinated by a Buddhist monk on September 26, 1959), and the agitation to give Buddhism special status in the 1972 constitution. But the equation of nation and religion also meant that any issue involving the welfare of the Sinhalese community, including issues of social equity, were fair game for activist monks and their supporters.

Thus, in 1986 leaders of the *sangha* (the community of Buddhist monks) joined with former Prime Minister Sirimavo Bandaranaike to establish the Movement for Defense of the Nation to deter President J.R. Jayewardene from making significant concessions to the Tamils. One Buddhist leader, the Venerable Palipane Chandananda, head of one of the major orders of monks, was labelled ''Sri Lanka's Khomeini'' both for his extremism and his predilection for getting involved in political issues. Lower-ranking monks also were frequent hardliners on the ethnic issue. A survey of monks taken during 1983 and 1984 by Nathan Katz, a Western student of Buddhism, revealed that 75 percent of his respondents refused to acknowledge that any Tamil grievances were legitimate. Many commented that the Tamils were an unjustly privileged minority and ''it is the Sinhalese who have the grievances.'' Because of the tremendous prestige and influence of Buddhist monks among Sinhalese villagers and the poorest, least Westernized urban classes, the government in the late 1980s could not ignore the monks' point of view, which could be summarized in a 1985 comment by Chandananda to the *Far Eastern Economic Review:* ''They [the Tamils] are saying that they have lived here for 1,000 years. But they are complete outsiders from India who have been living here temporarily.''

Tamil Exclusivism

The Sri Lankan Tamil community itself boasts an impressive mythology of cultural and religious uniqueness and superiority. This is particularly true of dominant-caste Vellala Tamils living in the Jaffna Peninsula, who regard their Tamil cousins living in India and the Indian Tamil residents of Sri Lanka, as well as the Sinhalese, as their less civilized inferiors (thus undermining, to some extent, the rationale behind Sinhalese fears of engulfment by the two Tamil communities). According to anthropologist Bruce Pfaffenberger, the Vellala Tamils place great importance on the correct observation of Hindu rituals, the chastity of their women, and the need to maintain precisely the hierarchical distinctions of caste. Pfaffenberger notes that the Vellala regard the Jaffna Peninsula as their *natu,* or country, and that states ruled by their kings existed there from the thirteenth century until the sixteenth-century arrival of the Portuguese. Although not all Sri Lankan Tamils were members of the Vellala caste, its members dominated local commercial and educational elites, and its values had strong influence on Tamils of other castes.

The 1978 Constitution and Government Institutions

Sri Lanka has benefited from the traditions of the rule of law and constitutional government that emerged during 150 years of British colonial rule. At least until the early 1970s, these traditions fostered the development of a political system characterized by broad popular participation in the political process, generally strict observance of legal guarantees of human and civil rights, and an orderly succession of elected governments without the intervention, as has occurred in several neighboring states, of the military. By the early 1980s, however, many observers feared for the future of Sri Lanka's democratic institutions. Some observers contended that constitutional government, rather than curbing the arbitrary use of political power, seemed itself to be shaped by aggressively narrow sectarian interests whose manipulation of the constitutional amendment process excluded large numbers of persons from politics and contributed to ethnic polarization and violence.

Historical Perspective, 1802-1978

After the Dutch ceded the island's maritime provinces to the British in 1802, these areas became Britain's first crown colony. The conquest and subjugation of the inland Kingdom of Kandy in 1815-18 brought the entire island under British control. Crown colony status meant that the island's affairs were administered by the Colonial Office in London, rather than by the East India Company that governed India until 1857. Even after the Indian Empire—ruled by a viceroy appointed by the British monarch—was established following the Indian Mutiny of 1857, Ceylon (as Sri Lanka was then called) was not included within its authority. The principal features of government and administration during the first century of British rule were a strong executive—the colonial governor—and a council of official and unofficial members who first served in a solely advisory capacity but were gradually granted legislative powers. An institution of central importance was the Ceylon Civil Service. In the early years, it was staffed primarily by British and other European personnel but then, increasingly and almost exclusively, by Sri Lankans.

A major turning point in the island's political development was implementation in 1931 of comprehensive reforms recommended by a royal commission headed by the Earl of Donoughmore. The most salient feature of the so-called Donoughmore Constitution, which attempted to reconcile British colonial control of the executive with Sri Lankan aspirations for self-government, was adoption of universal adult suffrage. This was, at that time, a bold experiment in representative government. Before 1931, only 4 percent of the male population, defined by property and educational qualifications, could vote. When elections to the legislature were held in 1932, the colony became the first polity in Asia to recognize women's suffrage. (Japan had adult male suffrage in 1925, but universal adult suffrage came only after World War II. The Philippines, a United States colony, achieved it in 1938.)

Toward the close of World War II, a second royal commission, headed by Lord Soulbury, was sent to Sri Lanka in order to consult with local leaders on the drafting of a new constitution. In its general contours, the Soulbury Constitution, approved in 1946, became the basic document of Ceylon's government when the country achieved independence on February 4, 1948. It established a parliamentary system modelled on that of Britain and quite similar to the constitution adopted by India in 1949. Like Britain and unlike India with its federal arrangement of states, independent Ceylon was, and in the late 1980s remained, a unitary state. The constitution established a parliament headed by the British monarch (represented by the governor general) and two houses, the Senate and the House of Representatives. The latter, like the House of Commons in Britain, had the preponderant role in legislation. The majority party or party coalition in the popularly elected House of Representatives designated the prime minister. Executive power, formally vested in the monarch (in the person of his or her representative, the governor general), was in actuality exercised by the prime minister and his or her cabinet.

The second constitution, adopted in 1972, represented an attempt on the part of the SLFP-led United Front coalition, which had been elected in May 1970, to create new political institutions that allegedly reflected indigenous values more perfectly than the 1946 constitution. It abolished the Senate and established a unicameral National State Assembly. The assembly was defined as the embodiment of the power of the state, and provisions in the constitution denied the judiciary the authority to challenge its enactments. In addition, the constitution changed the formal name of the country from Dominion of Ceylon to Republic of Sri Lanka. In a controversial measure, the United Front-dominated assembly gave itself two additional years in power beyond its constitutionally defined five-year term (elections were originally scheduled for 1975). Judicial curbs on the executive were also greatly restricted. Through the exercise of a wide range of emergency and special powers, the government of Sirimavo Bandaranaike exercised strict control over the political system.

Aside from the issue of authoritarianism, two extremely controversial aspects of the 1972 constitution were the abandonment of the idea of a secular state, which had been incorporated into the 1946 constitution, and designation of Sinhala as the sole national language. Although the constitution did not make Sri Lanka a Buddhist state, it declared that "the Republic of Sri Lanka shall give to Buddhism the foremost place and accordingly it shall be the duty of the state to protect and foster Buddhism while assuring to all religions the rights secured by Section 18 (i)(d) [religious freedom]." Tamils, a predominately Hindu minority, resented the special status given to Buddhism and the nonrecognition of a role for their language in national life.

In the July 1977 general election, the UNP was swept into power. The new ruling party, led by Jayewardehe, won 140 out of 168 seats in the assembly and thus was in a position to initiate substantial revisions of the 1972 constitution. This process it proceeded to undertake by passing the Second Amendment, which established the office of executive president in October 1977. Jayewardene assumed the presidency on February 4, 1978. In November 1977, the UNP and the major opposition parties, with the conspicuous absence of the Tamil United Liberation Front (TULF), convened a select committee to draft further revisions. After conducting a survey on the opinions of various Sri Lankan citizens, it concluded that changes embodied in the Second Amendment were not sufficient to promote substantial reform and recommended that a new constitution be drafted. The new document was adopted by the National State Assembly in mid-August 1978, and went into effect on September 7, 1978. Under its provisions, the legislature chosen in the July 1977 general election was designated the country's new Parliament.

Government Institutions

The 1978 Constitution changed the country's formal name from the Republic of Sri Lanka to the Democratic Socialist Republic of Sri Lanka and established a presidential form of government similar to that operating in France under the Fifth Republic. The document contains 172 articles divided into 24 chapters. Like the 1972 constitution, it recognizes the special status of the Buddhist religion (assuring it, again, "foremost place" while guaranteeing the freedom of other religious communities). It differs from its predecessor, however, in granting "national" status to the Tamil as well as Sinhala language although only Sinhala is recognized as the "official" language. The language provisions permit the use of Tamil in administrative business in Northern and Eastern provinces and allow applicants for government employment to use either Tamil or Sinhala in the examination process (though knowledge of Sinhala might be required subsequent to induction into the civil service). In February 1983, Jayewardene announced that English would be recognized as a third national language.

The Constitution recognizes and guarantees a broad range of fundamental rights including: freedom of thought and conscience; religious freedom; freedom from discrimination on the basis of race, religion, sex, or caste; freedom of speech; basic legal protection including freedom from arbitrary arrest or detention; freedom to engage in any lawful occupation; and freedom of movement and travel. These rights are guaranteed to stateless persons resident in Sri Lanka for ten years following promulgation of the Constitution. Exercise of the fundamental rights, however, can be restricted in situations where national security is at risk or when the otherwise legal actions of persons (such as speech or publication) detract from racial or religious harmony or endanger "public health and morality."

185

The Constitution contains a section devoted to directive principles of state policy. These encompass a broad range of policy goals, including the establishment of a "democratic socialist society" and a just distribution of wealth; economic development; and the raising of cultural and educational standards. The directive principles also include a commitment to decentralizing the country's administration and promoting national unity by eliminating all forms of discrimination. The duties of citizens (including the fostering of national unity) are also enumerated.

Amendment of the Constitution requires the vote of two-thirds of Parliament. In addition, measures that affect "the independent, unitary, and democratic nature of the state," the Buddhist religion, fundamental rights, or the length of the term of office of president or Parliament must be approved by a popular referendum. Bills judged "inconsistent with the Constitution" cannot become law unless two-thirds of Parliament approve, but such bills can be repealed by a simple majority vote.

With its five-sixths majority in Parliament following the July 1977 general election, the UNP government of Jayewardene was able to pass a number of controversial constitutional amendments over the objections of the opposition. Some political commentators have suggested that such measures as the Fourth Amendment (December 1982), which extended the life of Parliament for six years, or the Sixth Amendment (August 1983), which obliged members of Parliament to renounce support for separatism, were designed not to strengthen democratic institutions but to prolong the UNP's monopoly of power.

Presidency and Parliament

The most important national office is that of the president, who is defined in the Constitution as head of state, chief executive, and commander in chief of the armed forces. Although governmental institutions are divided in the customary way between the executive, legislative, and judicial branches, the president's powers as chief executive are formidable compared to those of the legislature. Thus, it cannot be said that the Constitution provides the political system with the benefits of a genuine separation of powers.

With Parliament's approval, the president appoints the prime minister and in consultation with the prime minister chooses the members of the cabinet. It is the chief executive, rather than the prime minister, who presides over the cabinet's deliberations, and who may assume any ministerial portfolio. The president also has the authority to dissolve Parliament at any time and call for new elections. The president cannot exercise this power, however, if the legislature has been in power for less than a year and does not consent to the dissolution, or if it is considering a resolution to impeach the president.

A striking feature of the governmental system is the huge size of cabinets. The Constitution designates twenty-eight minister-level portfolios, including two (the ministries of defense and plan implementation) held by the president. Additional ministers, however, may be appointed to take responsibility for special areas, such as the prevention of terrorism. District ministers, who play a major role in local government, are also designated. Including deputy ministers, a cabinet at one time may have more than eighty members chosen from the parliamentary ranks of the ruling party. In the late 1980s, ministerial rank and the resources made available through access to budgetary funds were, for individual legislators, an invaluable source of patronage and local level influence.

The president can announce a national referendum to seek popular approval of proposals of pressing national importance, including bills that have been rejected by Parliament. Other presidential prerogatives include declarations of war and peace, the granting of pardons, and the exercise of broad emergency powers. In the event of a public emergency, the president can invoke the power to enact measures without the consent of Parliament. The legislature, however, must convene no more than ten days after the chief executive's proclamation of an emergency. If a majority of the legislature fails to approve the state of emergency after two weeks, it automatically lapses; it lapses after ninety days if a simple majority of the members of Parliament do not approve its continuation.

The president is popularly elected for a term of six years. He or she may serve no more than two consecutive six-year terms. The Constitution stipulates, however, that the term of a chief executive who assumes office other than through a normal presidential election will not be counted as one of the two. Whether this means that Jayewardene's first term from 1977 to 1982, which began with his election as prime minister in the 1977 general election, would be counted toward the two-term total was unclear. The Third Amendment to the Constitution, approved in 1982, allows the president to hold a presidential election at any time following his fourth year in office.

The Constitution states that the president is responsible to Parliament and can be impeached by the legislature if that body approves the measure by a two-thirds vote and the Supreme Court also calls for his or her removal from office. Grounds for impeachment include mental or physical incapacitation, moral offenses, abuses of power, bribery, treason, and blatant violations of the Constitution.

The prime minister assumes the responsibilities of the president if the incumbent is disabled or is overseas. Parliament chooses a new president if the incumbent dies or leaves office before the end of his or her term.

During the mid-1980s, the powers vested by the Constitution in the chief executive, the unprecedented majority that the UNP won in the July 1977 election, the 1982 postponement of a new general election until 1989, and a strong tradition of party discipline provided Jayewardene virtually unchallenged control over Parliament. The Constitution gives the legislature a term of six years. But in November 1982, Jayewardene, elected the previous month to a second six-year presidential term, announced his decision to hold a popular referendum on a constitutional amendment, the fourth, which would extend the life of Parliament from six to twelve years (a general election was due by August 1983). As justification for the amendment, he cited both his popular mandate (he won 52.9 percent of the votes cast in the October 1982 presidential election compared to 39.1 percent for his nearest opponent) and the threat posed by an ''anti-democratic, violent and Naxalite group'' associated with the opposition SLFP that allegedly planned to seize power and ''[tear] up all constitutional procedures.'' (The term ''Naxalite'' refers to a leftist, revolutionary and violent movement that emerged in India during the 1960s.) After approval by Parliament and the Supreme Court, the amendment was supported by a narrow 54.7 percent of the voters on December 22, 1982. The fact that the referendum took place during a state of emergency and that there were widespread reports of voter fraud and intimidation caused many to doubt the legitimacy of this procedural exercise. Observers noted, however, that members of the opposition were allowed to express their opinions freely prior to the December 22 vote and were given access to the media, including television. The Constitution stipulates that when the next general election is held, the number of members of Parliament shall be increased from 168 to 196.

Local Government

Because Sri Lanka is a unitary rather than a federal state, local government institutions have had a very limited role in the political process. The country traditionally has been divided into nine provinces, which had played an important administrative role during the British colonial era. The principal local government subdivisions since the early 1980s have been the twenty-four administrative districts (see fig. 1). Before 1981 each district contained administrative offices representing most national-level ministries and known collectively as *kachcheri* (government offices). Two officers of major significance at the district level were the government agent and the district minister. Government agents, appointed by the central government, traced their origins to the colonial era, but the office of district minister, which was filled by individuals concurrently serving as members of Parliament, was created after 1978. Because of the district ministers' access to central government funds for patronage purposes, they tended to diminish the power and influence of the government agents.

In 1981 the *kachcheri* system and the subdistrict system of elective village and town councils were replaced by district development councils and subdistrict-level units known as *pradeshiya mandalaya* (divisional council) and *gramodaya mandalaya* (village council) (see fig. 11). The councils were created largely to satisfy minority aspirations for local self-government and were designed to exercise a significant measure of autonomy, especially—as the name implies—in the area of economic planning and development. Although the district development councils served in the late 1980s as conduits for central government funds, they also had been granted the authority to collect taxes and manage their own budgets and were given responsibility for educational and cultural activities within their spheres of jurisdiction. Each district council consisted of some members appointed by the central government and others elected by local constituents for four-year terms on the basis of proportional representation. Their deliberations were presided over by the district ministers who were, as mentioned, members of Parliament (they did not in all cases represent in Parliament the district in which they exercised this function); government agents served as council secretaries.

The subdistrict-level *mandalaya,* or councils, were designed to promote village-level democracy and provide support for district development council programs. The changes implemented in 1981 affected the 75 percent of the population living in rural areas. Twelve municipal and thirty-eight urban councils continued to function in urban areas in the late 1980s.

Electoral System

In the late 1980s, popular elections were held, in principle at regular intervals, for the office of president, members of Parliament, and positions on local government bodies such as municipal and urban councils, district development councils, and the *mandalaya.* The Constitution grants the right to vote to all citizens aged eighteen years and over who are of sound mind and have not been convicted of major crimes. All qualified voters have the right to run for Parliament unless they are members of the armed forces,

189

Figure 11. The Structure of Government, 1987

police, or certain branches of the civil service, hold other positions that might result in a conflict of interest, or have been convicted of bribery while serving in a previous term in Parliament within the past seven years. The qualifications for running for president are similar, though there is a minimum age requirement of thirty.

The president is chosen by a simple majority vote. In the election of October 20, 1982, the country was divided into twenty-two election districts (the Constitution provides for a maximum of twenty-four electoral districts). Citizens could mark their ballots for a maximum of three presidential candidates in order of preference. Under this "single transferable vote system," if no candidate received more than half the votes, all but the two candidates with the largest percentages of the total votes cast would be eliminated. Persons who voted their top preference for a candidate who had been eliminated would have their second or third preferences counted if they had chosen one of the top two vote-getters. In the 1982 balloting, six candidates contested the presidency but it was reported that only a small number of voters indicated a second or third preference on their ballots.

The 1946 and 1972 constitutions provided for the election of members of Parliament (or, between 1972 and 1978, the National State Assembly) from single-member constituencies similar to those found in Britain. Consequently, relatively small changes in the percentage of voters supporting a given party caused large variations in the number of seats that party won in Parliament, and majority parties were over-represented in terms of their percentage of the popular vote. For example, in the 1965 general election, the UNP won 39.3 percent of the vote and secured 66 out of 151 seats in Parliament; its share of the vote in the 1970 election dropped 1.4 percent to 37.9 percent, but it won only 17 seats. The 1978 Constitution replaced the single-member constituencies with a system of proportional representation in which the number of candidates returned from a single electoral district is determined on the basis of population. Although this system creates a closer correspondence between vote percentages and parliamentary representation, the equitable nature of proportional representation is diluted by a constitutional provision that grants the party with the largest percentage of votes in each district a "bonus" seat in addition to those gained through proportional representation.

The Constitution stated that by-elections to fill vacancies in Parliament before a general election were not necessary because the political parties themselves could appoint successors. On February 20, 1983, however, Parliament passed a constitutional amendment, the fifth, which provides for by-elections if the incumbent party fails to nominate a successor within thirty days of the seat becoming vacant. On May 18, 1983, by-elections for eighteen seats were held.

Judiciary

Although Sri Lanka's colonial heritage fostered a tradition of judicial freedoms, this autonomy has been compromised since independence by constitutional changes designed to limit the courts' control over the president and by the chief executive's power to declare states of emergency. Also, Parliament's willingness to approve legislation, such as the 1979 Prevention of Terrorism Act, vested the government in the late 1980s with broad powers to deal with subversives, or those deemed subversive, in an essentially extralegal manner. Observers in the late 1980s reported that the act facilitated widespread abuses of power, including the systematic torture of detainees, because it recognized the admissibility as evidence of confessions to the police not made in the presence of a magistrate.

Under the Constitution, the highest court is the Supreme Court, headed by a chief justice and between six and ten associate justices. Supreme and High Court justices are appointed by the president. Superior Court justices can be removed on grounds of incompetence or misdemeanor by a majority of Parliament, whereas High Court justices can be removed only by a judicial service commission consisting of Supreme Court justices. The Supreme Court has the power of judicial review; it can determine whether an act of Parliament is consistent with the principles of the Constitution and whether a referendum must be taken on a proposal, such as the 1982 extension of Parliament's life by six years. It is also the final court of appeal for all criminal or civil cases.

Civil Service

The civil service in Sri Lanka was established during the colonial period and in the late 1980s continued to operate in accordance with well-established British precedents. It was hierarchical in structure. At the apex of the hierarchy was a well-defined elite, the Sri Lanka Administrative Service, which was composed of talented men and women chosen by competitive examination. They were well-educated generalists, expected to take a broad perspective in their work in contrast to specialist personnel operating on the lower ranks of the hierarchy. They enjoyed tremendous prestige. Because government employment on practically all levels offered economic security as well as status, competition for civil service and other government positions remained intense. One of the most important sources of Tamil disaffection from the Sinhalese-dominated political system has been their perception that government service opportunities for members of their community were decreasing. This view is borne out by statistics: in the administrative service, the number of Tamil officeholders declined from 11.1 percent of the total during the 1970–77 period to only 5.7 percent during the 1978–81 period. Spokesmen for the Sinhalese majority have asserted that the British traditionally favored the employment of Tamils over Sinhalese in the colonial bureaucracy and that the declining Tamil percentages reflected an equitable redressing of the balance. The percentage during 1978–81, however, was substantially lower than Sri Lankan Tamils' percentage of the total population (12.6 percent in 1985).

Especially since the early 1970s, the civil service has been subject to intense political pressures. Under the British-style 1946 constitution, the highest-ranking appointed officials in the government were the secretaries attached to each ministry. But after the adoption of the 1972 constitution, secretaries have been political appointees. This change and the dynamics of patron-client politics have compromised both the bureaucracy's claim of political neutrality and the quality of its staff. The power of patronage means that each member of Parliament has jobs, ranging from professional positions like school teachers or engineers, to clerkships and menial labor, which the members can distribute freely to followers. The eclipse of Tamil influence in Parliament has meant that such benefits were not generally available to the Tamil community.

In the late 1980s, about 25 percent of all employment in Sri Lanka was in the public sector. In addition to the civil service, this proportion included the police, the armed forces, and public corporations, which continued to dominate the economy despite Jayewardene's liberalization policies since 1977 (see Nature of the Economy, ch. 3).

The Political Party System

One of the most striking features of the political system in the more than four decades since independence has been the existence of viable and generally stable political parties. In the general elections held between 1952 and 1977, a two-party system emerged in which the UNP and the SLFP alternately secured majorities and formed governments. Observers noted, however, that one major failure of the two-party system was the unwillingness or inability of the UNP and the SLFP to recruit substantial support among Tamils. As a result, this minority was largely excluded from party politics.

On the basis of ethnicity, three types of parties could be defined in the late 1980s: Sinhalese-backed parties including the UNP, the SLFP, Marxist parties, such as the Lanka Sama Samaja Party (LSSP) and the Communist Party of Sri Lanka, and the numerically insignificant splinter groups; a largely inoperative Tamil party system composed of the Tamil United Liberation Front (TULF); and other minority-oriented parties, such as the Ceylon Workers' Congress which enjoyed the support of the Indian Tamils, and the

Sri Lanka Muslim Congress. The situation was complicated by the fact that extremist groups, such as the Sinhalese-based People's Liberation Front (Janatha Vimukthi Peramuna—JVP) in southern Sri Lanka and the Tamil Tigers based in the Northern and Eastern provinces, challenged the legal parties for popular support. By the late 1980s, both the intransigence of the Jayewardene government and the use of intimidation tactics by extremists in Jaffna District and parts of Eastern Province dramatically reduced popular backing among Tamils for the relatively moderate TULF.

The political party system was also weakened by the determination of the UNP leadership to retain a solid parliamentary majority through the use of constitutional amendments (see Government Institutions, this ch.). During the 1980s, various UNP measures undermined the balance between the two major parties that had been an important factor behind the political stability of the years between 1952 and 1977. The extension of the life of Parliament until 1989 and the passage of the amendment prohibiting the advocacy of separatism, which resulted in the expulsion of TULF members from Parliament, created new political grievances. The Jayewardene government's decision to deprive SLFP leader Sirimavo Bandaranaike of her civil rights for seven years for alleged abuses of power in October 1980 also weakened the two-party system because it deprived the SLFP of its popular leader.

Despite drastic constitutional changes since 1972, the party system's British heritage is readily apparent in the clear distinction made between government and opposition legislators in Parliament (sitting, as in Westminster, on opposite benches) and provisions in the 1978 Constitution to prevent defections from one party to another, previously a common practice. Backbenchers are expected to follow the initiatives of party leaders and can be punished with expulsion from the party for failing to observe party discipline.

Sinhalese Parties

The UNP

The UNP was established in 1946 by prominent nationalist leaders such as Don Stephen Senanayake, who became the country's first prime minister, and S.W.R.D. Bandaranaike, who broke with Senanayake in 1951, establishing the SLFP. The UNP, originally a collection of disparate and jealous factions, was organized to compete in the first general elections in 1947 against leftist parties on the platform of communal harmony, parliamentary democracy, and anticommunism. Between 1946 and the early 1970s, the UNP was organized around power personalities and politically influential families rather than a consistent ideology or a strong party organization. In its early years it was known as the "uncle-nephew party" because of the blood ties between its major leaders. When the first prime minister, Don Stephen Senanayake, died in March 1952, he was succeeded by his son, Dudley. In September 1953, Sir John Kotelawala, Dudley Senanayake's uncle, assumed the leadership of the UNP government and remained in power until April 1956. In the March 1965 general election, Dudley Senanayake again became prime minister at the head of a UNP government. In 1970 leadership of the party passed to a distant relative, Junius Richard (J.R.) Jayewardene. A prominent activist in the preindependence Ceylon National Congress who was elected to the colonial era legislature in 1943, Jayewardene departed from the personality-dominated UNP status quo. Instead, he established a strong party organization and recruited members of the younger generation, traditionally attracted to the leftist parties, to fill UNP party ranks.

In keeping both with the privileged background of its leadership and the need to provide the electorate with a clear-cut alternative to the leftist orientation of the SLFP and other groups, the UNP has remained, since independence, a party of the moderate right. Despite the constitutional adoption of the term "Democratic Socialist Republic of Sri Lanka" as the country's formal name, the ruling party's policies under Jayewardene have included comprehensive economic liberalization designed to stimulate growth of a market economy, encouragement of foreign investment, a partial dismantling of the country's elaborate welfare state institutions, and closer and friendlier relations with the United States and other Western countries. Because the UNP's popular support is firmly anchored in the Sinhalese-majority regions of central, southern, and western Sri Lanka, it has had to compromise with rising grassroots sentiment against the Tamil minority as ethnic polarities intensified during the 1980s. Historically, however, it is less closely identified with Sinhalese chauvinism than its major rival, the SLFP.

The Sri Lanka Freedom Party

In 1951 S.W.R.D. Bandaranaike led his faction, the Sinhala Maha Sabha, out of the ruling UNP and established the SLFP. Bandaranaike had organized the Sinhala Maha Sabha in 1937 in order to promote Sinhalese culture and community interests. Since the 1950s, SLFP platforms have reflected the earlier organization's emphasis on appealing to the sentiments of the Sinhalese masses in rural areas. To this basis has been added the antiestablishment appeal of nonrevolutionary socialism. On the sensitive issue of language, the party originally espoused the use of both Sinhala and

Tamil as national languages, but in the mid-1950s it adopted a "Sinhala only" policy. As the champion of the Buddhist religion, the SLFP has customarily relied upon the socially and politically influential Buddhist clergy, the *sangha,* to carry its message to the Sinhalese villages.

Another important constituency has been the Sinhalese middle class, whose members have resented alleged Tamil domination of the professions, commerce, and the civil service since the British colonial era. In contrast to the free market orientation of the UNP, the SLFP's policies have included economic self-sufficiency, nationalization of major enterprises, creation of a comprehensive welfare state, redistribution of wealth, and a nonaligned foreign policy that favored close ties with socialist countries. It has, however, refused to embrace Marxism as its guiding ideology.

Like the UNP, the SLFP has been a "family party." S.W.R.D. Bandaranaike was assassinated in 1959. After a brief and somewhat chaotic interregnum, his widow, Sirimavo Bandaranaike, was chosen as party leader. In the July 1960 general election, the party won 75 out of 151 parliamentary seats, and in a coalition with Marxist parties, Mrs. Banaranaike became the world's first democratically elected female head of government. Although she was obliged to step down from party leadership after her civil rights were taken away in October 1980 on charges of corruption and abuse of power, she resumed leadership of the SLFP following a government pardon granted on January 1, 1986.

In 1977 six members of the SLFP left the party and formed a new group, the People's Democratic Party (PDP—Mahajana Prajathanthra). A second group, the Sri Lanka People's Party (SLPP—Sri Lanka Mahajana Pakshaya), was formed in 1984 by a daughter of Sirimavo Bandaranaike, Chandrika Kumaratunge, and her husband Vijay Kumaratunge. They claimed that the original SLFP, under the leadership of Sirimavo Bandaranaike's son, Anura, was excessively right wing and had become an instrument of the Jayewardene government. Although Sirimavo Bandaranaike reentered politics and assumed a leadership position within the SLFP after her 1986 pardon, Anura Bandaranaike remained leader of the parliamentary opposition. Neither the PDP nor the SLPP had representation in Parliament in 1988.

During the late 1980s, the SLFP and the breakaway SLPP remained split on the sensitive issue of negotiations with Tamil separatists. The former opposed the granting of significant concessions to the militants while the latter joined the UNP in supporting them. In 1986 Sirimavo Bandaranaike and politically active members of the Buddhist leadership established the Movement for

Defense of the Nation in order to campaign against proposed grants of regional autonomy to the Tamils.

The Marxist Parties

In the late 1980s, Sri Lanka had two long-established Marxist parties. The Lanka Sama Samaja Party (LSSP) was founded in 1935 and remained in the late 1980s one of the very few Marxist-Leninist parties in the world to associate itself with the revolutionary doctrines of Leon Trotsky. This connection made it attractive to independent-minded Marxists who resented ideological subservience to Moscow and who aspired to adapt Marxism to Sri Lankan conditions. During the late 1940s and early 1950s, the LSSP functioned as the primary opposition party, but its fortunes declined after the emergence of the non-Marxist SLFP. Like the SLPP, the LSSP joined with the ruling UNP in the mid-1980s to support a negotiated settlement with Tamil militants but in 1988 did not have members in Parliament. The New Equal Society Party (Nava Sama Samaja Party—NSSP) was in 1987 a breakaway faction of the LSSP.

The Communist Party of Sri Lanka (CPSL) was established in 1943 and continued in the late 1980s to follow the direction of the Soviet Union on matters of ideology. Banned briefly in July 1983 along with the JVP and the NSSP, in 1987 it had limited popular support.

The People's United Front

The People's United Front (Mahajana Eksath Peramuna—MEP) was a small party founded by veteran leftist Dinesh P. R. Gunawardene that since the early 1950s has attracted Sinhalese support with appeals to militant Buddhist and Sinhala chauvinist sentiments. In 1956 it formed a coalition on the left with the SLFP and Marxist parties, but in a shift to the right four years later joined forces with the UNP. During the late 1970s and the early 1980s, it maintained a formal association with the JVP, originally a Maoist group that was responsible for a bloody uprising in 1971 but operated as a legal political party between 1977 and 1983.

Tamil United Liberation Front

With very few exceptions, Sri Lankan Tamils have tended to support their own parties and candidates rather than vote for the UNP, SLFP, or the Marxist parties. In the July 1977 general election, for example, only 9 percent of the voters in the Tamil-majority Northern Province supported the two major parties (the UNP, less closely associated with Sinhalese chauvinism from the Tamil

197

Sri Lanka: A Country Study

viewpoint than the SLFP, won 8 of the 9 percent). In the years
following independence, the most important Tamil party was the
Tamil Congress, led by G.G. Ponnambalam, one of the major
figures in the independence movement. A breakaway group led
by another figure, S.J.V. Chelvanayakam, founded a second party,
the Federal Party, which began to make inroads into the Tamil
Congress' constituency by advancing proposals for a federal state
structure that would grant Tamils substantial autonomy.

In the early 1970s, several Tamil political groups, including the
Tamil Congress and the Federal Party, formed the Tamil United
Front (TUF). With the group's adoption in 1976 of a demand for
an independent state, a "secular, socialist state of Tamil Eelam,"
it changed its name to the Tamil United Liberation Front (TULF).
In the general election of July 1977, TULF won eighteen seats in
the legislature, including all fourteen seats contested in the Jaffna
Peninsula. In October 1983, all the TULF legislators, numbering
sixteen at the time, forfeited their seats in Parliament for refusing
to swear an oath unconditionally renouncing support for a separate
state in accordance with the Sixth Amendment to the Constitution. In an atmosphere of intensifying ethnic violence and polarization, their resignations deprived Sri Lankan Tamils of a role in
the legal political process and increased tremendously the appeal
of extremist groups such as the Liberation Tigers of Tamil Eelam
(see Tamil Militant Groups, this ch.). But in December 1985, the
TULF leadership softened its position and proposed that an
autonomous Tamil State could be established within the Sri Lankan
constitutional framework in a manner similar to the federal states
of India.

Other Parties

The Ceylon Workers' Congress, headed in 1988 by
Suvumyamoorthy Thondaman, originally joined with other Tamil
groups to form TULF, but withdrew from the party after the July
1977 general election, when Jayewardene offered Thondaman a
post in the UNP cabinet. In the late 1980s, the Ceylon Workers'
Congress, with one representative, Thondaman, in Parliament,
continued to cooperate with the ruling party. This was politically
feasible because its principal supporters, Indian Tamils located for
the most part in the central part of the country, were unrespon-
sive to the Sri Lankan Tamils' call for an independent state in the
north. In December 1986, the Sri Lanka Muslim Congress, based
in the Eastern Province, announced its determination to become
a national political party.

Electoral Performance

In general elections between 1952 and 1977, the two major parties have alternately secured majorities: the SLFP in 1956, July 1960 (elections were held in both March and July 1960), and 1970; and the UNP in 1952, March 1960, 1965, and 1977. To govern effectively, each party has formed coalitions with smaller groups. The two major parties, however, have together gained a progressively larger percentage of the popular vote at the expense of the smaller groups: from 59.5 percent of the total vote in 1952 to 80.6 percent in 1977 (see table 12, Appendix A). In the July 1977 general election, the UNP, benefiting from widespread public disaffection with the leftist policies of the SLFP, won the largest majority in history: 50.9 percent of the popular vote and 140 out of 168 seats contested. The SLFP's parliamentary representation dropped dramatically from 91 to 8 seats, though it garnered 29.7 percent of the vote. With its eighteen seats, the TULF became the principal opposition party. Two seats were won by the Ceylon Workers' Congress and an independent. The two Marxist parties, the LSSP and the CPSL, failed to win representation. Parliamentary elections have typically included a large number of independent candidates, but the number elected has steadily declined since 1947. In July 1977, there were 295 independents running without party affiliation, but only 1 secured a parliamentary seat.

By-elections for eighteen parliamentary seats that became vacant after the resignation of UNP members were held in May 1983 in tandem with local government elections. These were conducted under the system of proportional representation outlined in the Constitution. The UNP won fourteen of the contests, the SLFP won three, and the People's United Front won one. Further by-elections were held during the 1984–86 period.

Sri Lanka has had only one presidential election since promulgation of the 1978 Constitution. This occurred on October 20, 1982. Six candidates participated. The deeply divided SLFP, deprived of its most popular leader, Sirimavo Bandaranaike, put up Hector Kobbekaduwa, an obscure candidate who had served as minister of agriculture in a SLFP government. Kobbekaduwa won 39.1 percent of the vote, compared to the incumbent Jayewardene's 52.9 percent. The four other candidates, who together won only 8.1 percent of the vote, represented the JVP, LSSP, NSSP, and the Tamil Congress.

The Emergence of Extremist Groups

During the 1980s, extremist groups operating within both Tamil and Sinhalese communities were a grave threat to political stability

199

Sri Lanka: A Country Study

and democratic institutions. Like Northern Ireland and Lebanon, Sri Lanka had become a country in which the vicious cycle of escalating violence had become so deeply entrenched that prospects for a peaceful resolution of social and political problems seemed remote. Extremism was generationally as well as ethnically based: many youth, seeing a future of diminished opportunities, had little faith in established political and social institutions and were increasingly attracted to radical solutions and the example of movements abroad like the Popular Front for the Liberation of Palestine.

Perhaps surprisingly, the first major extremist movement in postindependence history was Sinhalese and Buddhist rather than Tamil and Hindu. The JVP, an ultra-leftist organization established in the late 1960s by Rohana Wijeweera, attracted the support of students and poor Sinhalese youth in rural areas. In April 1971, the JVP led an armed uprising that resulted in the death of thousands of the rebels at the hands of the security forces (one estimate is 10,000 fatalities). The historian, K.M. de Silva, calls the 1971 JVP insurrection "perhaps the biggest revolt by young people in any part of the world in recorded history, the first instance of tension between generations becoming military conflict on a national scale." Although it suppressed the poorly organized revolt with little difficulty, the Bandaranaike government was visibly shaken by the experience. Fears of future unrest within the Sinhalese community undoubtedly made it reluctant, in a "zero-sum" economy and society, to grant significant concessions to minorities.

Although the JVP was recognized as a legal political party in 1977 and Wijeweera ran as a presidential candidate in the October 1982 election, it was banned by the government after the summer 1983 anti-Tamil riots in Colombo and went underground. By the late 1980s, it was again active in Sinhalese-majority areas of the country. The JVP cadres organized student protests at Sri Lanka's universities, resulting in the temporary closure of six of them, and led sporadic attacks against government installations, such as a raid on an army camp near Kandy in 1987 to capture automatic weapons. But they were also suspected of establishing links with Tamil militant groups, especially the Eelam Revolutionary Organization of Students (EROS). Government intelligence analysts believed that the JVP, in tandem with EROS, was attempting to organize a leftist movement among Indian Tamils in the Central Highlands (see fig. 3). This was a disturbing development since the Indian Tamils had traditionally been docile and politically apathetic.

In 1987 a splinter group of the JVP, known as the Deshapremi Janatha Viyaparaya (DJV—Patriotic Liberation Organization),

200

emerged. The DJV threatened to assassinate members of Parliament who approved the conditions of the July 29, 1987 Indo-Sri Lankan Accord, which it described as a "treacherous sell-out to Tamil separatists and Indian expansionists" and said that it would take the lives not only of parliamentarians who approved it but also of their families (see The Janatha Vimukthi Peramuna, ch. 5).

Tamil Alienation

Moderate as well as militant Sri Lankan Tamils have regarded the policies of successive Sinhalese governments in Colombo with suspicion and resentment since at least the mid-1950s, when the "Sinhala Only" language policy was adopted (see Emergence of the Sri Lanka Freedom Party, ch. 1). Although limited compromises designed to appease Tamil sentiment were adopted, such as the 1959 Tamil Language Special Provision Act and the 1978 Constitution's granting of national language status to Tamil, the overall position of the minority community has deteriorated since Sri Lanka became an independent state. Pressured by militant elements within the Sinhalese community, the UNP and SLFP political leadership has repeatedly failed to take advantage of opportunities to achieve accords with the Tamils that could have laid the foundations for ethnic understanding and harmony. For example, in 1957 S.W.R.D. Bandaranaike reached an agreement with Tamil Federal Party leader Chelvanayakam that would have granted regional autonomy to Tamil-majority areas and recognized Tamil as a language of administration in those areas. The pact, however, was never honored by Bandaranaike or his widow. Tambiah called it "a great opportunity, fatefully missed, to settle the Tamil issue for all time." Three decades later, after thousands of people in both ethnic communities had met violent deaths, a similar accord was reached, but only with the intervention of India.

Several issues provided the focus for Sri Lankan Tamil alienation and widespread support, particularly within the younger generation, for extremist movements. Among the issues was the language problem, which was only partially resolved by the 1978 Constitution's conferral of national language status on Tamil. Sinhala still remained the higher-status "official language," and inductees into the civil service were expected to acquire proficiency in it. Other areas of disagreement concerned preference given to Sinhalese applicants for university admissions and public employment, and allegations of government encouragement of Sinhalese settlement in Tamil-majority areas.

Until 1970 university admissions were determined solely by academic qualifications. Because of the generally higher educational standards of Tamils, their percentage of university enrollments substantially exceeded their percentage of the general population. In 1969 for example, 50 percent of the students in the country's faculties of medicine and 48 percent of all engineering students were Tamil. During the 1970s, however, the government implemented a preferential admissions system known as the "policy of standardization." This was a geographically based criterion, but because the two ethnic communities tended to be regionally segregated, such a policy increased Sinhalese enrollments. The scheme established quotas for 70 percent of university places on the basis of revenue districts; this included a special allotment of 15 percent of all openings reserved for educationally underprivileged districts, which were predominantly Sinhalese. Only 30 percent of openings were allotted nationwide on merit considerations alone. By the early 1980s, the policy had proven a statistical success: in 1983 only 22 percent of medical students and 28 percent of engineering students were Tamils.

The limiting of educational opportunities for Tamils was reflected in declining percentages of Tamils in the skilled and professional areas of government service. State-employed Tamil physicians declined from 35 percent in the 1966-70 period to 30 percent in 1978-79; engineers from a 38 percent average in the 1971-77 period to 25 percent in 1978-79; and clerical workers from an 11 percent average in 1970-77 to a little more than 5 percent in 1978-79. By 1980 the percentage of Tamil employees in the public sector, excluding public corporations, was roughly equivalent to their percentage of the population, or 12 percent.

Political factors played a role in the decline in the number of Tamils in public service. Under the so-called chit system, which became pervasive when Sirimavo Bandaranaike was in power during the 1970s, the influence of a parliamentarian was needed to secure a government job (the chit being a memorandum written by the legislator to inform personnel authorities of the preferred candidate). The Jayewardene government made the machinery of patronage still more overt by giving each legislator "job banks" of lower level positions to be distributed to their followers. The expanding role of patronage on all levels of the civil service had two implications for Tamils: first, merit qualifications that would have benefited educated Tamils were sacrificed to patron-client politics; second, the patronage system provided Tamils with little or no access to public employment because their political representatives, especially after the 1977 general election, had very limited influence.

Government-sponsored settlement of Sinhalese in the northern or eastern parts of the island, traditionally considered to be Tamil

regions, has been perhaps the most immediate cause of intercommunal violence. There was, for example, an official plan in the
mid-1980s to settle 30,000 Sinhalese in the dry zone of Northern
Province, giving each settler land and funds to build a house and
each community armed protection in the form of rifles and machine
guns. Tamil spokesmen accused the government of promoting a
new form of "colonialism," but the Jayewardene government
asserted that no part of the island could legitimately be considered
an ethnic homeland and thus closed to settlement from outside.
Settlement schemes were popular with the poorer and less fortunate
classes of Sinhalese.

Indian Tamils, poorer and less educated than their Sri Lankan
Tamil cousins, since independence have endured an equally precarious situation. Although agreements with India largely resolved
the issue of their nationality, 100,000 Indian Tamils remained stateless in the late 1980s. Those holding Sri Lankan citizenship and
remaining loyal to Thondaman's progovernment Ceylon Workers'
Congress were largely indifferent to Sri Lankan Tamils' militant
demands for an independent state, but endemic poverty among
plantation workers and occasional harsh treatment at the hands
of the police and Sinhalese civilians made the people more recep-
tive to leftist ideology and threatened the traditional tranquility of
the inland hill country.

Tamil Militant Groups

The de facto policies of preference that the Sri Lankan government adopted in order to assist the Sinhalese community in such
areas as education and public employment affected most severely
middle class Tamil youth, who found it more difficult during the
1970s and 1980s to enter a university or secure employment than
had their older brothers and sisters. Individuals belonging to this
younger generation, often referred to by other Tamils as "the
boys," formed the core of an extremist movement that had become, by the late 1980s, one of the world's most violent. By the
end of 1987, they fought not only the Sri Lankan security forces
but also the armed might of the (Indian Peacekeeping Force) and
terrorized both Sinhalese and Tamil civilians with acts of random
violence. They also fought among each other with equal if not
greater brutality (see The Tamil Insurgency, ch. 5).

In a sense, the militant movement was not only a revolt against
the Sinhalese-dominated status quo but also an expression of in-
tergenerational tensions in a highly traditional society where obe-
dience to parental authority had long been sacrosanct. Militant
youth criticized their elders for indecisiveness at a time when they

felt the existence of their ethnic community clearly was in danger. The movement also reflected caste differences and rivalries. The membership of the largest and most important extremist group, for example, the Liberation Tigers of Tamil Eelam (LTTE), was generally drawn from the Karava or fisherman caste, while individuals belonging to the elite Vellala caste were found in considerable numbers in a rival group, the People's Liberation Organization of Tamil Eelam (PLOTE, also PLOT).

Liberation Tigers of Tamil Eelam

The Liberation Tigers of Tamil Eelam (LTTE) emerged in 1972 when Tamil youth espousing an independent Tamil state established a group called the Tamil New Tigers. At that time, the idea of secession was still considered radical by most Tamil leaders, though the TULF embraced it four years later. An incident of apparently unprovoked police brutality in 1974 started the LTTE on its career of insurgency. In January of that year, the World Tamil Research Conference, bringing delegates from many different countries, was held in Jaffna. Police seeing large crowds milling around the meeting hall attacked them ferociously. Nine persons were killed and many more injured. The incident was viewed by youthful militants not only as a provocative act of violence but as a deliberate insult to Tamil culture. It was, according to one Tamil spokesman, ''a direct challenge to their manhood.'' The Tigers' first act as an insurgent movement was to assassinate the progovernment mayor of Jaffna in 1975. Subsequently they went underground. As extremist movements in other countries have done, the LTTE apparently established contacts with similar groups, such as the Popular Front for the Liberation of Palestine, trained with Palestinians in Libya and Lebanon, and ran its own secret training camps in India's Tamil Nadu State. In 1988 Velupillai Prabhakaran, its undisputed military and political leader, and A.S. Balasingham, its ideological spokesman, were the LTTE's most important figures.

The Tamil militants' choice of the tiger as their symbol reflected not only the ferocity of that animal but a deliberate contrast with the lion (*singha*), which traditionally has been a symbol of the Sinhalese people and is depicted in the Sri Lankan flag.

Ideologically, LTTE theoreticians at times resorted to Marxist rhetoric to characterize their struggle. Overall, the creation of an independent Tamil state, irrespective of ideology, remained the movement's only goal. In pursuit of this objective, the LTTE seemed more wedded to direct and violent action than formulation of principles on which the independent state would operate.

LTTE leader Prabhakaran maintained friendly, though watch-ful, relations with the chief minister of India's Tamil Nadu State, M.G. Ramachandran, until the latter's death in 1987. Until India's intervention in 1987, he could count upon at least the moral sup-port of Ramachandran's political party, the All-India Anna Dravida Munnetra Kazhagam (AIADMK). Some of the LTTE's militant rivals maintained ties with the Tamil Nadu opposition party, the Dravida Munnetra Kazhagam, which was headed by Ramachan-dran's bitter rival, M. Karunaidhi.

Other Tamil Groups

Observers in the late 1980s counted at least thirty separate guer-rilla groups of which five, including the LTTE, were the most im-portant (see The Tamil Insurgency, ch. 5). The other four major groups were the Eelam People's Revolutionary Liberation Front (EPRLF), led by K. Padmanabha, the Tamil Eelam Liberation Organization (TELO), led by Sri Sabaratnam until he was killed by the LTTE assassins in May 1986, the Eelam Revolutionary Organization of Students (EROS), led by V. Balakumar, and the People's Liberation Organization of Tamil Eelam (PLOTE), headed by Uma Maheswaran. These groups differed significantly in terms of strategies and ideologies. EROS was said to prefer acts of economic sabotage. In March 1985, the LTTE, EPRLF, TELO, and EROS formed a united front organization, the Eelam National Liberation Front (ENLF). PLOTE, probably the most genuinely Marxist-Leninist of the five major guerrilla groups, remained out-side the coalition. By mid-1986, ENLF had become largely inoper-ative after the LTTE quit, although the other groups sought to form a front without its participation.

The Liberation Tigers proceeded to devour their rivals during 1986 and 1987. TELO was decimated in 1986 by repeated LTTE attacks. During 1987 the Tigers battled not only Indian troops but members of PLOTE and the EPRLF.

The year 1983 can be regarded as a psychological turning point in the ethnic crisis. The brutal anti-Tamil riots of July in Colombo and other towns, and the government's apparent lack of concern for Tamil safety and welfare seemed to rule out a peaceful resolu-tion of differences between Tamils and Sinhalese. The riots were touched off by the July 23 killing of thirteen Sinhalese soldiers by LTTE guerrillas on the Jaffna Peninsula. According to Tambiah, the mutilated corpses were brought to Colombo by their comrades and displayed at a cemetery as an example of the Tigers' barbarism. In an explosion of rage, local Sinhalese began attacks on Tamils and their property that spread out from Colombo District to other districts and resulted in at least 400 casualties (the official figure) and perhaps as many as 2,000 (an estimate by Tamil sources). Fifty-three Tamil prisoners were killed under questionable circumstances at the Welikade Prison outside Colombo. Damage to property, including Tamil-owned shops and factories, was initially estimated at the equivalent of US$150 million, probably a low figure.

The authorities, seemingly paralyzed during the bloody days of July 24 to July 31, did little or nothing to protect the victims of mob violence. Curfews were not enforced by security personnel even though they were required under a nationwide state of emergency in effect since the May by-elections. Jayewardene withdrew to his presidential residence, heavily guarded by government troops, and issued a statement after the riots that "the time has come to accede to the clamor and the national respect of the Sinhala People," that expressed little sympathy for the sufferings of the Tamils.

There was ample evidence, reported in the Indian and Western media, that the violence was more a carefully planned program than a totally spontaneous expression of popular indignation. According to a report in the New Delhi publication, *India Today,* "the mobs were armed with voters' lists, and detailed addresses of every Tamil-owned shop, house, or factory, and their attacks were very precise." Other sources mentioned the central role played by Minister of Industry and Scientific Affairs Cyril Mathew in providing personnel for the violence and the ease with which the mobs found transportation, including government vehicles, to move from place to place.

According to political scientist James Manor, the eagerness of powerful politicians such as Mathew to stir up ethnic trouble stemmed at least in part from factional struggles within the ruling UNP. Mathew reportedly used the riots to compromise the aging and seemingly indecisive Jayewardene and undermine support for the chief executive's all-but-designated successor, Prime Minister Ranasinghe Premadasa. According to *India Today* reporting in August 1983, five UNP factional groups, including Mathew's and Premadasa's, competed for influence. With deep reservoirs of anti-Tamil sentiment among poorer Sinhalese to draw upon, Mathew could not be ignored in any post-Jayewardene political arrangement within the UNP. His schemes, however, ultimately backfired. In December 1984, Mathew was obliged to resign from the cabinet for opposing negotiations between the government and the Tamils on regional autonomy, and he subsequently faced expulsion from the party.

The 1983 violence had a caste as well as ethnic dimension. Mathew was a leader of the Vahumpura caste. This group has a lower status than the politically dominant Goyigama caste but comprises more than one-third of the Sinhalese population. Traditionally, Vahumpura occupations included the making of jaggery (brown sugar derived from palm sap) and domestic service in higher caste households. Nevertheless, they trace their descent from the attendants of Mahinda, the brother or son of the Indian emperor Asoka, who came to Sri Lanka as a Buddhist missionary in the third century B.C. and thus claimed an esteemed status among Sinhalese Buddhists. The Vahumpura also had been actively involved in commerce, but in the 1970s and early 1980s they were forced out of the business by their Sinhalese Karava and Tamil competitors. The resultant decline in their fortunes was a source of much resentment toward the other groups.

Some observers speculated that the LTTE had moderated to a slight degree its attacks against government forces in the north, because of the presence of Tamil "hostages" in Colombo and other Sinhalese-majority urban areas, but that the July 1983 riots removed such inhibitions. The vicious cycle of violence intensified as attacks by the LTTE and other groups against troops brought harsh retaliation against Tamil civilians, especially in the Jaffna Peninsula. Reports issued by Amnesty International, the London-based human rights group, told of random seizures, tortures, and executions of hundreds of young Tamil men by the armed forces in Northern and Eastern provinces. These actions forced the great majority of Sri Lankan Tamils, whatever their point of view on the goals or methods of the guerrillas, into the arms of the extremists. In the words of one observer, the Tamil population in the north was "visibly afraid of the Tigers, but they disliked the [Sri Lankan] Army even more." As the civil war intensified, government troops were besieged inside the seventeenth-century Jaffna Fort, and most areas of Jaffna City and the surrounding countryside were under Tiger control. The government ordered serial bombings of the city. Thousands of Tamils sought refuge from government attacks across the Palk Strait in India's Tamil Nadu State. As indignation among Tamils in India grew over the atrocities, Colombo was filled with rumors of an impending Indian invasion that would have resulted in a permanent division of the island.

The 1984 All Party Conference

In January 1984, the Jayewardene government convened an All Party Conference to seek a resolution of the communal issue. Participants included the UNP, the SLFP, the TULF, and five smaller groups. The major issue under discussion was devolution. The government proposed the granting of autonomy to the country's districts through the creation of district councils and other changes in local government. Also, the government proposed establishment of a second house of Parliament, a council of state, whose members would include the chairmen and vice chairmen of the district councils and which would have both legislative and advisory roles. The Tamil spokesmen rejected these proposals. One reason was that they did not allow for special links between Northern and Eastern provinces. No compromise was reached and the conference broke up on December 21, 1984 and was not resumed, as had been planned, in 1985. Even if the All Party Conference had reached an agreement on devolution, it was unlikely that it could have been implemented because the SLFP and the Mahajana Eksath Peramuna had withdrawn from the negotiations. The proposals also were denounced by militant Sinhalese groups, such as politically active Buddhist monks, who viewed them as a sellout to the Tamils.

India's Perspective

By the close of 1984, it was becoming clear that the parties within Sri Lanka were incapable of reaching a workable compromise on their own. The new Congress (I), I for Indira Gandhi, government of Rajiv Gandhi in India assumed an active mediation role at the request of the government of Sri Lanka. Gandhi's own interest in containing the ethnic crisis was self-evident. Thousands of Sri Lankan Tamil refugees were fleeing to Tamil Nadu State, which was also a sanctuary for most of the militant groups and the now disenfranchised TULF (the number of Tamil refugees was more than 100,000 in early 1987). Local politicians, particularly Tamil Nadu's chief minister, M.G. Ramachandran, demanded initiatives on the part of New Delhi to halt the violence. Ramachandran's AIADMK was one of the few southern regional parties friendly to Gandhi's Congress (I). An appearance of insensitivity to Tamil suffering on the part of New Delhi might cost it the support of the AIADMK or strengthen the hand of the Dravida Munnetra Kazhagam, the state's major opposition party.

At the same time, Gandhi, whose predecessor as prime minister (his mother) had been assassinated by Sikh extremists on October 31, 1984, had no desire to encourage separatist forces within his own ethnically and religiously divided country by sponsoring separatist sentiments in Sri Lanka. New Delhi wished to rein in the Tigers without appearing to be too enthusiastic a backer of Jayewardene's government.

A third problem for Gandhi was strategic. As the ethnic crisis deepened, the Jayewardene government sought increasing military

Parliament, Colombo
Courtesy Doranne Jacobson

aid from countries of which India was suspicious or which seemed to challenge New Delhi's primacy in the Indian Ocean region. China, Britain, the Federal Republic of Germany (West Germany), and South Africa supplied Sri Lanka with arms. Israel operated a special interest section in the United States Embassy in Colombo, and Israeli experts provided training in counterinsurgency and land settlement strategies. Retired members of Britain's Special Air Service also trained Sri Lankan military personnel. India also feared that the United States naval forces might establish an Indian Ocean base at the strategic port of Trincomalee ("another Diego Garcia" charged India). The most ominous foreign presence, however, was Pakistan's. In March–April 1985, Jayewardene made an official visit to Islamabad to confer with President Mohammed Zia ul Haq and other top Pakistani officials. According to Indian sources, Sri Lankan forces were trained by Pakistani advisers both in Sri Lanka and Pakistan. Gandhi, like his mother before him, referred to Sri Lanka's inclusion within a "Washington-Islamabad-Beijing axis."

The Eastern Province Question

Indian pressure was apparently a major factor in persuading the four major guerrilla groups included within the Eelam National Liberation Front (the LTTE, TELO, EROS, and EPRLF) and the Tamil political party, TULF, to hold talks with a government

209

delegation headed by the president's brother, Hector Jayewardene. The meetings were convened in July and August 1985 in Thimpu, capital of Bhutan. Jayewardene advanced a proposal involving, as in the 1984 All Party Conference, the granting of autonomy to district councils. He also proposed the creation of a separate legislature for the Tamil-majority northern region of the island. The Tamil groups made four demands: recognition of the Tamils as a distinct national group, the creation of a Tamil state (Eelam) from Northern and Eastern provinces, the right of self-determination for the Tamil "nation," and full citizenship rights for all Tamils resident in Sri Lanka. The government rejected the first three on the grounds that they amounted to separatism, which was prohibited by the Constitution and the talks broke off abruptly on August 18, 1985, when Tamil delegates accused the armed forces of continuing to perpetrate atrocities against Tamil civilians. The fourth demand, for granting Sri Lankan citizenship to 96,000 Indian Tamils, was met in January 1986.

In December 1985, TULF broke ranks with the militants and announced support for a Tamil-majority federal state remaining within Sri Lanka with the devolution of substantial executive, legislative, and judicial powers. The government, however, objected to the controversial joining of Eastern Province with Northern Province in the proposed federal unit. Although Northern Province clearly had a Tamil majority and limited economic potential, the position in Eastern Province was ambiguous: 58 percent of its population was either Sinhalese or Muslim. Although Eastern Province Muslims spoke Tamil, the great majority were descended from Arab settlers. Also, Eastern Province contained large areas of fertile and economically exploitable land and the strategic port of Trincomalee. Although a second All Party Conference was held in June 1986, neither TULF nor the militants participated. Talks in Colombo between TULF and the government were snagged on the issue of the status of Eastern Province.

The Eastern Province issue brought the Muslims into the negotiations not only because they viewed themselves as a community quite separate from both the Tamils and Sinhalese but also because there had been communal violence involving Tamils and Muslims in Eastern Province during the 1980s, and the latter were not enthusiastic about being included in a separate, Tamil-dominated state. According to the leader of the Sri Lanka Muslim Congress, M. Ashraff, "we are a community being oppressed both by the Sinhalese and the Tamils." Some younger Muslims expressed sympathy for the LTTE, but the leadership of the community wanted the government to grant them some kind of autonomous status separate from any settlement with the Tamils.

By late 1986, Jayewardene's government found itself tied down by conflicting communal interests that included not only the Sri Lankan Tamils and Muslims but Sinhalese who rallied behind the nationalist appeal of Sirimavo Bandaranaike's Movement for Defense of the Nation. Against a background of unremitting violence that included bloody Tamil terrorist bombings in Colombo, the status of Eastern Province remained a major stumbling block. Given the stalemate, India's participation loomed larger in any formula that had a chance of achieving peace.

In November 1986, Sri Lankan and Indian leaders conferred at the annual summit meeting of the South Asian Association for Regional Cooperation (SAARC) in Bangalore, India. They outlined a settlement that included provincial councils for Northern and Eastern provinces and special provisions for Eastern Province that would entail the establishment of local councils for Sinhalese in Trincomalee, Tamils in Batticaloa District, and Muslims in the southern district of Amparai. This arrangement was scrapped in the face of Tamil opposition. On December 17–19, 1986, President Jayewardene met cabinet-level Indian officials in Colombo and agreed to another set of proposals, described as a "beginning point for further negotiations," which conceded the possible merger of Northern and Eastern provinces and the joining of Sinhalese-majority areas of Amparai District to the inland province of Uva. This proposal, too, was scrapped, because of the objections of Amparai Muslims.

By early 1987, India had grown impatient with the lack of progress on an accord and threatened to end its mediating role. A still more serious problem was the apparent determination of the Sri Lankan government to use military means to solve the crisis. In late May, a large-scale offensive, dubbed Operation Liberation, was launched against the LTTE in the Jaffna Peninsula. The offensive caused considerable hardship among local civilians. Indian efforts to bring relief supplies by boat were rebuffed by the Sri Lankan Navy on June 3, 1987, but an airdrop of supplies by the Indian Air Force took place the next day. Sri Lanka labelled this action a "naked violation" of its territorial integrity.

By July 1987, however, Jayewardene—weary of the bloodletting and sincere in his desire for a peaceful solution—and Prime Minister Gandhi, perceiving that he could not afford an indefinite prolongation of the crisis, had groped to within reach of a viable accord. In a July 1 letter, Gandhi urged Jayewardene to come up with some "new ideas" on a settlement. On July 16, Jayewardene, his cabinet,

Sri Lanka: A Country Study

and the Indian high commissioner in Colombo, Jyotindra Nath Dixit, conferred on an "improved version" of the December 19, 1986, proposals which were sent two days later to New Delhi and subsequently formed the basis for the July 29, 1987, Indo-Sri Lankan Accord.

The major task for Gandhi, acting as middleman, was to draw the Tamil militants into the settlement. On July 28, after a last minute meeting with the Indian prime minister, LTTE leader Prabhakaran announced his support for the accord. In an interview with *India Today,* he reconciled this decision with the long-standing LTTE demand for an independent state by citing the accord's recognition of the Northern and Eastern provinces' status as places of "historical habitation of Tamil-speaking people." But Prabhakaran also noted that he had not been a party to the accord and doubted that it would bring lasting peace. The four other major guerilla groups also gave their backing to the pact on July 28, though they expressed concern about its "deficiencies."

On July 30, 1987, Gandhi arrived in Colombo to sign a comprehensive settlement that had, as its main points the turn in of weapons by militant groups, a merger of Northern and Eastern provinces to create a single administrative unit; nationwide elections for eight (instead of the former nine) provincial councils before December 31, 1987 (not held until 1988); recognition of both Tamil and English as official (rather than national) languages on an equal status with Sinhala; amnesty for Tamil guerrillas and detainees; a cease-fire; return of Sri Lankan security forces to their barracks; the disbanding of Sinhalese militia units (who had acquired a reputation of viciousness toward Tamil civilians); and a referendum for Eastern Province, originally scheduled for December 31, 1988 but postponed until January 1990, to decide whether the merger of Northern and Eastern provinces should be permanent. India agreed to assist implementation of the accord by posting a peacekeeping force in the northern part of Sri Lanka (subsequently known as the Indian Peacekeeping Force) and helping to oversee the surrender of arms by Tamil militants, to be accomplished by August 3, 1987 (see Foreign Military Presence, ch. 5). New Delhi would also oblige Tamil militants to abandon their bases in Tamil Nadu State and assist the Sri Lankan Navy in patrolling the waters of the Palk Strait.

Rather predictably, the accord sparked the ire of the Sinhalese population. Gandhi was physically attacked by a rifle-wielding sailor while reviewing an honor guard in Colombo on July 30. Demonstrations against the accord in Colombo and other places resulted in nearly forty deaths. At the same time, the pact caused a cabinet

212

crisis. Several factions within the UNP opposed the merger of Northern and Eastern provinces and the alleged surrender of Sri Lankan independence to India. The opponents included Prime Minister Ramasinghe Premadasa, Minister of Defense and National Security Lalith Athulathmudali, and several other cabinet members. Premadasa signalled his displeasure by not attending the official functions held for Gandhi in Colombo on July 29 and 30. As the fighting in the north subsided following the cease-fire, however, so did the cabinet crisis.

Optimism over the accord soon turned to disappointment when the LTTE refused to turn in its weapons and hostilities flared up again, this time between the LTTE and the Indian Peacekeeping Force. By October 1987, approximately 20,000 Indian troops were engaged in pitched battles with between 2,000 and 3,000 LTTE guerrillas. The fighting represented a major loss of face for New Delhi. India had promised Sri Lanka that the Tigers would be completely disarmed, but it was apparent that the militants had surrendered only a fraction of their arsenal in August. In the face of mounting Indian military and Tamil civilian casualties, pessimists on the subcontinent speculated whether the accord signalled the beginning of India's "Vietnam" or "Afghanistan." In Colombo, SLFP leader Anura Bandaranaike declared that "the Indian Army is like the Trojan Horse. We accepted them and expected them to bring peace, and they then started watching as our people were butchered . . . . They have come here to stay. They won't take the President's orders."

Jayewardene, who survived a grenade attack in the Parliament building on August 18, 1987, was faced with the daunting task of obtaining the legislature's approval of the radical political changes outlined in the July 29 accord. Provincial autonomy was embodied in the Thirteenth Amendment to the 1978 Constitution, which the Supreme Court, in a five to four ruling, declared would not need to be submitted to a popular referendum if minor changes were made. Against the background of the JVP-instigated terrorist attacks in Sinhalese-majority areas and assassination threats against members of Parliament who approved the amendment, it was passed by 136 to 11, or substantially more than the required two-thirds majority. Few observers believed, however, that the establishment of new provincial political institutions would bring lasting peace to this strife-torn country.

Foreign Relations

The two most important factors in Sri Lanka's foreign relations since 1948 have been a commitment in principle to nonalignment and the necessity of preserving satisfactory relations with India without sacrificing independence. India had almost fifty times Sri Lanka's land area and population and forty times its gross national product in the late 1980s. Its point of view could not be ignored, but neither the country's political leaders nor the person in the street (especially if he or she were Sinhalese) wanted the island to become an appendage to India's regional power ambitions. The July 29, 1987, Indo-Sri Lankan Accord and the involvement of a large number of Indian troops in the northeast, however, seemed to many if not most Sri Lankans to be an unacceptable compromise of national independence.

Sri Lanka's first prime minister, Don Stephen Senanayake, had committed the country to a "middle path" of nonalignment to avoid entanglement in superpower rivalries (see Independence, ch. 1). But nonalignment has had its modulations in the decades since independence. UNP governments were generally friendlier to the West than those formed by the left-leaning SLFP. Sirimavo Bandaranaike deeply distrusted Washington's intentions and cultivated close and friendly relations with China in the early 1960s, a time when that country was vocally committed to the worldwide export of "wars of national liberation." Jayewardene gave Sri Lanka's foreign policy a decidedly Western orientation after he came to power in July 1977. This change was motivated largely by the desire to secure aid and investment in order to promote his government's economic liberalization program. At the same time, Sri Lanka shared with Western nations apprehensions concerning India's apparent determination to make the Indian Ocean region an Indian sphere of influence and its preservation of close ties with Moscow.

Although the 1972 constitution declared the nation a republic and ended its dominion status within the Commonwealth of Nations, Sri Lanka, like India, remained a Commonwealth member in the later 1980s. The country also belonged, like other South Asian states, to the seven-member South Asian Association for Regional Cooperation (SAARC), a group formed in the early 1980s to deliberate on regional problems. SAARC provided a context in which South Asian states other than India could discuss the Sri Lankan ethnic issue. But few observers regarded SAARC's role in any resolution of the crisis as anything more than peripheral. Some observers interpreted Sri Lanka's unsuccessful bid in 1982 to gain membership in the Association of Southeast Asian Nations (ASEAN) as an attempt to put a little comfortable distance between itself and India. The application was rejected, ostensibly on geographic grounds.

Relations with Western States

Ties with the United States in the late 1980s were based on a common democratic tradition, a mutual appreciation of the virtues of economic liberalization and market-oriented reforms, United States participation in major development projects such as the Accelerated Mahaweli Ganga Program, and seemingly convergent security interests in the Indian Ocean. The existence of a Voice of America relay facility on the island, used to transmit broadcasts within the South Asia region, was part of Washington-Colombo ties.

Large numbers of educated Sri Lankans, both Sinhalese and Tamil, lived in the United States, Britain, and Western Europe during the 1970s and 1980s. Overseas Tamils played a role in publicizing the plight of their countrymen in host country media and provided the militant movement with some financial support. An increasing number of Western countries expressed criticism of human rights violations by the government. For example, Norway halted all aid to Sri Lankan government bodies in June 1987 to protest abuses. The plight of Tamil refugees was highlighted in August 1986 when two lifeboats carrying 155 Sri Lankan Tamils were rescued off the coast of Newfoundland, Canada. It appeared that the Tamils had fled West Germany after being denied refugee status by the Bonn government and had been cast adrift from a West German-owned freighter (the Canadian government gave them one-year work permits and promised to consider applications for refugee status). At the same time, the fund-raising activities of many sympathizers in the West, including refugees, were not entirely within legal bounds. In January 1986, the Swiss government arrested seventy Tamil refugees on charges of selling heroin.

The Indo-Sri Lankan Accord and Foreign Relations

In an exchange of executive letters coinciding with the July 29, 1987, accord, President Jayewardene gave assurances to Gandhi that the port of Trincomalee would not be used by foreign powers, including the United States, and that agreements with the United States to upgrade the Voice of America facility and with Israel and Pakistan to provide military security would be reconsidered.

Indications in early 1988 were that although New Delhi wanted to avoid accusations that it was turning a formerly independent country into a client state, India was determined to prevent Sri Lanka from developing closer ties with unfriendly or potentially unfriendly foreign powers, such as Pakistan, Israel, and the United States. The *India Today* correspondent quoted a senior Indian military officer as asserting that "'Pakistan's military involvement

Sri Lanka: A Country Study

in Sri Lanka ended on July 29, 1987.'' But other observers wondered whether India, by cutting the Gordian knot of the Sri Lankan ethnic crisis and hoping at the same time to thwart Pakistan's ambitions, was finally exercising its full potential as one of the world's major nations or was being drawn into a military nightmare that would bring costs in men and money but few rewards.

* * *

S.J. Tambiah's *Sri Lanka: Ethnic Fratricide and The Dismantling of a Democracy* gives a critical account of both the ideological and socioeconomic bases of the ethnic crisis and forcefully argues that the Sinhalese-majority government bears a major responsibility for the violence and for the erosion of democratic institutions. A book by Craig Baxter et al., *Government and Politics in South Asia,* provides a detached but useful overview of Sri Lankan society, political dynamics, and governmental institutions. Janice Jiggins's *Caste and Family in the Politics of the Sinhalese, 1947–1976* provides analysis of the pre-Jayewardene era, giving an excellent description of the often neglected factor of caste in politics. On the evolution of political institutions and attitudes from the very earliest times to the 1970s, see K.M. de Silva's *A History of Sri Lanka.*

The biweekly *India Today* and the weekly *Far Eastern Economic Review* provide good coverage of the latest political developments. Articles on Sri Lanka are also frequently published in *Asian Survey, Pacific Affairs,* and journals covering comparative politics, such as the *Political Science Quarterly.* (For further information and complete citations, see Bibliography.)

Chapter 5. National Security

Sri Lankan soldiers

SRI LANKA HAS since earliest times been within the security orbit of its massive northern neighbor. Successive waves of invasion from the kingdoms of ancient India brought the majority of the Tamil and Sinhalese inhabitants to the island, while the overwhelming military power to the north historically has been the dominant external threat. In its distant past, Sri Lanka on a few occasions was able to project military power beyond its own shores to participate in the struggles of south India. For most of its history, however, and for all of the twentieth century, Sri Lanka's security posture has been a defensive one, responding with a greater or lesser degree of internal unity to the threats of the outside world. Together with India, Sri Lanka was swept along in the regional conflicts of world powers, undergoing domination in turn by the Portuguese, Dutch, and British.

Since independence in 1948, the nation has attempted to balance an external policy of nonalignment with an increasing reliance on Western development aid and an institutional affinity to British political and legal systems. While retaining membership in the Commonwealth, Sri Lanka reclaimed military bases granted to the British under a 1947 defense agreement and has attempted to insure its security by maintaining good ties with both the Western and communist worlds. Within the South Asian region, India continues to play a dominant role in Sri Lankan strategic consciousness and is perceived as the primary long-term external threat.

New Delhi's role in Sri Lankan national security has been further complicated by the direct involvement of Indian troops in the island nation's internal ethnic conflict in the late 1980s. Although this conflict is sometimes traced back to the mythical prehistory of ancient Sri Lanka, it emerged on the modern scene with the resurgence of Sinhalese nationalism in the 1950s, and by the early 1980s it constituted the single most serious threat to the nation's security. In addition to occasional outbreaks of large-scale civil violence between the Sinhalese and Tamil communities, the government has been faced with subversion and armed attacks from a changing array of terrorist organizations representing both Sinhalese and Tamil interests.

The armed forces were slow in responding to this threat. At the time of independence, Sri Lanka had only a small, volunteer reserve force led primarily by British officers. After the establishment of the Royal Ceylon Army, Navy, and Air Force in the years following

independence, the country continued to rely on volunteers to provide for its security; its small armed forces served mainly to assist
the police in the maintenance of public order. Two major events
in the 1970s and 1980s forced the government to break with this
past practice and to give a higher priority to defense issues. The
first was the 1971 insurrection by the People's Liberation Front
(Janatha Vimukthi Peramuna—JVP) that caught the army largely
unprepared and forced the government to rely on foreign military
assistance to restore order. The second event, the communal rioting of July 1983, left thousands of Tamil civilians dead and fueled
a Tamil insurgency strong enough to wrest control of the Jaffna
Peninsula from the Sri Lankan government. Faced with these
challenges, the government made important changes in the structure and size of the armed forces. It instituted a national draft in
1985, intensified its recruitment and training efforts, and devoted
a greater percentage of the budget to its growing military needs.

In spite of these improvements, the Sri Lankan government found
itself unable to deal with the military, political, and fiscal pressures
caused by the Tamil insurgency. In July 1987, President Junius R.
Jayewardene and Indian prime minister Rajiv Gandhi signed an
accord providing a political solution to the conflict and allowing
Indian peacekeeping troops to enforce the cease-fire and laying
down of arms in the Northern Province. Continuing conflict on
the terms of the accord led to a resumption of fighting in September 1987, with the Indian troops participating as active combatants in support of the Sri Lankan government. By December 1987,
the Indian Peacekeeping Force (IPKF) had increased to 30,000
troops, and Sinhalese political groups expressed a growing impa-
tience at the extended presence of Indian forces. Although these
troops were purportedly fighting on behalf of the Sri Lankan government, many Sinhalese still viewed them with grave suspicion
and saw their continued presence as a challenge to Sri Lankan
sovereignty.

Like the Sri Lankan armed forces, the national police experienced
major changes as a result of the deterioration of public order in
the 1970s and early 1980s. Previously an unarmed force organized
along British lines, the police force was greatly expanded and provided with a variety of firearms in the wake of the 1971 uprising.
The Tamil insurgency in the Northern and Eastern provinces
prompted the creation of the Special Task Force, a police field force
that played a major role in anti-insurgent operations in the 1980s.
At the same time, the regular police force was supplemented by
the formation of a local militia known as Home Guards.

The challenge of both Sinhalese and Tamil insurgent movements also brought substantial change to the criminal justice system. After an initial liberalization in the wake of the 1977 elections, the United National Party (UNP) government moved to expand the powers of the police, the armed forces, and the courts at the expense of civil liberties. Through emergency regulations and a variety of anti-terrorist provisions, the government imposed temporary restrictions on the fundamental freedoms embodied in the Constitution.

Primary Threats to National Security

The most immediate threats to Sri Lankan national security in 1988 were internal rather than external. The Tamil insurgency was the most severe of these, involving a changing number of heavily armed terrorist groups that carried out attacks on military and civilian targets throughout the island and, for most of 1986, actually controlled the Jaffna Peninsula (see fig. 1). A second source of instability came from leftist nationalist Sinhalese groups opposed to Tamil autonomy. The chief among these, the JVP, launched a short-lived insurrection in 1971 that came close to toppling the government of Sirimavo R. D. Bandaranaike. After a period of open participation in the political system, the JVP resumed its violent antigovernment activities in the 1980s, and expanded its following considerably at the time of the Indo-Sri Lankan Accord of July 1987. The government also faced a growing problem of civil violence that seriously threatened the democratic process. This unrest stemmed not only from the continuing ethnic conflict but also from a general economic malaise that increasingly prevented young men from playing productive roles in society (see Labor, ch. 3). The problem of a restless, unemployed youth, although separate from the ethnic difficulties, was instrumental in providing a fertile recruiting ground for extremists in search of a following.

Throughout the 1980s, external threats to the nation's security were long term rather than immediate and tended to involve the rivalry between regional and world superpowers for influence over the Indian Ocean. The port of Trincomalee, one of the best natural harbors in the world, has long been attractive to foreign nations interested in Indian Ocean bases. India has expressed a determination to prevent either the United States or the Soviet Union from establishing a naval presence there, and the Indo-Sri Lankan Accord helped confirm the Indian claim of regional leadership.

The Tamil Insurgency

Political and economic conflict between the Sinhalese and Tamil communities was a problem of growing urgency in the years following independence. In the face of an expanding Sinhalese ethnic nationalism, Tamil groups initially expressed their grievances through legally constituted political channels, participating in parliamentary debate through the Tamil Congress and the Federal Party. In the early 1970s, however, a number of events worked to create a new sense of alienation, especially among Tamil youths, and a new desire to seek redress through extralegal means. In 1970 the Ministry of Education introduced quotas for university admission that effectively reduced the number of places available for Tamil students. As a result, a contingent of young, educated Tamils was cut off from the traditional path to advancement and set loose on an economy ill-prepared to accommodate them.

Tamil interests received another blow in 1971 when the Constituent Assembly met to draft a new constitution. Federal Party delegates to the assembly proposed that the new republic be designed along federal lines to insure a large degree of autonomy for Tamil areas. In addition, the Tamils hoped to remove the special status that had been granted to the Sinhala language and Buddhism. The Constituent Assembly not only rejected both of these proposals, but even denied the minimal protection to minorities that had been guaranteed under the Soulbury Constitution of 1946. The Tamil delegates responded by walking out of the assembly.

The neglect of Tamil interests in the Constituent Assembly and the enactment of the new constitution in 1972 marked a turning point in Tamil political participation. The older generation of Tamil leaders had been discredited: their activity in the political process had accomplished little, and the Marxist JVP insurrection of 1971 had set a new model for political activism (see The Janatha Vimukthi Peramuna, this ch.). Two new groups emerged as an expression of the growing alienation and frustration in the Tamil community. The first, the Tamil United Front, was a coalition of Tamil interest groups and legal parties united by an urgent call for Tamil autonomy. The group espoused nonviolent means to achieve its goals—demonstrations, strikes, and roadblocks—and yet it offered tacit support to other, more confrontational tactics. The second of the new groups, the Tamil New Tigers (TNT), abandoned the political process altogether and geared itself for violence. The TNT was founded in 1972 by Velupillai Prabhakaran, an eighteen-year-old school dropout who was the son of a minor government official. Both the name and the emblem of the new group included the tiger, the traditional symbol of the ancient Tamil kingdoms and one that clearly opposed the lion symbol of Sinhalese nationalism. Despite this obvious ethnic affiliation, the TNT publicly espoused a Marxist ideology and claimed to represent the oppressed of all ethnic groups.

In July 1975, the TNT gained wide public attention with the assassination of the Tamil mayor of Jaffna, who had ordered the police to open fire on a Tamil rights demonstration outside city hall. Except for this act of violence, the activities of the TNT in this period are largely undocumented, and little evidence exists of widespread public support for its violent methods. Moreover, the prospects for a political solution had improved by 1976; the general elections scheduled for 1977 offered hope that the fiercely pro-Sinhalese Bandaranaike government could be ousted and replaced by the more moderate United National Party. At the local level, the Tamil United Liberation Front, a political party spawned by the Tamil United Front, launched a major campaign for a separate state in Tamil-dominated Northern and Eastern provinces.

The victory of the United National Party and the emergence of the Tamil United Liberation Front as the leader of the parliamentary opposition seemed to give substance to those political hopes. With the enactment of a new constitution, however, it became clear that no major party could turn its back on Sinhalese nationalism. In the Constitution of 1978, as in the previous one, Sinhala remained the sole official language, Buddhism retained "the foremost place" under law, and federal autonomy was denied the Tamil areas. The political disillusionment that emerged in the early 1970s increased after the 1977 elections and gained added impetus after the anti-Tamil riots of 1981 and 1983. A progressive radicalization of the Tamil population led to a growth in the size and level of activity of militant groups, and the insurgency emerged as a growing threat to the power of the government.

Insurgent Groups

The largest and most influential of the Tamil insurgent groups was the Liberation Tigers of Tamil Eelam (Eelam is the original Tamil name for Sri Lanka). Founded in 1972 as the Tamil New Tigers, the group changed its name in 1976 as it accelerated its violent campaign for Tamil independence. The growth of the insurgency in the late 1970s brought with it an increasing fragmentation as personal, caste, and tactical differences divided the original movement. One of the earliest groups to break away was the People's Liberation Organization of Tamil Eelam (known variously as PLOT or PLOTE). The group was formed in 1981 by Uma Maheswaran, a disgruntled member of the Liberation Tigers of Tamil Eelam (LTTE) who had major disagreements with LTTE leader Prabhakaran. The new group claimed to represent a purer form of Marxist orthodoxy. Although ideological disputes may have been involved in the split, caste also seems to have played an important role; LTTE members were largely from Karaiya and low-caste urban backgrounds, whereas PLOT contained mostly Vellala, a high-caste rural group (see Caste, ch. 2).

A host of other groups emerged in the early 1980s. Like the LTTE, most of these organizations espoused a Marxist ideology that appeared prominently in their publications but seemed to play only a minor role in their activities and indoctrination. Chief among these new groups were the Tamil Eelam Liberation Organization (TELO), the Eelam People's Revolutionary Liberation Front, the Tamil Eelam Liberation Army, the Tamil Eelam Army, and the Eelam Revolutionary Organization of Students (EROS). Known collectively as "Tigers" or simply "the boys," these groups operated in changing patterns of competition and cooperation, forming a variety of coalitions (such as the Eelam National Liberation Front and the Three Stars). Through a series of armed attacks, the LTTE eliminated TELO, a major rival, and by late 1986 had established itself as the dominant, if not the sole, spokesman of the Tamil insurgency.

Financial and technical support for the Tamil movement came from a variety of domestic and foreign sources. Internally, the Tigers relied on "taxes" either willingly donated or extorted from the local populace which were supplemented by a number of bank robberies. External support came from Tamils overseas, most notably in southern India, North America, and Western Europe. Many of the insurgent groups maintained headquarters and training facilities in the Indian state of Tamil Nadu, where the state government and a predominantly Tamil population were sympathetic to their insurgent brethren in Sri Lanka. Official Indian support was curtailed sharply, however, following the signing of the Indo-Sri Lankan Accord in July 1987. There were also unconfirmed reports that the Palestine Liberation Organization (PLO) had provided training at its installations in the Middle East.

Major Incidents of the Insurgency

After the assassination of Jaffna's mayor in 1975, the militant groups accelerated their campaign of violence and destabilization. Their early targets included policemen, soldiers, and a number of Tamil politicians who were seen as collaborators with the Sinhalese-dominated government. The attacks were sporadic, relying largely on hit-and-run tactics.

In July 1983, the LTTE ambushed a military convoy in Northern Province, killing thirteen soldiers. The attack sparked off a conflagration of communal violence in which approximately 350 Tamils were killed and as many as 100,000 were forced to flee their homes. Indiscriminate violence by Sinhalese mobs and members of the security forces led to insecurity and alienation among the Tamil population, and support for the insurgency grew dramatically. The year 1984 was marked by a substantial increase in terrorist attacks, and the militants turned increasingly against civilian targets. Major incidents included an armed attack against civilians in the ancient Sinhalese city of Anuradhapura (May 1985—146 dead); the detonation of a bomb aboard an Air Lanka jet at the Bandaranaike International Airport (May 1986—20 dead); and a massive explosion at the Pettah bus station in Colombo during rush hour (April 1987—110 dead).

As the Tamil movement grew and obtained more weapons, it changed tactics. A full-fledged insurgency that could confront the armed forces replaced the isolated terrorist incidents that had characterized the early period. By early 1986, the LTTE had won virtual control of the Jaffna Peninsula, confining the army to military bases and taking over the day-to-day administration of the city of Jaffna. In January 1987, the Tigers attempted to formalize their authority over the peninsula by establishing an ''Eelam Secretariat.'' LTTE leaders claimed that this was intended simply to consolidate functions that the insurgents were already performing, i.e., collecting taxes and operating basic public services. Nonetheless, the government interpreted this move as a unilateral declaration of independence and thus a challenge to governmental authority.

In response, the government launched a major offensive against Jaffna in May and June 1987. The security forces succeeded in destroying major insurgent bases and regaining control of most of the peninsula, but at the cost of growing political pressure from India. Reports of army brutality and high civilian casualties among the Tamil population made the offensive increasingly unacceptable to the Indian government, which had its own substantial Tamil minority to worry about. In early June, Indian Air Force planes invaded Sri Lankan airspace to drop relief supplies into embattled Tamil areas, sending a message to the Sri Lankan government that the offensive would not be allowed to continue. Within a week, the Sri Lankan government announced the successful completion of its campaign.

On July 29, 1987, President Jayewardene signed an accord with India designed to bring an end to the more than ten years of violence between the Sri Lankan government and the Tamil minority. The accord provided for the disarming of militant groups under the supervision of the Indian Peacekeeping Force and the granting of limited autonomy to the primarily Tamil regions in Northern and Eastern provinces. The terms of the accord provoked immediate criticism from a number of directions. For Sinhalese nationalists, including several high-level officials in Jayewardene's government, the agreement was a threat to the unitary nature of Sri Lanka, virtually sanctioning a separate Tamil nation within the island. Tamil militants questioned the basic validity of the accord; although prime participants in the conflict, they had not been included in the negotiations leading to the accord, and their later accession had been secured under extreme pressure from the Indian government. For the wider community of Tamils and Sinhalese, the presence of Indian troops, even in a peacekeeping role, represented an unacceptable compromise of sovereignty.

These criticisms became increasingly acute when, in October 1987, the Tamil militants and the Indian-Sri Lankan forces accused each other of violating the accord, and the fighting resumed. Indian forces were expanded from an initial 3,000 troops to more than 70,000, and the Indian Peacekeeping Force launched a major assault that succeeded in taking Jaffna in late October (see Foreign Military Presence, this ch.). Most of the insurgents managed to escape and, according to press reports, regrouped in Mannar in Northern Province and in Batticaloa and other areas of Eastern Province. Weakened and cut off from their original bases and sources of supply, the Tigers were no longer able to conduct positional warfare against the security forces, but they claimed that they would continue their struggle through terrorist attacks.

The intervention of Indian forces in the north allowed the Sri Lankan Army to concentrate on another crisis that was developing in the south; Sinhalese nationalist opposition to the Indo-Sri Lankan Accord had turned violent, breaking out in strikes and street demonstrations. In the midst of this disorder, an old Sinhalese extremist organization was gaining in support and threatened to launch its second bid for power.

The Janatha Vimukthi Peramuna

The leftist Sinhalese Janatha Vimukthi Peramuna drew worldwide attention when it launched an insurrection against the Bandaranaike government in April 1971. Although the insurgents were young, poorly armed, and inadequately trained, they succeeded in seizing and holding major areas in Southern and Central provinces before they were defeated by the security forces. Their attempt to seize power created a major crisis for the government and forced a fundamental reassessment of the nation's security needs.

The movement was started in the late 1960s by Rohana Wijeweera, the son of a businessman from the seaport of Tangalla, Hambantota District. An excellent student, Wijeweera had been forced to give up his studies for financial reasons. Through friends of his father, a member of the Ceylon Communist Party, Wijeweera successfully applied for a scholarship in the Soviet Union, and in 1960 at the age of seventeen, he went to Moscow to study medicine at Patrice Lumumba University. While in Moscow, he studied Marxist ideology but, because of his openly expressed sympathies for Maoist revolutionary theory, he was denied a visa to return to the Soviet Union after a brief trip home in 1964. Over the next several years, he participated in the pro-Beijing branch of the Ceylon Communist Party, but he was increasingly at odds with party leaders and impatient with its lack of revolutionary purpose. His success in working with youth groups and his popularity as a public speaker led him to organize his own movement in 1967. Initially identified simply as the New Left, this group drew on students and unemployed youths from rural areas, most of them in the sixteen-to-twenty-five age-group. Many of these new recruits were members of lower castes (Karava and Durava) who felt that their economic interests had been neglected by the nation's leftist coalitions. The standard program of indoctrination, the so-called Five Lectures, included discussions of Indian imperialism, the growing economic crisis, the failure of the island's communist and socialist parties, and the need for a sudden, violent seizure of power.

Between 1967 and 1970, the group expanded rapidly, gaining control of the student socialist movement at a number of major university campuses and winning recruits and sympathizers within the armed forces. Some of these latter supporters actually provided sketches of police stations, airports, and military facilities that were important to the initial success of the revolt. In order to draw the newer members more tightly into the organization and to prepare them for a coming confrontation, Wijeweera opened "education camps" in several remote areas along the south and southwestern coasts. These camps provided training in Marxism-Leninism and in basic military skills.

While developing secret cells and regional commands, Wijeweera's group also began to take a more public role during the elections of 1970. His cadres campaigned openly for the United Front of Sirimavo R. D. Bandaranaike, but at the same time they distributed posters and pamphlets promising violent rebellion if Bandaranaike did not address the interests of the proletariat. In a manifesto issued during this period, the group used the name Janatha Vimukthi Peramuna for the first time. Because of the subversive tone of these publications, the United National Party government had Wijeweera detained during the elections, but the victorious Bandaranaike ordered his release in July 1970. In the politically tolerant atmosphere of the next few months, as the new government attempted to win over a wide variety of unorthodox leftist groups, the JVP intensified both the public campaign and the private preparations for a revolt. Although their group was relatively small, the members hoped to immobilize the government by selective kidnapping and sudden, simultaneous strikes against the security forces throughout the island. Some of the necessary weapons had been bought with funds supplied by the members. For the most part, however, they relied on raids against police stations and army camps to secure weapons, and they manufactured their own bombs.

The discovery of several JVP bomb factories gave the government its first evidence that the group's public threats were to be taken seriously. In March 1971, after an accidental explosion in one of these factories, the police found fifty-eight bombs in a hut in Nelundeniya, Kegalla District. Shortly afterward, Wijeweera was arrested and sent to Jaffna Prison, where he remained throughout the revolt. In response to his arrest and the growing pressure of police investigations, other JVP leaders decided to act immediately, and they agreed to begin the uprising at 11:00 P.M. on April 5.

The planning for the countrywide insurrection was hasty and poorly coordinated; some of the district leaders were not informed until the morning of the uprising. After one premature attack, security forces throughout the island were put on alert and a number of JVP leaders went into hiding without bothering to inform their subordinates of the changed circumstances. In spite of this confusion, rebel groups armed with shotguns, bombs, and Molotov cocktails launched simultaneous attacks against seventy-four police stations around the island and cut power to major urban areas. The attacks were most successful in the south. By April 10, the rebels had taken control of Matara District and the city of Ambalangoda in Galle District and came close to capturing the remaining areas of Southern Province.

The new government was ill prepared for the crisis that confronted it. Although there had been some warning that an attack was imminent, Bandaranaike was caught off guard by the scale of the uprising and was forced to call on India to provide basic security functions. Indian frigates patrolled the coast and Indian troops guarded Bandaranaike International Airport at Katunayaka while Indian Air Force helicopters assisted the counteroffensive. Sri Lanka's all-volunteer army had no combat experience since World War II and no training in counterinsurgency warfare. Although the police were able to defend some areas unassisted, in many places the government deployed personnel from all three services in a ground force capacity. Royal Ceylon Air Force helicopters delivered relief supplies to beleaguered police stations while combined service patrols drove the insurgents out of urban areas and into the countryside.

After two weeks of fighting, the government regained control of all but a few remote areas. In both human and political terms, the cost of the victory was high: an estimated 10,000 insurgents—many of them in their teens—died in the conflict, and the army was widely perceived to have used excessive force. In order to win over an alienated population and to prevent a prolonged conflict, Bandaranaike offered amnesties in May and June 1971, and only the top leaders were actually imprisoned. Wijeweera, who was already in detention at the time of the uprising, was given a twenty-year sentence and the JVP was proscribed.

Under the six years of emergency rule that followed the uprising, the JVP remained dormant. After the victory of the United National Party in the 1977 elections, however, the new government attempted to broaden its mandate with a period of political tolerance. Wijeweera was freed, the ban was lifted, and the JVP entered the arena of legal political competition. As a candidate in the 1982 presidential elections, Wijeweera finished fourth, with more than 250,000 votes (as compared with Jayewardene's 3.2 million). During this period, and especially as the Tamil conflict to the north became more intense, there was a marked shift in the ideology and goals of the JVP. Initially Marxist in orientation, and claiming to represent the oppressed of both the Tamil and Sinhalese communities, the group emerged increasingly as a Sinhalese nationalist organization opposing any compromise with the Tamil insurgency. This new orientation became explicit in the anti-Tamil riots of July 1983. Because of its role in inciting violence, the JVP was once again banned and its leadership went underground.

The group's activities intensified in the second half of 1987 in the wake of the Indo-Sri Lankan Accord. The prospect of Tamil autonomy in the north together with the presence of Indian troops stirred up a wave of Sinhalese nationalism and a sudden growth of antigovernment violence. During 1987 a new group emerged that was an offshoot of the JVP—the Patriotic Liberation Organization (Deshapremi Janatha Viyaparaya—DJV). The DJV claimed responsibility for the August 1987 assassination attempts against the president and prime minister. In addition, the group launched a campaign of intimidation against the ruling party, killing more than seventy members of Parliament between July and November.

Along with the group's renewed violence came a renewed fear of infiltration of the armed forces. Following the successful raid of the Pallekelle army camp in May 1987, the government conducted an investigation that resulted in the discharge of thirty-seven soldiers suspected of having links with the JVP. In order to prevent a repetition of the 1971 uprising, the government considered lifting the ban on the JVP in early 1988 and permitting the group to participate again in the political arena. With Wijeweera still underground, however, the JVP had no clear leadership at the time, and it was uncertain whether it had the cohesion to mount any coordinated offensive, either military or political, against the government.

The Armed Forces

The armed forces of Sri Lanka bear the clear imprint of the British institutions and traditions that shaped them. The army was initially formed as a volunteer force to supplement the British military presence in the late nineteenth century, and British leadership of Sri Lankan troops continued through World War II. Even after independence, Britain continued to play a major role in training, equipping, and symbolically leading of the Sri Lankan armed forces.

During the 1970s and 1980s, the armed forces were greatly expanded and regularized in an attempt to cope with the growing problems of domestic instability. Despite these efforts, the military still lacked both the strength and the training to handle the crises that confronted the nation, and on two occasions the Sri Lankan government asked India to send in troops to restore internal order.

Because of their limited size and the pressing demands of internal security, the military forces have not been deployed overseas. Rare exceptions have been the dispatch of small military observer groups, in connection with international peacekeeping efforts, such as the United Nations force on the Indo-Pakistani border in 1966. In their largely domestic mission of internal defense, the armed forces resemble the paramilitary and police forces of larger nations. Since independence, their role has gradually expanded to include counterinsurgency and counterterrorism, controlling illegal immigration and smuggling, protecting vital institutions and government officials, and providing emergency relief during national disasters.

Historical Background

Ancient Military Traditions

Warfare plays a central role in the historical traditions of Sri Lanka. The two great literary works of this early period—the *Mahavamsa* and the *Culavamsa*—relate in great detail the battles and campaigns of the ancient kingdoms (see Ancient Legends and Chronicles, ch. 1). For most of Sri Lanka's history, these conflicts were confined to the island and its coastal waters as the various kingdoms battled with each other or attempted to repel new waves of immigrants and invaders from the mainland. In the twelfth century, however, Parakramabahu I was able to unify the island and assemble a military force strong enough to engage in conflicts overseas. In 1164 he sent a naval force to Burma to retaliate for the poor treatment his envoys had received. In another expedition, to southern India, his army took part in a succession struggle for the Pandyan throne.

Thirteenth-century manuscripts tell of "four-fold" armies in which divisions of elephants, chariots, cavalry, and infantry confronted each other in battle. Troops in this period were raised by local levies among ordinary citizens, while special corps of "moonlight archers" and mace-bearers were given extended training. Foreign mercenaries played an important role in these armies, with Indians (Tamils, Keralas, and Rajputs) especially prominent.

The Armed Forces under British Rule

Centuries of colonial rule by the Portuguese, Dutch, and British interrupted Sri Lanka's martial traditions (see European Encroachment and Dominance, 1500-1948, ch. 1). The kingdoms of Jaffna, Kotte, and Kandy, divided by bitter rivalries, were unable to mount a unified opposition to the colonial powers, and one by one, the native armies fell to the superior force of the invaders. The British defeat of the Kingdom of Kandy in 1815-18 marked the end of an independent Sri Lankan military force. The institution of colonial rule, however, soon created the need for a native, military force to maintain order. To fill this need, the colonial government raised a contingent of light infantry named the Ceylon Rifles. The force was composed largely of Malay soldiers under British officers, and was the only formation of regular, full-time troops established in Sri Lanka during the colonial period. As such, its existence was brief, and when the maintenance of the unit became too costly, it was disbanded. From 1873 until independence, the island's entire indigenous force consisted of a volunteer reservist army.

The first component of this new army, the Ceylon Light Infantry Volunteers, was established in 1881 by proclamation of the lieutenant governor. Like the Ceylon Rifles, the new volunteer force was commanded by British officers, while the ranks were filled out largely with Burghers, a highly Westernized group that adapted well to the demands of volunteer service (see Ethnic Groups, ch. 2). A mounted infantry company was added in 1892, and in 1900 this contingent was called to South Africa to assist the British army in the Boer War.

In 1910 the volunteer corps was redesignated as the Ceylon Defence Force. Although Sri Lankan units were not deployed outside the island in either of the world wars, individual soldiers served in the British and British Indian armies. In World War II, the British crown took direct control of the island's armed forces from the colonial government. During this period, the Ceylon Light Infantry grew from 1 battalion to 5 battalions, while the total number of troops in uniform increased to 12,000. Most of these were engaged in maintenance and transport functions. Their most direct contact with the war came in April 1942 when the Japanese launched an air attack on Colombo.

The Armed Forces after Independence

The advent of independence and dominion status in 1948 brought with it a series of changes in the designation and legal basis for the armed forces. In 1949 the legislature passed a bill authorizing the creation of the Royal Ceylon Army, Royal Ceylon Navy, and Royal Ceylon Air Force. The army was formed in October of that year, and the navy and air force were established in 1950 and 1951, respectively. These developments brought substantial changes at the highest levels of command, establishing an independent military force in the hands of an indigenous government for the first time in more than 100 years. At the level of individual units, however, the military order established by the British remained largely unchanged; the officers who took over as the force commanders had received their training under the British and, in many cases, in military academies in Britain. The basic structure of the colonial forces was retained, as were the symbolic trappings—the flags, banners, and regimental ceremonies (the Duke of Gloucester continued to serve as the honorary colonel of the Light Infantry until 1972).

Dutch fort, Galle
Courtesy Doranne Jacobson

In the early years following independence, military affairs received a relatively low priority; external security was guaranteed by a mutual security arrangement with Britain, while the function of internal security was usually left to the police. In this period, the armed forces served a largely ceremonial function, providing honor guards for state visits and occasionally helping to maintain public order. From 1949 to 1955, military expenses took up between 1 and 4 percent of the national budget (as compared with 20 percent for India and 35 to 40 percent for Pakistan in the same period), and the regular forces comprised only about 3,000 officers and enlisted personnel. (This represented a significant drop from the wartime high of 12,000, some of whom had been transferred into the reserve forces).

Even without sophisticated weaponry and training, this token military force was able to conduct the immigration-control and anti-smuggling operations that formed the bulk of its security missions in the 1950s and 1960s. Growing ethnic tensions after 1956 spawned a number of public disturbances in which the army was called to aid the civil powers, but these were largely local and small-scale events that offered no opportunity for traditional military operations. When the leftist Janatha Vimukthi Peramuna made its bid for power in April 1971, it confronted an army totally without combat experience and lacking the training necessary to deal with

233

a large-scale insurgency (see The Janatha Vimukthi Peramuna, this ch.).

In the wake of the 1971 insurrection, the government began to cope with some of the more glaring deficiencies of the armed forces. It immediately initiated a campaign to increase the size of each of the three services. In addition, the troops were reorganized to reflect the new concern with internal subversion; in 1972 the army was divided into area commands, and individual battalions were reinforced with larger rifle companies and additional support companies. Training in this period tended to focus on counterinsurgency and jungle warfare. At the same time, because of the army's greater operational commitments, collective training was suspended entirely for a year, and then resumed only at the platoon level.

Despite these reforms, the armed forces were once again unprepared for the outbreak of ethnic and political violence that shook the nation in 1983 (see The United National Party Returns to Power, ch. 1). This time, the military leadership was faced with a more complex set of problems, for the conflict threw into question not only the force's readiness, but also its reliability as a defender of public order. In responding to the anti-Tamil rioting that broke out in July 1983, the army was widely accused of failing to restrain the Sinhalese mobs and of actively participating in acts of intimidation, arson, and murder against the civilian population. A 1983 report issued by the International Commission of Jurists documents instances of army soldiers "going on the rampage," burning Tamil homes, and indiscriminately killing civilians in retaliation for Tamil militant attacks on army patrols.

Such reports played a major role in exacerbating the ethnic conflict and in fostering support for the Tamil Tigers among the Tamil civilian population. The perception of the armed forces as the ethnic army of Sinhalese nationalism stemmed from a number of sources. First, beginning in the early 1960s, the government adopted a military recruitment program that deliberately favored Sinhalese candidates (see Structure and Administration of the Armed Forces, this ch.). A force that had originally contained a disproportionately high number of minorities (especially Tamils and Burghers) came to be more than 95 percent Sinhalese by the early 1980s. Furthermore, the role of political and military leaders during the 1983 rioting suggested that the anti-Tamil violence of the security forces was receiving sympathy, if not outright support, at high levels. For several days after the rioting began, President Jayewardene refrained from any public condemnation of the violence. When he did finally speak out, it was to denounce the Tamil insurgents and the forces of separatism. Military leaders were similarly slow to call to account those soldiers responsible for atrocities.

In the face of a growing Tamil insurgency, the armed forces remained seriously understrength. The army's fighting force nominally consisted of five regiments, each consisting of one regular and two volunteer battalions. In fact, only one of these regiments had the full complement of volunteers, and these recruits were poorly trained and equipped. The regular forces themselves were below nominal staffing levels, and navy and air force personnel were frequently deployed to fill up the infantry ranks. Understaffing similarly plagued the signal, armored, and engineering units and hampered their support missions.

New and unaccustomed functions also impeded the Sri Lankan troop performance response. With the sudden growth of the Tamil separatist movement in the early 1980s, the role of the armed forces evolved from civil patrol to antiterrorism and eventually to counterinsurgency. The army and the Special Task Force of the police played the central role in these operations, launching attacks against suspected Tamil insurgent bases and rounding up Tamil men for questioning. The navy assisted with coastal patrols to interdict arms shipments from south India, and the air force was involved in transport and supply. Despite the creation of the Joint Operations Command in 1985, the coordination of anti-insurgent operations continued to be poor. During this period, the government failed to provide an effective strategy for isolating the insurgents and securing the Tamil civilian population.

By 1986 the insurgent movement had gained enough support to seize control of the entire Jaffna Peninsula. For more than a year, the armed forces in the area were confined to short ventures in the immediate vicinity of their base camps. Finally, spurred on by the threatened formation of a Tamil "Eelam Secretariat," the government launched an assault to regain the peninsula (see The Tamil Insurgency, this ch.). The offensive was preceded by a two-month fuel embargo to limit the mobility of the insurgents. Then, in May 1987, the armed forces began "Operation Liberation," a coordinated land, sea, and air attack involving 3,000 troops, the largest single force ever deployed by the Sri Lankan government. While air force helicopter gunships and fighter-bombers targeted known rebel strongholds, the army, under cover of artillery shelling, moved out of its camps in armored vehicles and expanded its area of operations. The task force gradually eliminated major Tamil bases along the northern coast with the assistance of gunfire from Sri Lankan naval vessels, and by the first week of June, succeeded in driving most of the insurgents into the city of Jaffna.

Because an assault on Jaffna itself would involve large-scale urban fighting that would cause numerous civilian casualties, the Indian government interposed its objections to the forthcoming offensive. Faced with a threat of Indian armed intervention on behalf of the insurgents, the Sri Lankan government declared a successful end to the operation. The Indo-Sri Lankan Accord that followed provided for Indian troops to supervise the disarming of the insurgents in the north, and the Sri Lankan armed forces accordingly took up positions in the southern and eastern parts of the island. When Tamils resumed armed assaults in September 1987, the security forces returned to the antiterrorist activities that had been their primary function before 1985.

Structure and Administration of the Armed Forces

The armed forces consist of the Sri Lankan Army, Navy, and Air Force. As stipulated in the 1978 Constitution, the president of Sri Lanka is the commander in chief of the armed forces and has the sole authority to declare war and peace. Under the president, the formal chain of command includes the prime minister, the minister of defense, and the individual service commanders. In order to consolidate control over the armed forces, Jayewardene also assumed the portfolio of minister of defense when he took office in 1977. In March 1984, the additional position of minister of internal security was created in response to the ethnic turmoil of the previous summer. Its incumbent was primarily responsible for the coordination of government efforts in the eradication of Tamil extremist violence and reported directly to the president. On the operational level, the government created a Joint Operations Command in 1985 to coordinate the anti-insurgent and antiterrorist activities of the army, navy, air force, and police. This council was chaired by the president and included, among others, the prime minister, the minister of internal security, the three service commanders, the inspector general of police, the director of the National Intelligence Bureau, and the general officer commanding joint operations.

The Army

The Sri Lankan Army is the oldest and largest of the nation's three armed services. It was established as the Royal Ceylon Army in 1949, and was renamed when Sri Lanka became a republic in 1972. The commander of the army exercises direct operational control over the force. In early 1988, the government announced a major reorganization of the army, creating several high-level posts to accommodate the new structure. Under this revised chain of command, the commander of the army (upgraded from lieutenant general to general) will be assisted by a deputy commander (a lieutenant general) and a chief of staff (a major general). Apart from the Colombo District, which will be under the direct authority of Army Headquarters, the island will be divided into two area commands and twenty-one sectors. Each area command is scheduled to have 12,000 troops under the authority of a major general, with a brigadier as chief of staff. When the reorganization is completed, each sector will have a full battalion of troops dedicated to its defense.

Like the Indian Army, the Sri Lankan Army has largely retained the British-style regimental system that it inherited upon independence. The individual regiments (such as the Sri Lanka Light Infantry and the Sinha Regiment) operated independently and recruited their own members. Officers tended to remain in a single battalion throughout their careers. The infantry battalion, the basic unit of organization in field operations, included five companies of four platoons each. Incomplete reports suggest that a typical platoon had three squads (sections) of ten personnel each. In addition to the basic infantry forces, a commando regiment was established in 1986. Support for the infantry was provided by two reconnaissance regiments (one regular, one reserve), two field artillery regiments (one regular, one reserve), one antiaircraft regiment, one field engineering regiment, one engineering plant regiment, one signals battalion, a medical corps, and a variety of logistics units.

In late 1987, the army had a total estimated strength of up to 40,000 troops, about evenly divided between regular army personnel and reservists on active duty. The approximately 20,000 regular army troops represented a significant increase over the 1983 strength of only 12,000. Aggressive recruitment campaigns following the 1983 riots raised this number to 16,000 by early 1985.

After the 1971 uprising, the army expanded its range of weapons from the original stock of World War II-era British Lee Enfield rifles and 4.2-inch heavy mortars. New sources of weaponry in the mid-to-late 1970s included the Soviet Union, Yugoslavia, and China, countries with which the left-leaning Bandaranaike government had the closest ties. China continued to be an important source into the 1980s, and was joined by Australia, Italy, South Africa, Israel,and the United States. New equipment included 85mm field guns, light trucks, and armored personnel carriers. Chinese copies of Soviet small arms were the basic weapons used by the infantry. Of particular note were the Type 56 semiautomatic rifle (based on the Soviet AK), the Type 69 rocket launcher (like the Soviet

RPG-7), and the Type 56 light machine gun, a copy of the Soviet 7.62mm RPD.

Despite the rapid acquisition of trucks and armored personnel carriers, individual units of the army had no transportation capability of their own, and most patrols were carried out on foot. Helicopters were available only for special operations, and most troop transport was by ordinary buses or minibuses. This situation frequently left troops vulnerable to mines, and many of the army's casualties occurred in this fashion, rather than in face-to-face combat with the insurgents. Because of the small geographical area within which the forces were deployed, long supply lines were not necessary, and individual units frequently made their own decisions about what rations to carry on a given operation.

Most training is provided at the Army Training Centre in Diyatalawa, Badulla District, Uva Province. The center encompasses three separate facilities: the Sri Lankan Military Academy, the Non-Commissioned Officers' School, and the Recruit Training School. The Military Academy was founded in 1981 and absorbed the earlier Officers' Cadet School and the Officers' Study Center. In the late 1980s, it was providing training in tactics and administration, and its graduates were commissioned as officers in the regular forces. The officer cadets' course lasted ninety weeks and prepared cadets to serve as platoon commanders. It included military and academic subjects as well as physical training, and placed a special emphasis on fostering leadership qualities and an understanding of the role of the officer as a servant of the state. Because of an extreme shortage of officers at the lower levels, a short commission course was developed to speed the training process. Cadets in this course received fifty-six weeks of training and committed themselves to five years of service with the option of continuing their careers in the military. The Army Training Centre handled approximately 300 recruits at a time and, in 1982, reportedly trained 18 officers. Additional training is provided by individual field units.

Cadet training was offered at the Sir John Kotelawala Defence Academy established in 1981 in Ratmalana, fourteen kilometers south of Colombo. (The academy was named after the nation's third prime minister.) Each year, the academy admits fifty cadets (ages seventeen to nineteen) for a three-year program of academic work and basic training. Graduates continue their studies at a regular university before taking up a full-time career in the military services.

With the limited capacity of indigenous training facilities, the armed forces have relied extensively on foreign military training.

The British played a central role in the early years following independence and have continued to be an important source of military expertise. Other sources have included Pakistan, Australia, Malaysia, and the United States. In addition, in an agreement reached in 1984, Israeli security personnel (reportedly from Shin Bet, the Israeli counterespionage and internal security organization) went to Sri Lanka to train army officers in counterinsurgency techniques (see Foreign Military Relations, this ch.).

The Navy

The Sri Lankan Navy, originally established in December 1950 as the Royal Ceylon Navy, is the smallest of the nation's armed services. It consists of a regular and a volunteer force, each with its own reserve component. The navy is under the direct operational control of a service commander who is equal in authority to the army and air force commanders. The force is divided into three Naval Area Commands—Northern, Eastern, and Western—with a fourth (Southern Command) to be established at a later date. The navy maintains major bases in Colombo and Trincomalee, with secondary bases at Karainagar (Jaffna District), Welisara (Colombo District), Tangalla (Hambantota District), and Kalpitiya (Puttalam District).

The navy's primary mission is to prevent illegal immigration and smuggling across the Palk Strait, the narrow body of water that separates the island from the Indian state of Tamil Nadu. With the growth of the Tamil separatist movement in the late 1970s, the strait became a major conduit for armaments and insurgents traveling from training bases in south India, and the naval mission was therefore expanded to include counterinsurgency patrols.

In the late 1980s, the navy had an approximate total strength of 4,000, including active reservists. By 1985 estimates, the regular force contained 243 officers and 3,072 ratings, and the Volunteer Naval Force had 64 officers and 427 men, a substantial increase over the 1977 figures (200 officers, 2,400 ratings).

In late 1987, the navy had a fleet of approximately seventy vessels, more than half of them coastal patrol craft. Building on an original fleet of mostly British ships, the government took aggressive steps to expand its sources of supply and at the same time develop a domestic shipbuilding industry sufficient to meet national defense needs. As a result, the Colombo dockyards began production of the 40-ton Pradeepa coastal patrol craft in 1980, followed by the 330-ton Jayasagara large patrol craft. The original fleet of six Sooraya fast attack craft (the Chinese Shanghai-II, bought in 1972 and 1975) was supplemented in 1985 with six Israeli Super

Dvora craft, and eight more were reportedly on order. One serious gap in the fleet was the lack of shallow-draft vessels suitable for surveying purposes. Palk Strait, although relatively narrow, is infamously difficult to navigate because of the large number of uncharted coral reefs.

A cumbersome bureaucratic structure prevented the navy from fully carrying out the basic elements of its intended mission. Although the fleet inventory improved steadily, logistical support to naval vessels was a continuing problem that resulted in poor performance and low morale throughout the service. The matériel procurement process was reportedly complex and inefficient, and spare parts for foreign-made vessels were frequently in short supply. Even where the necessary parts were available, poorly trained maintenance personnel were not always able to repair breakdowns, and inadequate administrative support compounded the difficulties.

Full maintenance facilities were available at the Colombo dockyard, where dry-dock equipment was expanded to allow construction of large patrol vessels in the 1980s. In addition, the base in Trincomalee was fitted out to perform slipway repairs. At both facilities, a shortage of qualified maintenance personnel continued to hamper effective repair work.

General training for officers and ratings was being provided at the Naval and Maritime Academy in Trincomalee in the 1980s. The academy was established in 1967, and offered a fifteen-month basic course in navigation, seamanship, and engineering. Seamen were given practical training on commercial cargo ships. For postgraduate technical training, recruits were sent overseas, mainly to India, Pakistan, Australia, the United States, and Britain.

The Air Force

The Sri Lankan Air Force is the youngest of the three armed services. Founded in 1951 as the Royal Ceylon Air Force, it relied totally on the British Royal Air Force for its earliest equipment, training, and leadership. The service was led by a force commander and its operational headquarters were located in Ratmalana, south of Colombo. The air force operates major air bases at Katunayaka in Colombo District and China Bay (Trincomalee), with a secondary base in Jaffna.

In 1988 the air force was divided into four functionally defined squadrons, with a variety of support units: Number One (Flight Training School) Squadron, China Bay Air Base; Number Two (Transport) Squadron, Katunayaka Air Base; Number Three (Navigation) Squadron, China Bay Air Base; and Number Four (Helicopter) Squadron, Katunayaka Air Base. Support units included an electronic engineering division, an aeronautical division, and administrative, operations, medical, logistics, and procurement units. In addition, the force operated two antiaircraft gun battery sections and a small Air Force Security Force.

In its early years, the air force was engaged primarily in immigration patrol, with occasional assistance in emergency relief. During the insurgency of 1971, the air force played a major role in restoring internal order; in addition to providing transport of ammunition, food, and troops, it participated in assaults against insurgent strongholds. Following the ethnic rioting of 1983, the air force was placed on permanent active status and participated in counterinsurgent activities in Northern Province. Because of a severe shortage of hard currency for military expenditures in the wake of the 1971 uprising, the Number Four (Helicopter) Squadron began operating commercial transportation services for foreign tourists under the name of Helitours. In 1987 the air force had a total strength of 3,700 personnel, including active reserves. The force had grown gradually during its early years, reaching a little over 1,000 officers and recruits in the 1960s. Rapid growth began in the mid-1980s, when the ethnic disturbances drew the service into a major, long-term security role. Between 1983 and 1987, the force grew by nearly 50 percent.

The air force had a fleet of approximately eighty aircraft, of which sixty-four were reported to be operational in early 1988. The earliest aircraft—small transport airplanes and trainers—were provided by the British and were supplemented in the late 1960s with United States Bell helicopters. During the 1971 insurgency, the left-leaning Bandaranaike government turned to the Soviet Union for more sophisticated weaponry, and received five MiG-17 F fighter bombers, a MiG-15UTI Midget trainer, and two Ka-26 helicopters. The British also assisted with five BAC Jet Provosts. By the early 1980s, the Provosts and all of the Soviet aircraft had been taken out of active service and were relegated to long-term storage, leaving the air force without any bomber capability.

After the 1983 riots, the government worked rapidly to expand the inventory, relying largely on sources in Italy, Britain, and the United States. Because of tight budget constraints, the air force was compelled to refit a number of noncombat aircraft for military uses in counterinsurgency operations against Tamil separatists. Central in the government's security efforts were six SIAI-Marchetti SF–260 turboprop trainers which were used for rocket attacks and strafing. Additionally, the air force, with the help of Heli Orient of Singapore, equipped twelve Bell 212 and 412 helicopters to serve as gunships and as transport vehicles for commando assault

241

Sri Lanka: A Country Study

operations. Government forces reportedly also used helicopters on "bombing" missions; frequently operating without conventional bombs, air force troops reportedly dropped hand grenades stuffed in wine glasses so that the lever would not be released until the glass shattered on the ground. A more effective bombing capability was provided by a small fleet of Chinese Yun-12 turboprop transport aircraft. These were equipped with bomb racks that had been fitted to carry up to 1,000 kilograms of fragmentation and anti-personnel bombs. Transport, training, and surveying functions were carried out by a variety of Cessna and DeHavilland aircraft.

As in the other services, a shortage of spare parts plagued maintenance efforts, forcing the service to send a number of aircraft to Singapore and elsewhere for repairs. After the purchase of equipment from Canada in 1986, the air force gained the capability to make structural repairs on its fleet of Bell helicopters, several of which had been damaged in operations against the Tamil insurgents. Maintenance of electronic equipment was performed at the communications station at Ekala, in the north of Colombo District.

Under the auspices of the British Royal Air Force, flight training was first offered to Ceylon Air Force pilots at Katunayaka Air Base in 1952. In addition, a number of recruits received flight training at the Royal Air Force college in Cranwell, England. After the British withdrew from Sri Lankan military facilities in 1967, the Number One (Flight Training School) Squadron was established at the China Bay Air Base in Trincomalee. With the increase in insurgent activities in the mid-1980s, the air force stepped up its training activities, bringing in foreign pilots to assist in the helicopter training program.

Officer training is provided at the Air Force Academy at the China Bay Air Base. The academy offers a two-year program of basic flight training and a variety of specialized courses. Air traffic controllers receive schooling at special facilities in Colombo, and weapons familiarity training is conducted in conjunction with the other services at the Army Training Centre in Diyatalawa. In addition, approximately twenty-five officers a year receive advanced training abroad, most commonly in Britain and India.

Conditions of Service

The regular forces of the army, navy, and air force were recruited by voluntary enlistment (see fig. 12). Despite the influence of Buddhist pacifist traditions, the prestige of government service and the possibility of a stable income have insured a sufficient flow of new recruits into the three services even prior to the establishment of a national draft in 1985. As a result of stringent Sinhala language requirements, noncommissioned (NCO) ranks of all services were virtually all Sinhalese. In the army, regular enlisted personnel were required to sign contracts that were renewable after the fifth and twelfth years of service. Renewal was contingent on the receipt of good performance ratings. After twenty-two years of service, individuals became eligible for pensions, and in the 1980s the average age of retirement for the enlisted ranks was forty-two. After completing regular service, recruits were required to fulfill seven years of obligatory service in the reserves. Officers were allowed to serve in each rank for a specified number of years, after which they had either to qualify for the next higher rank or retire. Because of the small number of positions available at the higher levels, most officers were forced to leave the service at about forty-five years of age (see fig. 13).

Separate recruiting was conducted for the First Commando Regiment of the army. Applicants for NCO positions had to be single and between eighteen and twenty-two years old, and must have passed the Ordinary Levels of the General Common Entrance examination in six subjects. Candidates were offered the possibility of specialized training overseas in such fields as intelligence, parachuting, and dog handling. Within the navy, the small size of the total force enabled the leadership to remain highly selective in its recruitment, and naval personnel had a uniformly high literacy rate. Recruits committed themselves to ten years of obligatory service.

After retiring from active service, officers and enlisted personnel reportedly had considerable difficulty finding suitable employment. Priority placement in civil service jobs, commonly offered under the British administration, was no longer available to military retirees in the 1980s, and former officers spoke out with bitterness on the failure of the nation to repay its soldiers for their years of service. In addition, military pensions reportedly have not kept pace with inflation.

In October 1985, the Parliament passed the Mobilization and Supplementary Forces Act, which gave the government the power to draft citizens into the National Armed Reserve. Under this law, the prime minister, with the approval of Parliament, was authorized to conscript Sri Lankan citizens eighteen years or older for one year of basic training and a total of ten years of reserve service. Under normal conditions, reserves could be called into active service for up to twenty-one days per year. At the request of the president, however, reserves could be deployed in active service for an indefinite period of time in the event of a war or ''in the

SRI LANKAN RANK	PRIVATE	NO RANK	LANCE CORPORAL	CORPORAL	SERGEANT	STAFF SERGEANT	WARRANT OFFICER CLASS II	WARRANT OFFICER CLASS I
ARMY	NO INSIGNIA							
U.S. RANK TITLES	BASIC PRIVATE	PRIVATE	PRIVATE 1ST CLASS	CORPORAL	STAFF SERGEANT	SERGEANT 1ST CLASS	MASTER SERGEANT	COMMAND SERGEANT MAJOR
SRI LANKAN RANK	NO RANK	LEADING AIRCRAFTSMAN	NO RANK	CORPORAL	SERGEANT	FLIGHT SERGEANT	NO RANK	WARRANT OFFICER
AIR FORCE								
U.S. RANK TITLES	AIRMAN BASIC	AIRMAN	AIRMAN 1ST CLASS	SERGEANT	TECHNICAL SERGEANT	MASTER SERGEANT	SENIOR MASTER SERGEANT	CHIEF MASTER SERGEANT
SRI LANKAN RANK	NO RANK	NO RANK		LEADING SEAMAN	NO RANK	CHIEF PETTY OFFICER		MASTER CHIEF PETTY OFFICER
NAVY								
U.S. RANK TITLES	SEAMAN RECRUIT	APPRENTICE SEAMAN	SEAMAN	PETTY OFFICER 3D CLASS	PETTY OFFICER 1ST CLASS	CHIEF PETTY OFFICER	SENIOR CHIEF PETTY OFFICER	MASTER CHIEF PETTY OFFICER

Figure 12. Enlisted Rank Insignia, 1988

prevention or suppression of any rebellion or insurrection or other civil disturbance.''

Ethnic Composition of the Armed Forces

At independence the government inherited from the British a military establishment that was neither ethnically nor religiously representative of the population at large. Minorities, for example, were heavily overrepresented in the officer corps. Christians, who comprised about 8 percent of the population, accounted for about 50 percent of all officers. Ethnically, Tamils and Burghers, who together comprised less than 20 percent of the population, accounted for 40 percent of the officer corps. This unbalanced representation was the result of a number of deliberate policies and incidental developments under the British. As in India, the colonial government in Sri Lanka tended to favor certain minorities in the selection of both military and civil service posts. In addition, the greater willingness of the Tamils to attend Christian missionary schools gave them the advantage of knowing the language, faith, and value system of the colonial administration. These Christian schools were also more likely than their Buddhist counterparts to offer rigorous physical training; the student cadet corps that were common in the colonial tradition were anathema to the Buddhist pacifist orthodoxy. Finally, the largely Westernized Burgher population adapted more easily to the social and public values of a colonial force.

In the first few years of independence, the high representation of Christians and minorities in the military leadership was fully in step with the political currents of the time; the governments of Don Stephen Senanayake and Sir John Kotelawala were dominated by a Westernized elite that preached accommodation with all ethnic groups. Starting in the mid-1950s, however, a new Sinhalese and Buddhist nationalism turned increasingly against the British-sponsored elite of the colonial period. Within the government, this tendency was reflected in the victory of S.W.R.D. Bandaranaike in the 1956 elections. In the military, however, changes were much more gradual; most of the commissions that had become available in the newly created services were already filled, and the relatively young army had few officers approaching retirement age. As a result, this period was marked by an increasing strain between the civil and the military authorities. The government's program of nationalization and its attempt to establish a privileged place for Buddhism and the Sinhala language caused increasing conflict around the island. In January 1962, several high-ranking military officers were arrested and accused of planning a coup d'état. They

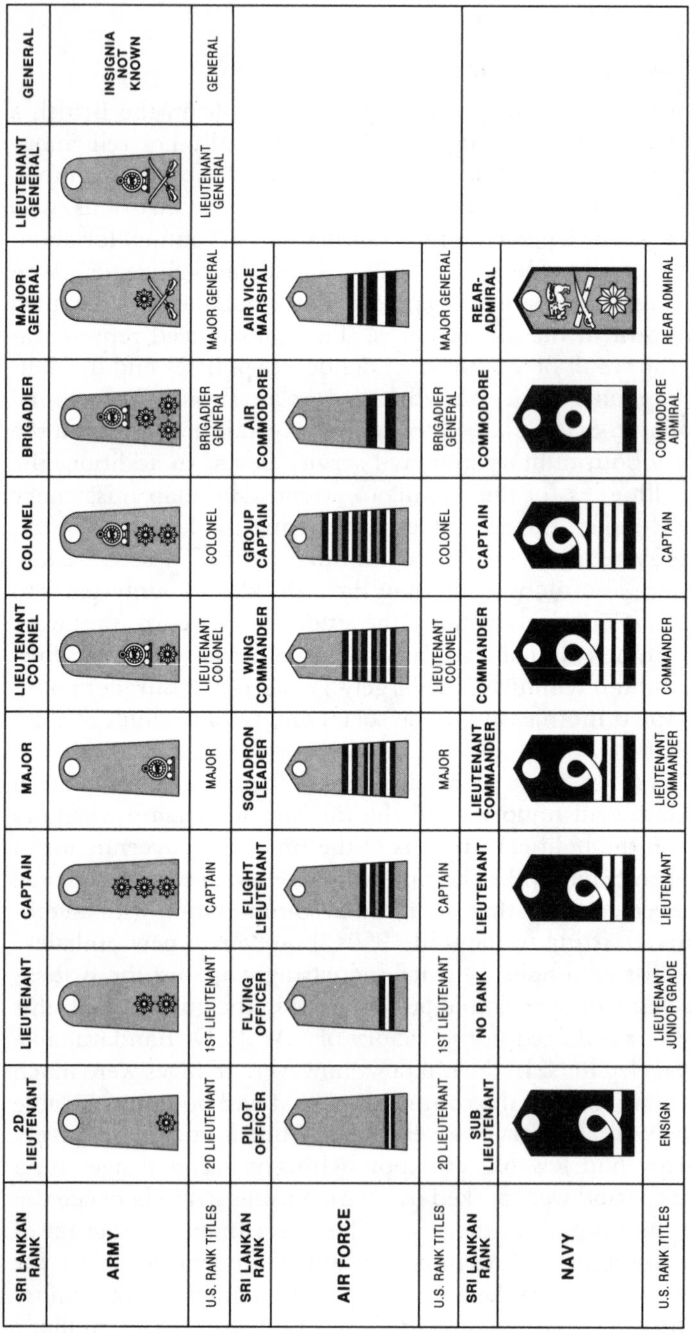

SRI LANKAN RANK	2D LIEUTENANT	LIEUTENANT	CAPTAIN	MAJOR	LIEUTENANT COLONEL	COLONEL	BRIGADIER	MAJOR GENERAL	LIEUTENANT GENERAL	GENERAL
ARMY										
U.S. RANK TITLES	2D LIEUTENANT	1ST LIEUTENANT	CAPTAIN	MAJOR	LIEUTENANT COLONEL	COLONEL	BRIGADIER GENERAL	MAJOR GENERAL	LIEUTENANT GENERAL	GENERAL
SRI LANKAN RANK	PILOT OFFICER	FLYING OFFICER	FLIGHT LIEUTENANT	SQUADRON LEADER	WING COMMANDER	GROUP CAPTAIN	AIR COMMODORE	AIR VICE MARSHAL		INSIGNIA NOT KNOWN
AIR FORCE										
U.S. RANK TITLES	2D LIEUTENANT	1ST LIEUTENANT	CAPTAIN	MAJOR	LIEUTENANT COLONEL	COLONEL	BRIGADIER GENERAL	MAJOR GENERAL		
SRI LANKAN RANK	SUB LIEUTENANT	NO RANK	LIEUTENANT	LIEUTENANT COMMANDER	COMMANDER	CAPTAIN	COMMODORE	REAR-ADMIRAL		
NAVY										
U.S. RANK TITLES	ENSIGN	LIEUTENANT JUNIOR GRADE	LIEUTENANT	LIEUTENANT COMMANDER	COMMANDER	CAPTAIN	COMMODORE ADMIRAL	REAR ADMIRAL		

Figure 13. Officer Rank Insignia, 1988

reportedly had planned to restore order by detaining a number of prominent left-wing politicians from the Bandaranaike coalition and returning the UNP to office. By the time the conspiracy was made public, the original plans had already been abandoned. Nonetheless, the Bandaranaike government used the potential threat to bolster its pro-Buddhist campaign, making political capital from the fact that all of the conspirators had been Christians.

Despite the initial resistance from a number of military officers, the government succeeded gradually in recasting the armed forces in its own image. Recruitment at all levels became increasingly dominated by Sinhalese Buddhists, and by mid-1983 Tamils accounted for less than 5 percent of all military personnel. Military training that previously had been conducted in a variety of languages was now limited to Sinhala and English. Also, under the leadership of S.W.R.D. Bandaranaike, the army was supplemented with the new Sinha Regiment, whose name and unprecedented lack of regimental colors stood in clear opposition to the British colonial regalia of the Ceylon Light Infantry. Even the Light Infantry took on a new Sinhalese cast when in 1961 it adopted an elephant named Kandula as its regimental mascot; as the *Times of Ceylon* was quick to point out, Kandula was the battle elephant of Dutthagamani (or Duttugemunu), the ancient Sinhalese king who was credited with driving the Tamils out of Sri Lanka in the second century B.C.

The Sinhalization of the armed forces continued under the United National Party government of President Jayewardene. The retirement of the British-educated cadre of Tamil and Burgher officers gradually depleted the ranks of minority members. At the same time, the growing ethnic divisions in the country and the deployment of the armed forces against the Tamil population in the Northern Province tended to discourage young Tamil males from pursuing a career in the military. By 1985 almost all enlisted personnel in the armed services were Sinhalese.

Women in the Armed Forces

The Sri Lankan Army Women's Corps was formed in 1980 as an unarmed, noncombatant support unit. Set up with the assistance of the British Women's Reserve Army Corps, it was identical in structure to its parent organization, and its first generation of officer cadets was trained in Britain. Candidates were required to be between eighteen and twenty years old and to have passed the lowest level of the General Common Entrance examinations. (Officer candidates must have passed the Advanced Level.) Enlistment entailed a five-year service commitment (the same as for men), and recruits were not allowed to marry during this period. In the sixteen-week training course at the Army Training Centre at Diyatalawa, cadets were put through a program of drill and physical training similar to the men's program, with the exception of weapons and battlecraft training. Women recruits were paid according to the same scale as the men, but were limited to service in nursing, communications, and clerical work. In late 1987, the first class of women graduates from the Viyanini Army Training Center were certified to serve as army instructors.

Women were first admitted into the navy in 1985. New recruits were given six weeks of training with the Sri Lankan Army Women's Corps. Although they were trained in the use of weapons, they were not assigned to combat positions or shipboard duty. Instead, they assisted in nursing, communications, stores, and secretarial work.

Awards in the Armed Forces

In the period between independence and the establishment of the republic, members of the Sri Lankan armed services were eligible for awards from the British government, including the Order of the British Empire (O.B.E.) and the Member of the British Empire (M.B.E.). After 1972 however, the nation established its own system of decorations, which was modified in 1979 to conform more closely with the practices of other South Asian nations. Under the system in place in 1988, the nation's highest decoration was the Parama Veera Vibushanaya, equivalent to the Victoria Cross of Britain and the Param Vir Chakra of India, and awarded "for individual acts of gallantry of the most exceptional order." For acts of bravery performed outside a military context, individuals were awarded the Veerodhara Vibushanaya, a decoration equivalent to the British George Cross and the Indian Asoka Chakra. Other awards include the Visiatha Seva Vibushanaya for twenty years of service with an "unblemished record of moral and military conduct;" the Uttama Seva Padakkama, equivalent to India's Meritorious Service Medal, and given to a soldier with not fewer than fifteen years of service marked by exceptional ability and exemplary conduct; the Videsha Seva Padakkama, for active service in a foreign military mission; and the Veera Vickrama Vibushanaya, equivalent to the Military Cross of Britain, and given for acts of gallantry in saving the lives of others.

Foreign Military Relations

Sri Lanka's oldest and most enduring military relationship has been with Britain. As a British colony, the island was garrisoned with British troops and, following independence, its own indigenous armed forces were organized, trained, armed, and led by British military personnel. Under a mutual defense arrangement dating from 1947, the two nations have agreed to give each other "such military assistance for the security of their territories for defense against external aggression and for the protection of essential communications as it may be in their mutual interests to provide." The vague wording of this treaty has allowed it to survive a number of political swings in Sri Lanka's domestic arena, and it remained in force in 1988. Even after the government of S.W.R.D. Bandaranaike withdrew island base rights from British forces in 1957, the British continued to be a major supplier of military hardware. Although the British government has denied any direct involvement, for a time former British Special Air Service personnel under the auspices of the private firm of Keeny Meeny Services were instrumental in training Sri Lankan troops in counterterrorist and counterinsurgency techniques.

After the anti-Tamil riots of 1983 and as the ethnic insurgency increased in the north, the government turned to a variety of foreign nations to assist in its counterinsurgency campaign. In May 1984, at considerable cost to its standing among Third World nations, the government arranged for the establishment of an Israeli special interest section in Colombo. Operating out of the United States embassy, agents from Shin Bet, the Israeli counterespionage and internal security organization, trained members of the Sri Lankan Special Task Force and other groups in intelligence gathering and internal security techniques.

Other nations that have reportedly provided training include Australia, India, Malaysia, Pakistan, and the United States. Unconfirmed press reports suggest that a number of foreign advisers, including Englishmen, Pakistanis, and South Africans, have actually taken part in combat operations against the Tamil insurgents. In April 1986, the Indian press announced that a Pakistani Air Force officer had been killed in an airplane crash shortly after participating in an air assault in Northern Province.

Military relations between Sri Lanka and India underwent a major change in mid-1987. For almost ten years, the Tamil insurgency in Northern and Eastern provinces had been a major source of friction between the two nations because India provided shelter, training, and weapons to the insurgent groups. The Sri Lankan insurgents found abundant sympathy and support for their cause within the Tamil-dominated Indian state of Tamil Nadu, and Madras served as the headquarters from which they regularly issued condemnations of the government. Beginning in May 1987, the

249

Indian government changed its official role from that of intermediary to active participant as it sought to abate the turmoil in the island and bring together the Tamil separatists and the Sri Lankan government. Although the resulting Indo-Sri Lankan Accord, which was signed in July 1987, offered an equitable formula for restoring peace to the troubled nation, a subsequent exchange of executive letters accorded to India a substantial voice in Sri Lankan military affairs. In particular, Sri Lanka acceded to three major concessions. First, it agreed to consult New Delhi on the employment of all foreign military and intelligence personnel in Sri Lanka "with a view to insuring that such presences will not prejudice Indo-Sri Lankan relations." Second, it guaranteed that no Sri Lankan ports would be made available "for military use by any country in a manner prejudicial to India's interests." Third, Sri Lanka agreed to review its contracts with foreign broadcasting organizations to insure that none of their facilities in Sri Lanka would be used for military or intelligence purposes. This latter concession was specifically aimed at Voice of America broadcasting operations on the island. In return, New Delhi agreed to deport all Sri Lankan terrorists and insurgents operating on Indian soil and to provide military training and supplies to the Sri Lankan armed forces. Press reports in early 1988 suggested that Sri Lanka was prepared to expand and formalize its military relationship with India through a treaty of friendship and cooperation similar to that linking India with the Soviet Union.

Foreign Military Presence

Under the provisions of the Indo-Sri Lankan Accord, an Indian military contingent was dispatched to northern Sri Lanka. This contingent, named the Indian Peacekeeping Force was composed of army and paramilitary units from the Indian Army's Southern Command, headquartered in Madras. The IPKF, when it was initially dispatched to Sri Lanka, numbered about 1,600 personnel. As the cease-fire failed to take hold, and as the tenacity of the Tamil insurgents became increasingly evident, the force was steadily augmented. Within three months of its deployment, the IPKF presence in Sri Lanka had grown to 20,000 personnel. At the end of the year, two brigades of Muslim troops were introduced into Eastern Province to deal with growing tension in the Islamic community of that area. By January 1988, the overall force had a total strength of 50,000 personnel from three Indian Army divisions, plus supporting units. The following month it was announced in the Indian Parliament that the IPKF would be increased to 70,000 personnel organized tactically into fifteen brigades. Some Sri

Lankan sources said privately that the force had grown well in excess of this total, possibly surpassing 100,000 troops, and that its presence in Sri Lanka might well exceed the duration of the insurgency. In mid-1988, however, the Indian government did withdraw from Sri Lanka some of its more heavily armed artillery and armored units that were obviously unsuitable for fighting a counterinsurgency war.

At the time of its deployment, the IPKF was intended as a truce supervisory force that would oversee the disarming of the Tamil insurgents and the disengagement of the Sri Lankan government forces. As the cease-fire between the two sides broke down, however, the Indians were compelled to assume a combat role and were sent into action against the Tamil guerrillas overrunning the Jaffna Peninsula. In this operation, codenamed Operation Parwan, IPKF units of the 54th Indian Army division launched a five-pronged attack to clear the area of insurgents. After sixteen days of fighting, Jaffna fell to the Indians, and the Tamil combatants retreated to the more inaccessible areas of Northern and Eastern provinces.

Among the residents of Jaffna, the assault on the city provoked widespread bitterness toward the Indian troops, as reports spread of atrocities and high civilian casualties caused by careless bombardment of populated areas. Many of these reports were believed to be the result of Tamil insurgent propaganda. Nonetheless, in early 1988 the Indian Army acknowledged that there had been serious disciplinary problems during the campaign, and a number of soldiers were sent back to India after conviction on rape charges. Such gestures also hinted that the IPKF seemed disposed to apply the lessons learned from the Jaffna offensive and to abandon its previous hamfisted tactics and insensitivity to the civilian population. When continued insurgent activity required redeployment of IPKF units to Eastern Province and the inland districts of Northern Province, the Indian forces embarked on an aggressive civic action program to restore the infrastructure in war-ravaged areas, and on an intensive campaign of heavy patrolling to keep the guerrillas off balance. The Indians gained experience in both urban and counterinsurgency warfare and made some progress in keeping the Tamil insurgents at bay. However, the guerrillas were proving a more intractable foe than anticipated, and observers were not optimistic about an early conclusion to the conflict.

The Defense Budget

The intervention of the Indian Peacekeeping Force in 1987 permitted the Sri Lankan government to decrease its defense outlays for the first time in ten years. Since the United National Party came to power in 1977, Colombo's efforts to quell the Tamil insurgency and the radical Sinhalese movement in the south had demanded an increasing share of the nation's resources; in the early 1980s, defense expenditures represented only 1 percent of the gross domestic product (GDP—see Glossary). By 1986 this figure had risen to 3.5 percent, and by 1987 it was estimated at over 5 percent. After a number of supplemental appropriations, 1987 defense costs were estimated at Rs10.6 billion (for value of the rupee—see Glossary), including Rs3.5 billion for the army, Rs1.3 billion for the navy, Rs1.9 billion for the air force, and Rs1.7 billion for the police (see National Police and Paramilitary Forces, this ch.). The dramatic growth in defense outlays took place at a time when Sri Lanka's major exports were realizing significantly lower prices on the international market and in 1986, for the first time, the government was forced to resort to large-scale commercial borrowing. A continuation of this trend promised to undermine the government's development efforts and aggravate an already sizable trade deficit (see Trade, ch. 3). After the arrival of Indian troops in July 1987, the Sri Lankan government withdrew most of its forces from Northern and Eastern provinces, saving significantly on operational costs. As a result, Sri Lanka projected a 37 percent cut in army expenditures and a total military budget of Rs9.2 billion, 13 percent below 1987 levels.

National Police and Paramilitary Forces

The Sri Lankan National Police is an integral part of the nation's security forces, with primary responsibility for internal security. Specially trained commando units of the police are regularly deployed in joint operations with the armed forces, and the police command structure in Northern and Eastern provinces is closely integrated with the other security organizations under the authority of the Joint Operations Command. The police is headed by an inspector general of police who reports to the minister of defense.

Organization

In 1988 the police force was divided into three geographic commands—known as ranges—covering the northern, central, and southern sectors of the island. The ranges were subdivided into divisions, districts, and stations, and Colombo was designated as a special division. In 1974 there were a total of 260 police stations throughout the country. In more remote rural areas beyond the immediate range of existing police stations, law enforcement functions are carried out by locally elected village headmen (*grama seva niladhari*, literally "village service officers"). In addition to its regular

252

forces, the national police operated a small reserve contingent and a number of specialized units responsible for investigative and paramilitary functions. Routine criminal activity was handled by the Criminal Investigation Department under the command of an assistant superintendent of police. More coordinated threats to internal security, such as that posed by the radical Sinhalese Janatha Vimukthi Peramuna were the responsibility of the Countersubversive Division, which was primarily an investigative division. Special operational units included the Commando Squad of the Colombo police and the Special Task Force. The former, a 200-strong riot control force, was established following the anti-Tamil riots of 1983. The Special Task Force is a police field force. It was set up in 1984 with the assistance of foreign advisers (primarily former British Special Air Service personnel under the auspices of Keeny Meeny Services, see Foreign Military Relations, this ch.). Its 1,100-member force was organized into 7 companies and trained in counterinsurgency techniques. It played a major role in the government's combined force operations against the Tamil Tigers in Eastern Province before July 1987. Following the signing of the Indo-Sri Lankan Accord, the Special Task Force was redesignated the Police Special Force, and deployed in Southern Province, where it immediately went into action against the JVP terrorists. Companies of the force also served in rotation as part of the presidential security guard.

Until 1984 the police were responsible for national intelligence functions, first under the Special Branch, and later under the Intelligence Services Division. The perceived failure of the Intelligence Services Division during the riots of July 1983 led the Jayewardene government to reevaluate the nation's intelligence network, and in 1984 the president set up a National Intelligence Bureau. The new organization combined intelligence units from the army, navy, air force, and police. It was headed by a deputy inspector general of police who reported directly to the Ministry of Defence.

Strength

By late 1987, the police had an estimated total strength of 21,000 personnel, with plans to increase to 28,000. The force expanded most rapidly in the years following the 1971 uprising, an event that constituted the nation's first major challenge to internal security; between 1969 and 1974, the police grew from 11,300 to 16,100, an increase of over 42 percent. According to the United States Department of State's *Country Reports on Human Rights Practices,* the force was less than 5 percent Tamil.

Equipment and Training

Following the British tradition, Sri Lankan police were customarily unarmed during routine patrol duty in the years following independence. With the growth of ethnic tensions in the late 1970s and the increasing tendency of both Sinhalese and Tamil extremist groups to target the police, the government decided in 1982 to issue handguns to all sergeants and constables. Chinese copies of Soviet pistols formed an important component of the police arsenal, and included the 7.62mm Type 54 (modeled on the Soviet TT–M1933) and the 9mm Type 59 (based on the Soviet PM). For emergencies, the police also used the British Lee Enfield .303 carbine. The Commando Squadron was equipped with Sterling submachineguns, repeater shotguns, revolvers, and tear gas.

Regular force training in the 1980s was conducted at the Police College in Katukurunda, Western Province. Separate training facilities for the Special Task Force have been established in Kalutara, 96 kilometers south of Colombo. Starting in 1984, foreign trainers affiliated with Keeny Meeny Services offered counterinsurgency pilot training in the use of Bell 212 and 412 helicopter gunships.

The Home Guard

As the Tamil insurgents accelerated their campaign for a separate state in the early 1980s, they turned increasingly against those Sinhalese settlers who, through government-sponsored resettlement programs, had "infringed" on traditional Tamil areas in the north and east. In response, the government authorized the formation and arming of small militias for local self-defense. These armed groups, known as Home Guards, were generally composed of poorly educated Sinhalese villagers with little or no military training. Armed with shotguns that had been provided by the government, they frequently exceeded their original mandate of self-defense, avenging terrorist attacks with indiscriminate killings of Tamil civilians. This violence was an important factor in the increasing radicalization of the Tamil population. By April 1987, there were reportedly 12,000 Home Guards throughout the country, and the National Security Council, a consultative body that meets on defense matters, had announced its intention of increasing the number to 20,000. With the successful negotiation of the Indo-Sri Lankan Accord in July, however, the government moved to dismantle this poorly disciplined paramilitary force. The Home Guards in Northern and Eastern provinces were ordered to surrender their weapons to the authorities, and by August the police claimed to have collected 8,000 of the more than 10,000 shotguns that had been issued 3 years earlier. When the Tamil terrorist attacks resumed in late 1987, however, the government reportedly reversed its decision and allowed a partial rearming of the force. At the same time that it was acting to limit the Home Guards in the north, the government authorized an expansion of local and private militias in the south. The signing of the accord had unleashed a wave of violence among militant Sinhalese groups who opposed both the accommodation with the Tamil separatists and the presence of Indian troops on Sri Lankan soil. As Jayewardene moved to force passage of the provisions of the accord in Parliament, the Janatha Vimukthi Peramuna launched a campaign against members of the ruling United National Party who supported the pact. In the second half of 1987, the party chairman and more than seventy United National Party legislators were killed by Sinhalese extremists. The government responded by allocating 150 Home Guards to each Member of Parliament, leaving the legislators themselves responsible for the arming and training of these personal militias. At the same time, the press reported that pro-government gangs of thugs known as Green Tigers (named for the colors of the ruling party) had begun to attack opponents of the accord.

The Criminal Justice System

Founded on the principles of British law, the Sri Lankan criminal justice system underwent major changes in the 1970s as the government attempted to cope with the challenges posed by both Sinhalese and Tamil insurgencies. Through a series of new laws, constitutional provisions, and emergency regulations, Sri Lanka acted to enlarge the legal powers of the police and armed forces and to increase the capacity of the courts to deal with the growing number of cases. These changes were at the expense of individual civil liberties, and the new powers of the state evoked strong criticism from all ethnic communities. The most significant changes affected the rules of search, arrest, and seizure and the procedures by which criminal cases were investigated and tried. Through all this flux, the one element that remained relatively constant was the Penal Code, established in the late nineteenth century by the British colonial government. Although various individual provisions were amended to suit changing social conditions, in 1988 the general classification and definition of crime and punishment set forth in the code remained the basis of criminal law.

Criminal Justice and the Effects of Insurgency

Following the insurrection of 1971, the judicial system was flooded with thousands of young insurgents who had played varying roles in the attempt to overthrow the government. The established legal channels—holdovers from the colonial era—were clearly insufficient to deal with the crisis. At the same time, the government realized that any significant delay in the trial and settlement of cases would only serve to increase the alienation that had led to the rebellion. As a temporary measure, the parliament passed the Criminal Justice Commissions Act of 1972, providing for the establishment of special commissions outside the normal judicial structure and empowered to conduct cases free from the usual stringent rules of procedure.

The judicial crisis of the early 1970s also served to promote long-term reforms that had been under consideration for more than twenty years. In 1973 the parliament passed the Administration of Justice Law, a bill to reorganize the entire judicial system. Heralded as a major break with inherited British colonial traditions, the new law was intended to simplify the court structure and speed the legal process. It repealed thirteen acts and ordinances, including the Courts Ordinance and the Criminal Procedure Code of 1898, replacing them with five chapters covering the judicature, criminal, testamentary, and appeals procedures and the destruction of court records. The seven levels of the British court structure were replaced with four levels, including a Supreme Court that held only appellate jurisdiction. The high courts, district courts, and magistrate's courts were assigned jurisdiction respectively over the island's sixteen judicial zones and their respective forty districts and eighty divisions.

After Bandaranaike's defeat in the 1977 elections, the new United National Party government moved quickly to revise the workings of the criminal justice system. Of the five chapters of the Administration of Justice Law, two (on criminal procedure and appeals) were replaced by the Code of Criminal Procedure Act of 1979, and a third (on the judiciary) was substantially amended by the 1978 Constitution. These radical changes, coming on the heels of the previous reforms, were motivated by a variety of concerns. First, there were political considerations. Jayewardene's electoral success had been based in part on a popular reaction against the extraordinary legal and judicial powers assumed by the Bandaranaike government; the previous six years had been marked by an unbroken state of emergency, the creation of the highly powerful Criminal Justice Commissions, and a growing constriction of the freedom of the press. In his first year in office, Jayewardene declared an end to emergency rule, repealed the Criminal Justice Commissions Act, and engineered a new constitution with explicit safeguards of fundamental rights. These rights, set forth in Article 13, included free speech, the right to a fair trial, and freedom from arbitrary arrest and detention. Although many of these rights had appeared in the previous constitution, the new document put them under the jurisdiction of the courts for the first time.

A second motive for the changes stemmed from the sudden expansion of the Tamil insurgency in the late 1970s. Faced with a growing number of terrorist activities in the north, the Jayewardene government moved to streamline the judicial system and establish clearer lines of jurisdiction between the various levels of courts. Primary jurisdiction over criminal cases, previously the concurrent right of three levels of the judiciary, was now confined to two levels, the high court and the magistrate's courts, with their respective domains clearly demarcated in the new criminal procedure code.

The liberalizations of the Jayewardene government soon fell prey to the nation's deteriorating security situation. Hampered by the civil liberties embedded in the new laws and codes, the police and armed forces were unable to deal with an insurgent movement that involved a growing portion of the Tamil civilian population. Legal sanctions against terrorism began with the Prevention of Terrorism Act of 1979, followed by further antiterrorist provisions in 1982 and full-scale emergency regulations in 1983. With the consent of Parliament, these regulations were renewed on a monthly basis. By early 1988, the existing criminal justice system was a composite of permanent and provisional legislation. In contrast with the relatively stable Penal Code, the judicial structure and the procedures for criminal cases reflected the complex and sometimes contradictory interweavings of the Administration of Justice Law, the Constitution, the Code of Criminal Procedure, and the emergency and antiterrorist provisions enacted to cope with the Tamil insurgency (see Judiciary, ch. 4).

The Penal Code

The passage of the Penal Code, Ordinance Number 2 of 1883, marked an important stage in the island's transition from Roman-Dutch to British law. Despite the wide variety of amendments to the code, from 1887 to as recently as 1986, it remained substantially unchanged, and established a humane and unambiguous foundation for criminal justice. Crimes are divided into eighteen categories that include offenses against the human body, property, and reputation; various types of forgery, counterfeit, and fraud; offenses against public tranquillity, health, safety, justice, and the holding of elections; and offenses against the state and the armed forces. The code provides for six different types of punishment:

death by hanging, rigorous imprisonment (with hard labor), simple imprisonment, whipping, forfeiture of property, and fine. For sentences that involve whipping, the provisions of the Penal Code have been modified by the Code of Criminal Procedure, which sets a maximum sentence of twenty-four strokes, and requires that a medical officer be present during the execution of the sentence. Offenders under sixteen are given a maximum of six strokes with a light cane, and the sentence must be carried out in the presence of the court and, optionally, of the parents. In cases of imprisonment, the Penal Code specifies a maximum sentence permissible for each offense, leaving the specific punishment to the discretion of the judge. Imprisonment for any single offense may not exceed twenty years. The death penalty is limited to cases involving offenses against the state (usually of open warfare), murder, abetment of suicide, mutiny, and giving false evidence that leads to the conviction and execution of an innocent person. If the offender is under eighteen years of age or pregnant, extended imprisonment is substituted for a death sentence.

An attempt by the government to eliminate capital punishment received mixed reactions. In April 1956, the Bandaranaike government proposed the suspension of the death penalty for murder and abetment of suicide for a trial period of three years; this experiment was to be reviewed thereafter with the aim of abolishing capital punishment from the statute book. Parliament passed the Suspension of Death Penalty Bill in May 1956.

In October 1958, the government appointed a commission on capital punishment to examine the question of whether the suspension had contributed to any increase in the incidence of murder. The commission released a provisional report shortly before Prime Minister S.W.R.D. Bandaranaike was assassinated in September 1959 (see Sri Lanka Freedom Party Rule, 1956–65, ch. 1). Concluding that there was no immediate evidence to support a resumption of capital punishment, the commission recommended that the suspension be continued until April 1961 to permit a more extensive and conclusive study. As a result of the assassination, however, the commission's recommendation was set aside. In October 1959, the government decided to restore the death penalty, and a bill to this effect was passed in November 1959.

Criminal Procedure and the Structure of the Courts

As defined by the Constitution of 1978, the judiciary consists of a Supreme Court, a Court of Appeal, a High Court, and a number of magistrate's courts (one for each division, as set out in the Administration of Justice Law). In cases of criminal law, the magistrate's courts and the High Court are the only courts with primary jurisdiction, and their respective domains are detailed in the Code of Criminal Procedure. Appeals from these courts of first instance can be made to the Court of Appeal and, under certain circumstances, to the Supreme Court, which exercises final appellate jurisdiction. In all cases, the accused has the right to representation by an attorney, and all trials must be public unless the judge determines, for reasons of family privacy, national security, or public safety, that a closed hearing is more appropriate.

The vast majority of the nation's criminal cases are tried at the lowest level of the judicial system, the magistrate's courts. Cases here may be initiated by any police officer or public servant, or by any oral or written complaint to the magistrate. The magistrate is empowered to make an initial investigation of the complaint, and to determine whether his court has proper jurisdiction over the case, whether it should be tried by the High Court, or whether it should be dismissed. Magistrates' courts have exclusive original jurisdiction over all criminal cases involving fines of up to Rs1,500 or prison sentences of up to two years. If the magistrate's court is determined to have the necessary jurisdiction, prosecution may be conducted by the complainant (plaintiff) or by a government officer, including the attorney general, the solicitor general, a state counsel, a pleader authorized by the attorney general, or any officer of any national or local government office. At the trial, the accused has the right to call and cross-examine witnesses. Trials are conducted without a jury, and the verdict and sentence are given by the magistrate. Any person unsatisfied with the judgment has the right to appeal to the Court of Appeal on any point of law or fact.

For criminal cases involving penalties over Rs1,500 or two years imprisonment, original jurisdiction resides with the High Court. The High Court is the highest court of first instance in criminal law, and exercises national jurisdiction. Prosecution must be conducted by the attorney general, the solicitor general, a state counsel, or any pleader authorized by the attorney general. During the trial, the accused or his or her attorneys are allowed to present a defense and call and cross-examine witnesses. For more serious offenses, including crimes against the state, murder, culpable homicide, attempted murder, and rape, the law provides for trial by jury. In such cases, a jury of seven members is chosen by lot from a panel elected by the accused unless the court directs otherwise. Both the prosecution and the defense have the opportunity to eliminate proposed members of the jury. The jury is required to reach a verdict by a majority of no less than five to two. (Under the Prevention of Terrorism Act of 1979, the right to a jury was suspended for a wide variety of offenses involving violations of communal harmony defined as incitement of one ethnic group against another.) In cases where the law does not prescribe trial by jury, the judge gives the verdict and passes sentence at the conclusion of the hearings. As in the magistrate's courts, the accused has the right of appeal to the Court of Appeal on any matter of law or fact.

As its name suggests, the Court of Appeal has only appellate jurisdiction in matters of criminal law. Cases before the court are conducted without a jury. Appeals from the High Court must be heard by a bench of at least three judges, whereas appeals from a magistrate's court require at least two judges. Verdicts are reached by majority decision, and therefore a supplemental judge is added in cases of a split vote. As in other courts, appellants are entitled to representation by an attorney, but if they cannot afford legal counsel, the Court of Appeal may, at the discretion of the judges, assign an attorney at the court's expense. After the court has handed down its decision, further appeal to the Supreme Court may be made on any matter involving a substantial question of law, but an appeal requires the approval of either the Court of Appeal or the Supreme Court itself.

The Supreme Court was substantially refashioned by the 1978 Constitution, with many of its former functions reverting to the Court of Appeal. The Supreme Court in the 1980s consisted of a chief justice and between six and ten other justices who sit as a single panel on all cases before the court. Cases are conducted without a jury, and the court exercises final appellate jurisdiction for all errors in fact or in law.

Rules of Search, Arrest, and Detention

Despite the numerous protections of individual liberties embodied in the Constitution and the Code of Criminal Procedure, the government has succeeded in greatly expanding the discretionary powers of the armed forces and police through a variety of regulations and temporary provisions. The legal basis for these provisions comes from the Constitution itself, which sets conditions under which the government may act to restrict fundamental rights. Article 15 states that freedom of speech, assembly, and association may be subject to restrictions "in the interests of racial and religious harmony." It also allows the government, for reasons of national security, to suspend the right of a suspect to be presumed innocent until proven guilty. In addition, Article 155 authorizes the Parliament and, in certain circumstances, the president, to make emergency regulations which override or amend existing legislation.

Under these special provisions, the government passed the Prevention of Terrorism Act of 1979. The act empowered a superintendent of police, or an officer at or above the rank of subinspector authorized by the superintendent, to enter and search any premises and to arrest without a warrant upon reasonable suspicion of a crime. Although this act was originally slated as a temporary provision to be in effect for three years, the parliament voted in March 1982 to continue it indefinitely. In addition, an amendment passed in 1983 extended the police powers detailed in the act to members of the armed forces, and provided legal immunity for arrests and deaths occurring in the course of security operations.

The Code of Criminal Procedure allows the police to detain suspects without a hearing for a maximum of twenty-four hours. Under the Prevention of Terrorism Act, however, this period has been extended to seventy-two hours, and if the subsequent hearing leads to an indictment, the magistrate is required to order continued detention until the conclusion of the trial. The act further provides that the minister of internal security may, upon reasonable suspicion, order a suspect to be detained for a period of three months, extendable by three-month intervals up to a total of eighteen months. These provisions have been supplemented by the state of emergency regulations, first put into effect in May 1983 and renewed on a monthly basis thereafter. Under these regulations, police are given broad powers of preventive detention. In addition, a suspect may be detained for up to ninety days by order of the attorney general. At the end of this period, the suspect must appear before a magistrate's court which, with or without an indictment, is required by law to remand the suspect to prison. Subsequent detention may continue for an indefinite period of time.

Executive Powers of Pardon and Commutation

The president has the power to grant a pardon or a stay or commutation of sentence to any offender convicted in any court in Sri Lanka. In cases involving a sentence of death, however, the president is required to seek the advice of both the attorney general and the minister of justice before issuing a pardon. The president also has the authority to pardon the accomplice to any offense, whether before or after the trial, in exchange for information leading to the conviction of the principal offender.

Penal Institutions and Trends in the Prison Population

All correctional institutions were administered by the Department of Prisons under the Ministry of Justice. In 1980 the department had a reported staff of approximately 4,000 officers and a

261

total of 28 prisons, including conventional prisons, open prison camps, and special training schools for youthful offenders. The facilities were regulated by the Prisons Ordinance of 1878, and each was headed by a superintendent or assistant superintendent of prisons. Departmental staff are trained at the Centre for Research and Training in Corrections in Colombo. The center, which was established in 1975, provided new recruits a ten-week training course in law, human relations, unarmed combat, first aid, and the use of firearms.

Between 1977 and 1985, the prison population remained relatively stable, averaging 11,500 new admissions each year. More than 75 percent of the new inmates in 1985 had been convicted of minor crimes, and 62 percent were serving sentences of less than six months. Those convicted of serious crimes (including murder, culpable homicide, rape, and kidnaping) represented less than 2 percent of the prison population and, although the number of new convicts sentenced to death fluctuated over this period (between 33 and 81), no prisoners were executed. Men represented more than 95 percent of the prison population, and more than one-third of the nation's prisoners were being held in the Colombo District.

In the 1980s, convicted offenders between the ages of sixteen and twenty-two were being housed at separate correctional facilities and open work camps. Many of them were eligible for admission to the Training School for Youthful Offenders, which provided a special program of rehabilitation. Offenders under sixteen were not accepted into the correctional system.

Because of the small number of female prisoners at any one time, in the 1980s there were no separate institutions exclusively for women. Instead, each of the major prisons had a small women's section staffed by female attendants. All female convicts with terms longer than six weeks were transferred to Welikade Prison in Colombo. Mothers with infants were allowed to keep their children in prison, and a preschool program was established to provide child care during daytime hours.

In the 1980s, all male and female prisoners with terms longer than six months received vocational training during their stay in prison. Training was offered in twenty-two trades, including agriculture, animal husbandry, rattan work, carpentry, and tailoring. Every convicted offender was required to work eight hours each day and received a wage calculated according to the level of skill.

Apart from the correctional system maintained by the Department of Prisons, the armed forces and the police have operated a number of detention camps for suspects arrested under the Prevention of Terrorism Act. According to the United States State

Department's *Country Reports on Human Rights Practices,* "there have been persistent reports of torture or ill-treatment by military and police" at these camps, and detainees have been deprived of the legal rights and conditions of incarceration that apply to conventional detention facilities.

Drug Abuse and Drug Legislation

Because of the traditionally accepted roles of both opium and hashish in indigenous *ayurvedic* medicine, the population of Sri Lanka has historically been tolerant of the use of a variety of psychoactive drugs (see Health, ch. 2). As a result, the government has been slow to identify drug abuse as an issue meriting national attention, and until the late 1970s, no efforts were made to quantify the problem. In 1978 the Narcotics Advisory Board of Sri Lanka coordinated the first systematic field investigation of drug abuse. The survey revealed that opium, cannabis, and barbiturates were the drugs most commonly used for nonmedical purposes, and that the majority of drug abusers were under forty years old (for cannabis, 48 percent were between the ages of fifteen and twenty-five). Between 1975 and 1979, an average of 4,000 persons per year were arrested for drug-related offenses, while an additional 3,000 people sought help for drug problems. A 1980 government survey estimated between 3,500 and 5,800 opium dependents and between 16,000 and 18,000 chronic cannabis users. Based on the World Health Organization conversion factor of ten actual drug abusers for every one identified, the government estimated a total usage level as high as 1.5 percent of the population.

The delayed appearance of drug abuse among the issues of national concern is reflected in the state of antidrug legislation. As of 1981, one of the major statutes on the books was the Poisons, Opium, and Dangerous Drugs Ordinance. Although it has been amended several times since its enactment in 1929, the ordinance was seriously outdated for a society in the 1980s. It divides drugs into five categories (poisons; poppy, coca, and hemp; opium; dangerous drugs; and other drugs) and regulates their import, export, and domestic trade. Rather than attempting to define dangerous drugs, the ordinance simply appends a list of forbidden substances, and this has permitted greater flexibility in amending the law to suit changes in society. More recent efforts to regulate drug abuse include the Cosmetics, Devices, and Drugs Act of 1980, which requires companies trading legal drugs to obtain a license from the director of health services. This provision has given an important avenue for the authorities to monitor the import and export of pharmaceuticals. In spite of the government's efforts to eliminate illegal drugs, the strong Buddhist constituency has insisted on the legitimacy of traditional medical practices, and the Ayurvedic Act of 1961 assures *ayurvedic* physicians of continued legal access to opium. Because drug addiction in Sri Lanka has been far less prevalent than in the West, and because terrorism and insurgency have strained to the utmost the nation's security assets, a concerted campaign on illegal substance abuse is likely to await a return to normal conditions in the country.

*   *   *

As this chapter goes to press, the security crisis in Sri Lanka is more appropriately the subject of current events than of history; the analyses of scholarly journals are quickly outpaced by happenings in the field. Recent changes in the structure of the nation's legal and military institutions have yet to be reflected in any major monographs, and, as a result, this study has relied to an unusual degree on the piecemeal reportage of daily newspapers and weekly magazines.

The most comprehensive survey of the nation's armed forces appears in a special report by G. Jacobs in the July 1985 issue of *Asian Defence Journal*. Entitled ''Armed Forces of Sri Lanka,'' the report deals with the strength, organization, training, and equipment of the three armed services and the police, and provides valuable information on the difficulties that the security forces have faced in dealing with the insurgency. For treatment of the Tamil separatist movement, Dagmar Hellmann-Rajanayagam's ''The Tamil 'Tigers' In Northern Sri Lanka: Origins, Factions, Programmes'' (*Internationales Asienforum*) and Robert Kearney's ''Ethnic Conflict and the Tamil Separatist Movement In Sri Lanka'' (*Asian Survey*) provide excellent background material on the origins and organization of the insurgency. Hellmann-Rajanayagam focuses more on the composition and leadership of the individual groups, while Kearney delves into the political environment that gave rise to the movement. S.J. Tambiah's *Sri Lanka: Ethnic Fratricide and the Dismantling of Democracy* focuses on the anti-Tamil riots of July 1983 and offers insights into the role of the government and the armed forces in intensifying the ethnic conflict. Similar background material on the Janatha Vimukthi Peramuna appears in A.C. Alles' *Insurgency—1971*. The author was himself a member of the Criminal Justice Commission that investigated the uprising, and his blow-by-blow account, although sometimes excessively detailed, provides a fascinating picture of the rebel group—its ideology, leadership, and the haphazard nature of its attempt to seize power.

The United States Department of State's *Country Reports on Human Rights Practices* offers an annual update on the treatment of prisoners and the effect of the emergency regulations and antiterrorist provisions on the administration of criminal justice. Information on the nation's prison system appears in the annual proceedings of the Asian and Pacific Conference of Correctional Administrators published by the Australian Institute of Criminology. In his report to the first, third and sixth conferences, the Sri Lankan Commissioner of Prisons, J.P. Delgoda, summarizes the major changes of the previous year and offers information on the structure of the prison administration, the treatment of women and minors, and the vocational training program. (For further information and complete citations, see Bibliography.)

Appendix A

Table

Appendix A

Table 1. *Metric Conversion Coefficients and Factors*

When you know	Multiply by	To find
Millimeters	0.04	inches
Centimeters	0.39	inches
Meters	3.3	feet
Kilometers	0.62	miles
Hectares (10,000 m²)	2.47	acres
Square kilometers	0.39	square miles
Cubic meters	35.3	cubic feet
Liters	0.26	gallons
Kilograms	2.2	pounds
Metric tons	0.98	long tons
....	1.1	short tons
....	2,204	pounds
Degrees Celsius	9	degrees Fahrenheit
(Centigrade)	divide by 5 and add 32	

Table 2. *Projected Population Growth, Selected Years, 1991–2001* *
(in thousands)

Year	Low Estimate			Medium Estimate			High Estimate		
	Male	Female	Total	Male	Female	Total	Male	Female	Total
1991	8,931	8,776	17,707	9,018	8,862	17,880	9,099	8,940	18,039
1996	9,501	9,434	18,935	9,695	9,624	19,319	9,875	9,794	19,669
2001	9,980	10,021	20,001	10,320	10,354	20,674	10,644	10,665	21,309

* Sri Lankan government figures.

Source: Based on information from Federal Republic of Germany, Federal Statistical Office, *Länderbericht: Sri Lanka, 1988,* Wiesbaden, 1988, 17.

269

Table 3. Population According to Age-group, 1986
(in percentage of total population)

Age-group	1986 [1]	
	Male	Total
Below 5	6.4	12.5
5-10	5.8	11.4
10-15	5.8	11.4
15-20	5.5	10.8
20-25	5.1	10.2
25-30	4.3	8.6
30-35	3.8	7.6
35-40	2.8	5.6
40-45	2.4	4.7
45-50	2.1	4.1
50-55	1.9	3.7
55-60	1.5	2.8
60-65	1.2	2.3
65-70	0.9	1.7
70-75	0.7	1.2
75-80	0.4	0.7
80-85	0.4	0.7
85 and over	0.4	0.7
TOTAL	51.4	100.7 [2]

[1] Based on population estimates as of June 1986.
[2] Percentage does not add to 100 because of rounding.

Source: Based on information from Federal Republic of Germany, Federal Statistical Office, *Länderbericht: Sri Lanka, 1988,* Wiesbaden, 1988, 18.

Table 4. Schools and Other Education Institutions, Selected Years, 1975–86

Institution	1975	1980	1984	1986
General, all-purpose schools	9,386	9,117	9,556	9,656
Elementary schools [1]	7,656	4,156	4,000	3,938
Intermediate and upper level schools [2]	1,730	4,961	5,556	5,718
Other schools	1,058	677	358	421
Buddhist temple schools (*pirivena*)	289	282	307	372
Trade schools [3]	n.a.	36	31	36
Universities	7 [4]	8	9	9

n.a.—not available.
[1] Grades 1-5.
[2] Grades 6-12.
[3] Including technical and farm schools.
[4] Until the late 1970s, there was one university with seven parts; each became independent in 1979.

Source: Based on information from Federal Republic of Germany, Federal Statistical Office, *Länderbericht: Sri Lanka, 1988,* Wiesbaden, 1988, 29.

Table 5. Summary of Major Exports, Selected Years, 1976–86

Export Sector	1976	1984	1985	1986	1986 [1]
	(in percentage of annual total)				
Agricultural					
Tea	43.4	42.2	33.1	27.2	9,253
Rubber	18.4	8.8	7.1	7.7	2,622
Coconuts	10.2	5.7	8.5	7.0	2,389
Other agricultural	4.2	3.7	3.8	4.4	1,500
Total agricultural	76.2	60.4	52.5	46.3	15,764
Industrial					
Textiles	1.4	20.3	22.0	28.3	9,629
Oil products	10.5	8.8	10.7	6.9	2,358
Other industrial	3.0	5.5	6.8	11.4	3,891
Total industrial	14.9	34.6	39.5	46.6	15,878
Minerals					
Gems	5.4	1.6	1.6	2.2	755
Other minerals	0.6	0.6	0.8	1.3	427
Total minerals	6.0	2.2	2.4	3.5	1,182
Miscellaneous	2.8	2.7	5.6	3.7	1,249
TOTAL [2]	100.0	100.0	100.0	100.0	34,073

[1] In millions of SL rupees. For value of rupee—see Glossary.
[2] Figures may not add to total because of rounding.

Source: Based on information from Central Bank of Sri Lanka, *Review of the Economy, 1987,*
Colombo, 1988, 157–59.

Table 6. Gross National Product, Selected Years, 1975, 1980, and 1986
(current factor cost prices in millions of rupees) [1]

Sector	1975	1980	1986 [2]
Agriculture, forestry, and fishing	8,643	17,151	44,355
Banking, insurance, and real estate	336	1,785	6,840
Construction	1,018	5,552	12,272
Manufacturing	3,217	11,048	24,869
Mining and quarrying	316	1,249	4,155
Ownership of property	463	1,457	4,578
Public administration and defense	798	1,965	7,945
Transport, storage, communications, and utilities	1,889	5,894	20,163
Wholesale and retail trade	3,076	10,898	31,808
Other services	2,320	5,247	6,728
GDP at factor cost	22,076	62,246	163,713
Net income factor, from abroad	-140	-432	-3,861
GNP TOTAL	21,936	61,814	159,852

[1] For value of SL rupee—see Glossary.
[2] Provisional.

Source: Based on information from Economist Intelligence Unit, *Country Profile: Sri Lanka,
1987-88,* London, 1987, 8-9; and *Quarterly Economic Review: Annual Supplement, 1977,*
London, 1978, 8.

Table 7. Growth of Gross Domestic Product, Selected Years, 1960-87
(in percentages)

Sector	1960-65 [1]	1970-77 [1]	1977-84 [1]	1987 [2]
Agriculture	2.7	2.2	3.8	0.8
Industry	5.2	1.6	5.6	6.0
Services [3]	4.6	3.2	6.1	3.2
Gross Domestic Product Total	4.0	2.9	6.0	3.0
Gross Domestic Product Per Capita ..	1.5	1.3	4.3	1.3

[1] Annual averages.
[2] Estimated.
[3] Including construction.

Table 8. Industrial Production, Selected Years, 1980, 1985, and 1986
(in millions of rupees) [1]

Sector	1980	1985	1986 [2]
Basic metal products	478	123	281
Chemicals, oil, coal, rubber, and plastics ..	9,416	13,104	11,088
Fabricated metal products, machinery,			
and transport equipment	620	1,592	1,754
Food, beverages, and tobacco	3,899	10,497	12,169
Nonmetallic mineral products (except oil			
and coal)	1,156	1,854	2,053
Paper products	476	1,187	1,289
Textiles, clothing, and leather	1,923	9,505	12,088
Wood products	289	705	632
Others	54	125	136
TOTAL	18,311	38,692	41,490

[1] For value of SL rupee—see Glossary.
[2] Provisional.

Source: Based on information from Economist Intelligence Unit, *Country Profile: Sri Lanka, 1987–88,* London, 1987, 17; and *Country Profile: Sri Lanka, 1986–87,* London, 1986, 15.

*Table 9. Medium-Wave AM Radio Stations of Sri Lanka
Broadcasting Corporation, 1988*

Location	Frequency (kHz)	Power (kw)	Language	Network
Ambawela	531	40	Sinhala	National—Channel 1
Ambawela	648	40	Sinhala	National—Channel 2
Amparai	693	20	Sinhala	National—Channel 2
Amparai	855	20	Sinhala	National—Channel 1
Amparai	972	20	Tamil	National—Tamil
Anuradhapura	774	10	Sinhala	National—Channel 2
Diyagama [1]	558	10	Tamil	National—Tamil
Diyagama	621	20	Sinhala	National—Channel 1
Diyagama	873	20	English	none
Diyagama	918	25	n.a.	n.a.
Diyagama	702	25	Sinhala	National—Channel 2
Galle	1026	10	Sinhala	National—Channel 1 National—Channel 2
Kandy	567	10	Sinhala	National—Channel 2
Kandy	819	10	Sinhala	National—Channel 1
Kantalai	585	20	Tamil	National—Tamil
Kantalai	747	20	Sinhala	National—Channel 1
Mahiyangana	1485	1	Sinhala	National—Channel 1
Mahiyangana	1602	1	Sinhala	National—Channel 2
Maho	639	50	various [2]	Regional
Maho	801	40	Sinhala	National—Channel 1
Ratnapura	603	10	Sinhala	National—Channel 1
Ratnapura	729	10	Sinhala	National—Channel 2
Wiraketiya	675	40	Sinhala	National—Channel 1
Wiraketiya	594	50	various [2]	Regional

n.a.—not available.
[1] Diyagama is in Colombo District.
[2] Probably Sinhala.
Source: Based on information from *World Radio-TV Handbook, 1987,* Amsterdam, 1987, 229–30.

Table 10. Balance of Trade and Terms of Trade, Selected Years, 1970–86
(in millions of rupees) [1]

	1970	1975	1980	1985	1986 [2]
Imports	2,313	5,196	33,942	54,049	54,609
Exports	2,033	3,968	17,595	36,207	34,072
Balance of Trade ..	−280	−1,228	−16,347	−17,843	−20,537
Terms of Trade ... (1981 = 100)	194	107	106	108	102

[1] For value of SL rupee—see Glossary.
[2] Provisional.

Table 11. Government Fiscal Operations, 1982–86
(in millions of rupees) [1]

	1982	1983	1984	1985 [2]	1986 [2]
Revenue					
Income taxes	2.9	3.4	5.5	5.6	4.8
Sales and turnover taxes	6.4	9.5	13.9	14.2	14.6
Import and export duties	6.1	7.3	11.1	10.3	11.6
Other revenue	2.3	5.1	7.2	9.0	10.7
Total Revenue	17.7	25.3	37.7	39.1	41.7
Expenditure					
Recurrent	19.2	25.1	31.8	34.2	34.6
Capital	18.7	21.7	21.8	30.5	35.1
Total Expenditure	37.9	46.8	53.6	64.7	69.7
Budget Deficit	20.1	21.6	15.9	25.7	26.6
Financing of deficit					
Domestic bank borrowing	4.0	1.2	-2.7	7.5	2.3
Domestic non-bank borrowing	7.6	10.1	6.6	8.5	9.2
Foreign grants	3.4	3.5	3.3	3.3	3.8
Foreign loans	5.4	7.5	8.0	8.9	12.1
Use of cash balances	-0.3	-0.7	0.7	-2.5	-0.8
Public debt outstanding	71.3	86.4	95.7	123.7	150.3

[1] For value of SL rupee—see Glossary.
[2] Estimated—figures rounded.

Source: Based on information from Central Bank of Sri Lanka, *Review of the Economy, 1986*, Colombo, 1987, 232; and Economist Intelligence Unit, *Country Profile: Sri Lanka: 1987–1988*, London, 1987, 22.

Table 12. Party Performance in General Elections, 1947–77
(showing percentage of popular vote and number of seats won)

	1947		1952		1956		March 1960	
	% Votes Won	No. of Seats	% Votes Won	No. of Seats	% Votes Won	No. of Seats	% Votes Won	No. of Seats
UNP [1]	39.9	42	44.0	54	27.9	8	29.6	50
SLFP [2]	—	—	15.5	9	40.0	51	20.9	46
LSSP [3]	16.8 [4]	15 [4]	13.1	9	10.5	14	10.5	10
CPSL [5]	3.7	3	5.8	4	4.6	3	4.8	3
MEP [6]	—	—	—	—	—	—	10.6	10
TC [7]	4.4	7	2.8	4	0.3	1	1.2	1
FP [8]	—	—	1.9	2	5.4	10	5.7	15
CIC [9]	3.8	6	—	—	—	—	—	—
Other	2.3	1	2.9	1	0.3	0	7.6	9
TULF [10] ...	—	—	—	—	—	—	—	—
Ind. [11]	29.1	21	14.0	12	11.0	8	9.1	7
TOTAL * ...	100.0	95	100.0	95	100.0	95	100.0	151

	July 1960		1965		19700		1977	
	% Votes Won	No. of Seats	% Votes Won	No. of Seats	% Votes Won	No. of Seats	% Votes Won	No. of Seats
UNP [1]	37.6	30	39.3	66	37.9	17	50.9	140
SLFP [2]	33.6	75	30.2	41	36.9	91	29.7	8
LSSP [3]	7.4	12	7.5	10	8.7	19	3.6	0
CPSL [5]	3.0	4	2.7	4	3.4	6	2.0	0
MEP [6]	3.4	3	2.7	1	0.9	0	0.4	0
TC [7]	1.5	1	2.4	3	2.3	3	—	—
FP [8]	7.2	16	5.4	14	4.9	13	—	—
CIC [9]	—	—	—	—	—	—	—	—
Other	5.3	7	6.7	7	1.3	0	1.8 [12]	1
TULF [10] ...	—	—	—	—	—	—	6.4	18
Ind. [11]	4.4	6	5.8	6	4.6	2	5.6	1
TOTAL * ...	100.0	151	100.0	151	100.0	151	100.0	168

— Means did not particpate.
* Figures may not add to total because of rounding.
[1] UNP - United National Party.
[2] SLFP - Sri Lanka Freedom Party.
[3] LSSP - Lanka Sama Samaja Party.
[4] Includes both factions of LSSP, which ran separately in 1947.
[5] CPSL - Communist Party of Sri Lanka.
[6] MEP - Mahajana Eksath Peramuna.
[7] TC - Tamil Congress. With FP, formed the TULF to contest the 1977 election.
[8] FP - Federal Party. With TC, formed the TULF to contest the 1977 election.
[9] CIC - Ceylon Indian Congress.
[10] TULF - Tamil United Liberation Front.
[11] Ind. - Independents.
[12] The Ceylon Workers' Congress.

Source: Based on information from Craig Baxter, et al. *Government and Politics in South Asia,*
Boulder, 1987, 330; and Robert N. Kearney, 'The Political Party System in Sri
Lanka,' in *Political Science Quarterly,* 98, No. 1, Spring 1983, 19.

Appendix B

Political Parties and Groups

All Ceylon Tamil Congress—also known as the Tamil Congress. Founded in 1944 to champion the cause of the Tamils against Sinhalese Buddhist domination. A faction broke away in 1949 to form the more aggressive Tamil Federal Party.

Ceylon Equal Society Party (Lanka Sama Samaja Party—LSSP)— Trotskyite-oriented party founded in 1935. Though touted as the world's only successful Trotskyite party, in recent years the LSSP has been considered politically spent.

Ceylon Indian Congress—founded in 1939. Political group representing Indian Tamils that sought to revive Buddhism.

Ceylon Workers' Congress—a minority-oriented party which enjoyed the support of the Indian Tamils and the Sri Lanka Muslim Congress in the late 1980s.

Communist Party of Sri Lanka (CPSL)—began as a Stalinist faction of the LSSP, but was later expelled and founded as a separate party in 1943, remaining faithful to the Communist Party of the Soviet Union.

Deshapremi Janatha Viyaparaya (DJV)—Patriotic Liberation Organization—emerged in 1987 as a splinter group of the JVP.

Eelam National Liberation Front (ENLF)—a united front organization formed in March 1985 by the LTTE, EPRLF, TELO, and EROS, which became largely inoperative by mid-1986 when LTTE quit, although the other groups sought to form a front without LTTE participation.

Eelam People's Revolutionary Liberation Front (EPRLF)—a guerrilla group that emerged in the early 1980s, part of the ENLF.

Eelam Revolutionary Organization of Students (EROS)—militant Tamil guerrilla group that emerged in the early 1980s, part of the ENLF.

Janatha Vimukthi Peramuna (JVP—People's Liberation Front)— insurgent extremist political group founded in the late 1960s by Rohana Wijeweera. A Maoist and primarily rural Sinhalese youth movement based in southern Sri Lanka, it initially sympathized with the "oppressed" of both the Tamil and Sinhalese communities, but by the early 1980s, became increasingly a Sinhalese nationalist organization opposing any compromise with the Tamil insurgency.

Liberation Tigers of Tamil Eelam (LTTE)—strongest of Tamil
separatist groups, founded in 1972 when Tamil youth espousing a Marxist ideology and an independent Tamil state established a group called the Tamil New Tigers; name changed
in 1976. Competitors include People's Liberation Organization of Tamil Eelam (PLOTE), Tamil Eelam Liberation Army
(TELA), and the Tamil Eelam Liberation Organization
(TELO). Membership generally drawn from the Karava or
fisherman caste. By late 1986 LTTE had eliminated TELO
and established itself as the dominant spokesman of the Tamil
insurgency.

New Equal Society Party (Nava Sama Samaja Party—NSSP)—a
breakaway faction of the LSSP.

People's Democratic Party (PDP—Mahajana Prajathanthra)—
Sinhalese, founded in 1977 by six members of the SLFP.

People's Liberation Organization of Tamil Eelam (PLOTE, also
PLOT)—insurgent political group with large percentage of
members belonging to elite Vellala caste; a rival of the LTTE,
from whom it broke away in 1981 claiming a purer form of
Marxist orthodoxy.

People's United Front (Mahajana Eksath Peramuna—MEP)—
political party founded by Dinesh P.R. Gunawardene in 1955
that has attracted Sinhalese support with its appeals to militant Buddhist and Sinhala chauvinist sentiments. Originally
opposed to the UNP, it is basically an SLFP-Marxist coalition.

Sinhala Maha Sabha—Great Council of the Sinhalese. It was founded in 1937 to represent the interest of Sinhala-language speakers in the Ceylon National Congress and to mobilize popular
support for the liberation of the country from foreign rule.

Sri Lanka Freedom Party (SLFP)—first major non-Marxist left-
of-center political party to oppose the UNP; founded in July
1951 when S.W.R.D. Bandaranaike's left-of-center bloc split
with D.S. Senanayake and seceded to form the SLFP.

Sri Lanka People's Party (SLPP—Sri Lanka Mahajana Pakshaya)—
political party formed in 1984 by a daughter of Sirimavo Bandaranaike, Chandrika Kumaratunge, and her husband Vijay
Kumaratunge, who claimed that the original SLFP, under the
leadership of Bandaranaike's son, Anura, was excessively right
wing and had become an instrument of the Jayewardene
government.

Tamil Eelam Army (TEA)—insurgent group.

Tamil Eelam Liberation Army (TELA)—insurgent group.

Tamil Eelam Liberation Organization (TELO)—guerrilla group
decimated in 1986 by repeated LTTE attacks.

Tamil Federal Party—also known as the Federal Party. Formally established in December 1949. Competitor of the more conciliatory Tamil Congress, also known as the All Ceylon Tamil Congress, the party desired a federal system of government and the right to political autonomy—an independent Tamil state. Renamed the Tamil United Liberation Front (TULF) in 1971.

Tamil New Tigers—guerrilla group, formed in 1972, that abandoned the political process and geared itself for violence. The New Tigers espoused Marxist ideology and claimed to represent the oppressed of all ethnic groups despite its obvious ethnic affiliation; see also LTTE.

Tamil Tigers—Tamil separatist underground of rival and sometimes violently hostile groups based in the Northern and Eastern provinces and known collectively as Tamil Tigers.

Tamil United Front—founded in May 1972 as a reaction against the 1972 constitution, a coalition of Tamil interest groups and legal parties including the Tamil Congress and the Federal Party; united by the goal of Tamil autonomy and espousing nonviolent means, called the Tamil United Liberation Front (TULF) in 1976. Tamil United Liberation Front (TULF)—political party spawned by the Tamil United Front.

Three Stars—insurgent Tamil coalition.

United Front (Samagi Peramuna)—three-party political coalition (LSSP, CPSL, and SLFP), formed in 1968 by Sirimavo Bandaranaike to prepare for the 1970 general election and to oppose the UNP.

United National Party—conservative, umbrella party founded by Don Stephen Senanayake in 1946 as a partnership of many disparate groups—including the Ceylon National Congress, the Sinhala Maha Sabha, and the Muslim League. Political party in power in Sri Lanka for ten years beginning in February 1948 when the new constitution went into effect, and again from 1977 to 1988; nickname is "uncle-nephew party" because of kinship ties among the party's top leadership.

Bibliography

Chapter 1

Arasaratnam, Sinnappah. *Ceylon.* Englewood Cliffs, New Jersey: Prentice-Hall, 1984.

Baxter, Craig, Yogendra K. Malik, Charles H. Kennedy, and Robert C. Oberst. "Sri Lanka." Pages 295–352 in *Government and Politics in South Asia.* Boulder, Colorado: Westview Press, 1987.

Canararetna, Surjit M. "Nation Building in a Multiethnic Setting: The Sri Lankan Case," *Asian Affairs,* 14, Spring 1987, 1–19.

Codrington, Humphrey William. *A Short History of Ceylon.* Freeport, New York: Books for Libraries Press, 1970.

de Silva, Chandra Richard. *Sri Lanka: A History.* New Delhi: Vikas, 1987.

———. "Sri Lanka: The Ethnic Crisis," *Asian Thought and Society: An International Review,* 10, July 1985, 137–41.

de Silva, K.M. *A History of Sri Lanka.* Delhi: Oxford University Press, 1981.

de Silva, K.M. (ed.). *Sri Lanka: A Survey.* London: C. Hurst, 1977.

Ellawala, H. *Social History of Early Ceylon.* Colombo: Department of Cultural Affairs, 1969.

Geiger, Wilhelm (ed.). *Culavamsa, Being the More Recent Part of the Mahavamsa.* London: Pali Text Society, 1980.

———. (trans.). *The Mahavamsa or the Great Chronicle of Ceylon.* London: Oxford University Press, 1912.

Hart, Judith. *Sri Lanka: An Island in Crisis.* London: International Emergency Committee on Sri Lanka, 1986.

Hettiarachchy, Tilak. *History of Kingship in Ceylon up to the Fourth Century A.D.* Colombo: Lake House Investments, 1972.

Jeffries, Charles. *Ceylon: The Path to Independence.* New York: Praeger, 1963.

Kearney, Robert N. "Ethnic Conflict and the Tamil Separatist Movement in Sri Lanka," *Asian Survey,* 25, No. 9, September 1985, 898–917.

Knighton, William. *The History of Ceylon from the Earliest Period to the Present Time.* London: Longman, Brown, Green, and Longmans, 1845.

Ludowyk, E.F.C. *A Short History of Ceylon.* New York: Praeger, 1967.

Mahendran, Sharmini. "Sri Lanka: A Country in Crisis," *Harvard International Review,* 9, November–December 1986, 48, 50, 55.

Manor, James (ed.). *Sri Lanka: In Change and Crisis.* New York: St. Martin's Press, 1984.

Matthews, Bruce. "Radical Conflict and the Rationalization of Violence in Sri Lanka," *Pacific Affairs,* 59, Spring 1986, 28-44.

Mendis, Garrett Champness. *Ceylon Today and Yesterday: Main Currents of Ceylon History.* Colombo: Associated Newspapers of Ceylon, 1963.

_____. *The Early History of Ceylon.* Calcutta, Y.M.C.A. Publishing House, 1932.

Misquita, Michelle. "Sri Lanka." Pages 311-15 in *Asia and Pacific, 1984.* Saffron Walden, Essex, United Kingdom: World of Information, 1984.

Nagarajan, K.V. "Troubled Paradise: Ethnic Conflict in Sri Lanka," *Conflict,* 6, No. 4, 1986, 333-53.

Nicholas, Cyril Wace, and S. Paranavitana. *A Concise History of Ceylon: From the Earliest Times to the Arrival of the Portuguese in 1505.* Colombo: Ceylon University Press, 1961.

Obeyesekere, Gananath. "Political Violence and the Future of Democracy in Sri Lanka," *Internationales Asienforum* [Munich], 15, Nos. 1-2, May 1984, 39-60.

Pfaffenberger, Bryan. "Sri Lanka in 1986: A Nation at the Crossroads," *Asian Survey,* 27, February 1987, 155-62.

Pieris, Paulus Edward. *Ceylon, The Portuguese Era: Being a History of the Island for the Period, 1505-1658.* Dehiwala, Sri Lanka: Tisara Prakasakayo, 1983.

Rahula, Walpola. *History of Buddhism in Ceylon: The Anuradhapura Period, 3rd Century B.C.-10th Century A.D.* Colombo: M.D. Gunasena, 1966.

Tambiah, S.J. *Sri Lanka: Ethnic Fratricide and the Dismantling of Democracy.* Chicago: The University of Chicago Press, 1986.

Tennent, Sir James Emerson. *Ceylon: An Account of the Island.* London: Longman, Green, Longman, and Roberts, 1860.

Tresidder, Argus John. *Ceylon: An Introduction to the "Resplendent Land."* Princeton, New Jersey: D. Van Nostrand, 1960.

Whittington, Sherrill. *Ethnic Conflict in Sri Lanka: Background, Recent Developments and the Prospects for Resolution.* (Current Issues Paper No. 3.) Canberra: Legislative Research Service, Department of the Parliamentary Library, October 1987.

Wilber, Donald N. *The Land and the People of Ceylon.* (rev. ed.) Philadelphia: Lippincott, 1972.

Wilson, A. Jeyaratnam. *Politics in Sri Lanka, 1947-1979.* (2d. ed.) London: Macmillan, 1979.

Winnius, George Davison. *The Fatal History of Portuguese Ceylon: Transition to Dutch Rule.* Cambridge: Harvard University Press, 1971.

Wriggins, W. Howard. *Ceylon: Dilemmas of a New Nation.* Princeton, New Jersey: Princeton University Press, 1960.

Zeylanicus. *Ceylon: Between Orient and Occident.* London: Elek Books, 1970.

Chapter 2

Agro-Bio-Environmental Chart of Sri Lanka. Tokyo: Resources Council, Science and Technology Agency, 1977.

Arumugam, Shanmugam. *Some Ancient Hindu Temples of Sri Lanka.* Colombo: Ranco Printers and Publishers, 1980.

Attanayake, Abhaya, et al. *Mahaweli Saga: Challenge and Response.* (Ed., Lucien Rajakarunanayake.) Colombo: Mahaweli Authority of Sri Lanka, 1985.

Bandaranayake, Senake. "Form and Technique in Traditional Rural Housing in Sri Lanka." Pages 61–73 in *Proceedings of the National Symposium on the Traditional Rural Culture of Sri Lanka.* Colombo: Department of Government Printing, 1977.

Barrett, David B. (ed.). *World Christian Encyclopedia: A Comparative Study of Churches and Religions in the Modern World, A.D. 1900–2000.* Nairobi: Oxford University Press, 1982.

Bechert, Heinz. "On the Popular Religion of the Sinhalese." Pages 217–33 in Heinz Bechert (ed.), *Buddhism in Ceylon and Studies on Religious Syncretism in Buddhist Countries.* Gottingen, West Germany: Vandehoeck and Ruprecht, 1978.

––––––. "S.W.R.D. Bandaranaike and the Legitimation of Power Through Buddhist Ideals." Pages 199–211 in Bardwell L. Smith, *Religion and Legitimation of Power in Sri Lanka.* Chambersburg, Pa.: ANIMA Books, 1978.

Bechert, Heinz, and Richard Gombrich (eds.). *The World of Buddhism: Buddhist Monks and Nuns in Society and Culture.* New York: Facts on File, 1984.

Cartman, James. *Hinduism in Ceylon.* Colombo: M. D. Gunasena, 1957.

Central Bank of Sri Lanka. Statistics Department. *Economic and Social Statistics of Sri Lanka,* VIII. Colombo: December 1985.

Chen, Kenneth K.S. *Buddhism: The Light of Asia.* Woodbury, New York: Barron's Educational Series, 1968.

Coomaraswamy, Ananda K. *The Dance of Shiva.* New York: Noonday Press, 1958.

Dayal, Rekha. *Women in Health and Development in South-East Asia.* (SEARO Regional Health Papers, No. 8.) New Delhi: World Health Organization, Regional Office for South-East Asia, 1985.

de Bary, William Theodore (ed.). *The Buddhist Tradition in India, China, and Japan.* New York: Vintage, 1972.

de Silva, Chandra Richard. "Sinhala-Tamil Relations and Education in Sri Lanka: The University Admissions Issue—The First Phase, 1971-77." Pages 125-46 in Robert B. Goldmann and A. Jeyaratnam Wilson (eds.). *From Independence to Statehood: Managing Ethnic Conflict in Five African and Asian States.* New York: St. Martin's Press, 1984.

de Silva, Chandra Richard, and Daya de Silva. *Education in Sri Lanka, 1948-1985: An Analysis of the Structure and a Critical Survey of the Literature.* Colombo: The Asia Foundation, 1986.

de Silva, K.M. "University Admissions and Ethnic Tension in Sri Lanka, 1977-82." Pages 97-110 in Robert B. Goldmann and A. Jeyaratnam Wilson (eds.). *From Independence to Statehood: Managing Ethnic Conflict in Five African and Asian States.* New York: St. Martin's Press, 1984.

———. (ed.). *Sri Lanka: A Survey.* London: C. Hurst, 1977.

de Silva, Lynn. *Buddhism: Beliefs and Practices in Sri Lanka.* Colombo: Wesley Press, 1980.

Dhavamony, Mariasusai. *Love of God According to Saiva Siddhanta.* Oxford: Clarendon Press, 1971.

Dieter-Evers, Hans. *Monks, Priests, and Peasants: A Study of Buddhism and Social Structure in Central Ceylon.* Leiden, Netherlands: E.J. Brill, 1972.

Dimmit, Cornelia, and J.A.B. van Buitenen. *Classical Hindu Mythology.* Philadelphia: Temple University Press, 1978.

Edirisinghe, Neville. *The Food Stamp Scheme in Sri Lanka: Costs, Benefits, and Options for Modification.* (IFPRI Research Report, No. 58.) Washington: International Food Policy Research Institute, 1987.

Geological Society of Sri Lanka. *Geological Survey of Sri Lanka.* (L.J.D. Fernando Felicitation Volume.) Peradeniya, Sri Lanka: Department of Geology, University of Peradeniya, 1986.

Germany, Federal Republic of. Federal Statistical Office. *Länderbericht: Sri Lanka, 1988.* Wiesbaden: W. Kohlhammer GmbH, 1988.

Gibb, H.A.R. *Muhammedanism: An Historical Survey.* London: Oxford University Press, 1980.

Glen, William. *Continental Drift and Plate Tectonics.* Columbus, Ohio: Charles E. Merrill, 1975.

Gombrich, Richard F. *Precept and Practice: Traditional Buddhism in the Rural Highlands of Ceylon.* Oxford: Clarendon Press, 1971.

Hardy, Friedhelm. *Viraha-Bhakti: The Early History of Krsna Devotion in South India.* Delhi: Oxford University Press, 1983.

Hawley, John Stratton, and Donna Marie Wulff (eds.). *The Divine Consort: Radha and the Goddesses of India.* Boston: Beacon Press, 1986.

Herath, J.W. *Mineral Resources of Sri Lanka.* (Geological Survey Department Economic Bulletin, No. 2.) Colombo: Geological Survey Department, 1975.

Hopkins, Thomas J. *The Hindu Religious Tradition.* Encino, California: Dickenson, 1971.

Kingsbury, F., and G.E. Phillips (trans.). *Hymns of the Tamil Saivite Saints.* Calcutta: Association Press, 1921.

Kurian, Rachel. *Women Workers in the Sri Lanka Plantation Sector: An Historical and Contemporary Analysis.* (Women, Work and Development Series, No. 5.) Geneva: International Labour Office, 1982.

Marks, Thomas A. " 'People War' in Sri Lanka: Insurgency and Counterinsurgency," *Issues & Studies* [Taipei], 22, No. 8, August 1986, 63–100.

McKenzie, D.P., and J.G. Sclater. "The Evolution of the Indian Ocean." Pages 139–48 in *Continents Adrift and Continents Aground.* San Francisco: W.H. Freeman, 1976.

Mohan, Vasundhara. "The Dilemma of a Minority in a Multi-Racial Society: The Muslims of Sri Lanka," *South Asian Studies* [Jaipur], 21, No. 2, July–December 1986, 68–87.

Namamalvar. *Hymns for the Drowning: Poems for Visnu.* (Trans. A.K. Ramanujan.) Princeton: Princeton University Press, 1981.

Obeyesekere, Gananath. *The Cult of the Goddess Pattini.* Chicago: University of Chicago Press, 1984.

————. "The Impact of Ayurvedic Ideas on the Culture and the Individual in Sri Lanka." Pages 201–26 in Charles Leslie (ed.), *Asian Medical Systems: A Comparative Study.* Berkeley: University of California Press, 1976.

Paranavitana, Senarat. *The Stupa in Ceylon.* (Reissue of 1946 Memoirs of the Archaeological Survey of Ceylon, Vol. 5.) Colombo: Colombo Museum, 1980.

Rahman, Fazlur. *Islam.* New York: Holt, Rinehart, and Winston, 1966.

Ratnapala, Nandasena. *Sinhalese Folklore, Folk Religion, and Folk Life.* Dehiwala, Sri Lanka: Sarvodaya Research, 1980.

Renou, Louis. *Religions of Ancient India.* New York: Schocken Books, 1968.

Robert, Michael. *Caste Conflict and Elite Formation: The Rise of a Karava Elite in Sri Lanka, 1500–1931.* Cambridge: Cambridge University Press, 1982.

Ruberu, Tantrige Ranjit. *Education in Colonial Ceylon.* Kandy, Sri Lanka: Kandy Printers, 1962.

Ryan, Bruce. *Caste in Modern Ceylon: The Sinhalese System in Transition.* New Brunswick, New Jersey: Rutgers University Press, 1953.

Schulman, David. *Tamil Temple Myths.* Princeton, New Jersey: Princeton University Press, 1980.

Seligmann, C.G., and Brenda Z. Seligmann. *The Veddas.* Cambridge: The University Press, 1911.

Shukri, M.A.M. (ed.). *Muslims of Sri Lanka: Avenues to Antiquity.* Beruwala, Sri Lanka: Jamiah Naleemia Institute, 1986.

"Special Report: Sri Lanka," *Journal of Defense and Diplomacy,* 6, No. 1, January 1988, 25–37.

Sri Lanka, Democratic Socialist Republic of. Ministry of Land, Land Development, and Mahaweli Development. *Mahaweli, Projects and Programme, 1985.* Colombo: 1984.

_____. Ministry of Local Government, Housing, and Construction. *International Drinking Water Supply and Sanitation Decade, 1981–1990.* Colombo: 1980.

_____. Ministry of Local Government, Housing, and Construction. Urban Development Authority. *Sri Lanka's New Capital, Sri Jayawardanapura.* Colombo: 1982.

_____. Ministry of Plan Implementation. Department of Census and Statistics. *Population and Housing, 1981: General Report,* III. Colombo: 1986.

_____. Ministry of Plan Implementation. Department of Census and Statistics. *Report of the Registrar General on Vital Statistics, 1981.* Colombo: 1986.

_____. Ministry of Plan Implementation. Department of Census and Statistics. *Socio-Economic Indicators of Sri Lanka.* Colombo: 1983.

Sri Lanka, Republic of. Ministry of Health. *A Note on the Ancient Hospitals with Special Reference to That at Mihintale.* Colombo: 1974.

Secretaria Status. Rationarium Generale Ecclesiae. *Statisticum Ecclesiae.* (Statistical Yearbook of the Church.) Vatican City: 1985.

Swearer, Donald K. "The Kataragama and Kandy Asala Peraharas: Juxtaposing Religious Elements in Sri Lanka." Pages 295–311 in Guy R. Welbon and Glenn E. Yocum (eds.), *Religious Festivals in South India and Sri Lanka.* New Delhi: Manohar Publications, 1982.

Tefft, Sheila. "War's Refugees Engulf Sri Lanka," *Christian Science Monitor,* October 20, 1987, 1.

United Nations. Economic and Social Commission for Asia and the Pacific (ESCAP). *Economic and Social Survey for Asia and the Pacific, 1983.* Bangkok: 1984.

United States. Department of State. Bureau of Public Affairs. *Background Notes: Sri Lanka.* Washington: GPO, June 1983.

Wickramasekara, Piyasiri. "An Evaluation of Policies and Programmes for the Alleviation of Poverty in Sri Lanka." Pages 243–86 in Rizwanul Islam (ed.). *Strategies for Alleviating Poverty in Rural Asia.* Bangkok: International Labour Organisation, Asian Employment Programme, 1985.

Yalman, Nur. *Under the Bo Tree: Studies in Caste, Kinship, and Marriage in the Interior of Ceylon.* Berkeley: University of California Press, 1967.

Zvelebil, Kamil. *The Smile of Murugan: On Tamil Literature of South India.* Leiden, Netherlands: E.J. Brill, 1973.

Chapter 3

Agro-Bio-Environmental Chart of Sri Lanka. Toyko: Resources Council, Science and Technology Agency, 1977.

Attanayake, Abhaya, et al. *Mahaweli Saga: Challenge and Response.* (Ed., Lucien Rajakarunanayake.) Colombo: Mahaweli Authority of Sri Lanka, 1985.

Balakrishnan, N. "Industrial Policy and Development since Independence." Pages 192–212 in K.M. de Silva (ed.), *Sri Lanka: A Survey.* Honolulu: University of Hawaii Press, 1977.

————. "A Review of the Economy." Pages 101–30 in Tissa Fernando and Robert N. Kearney (eds.), *Modern Sri Lanka: A Society in Transition.* Syracuse, New York: Maxwell School of Citizenship and Public Affairs, 1979.

Bansil, P.C. *Ceylon Agriculture: A Perspective.* Delhi: Dhanpat Rai & Sons, 1971.

Bhalla, Surjit S., and Paul Glewwe. "Growth and Equity in Developing Countries: A Reinterpretation of the Sri Lankan Experience," *World Bank Economic Review,* 1, No. 1, September 1986, 35–63.

Central Bank of Sri Lanka. *Annual Report of the Central Bank of Sri Lanka, 1986.* Colombo: 1987.

————. *Review of the Economy, 1986.* Colombo: 1987.

"Colombo's Slipping Grip," *Asiaweek* [Hong Kong], 13, No. 17, April 26, 1987, 56–57.

Country Profile: Sri Lanka, 1986–87. London: Economist Intelligence Unit, 1986.

Country Profile: Sri Lanka, 1987–88. London: Economist Intelligence Unit, 1987.

De Mel, Ronnie. "Economic Targets, 1983–89" *Daily News* [Colombo], November 17, 1983, 8–12.

de Silva, Chandra Richard. *Sri Lanka: A History.* New Delhi: Vikas, 1987.

de Silva, K.M. *A History of Sri Lanka.* Delhi: Oxford University Press, 1981.

de Silva, K.M. (ed.). *Sri Lanka: A Survey.* London: C. Hurst, 1977.

de Valk, Peter. *The State and Income Distribution: With a Case Study of Sri Lanka.* The Hague: Institute of Social Studies, 1981.

Duke, James A. *CRC Handbook of Agricultural Energy Potential of Developing Countries.* (4 vols.) Boca Raton, Florida: CRC Press, 1987.

Economist Intelligence Unit. *Quarterly Economic Review of Sri Lanka (Ceylon) Annual Supplement, 1977.* London: The Unit, 1977.

Gunasekera, H.M. "Foreign Trade of Sri Lanka." Pages 172–91 in K.M. de Silva (ed.), *Sri Lanka: A Survey.* Honolulu: University of Hawaii Press, 1977.

Herring, Ronald J. "Economic Liberalisation Policies in Sri Lanka: International Pressures, Constraints, and Supports," *Economic and Political Weekly* [Bombay], 22, No. 8, February 21, 1987, 325–33.

———. *Land to the Tiller: The Political Economy of Agrarian Reform in South Asia.* New Haven: Yale University Press, 1983.

Hewavitharana, B. "New Patterns and Strategies of Development for Sri Lanka," *Economic Bulletin for Asia and the Pacific,* 31, No. 1, June 1980, 20–44.

Isenman, Paul. "Basic Needs: The Case of Sri Lanka," *World Development* [Oxford], 8, No. 3, March 1980, 237–58.

———. "A Comment on 'Growth and Equity in Developing Countries: A Reinterpretation of the Sri Lankan Experience'," *World Bank Economic Review,* 1, No. 3, May 1987, 521–31.

James, William E. *Asian Agriculture in Transition: Key Policy Issues.* (Asian Development Bank Economic Staff Paper.) Manila: Asian Development Bank, 1983.

Karunatilake, H.N.S. *Economic Development in Ceylon.* New York: Praeger, 1971.

Kearney, Robert N. *Trade Unions and Politics in Ceylon.* Berkeley: University of California Press, 1971.

Masannif, Yazgan, and Roland Edirisinghe. *Sri Lanka: An Emerging Business Centre.* London: Economist Intelligence Unit, 1980.

Meyer, Eric. "The Plantation System in British Ceylon: Involution or Evolution?" Pages 23–56 in Peter Robb (ed.), *Rural South Asia: Linkages, Change, and Development.* London: Curzon Press, 1983.

Moore, Mick. *The State and Peasant Politics in Sri Lanka.* Cambridge: Cambridge University Press, 1985.

Morrison, Barrie M., and Nancy E. Waxler. "Three Patterns of Basic Needs Distribution Within Sri Lanka: 1971-73," *World Development* [Oxford], 14, No. 1, January 1986, 97-114.

Obeyesekere, Gananath. "The Origins and Institutionalisation of Political Violence." Pages 153-74 in James Manor (ed.), *Sri Lanka in Change and Crisis.* New York: St. Martin's Press, 1984.

Papanek, Gustav Fritz. *Fiscal Policy and Development Strategy in Southern Asia.* (Report No. DRD278.) New York: World Bank, 1987.

Peebles, Patrick. *Sri Lanka: A Handbook of Historical Statistics.* Boston: G.K. Hall, 1982.

Peiris, Gerald. "Plantation Agriculture." Pages 3-30 in K.M. de Silva (ed.), *Sri Lanka: A Survey.* London: C. Hurst, 1977.

Pyatt, Graham. "Comments on 'Growth and Equity in Developing Countries: A Reinterpretation of the Sri Lankan Experience' by Bhalla and Glewwe," *World Bank Economic Review*, 1, No. 3, May 1987, 515-20.

Richards, Peter, and E.J. Stoutjesdijk. *Agriculture in Ceylon until 1975.* Paris: Development Centre of the Organization for Economic Cooperation and Development, 1970.

Ross, Lee Ann, and Tilak Samaranayake. "The Economic Impact of the Recent Ethnic Disturbances in Sri Lanka," *Asian Survey*, 26, No. 11, November 1986, 1240-55.

Seabright, Paul. "Effects of Conflict on Economy in Northern Sri Lanka," *Economic and Political Weekly* [Bombay], 21, No. 2, January 11, 1986, 78-83.

Sennitt, Andrew G. (ed.). *World Radio-TV Handbook.* (Vol. 43.) Billboard: Amsterdam, 1989.

Snodgrass, Donald R. *Ceylon: An Export Economy in Transition.* Homewood, Illinois: Richard D. Irwin, 1966.

"South Survey—Sri Lanka," *South* [London], No. 79, May 1987, 41.

Sri Lanka, Democratic Socialist Republic of. Ministry of Finance and Planning. *Public Investment, 1983-87.* Colombo: 1983.

_____. National Planning Division. Ministry of Plan Implementations. Department of Census and Statistics. *Statistical Abstract of the Democratic Socialist Republic of Sri Lanka, 1982.* Colombo: 1983.

Tefft, Shelia. "War-Torn Sri Lanka Sees Hope for Recovery in Economic Aid," *Christian Science Monitor*, December 7, 1987, 2.

Tveite, Per. *Sri Lanka: Problems of Economic Growth During the Bandaranaike Government, 1970-77.* Bergen, Norway: Chr. Michelsen Institute, Development Research and Action Programme, 1981.

United Nations. Economic and Social Commission for Asia and the Pacific. *Migration, Urbanization, and Development in Sri Lanka.* New York: 1980.

289

United States. Department of Agriculture. Economic Research Service. *South Asia: Situation and Outlook Report.* Washington: 1982–83.

_____. Department of Agriculture. Economic Research Service. *South Asia: Situation and Outlook Report.* Washington: 1984–85.

_____. Department of Agriculture. Economic Research Service. *South Asia: Situation and Outlook Report.* Washington: 1986–87.

Wickremeratne, L.A. "The Economy in 1948." Pages 131–43 in K.M. de Silva (ed.), *Sri Lanka: A Survey.* Honolulu: University of Hawaii Press, 1977.

_____. "Peasant Agriculture." Pages 236–55 in K.M. de Silva (ed.), *Sri Lanka: A Survey.* Honolulu: University of Hawaii Press, 1977.

_____. "Planning and Economic Development." Pages 144–71 in K.M. de Silva (ed.), *Sri Lanka: A Survey.* Honolulu: University of Hawaii Press, 1977.

Wilson, A. Jeyaratnam. *The Gaullist System in Asia: The Constitution of Sri Lanka, 1978.* London: Macmillian, 1980.

(Various issues of the following publications also were used in the preparation of this chapter: *Asian Wall Street Journal;* Country Report: Sri Lanka [London]; *Far Eastern Economic Review* [Hong Kong]; *Quarterly Economic Review of Sri Lanka* [London].)

Chapter 4

Abraham, A.S. "Gathering Sri Lanka Crisis—Colombo's Dangerous Ambivalence," *Times of India* [Bombay], April 13, 1984, 8.

Ali Khan, Ahsan. "Is Sri Lanka Heading Towards Partition?" *Muslim* [Islamabad], June 22, 1986, 4.

Ali, Salamat. "The Price of Power," *Far Eastern Economic Review* [Hong Kong], 138, No. 48, November 26, 1987, 28.

_____. "Smoothed-Over Summit," *Far Eastern Economic Review* [Hong Kong], 138, No. 47, November 19, 1987, 39–41.

" 'All Hell Broke Loose'," *Asiaweek* [Hong Kong], 13, No. 35, August 30, 1987, 10, 15.

"An Angry Old Man's Folly," *Telegraph* [Calcutta], July 26, 1984, 6.

"At Last, a Farewell to Arms," *Asiaweek* [Hong Kong], 13, No. 32, August 9, 1987, 10–11, 13.

Balasingham, A.S. *Liberation Tigers and Tamil Eelam Freedom Struggle.* Madras: Makkal Acchakan, 1983.

Baxter, Craig, Yogendra K. Malik, Charles H. Kennedy, an Robert C. Oberst. "Sri Lanka." Pages 295–352 in *Governmer and Politics in South Asia*. Boulder, Colorado: Westview Pres: 1987.

"Bearing the Blockade," *India Today* [New Delhi], 12, No. 3 February 15, 1987, 80–83.

Bjorkman, James Warner. *The Changing Division of Labor in South Asia: Women and Men in India's Society, Economy, and Politics*. New Delhi: Manohar, 1987.

Blackton, John Stuart. *Local Government and Rural Development in Sri Lanka*. (Special Series on Rural Local Government, No. 14.) Ithaca: Cornell University Press, 1974.

"Blasting Peace," *Asiaweek* [Hong Kong], 13, No. 47, November 20, 1987, 20.

Burger, Angela S. "Policing a Communal Society: The Case of Sri Lanka," *Asian Survey*, 27, No. 7, July 1987, 822–33.

Canagaretna, Surjit M. "Nation Building in a Multiethnic Setting: The Sri Lankan Case," *Asian Affairs*, 14, Spring 1987, 1–19.

Claude, Patrice. " 'Old Man' Beset by Chaos," *Manchester Guardian Weekly* [Manchester], May 10, 1987, 11.

_____. "Sri-Lanka menacé par la guerre civile," *Le Monde* [Paris], April 21, 1984, 1.

"Colombo's New Challenge," *Asiaweek* [Hong Kong], 12, No. 40, October 5, 1986, 23.

"Conciliation in Colombo," *Times* [London], May 25, 1985, 7.

Corea, Ernest. *Background Note: Sri Lanka—Beyond Conflict*. Washington: Embassy of the Democratic Socialist Republic of Sri Lanka, 1983.

"Crisis Month for Sri Lanka," *Times* [London], January 9, 1986, 15.

de Silva, Chandra Richard. *Sri Lanka: A History*. New Delhi: Vikas, 1987.

_____. "Sri Lanka: The Ethnic Crisis," *Asian Thought and Society: An International Review*, 10, No. 29, July 1985, 137–41.

de Silva, K.M. *A History of Sri Lanka*. Delhi: Oxford University Press, 1981.

de Silva, Manik. "The Domestic Equation," *Far Eastern Economic Review* [Hong Kong], 135, No. 9, February 9, 1987, 16.

_____. "Peace Eludes Devolution," *Far Eastern Economic* Review [Hong Kong], 138, No. 48, November 26, 1987, 26–27.

_____. "Pressed to Print," *Far Eastern Economic Review* [Hong Kong], 138, No. 50, December 10, 1987, 104.

de Silva, Mervyn. "The Anxious Neighbor," *Far Eastern Economic Review* [Hong Kong], 135, No. 9, February 26, 1987, 17.

_____. "Solution to Sri Lanka Strike Seems Distant," *Christian Science Monitor,* June 13, 1986, 12.

_____. "Sri Lanka—Uneasy Calm," *India Today* [New Delhi], 11, No. 12, June 30, 1986, 135.

Dubey, Suman. "The Coming Crunch," *India Today* [New Delhi], 8, No. 4, February 16, 1983, 54–55.

Frances, Patrick. "Les troubles a Sri Lanka: Déchirée par les luttes ethniques," *Le Monde* [Paris], August 4, 1983, 1–3.

Gupte, Shekhar. "Ominous Presence in Tamil Nadu," *India Today* [New Delhi], 9, No. 6, March 31, 1984, 88–94.

Hamlyn, Michael. "Buddhist Threat to Tamils," *Times* [London], August 24, 1987, 7.

_____. "Sri Lanka Peace Talks Face Hostility from Both Sides," *Times* [London], August 29, 1986, 8.

Heginbotham, Stanley J. "Sri Lanka's Gamble for Ethnic Peace." (Library of Congress, Congressional Research Service, Major Issues System, IB87183.) January 22, 1988.

"India Cracks the Whip," *Asiaweek* [Hong Kong], 12, No. 47, November 23, 1986, 33.

Jack, Ian. "Sri Lanka's Last Bid to Woo Tamils from Terror," *Sunday Times* [London], December 16, 1984, 21.

Jayewardene, Junius R. *Address to Parliament by the President on 20th February, 1986.* Colombo: Government Press, 1986.

Jenkins, Loren. "Gandhi Brokering Derailed by Tamils," *Washington Post,* August 30, 1985, A25, A33.

Jiggins, Janice. *Caste and Family in the Politics of the Sinhalese, 1947–1976.* Cambridge: Cambridge University Press, 1979.

Jofferand, Marie. "The Political Party System in Sri Lanka," *Political Science Quarterly,* 98, No. 1, Spring 1983, 17–33.

_____. "Sri Lanka: La longue marche vers l'unité," *Afrique-Asie* [Paris], No. 316, February 27, 1984, 38–39.

Kearney, Robert N. "Sri Lanka in 1985: The Persistence of Conflict," *Asian Survey,* 27, No. 2, February 1986, 219–23.

Kulkarni, V.G. "The Island of Tears," *Far Eastern Economic Review* [Hong Kong], 122, No. 46, November 17, 1983, 30–36.

_____. "Tigers in a Corner," *Far Eastern Economic Review* [Hong Kong], 138, No. 44, October 29, 1987, 36–37.

Mahendran, Sharmini. "Sri Lanka—A Country in Crisis," *Harvard International Review,* 9, November–December 1986, 48.

Manor, James, and Gerald Segal. "Causes of Conflict: Sri Lanka and Indian Ocean Strategy," *Asian Survey,* 25, No. 12, December 1985, 1165–85.

Manor, James (ed.). *Sri Lanka in Change and Crisis.* New York: St. Martin's Press, 1984.

Matthews, Bruce. "Devolution of Power in Sri Lanka," *Round Table* [London], No. 301, January 1987, 74–91.

_____. "District Development Councils in Sri Lanka," *Asian Survey*, 22, No. 11, November 1982, 1117–34.

_____. "President Jayewardene: Half-Term Report," *Round Table* [London], No. 282, April 1981, 149–62.

_____. "Radical Conflict and the Rationalization of Violence in Sri Lanka," *Pacific Affairs* [Vancouver], 59, No. 1, Spring 1986, 28–44.

_____. "Recent Developments in Sri Lanka Politics," *Public Affairs*, 51, Spring 1978, 84–100.

_____. "The Situation in Jaffna—And How It Came About," *Round Table* [London], No. 290, April 1984, 188–204.

Menon, Appan. "Getting Around Imponderables," *Frontline* [Madras], 5, No. 3, February 6, 1988, 20–22.

Misquita, Michelle. "Sri Lanka." Pages 311–15 in *Asia and Pacific, 1984*, Saffron Walden, Essex, United Kingdom: World of Information, 1984.

"The Monks Take a Stand," *Asiaweek* [Hong Kong], 12, No. 40, October 5, 1986, 23.

Narayan, S. Venkat. "Breakthrough at Last," *India Today* [New Delhi], 8, No. 22, November 16–30, 1983, 69.

Nyrop, Richard F. (ed.). *India: A Country Study*. Washington: GPO, 1985.

Oberst, Robert. *Legislators and Representation in Sri Lanka: The Decentralization of Development Planning*. (Westview Special Studies on South and Southeast Asia.) Boulder, Colorado: Westview Press, 1985.

Obeyesekere, Gananath. "Political Violence and the Future of Democracy in Sri Lanka," *Internationales Asienforum* [Munich], 15, Nos. 1–2, January–February 1984, 39–60.

Peebles, Patrick. *Democracy and Violence in Sri Lanka*. Hanover, New Hampshire: Universities Field Staff International, 1983.

Pfaffenberger, Bryan. *Caste in Tamil Culture: The Religious Foundations of Sudra Domination in Tamil Sri Lanka*. (Foreign and Comparative Studies, South Asian Series No. 7.) Syracuse, New York: Syracuse University, 1982.

_____. "Sri Lanka in 1986: A Nation at the Crossroads," *Asian Survey*, 27, No. 2, February 1987, 155–62.

Samarasinghe, S.W.R. de A. "Sri Lanka in 1982: A Year of Elections," *Asian Survey*, 23, No. 2, February 1983, 158–64.

Sebastian, Rita. "None Can Win Lanka Civil War," *Indian Express* [New Delhi], December 27, 1985, 8.

Silver, Eric. "Colombo Peace Moves Collapse," *Guardian* [Manchester], November 9, 1985, 5.

"Sri Lanka." Pages 1811-31 in George Thomas Kurian (ed.), *Encyclopedia of the Third World.* (3rd ed.) New York: Facts on File, 1987.

"Sri Lanka 'Clarifications' to India," *Hindu* [Madras], July 5, 1986, 8.

"Sri Lanka: de la féerie cinghalaisé a la guerre civile," *Le Monde* [Paris], May 5, 1985, 4-5.

Sri Lanka, Democratic Socialist Republic of. Ministry of Information. *This Is the Truth . . . Sri Lanka.* Colombo, 1983.

_____. Ministry of Local Government, Housing, and Construction. Urban Development Authority. *Sri Lanka's New Capital, Sri Jayawardanapura.* Colombo; 1982.

_____. "Sri Lanka Refutes Statement of Indian Minister of External Affairs." Statement of Sri Lankan High Commissioner, New Delhi, March 1, 1986.

"Sri Lanka: War or Peace?" *Frontline* [Madras], 3, No. 14, July 12, 1986, 4-16.

Tambiah, Stanley Jeyaraja. *Sri Lanka: Ethnic Fratricide and the Dismantling of Democracy.* Chicago: University of Chicago Press, 1986.

Tasker, Rodney. "Brink of Civil War," *Far Eastern Economic Review* [Hong Kong], 127, No. 7, February 21, 1985, 36-41.

_____. "Continuing Impasse on the Autonomy Issue," *Far Eastern Economic Review* [Hong Kong], 135, No. 9, February 26, 1987, 15.

_____. "Coping with Containment," *Far Eastern Economic Review* [Hong Kong], 135, No. 9, February 26, 1987, 18-19.

_____. "Militants and Military Wage Undisciplined War," *Far Eastern Economic Review* [Hong Kong], 135, No. 9, February 26, 1987, 18-19.

_____. "The Point of No Return," *Far Eastern Economic Review* [Hong Kong], 125, No. 38, September 20, 1984, 23-27.

_____. "Trouble from the South," *Far Eastern Economic Review* [Hong Kong], 136, No. 21, May 21, 1987, 46-47.

_____. "Under the Surface Calm," *Far Eastern Economic Review* [Hong Kong], 136, No. 22, May 28, 1987, 18.

Tenorio, Vyvyan. "Rising Racism in Sri Lanka's Ethnic Strife Weakens Fabric of Nation," *Christian Science Monitor,* November 22, 1985, 18.

_____. "Sri Lankans Doubt Military Can End War," *Christian Science Monitor,* September 22, 1986, 9.

_____. "Sri Lanka Peace Process at Delicate Point," *Christian Science Monitor,* September 2, 1986, 11-14.

"Text of Indo-Sri Lanka Agreement," *Frontline* [Madras], 4, No. 16, August 8, 1987, 116–17.

"Time of Troubles and Trial," *Frontline* [Madras], 3, No. 24, November 29, 1986, 16–20.

"A Very Mixed Up Picture," *Frontline* [Madras], 3, No. 10, May 17, 1986, 4–10.

Viswam, S. "India-Sri Lanka Agreement: Triumph of Statesmanship," *Indian and Foreign Review* [New Delhi], 24, September 30, 1987, 4–30.

"Waging Peace in Sri Lanka," *Frontline* [Madras], 4, No. 16, August 8, 1987, 4–19, 21–26, 115–19.

Weintraub, Richard M. "India, Sri Lanka Await Result of Gamble," *Washington Post,* August 3, 1987, A1, A18.

_____. "Sri Lanka, India Await Rebel Truce," *Washington Post,* August 1, 1987, A15, A17.

_____. "Sri Lankan Lists Reforms to End Ethnic Violence," *Washington Post,* June 26, 1986, A27.

_____. "Sri Lanka's War Grows," *Washington Post,* April 26, 1987, A1, A30.

Weisman, Steven R. "A Centuries-Old Struggle Keeps Sri Lanka on Edge," *New York Times,* February 17, 1985, E2.

_____. "India Talks Cover Crisis in Sri Lanka," *New York Times,* June 3, 1985, 1.

_____. "Sri Lanka: A Nation Disintegrates," *New York Times Magazine,* December 13, 1987, 34–38, 80–81, 85.

Wickremasinghe, W.G. "The Cry for Eelam," *Daily News* [Colombo], February 11, 1983, 4.

Wiswa Warnapala, W.A. *Recent Politics in Sri Lanka: The Presidential Election and the Referendum of 1982: A Study of Electoral Practice and Behaviour in an Asian Democracy.* New Delhi: Navrang, 1983.

(Various issues of the following periodicals also were used in the preparation of this chapter: *India Today* [Madras], 1983–88 and *Far Eastern Economic Review* [Hong Kong], 1983–88.)

Chapter 5

"Administration of Justice Law, No. 44 of 1973," in *Bills and Laws of the National State Assembly, Nos. 1–55 of 1973.* Colombo: Department of Government Printing, 1973.

Alles, A.C. *Insurgency—1971: An Account of the April Insurrection in Sri Lanka.* Colombo: Trade Exchange (Ceylon), 1976.

Ariyapala, M.B. *Society in Mediaeval Ceylon: The State of Society in Ceylon as Depicted in the Saddharma-ratnavaliya and Other Literature of the Thirteenth Century.* Colombo: K.V.G. de Silva, 1956.

"Asian Air Forces Survey—Part 5: Sri Lanka," *Asian Aviation* [Singapore], August 1986, 28.

Asian Recorder, 1985. New Delhi: Recorder Press, 1985.

Athas, Iqbal. "Sri Lanka Strengthens Defence Forces," *Jane's Defence Weekly* [London], 3, No. 2, January 12, 1985, 45.

Bobb, Dilip. "The Colombo Chill," *India Today* [New Delhi], 11, No. 6, March 31, 1986, 94-95.

Bobb, Dilip, S.H. Venkatramani, and M. Rehman. "A Bloodied Accord," *India Today* [New Delhi], 12, No. 21, November 15, 1987, 33-39.

Canagaretna, Sujit M. "Nation Building in a Multiethnic Setting: The Sri Lankan Case," *Asian Affairs,* 14, No. 1, Spring 1987, 1-19.

The Ceylon Light Infantry: History of the First Battalion (Regular Force), 1949-1975. Panagoda, Sri Lanka: Ceylon Army, 1976.

Code of Criminal Procedure Act, No. 15 of 1979. Colombo: Department of Government Printing, 1979.

"Come Join the Elite," *Daily News* [Colombo], July 4, 1986, 22.

"Constitution of the Democratic Socialist Republic of Sri Lanka." Pages 125-94 in *Ferguson's Sri Lanka Directory, 1983-1985.* (122d ed.) Colombo: Associated Newspapers of Ceylon, 1983.

Couhat, Jean Labayle (ed.). *Combat Fleets of the World, 1986-87.* Annapolis, Maryland: Naval Institute Press, 1986.

"Crack Anti-Hijack Squad Formed," *Daily News* [Colombo], March 18, 1986, 1.

Dasgupta, Swapan. "JVP's Terror Tactics Keep Jayewardene on His Toes," *Statesman* [Calcutta], September 10, 1987, 1.

Deen, Thalif. "Sri Lanka: Defence Budget Still Up," *Jane's Defence Weekly* [London], 8, No. 4, August 1, 1987, 172.

Defense Market Profiles: South and Southeast Asia. Geneva: Interavia, 1984.

Delgoda, J.P. "Management Services." Pages 235-37 in Peter Kay and Tim Isles (eds.), *Corrections in Asia and the Pacific: Proceedings of the First Asian and Pacific Conference of Correctional Administrators.* Canberra, Australia: Australian Institute of Criminology, 1980.

_____. "Sri Lanka." Pages 259-61 in Jack Sandry and Barry Looms (eds.), *The Management of Corrections in Asia and the Pacific: Proceedings of the Third Asian and Pacific Conference of Correctional Administrators.* Canberra, Australia: Australian Institute of Criminology, 1983.

_____. "Sri Lanka." Pages 236–37 in Jane Mugford (ed.), *Corrections in Asia and the Pacific: Proceedings of the Sixth Asian and Pacific Conference of Correctional Administrators.* Canberra, Australia: Australian Institute of Criminology, 1986.

Dep, A.C. *History of the Ceylon Police.* Colombo: Times of Ceylon, 1969.

de Silva, K.M. (ed.). *Sri Lanka: A Survey.* London: C. Hurst, 1977.

de Silva, Manik. "Terrorists in the South," *Far Eastern Economic Review* [Hong Kong], November 12, 1987, 22–23.

_____. "Treaty in the Making," *Far Eastern Economic Review* [Hong Kong], February 11, 1988, 29.

Central Bank of Sri Lanka. Statistics Department. *Economic and Social Statistics of Sri Lanka,* VIII. Colombo: December 1985.

Economist Intelligence Unit. *Sri Lanka: A Country Profile.* London: 1986.

Edirisinghe, Roland. "Britain Is Reminded of Sri Lanka Treaty," *Guardian* [Manchester], April 9, 1984, 6.

"Estimates Slash Defence Vote," *Daily News* [Colombo], November 4, 1987, 1.

Gunasekera, Rohan. "Sri Lankan Armed Forces Switch Focus," *International Defense Review* [Geneva], 21, No. 5, May 1988, 509–12.

Gunatilleke, Godfrey, Neelan Tiruchelvam, and Radhika Coomaraswamy (eds.). *Ethical Dilemmas of Development in Asia.* Lexington, Massachusetts: Lexington Books, 1983.

Hellmann-Rajanayagam, Dagmar. "The Tamil 'Tigers' in Northern Sri Lanka: Origins, Factions, Programmes," *Internationales Asienforum* [Munich], 17, Nos. 1–2, May 1986, 63–85.

Hewish, Mark, et al. *Air Forces of the World.* New York: Simon and Schuster, 1979.

Horowitz, Donald L. *Coup Theories and Officers' Motives: Sri Lanka in Comparative Perspective.* Princeton: Princeton University Press, 1980.

Jacobs, G. "Armed Forces of Sri Lanka: Small and Inadequate for Its Needs," *Asian Defence Journal* [Kuala Lumpur], July 1985, 4–16.

Jayasuriya, D.C. "Basic Elements of Drug Legislation and Regulatory Controls with Special Reference to Sri Lanka," *Survey of Sri Lankan Law* [Colombo], 1, 1980–81, 57–68.

Jayewardene, C.H.S., and H. Jayewardene. *Tea for Two: Ethnic Violence in Sri Lanka.* Ottawa: Crimcare, 1984.

Jeffries, Charles. *Ceylon: The Path to Independence.* New York: Praeger, 1963.

Sri Lanka: A Country Study

Judicature Act, No. 2 of 1978. Colombo: Department of Government
    Printing, 1978.
Kearney, Robert N. "Ethnic Conflict and the Tamil Separatist
    Movement in Sri Lanka," *Asian Survey*, 25, No. 9, September
    1985, 898–917.
Keegan, John. *World Armies*. (2d ed.) Detroit: Gale Research Com-
    pany, 1983.
Kodagoda, N. "Drug Abuse—A Barrier to Development," *Progress*
    [Colombo], 2, No. 1, March 1982, 8–12.
Kurian, George Thomas. *Encyclopedia of the Third World*. Oxford:
    Facts on File, 1987.
Leary, Virginia, A. *Ethnic Conflict and Violence in Sri Lanka*. Geneva:
    International Commission of Jurists, 1983.
McDonald, Robert. "Eyewitness in Jaffna," *Pacific Defense Reporter*
    [Kunyung, Australia], 14, No. 2, August 1987, 25–9.
Marks, Tom A. "Counter-Insurgency in Sri Lanka: Asia's Dirty
    Little War," *Soldier of Fortune*, 12, No. 2, February 1987, 38–47.
Marks, Thomas A. " 'People's War' in Sri Lanka: Insurgency
    and Counterinsurgency," *Issues & Studies* [Taipei], 22, No. 8,
    August 1986, 63–100.
_____. "Sri Lankan Minefield," *Soldier of Fortune*, 13, No. March
    1988, 36–45.
_____. "Sri Lanka's Special Force," *Soldier of Fortune*, 13, No. 7,
    1988, 32–39.
The Military Balance, 1987–1988. London: International Institute
    for Strategic Studies, 1987.
"Military Operations in the North," *Asian Defence Journal* [Kuala
    Lumpur], May 1987, 122.
Miller, Matt. "Sri Lanka Mounts Crucial Jaffna Assault," *Asian
    Wall Street Journal* [Hong Kong], May 28, 1987, 1.
Mills, Lennox A. *Ceylon under British Rule: 1795–1932*. New York:
    Barnes and Noble, 1965.
Mobilization and Supplementary Forces Act, No. 40 of 1985. Colombo:
    Department of Government Printing, 1985.
Nuri, Maqsud ul Hasan. "Sri Lanka: Profile of Guerrilla Groups,"
    Muslim Magazine International [Islamabad], January 30, 1987, 3.
O'Ballance, Edgar. "Sri Lanka and Its Tamil Problem," *Armed
    Forces* [Shepperton, United Kingdom], 5, December 1986, 542.
Pasupati, Shiva. "Some Reflections on the Criminal Justice Sys-
    tem in Sri Lanka," *Survey of Sri Lankan Law* [Colombo], 1,
    1980–81, 28–40.
Peiris, Gamini Lakshman. *Criminal Procedure in Sri Lanka under the
    Administration of Justice, Law No. 44 of 1973*. Colombo: Lake House
    Investments, 1975.

"The Penal Code, Ordinance No. 2 of 1883." Pages 281–433 in Hema Henry Basnayake, *The Legislative Enactments of Ceylon in Force on the 30th Day of June, 1956,* I. (rev. ed.) Colombo: Government Press, 1958.

Prakash, Sanjiv. "Indian Troops in Sri Lanka until 1989?" *Defense and Foreign Affairs Daily,* 16, No. 159, August 20, 1987, 1.

Pratap, Anita. "The Killing Fields," *Telegraph Colour Magazine* [Calcutta], June 1, 1986, 5.

_____. "A Winning Strategy," *India Today* [New Delhi], 13, No. 11, June 15, 1988, 98–101.

Prevention of Terrorism (Temporary Provisions) Act, No. 48 of 1979. Colombo: Department of Government Printing, 1979.

Prevention of Terrorism (Temporary Provisions) (Amendment) Act, No. 10 of 1982. Colombo: Department of Government Printing, 1982.

"Sri Lanka," *Asian Defence Journal* [Kuala Lumpur], December 1984, 53–54.

"Sri Lanka Air Force: A Most Pacific Air Arm," *Air International* [Bromley, United Kingdom], 24, No. 3, March 1983, 111–15.

"Sri Lanka Disarms Thousands of Sinhalese Home Guards," *China Post* [Taipei], August 13, 1987, 3.

"Sri Lankan Army in Major Reorganization," *Jane's Defence Weekly* [London], 9, No. 17, April 30, 1988, 827.

"Sri Lanka Revamps Its Intelligence Services," *Jane's Defence Weekly* [London], 2, No. 23, December 15, 1984, 1059.

Stares, Judith. "Birth of a New Model Army," *Soldier* [London], 36, No. 11, November 1980, 6–9.

Tambiah, Stanley Jeyaraja. *Sri Lanka: Ethnic Fratricide and the Dismantling of Democracy.* Chicago: University of Chicago Press, 1986.

Tasker, Rodney. "Trouble from the South," *Far Eastern Economic Review* [Hong Kong], 136, No. 21, May 21, 1987, 46–47.

Tefft, Sheila. "Sri Lanka Conflict Takes New Twist," *Christian Science Monitor,* January 7, 1987, 7.

Tennent, James Emerson. *Ceylon: An Account of the Island—Physical, Historical and Topographical.* (5th ed.) London: Longman, Green, Longman and Roberts, 1860.

"Tigers Still Able to Fight a Long War," *Muslim* [Islamabad], November 27, 1987, 5.

Tucker, Anthony R. "The Indian Army in Sri Lanka," *Armed Forces* [London], 7, No. 6, June 1988, 279–81.

United States. Department of State. *Country Reports on Human Rights Practices for 1984.* Washington: GPO, 1985.

_____. Department of State. *Country Reports on Human Rights Practices for 1985.* Washington: GPO, 1986.

Weintraub, Richard M. "Bomb Kills Up to 150 in Sri Lanka," *Washington Post,* April 22, 1987, A1.

_____. "Indian Troops Enforce Pact in Sri Lanka," *Washington Post,* July 30, 1987, A1.

Wilson, A. Jeyaratnam. *Politics in Sri Lanka, 1947–1979.* (2d ed.) London: Macmillan, 1979.

Wriggins, W. Howard. *Ceylon: Dilemmas of a New Nation.* Princeton: Princeton University Press, 1960.

Yapa, Vijitha. "Colombo MPs Fear More Attacks after Official Is Murdered," *Times* [London], November 4, 1987, 12.

(Various issues of the following publications also were used in the preparation of this chapter: *Asiaweek* [Hong Kong]; *Ceylon Daily News* [Colombo]; *Daily News* [Colombo]; Foreign Broadcast Information Service *Daily Report: Near East and South Asia;* Foreign Broadcast Information Service *Daily Report: South Asia; Frontline* [Madras]; *Hindu* [Madras]; *India Today* [New Delhi]; *Keesing's Record of World Events* [London]; *Manchester Guardian Weekly* [Manchester]; *New York Times; Times* [London]; *Times of India* [Bombay] and *Washington Post.*)

Glossary

Accelerated Mahaweli Program—Begun in the 1960s as the Mahaweli Ganga Program, it "accelerated" in the 1980s. The project, damming the Mahaweli Ganga (river), was expected to make Sri Lanka self-sufficient in rice and generate enough hydroelectric power to supply the entire nation.

ayurveda—System of healing based on homeopathy and naturopathy, with an extensive use of herbs. There are *ayurvedic* doctors, hospitals, and colleges, all recognized by the government.

bhikku—Buddhist monk. When capitalized, an honorific title. The *bhikkus* are not priests or ministers in the Western sense of the terms.

chena—Slash-and-burn agriculture. Forest or shrub undergrowth is cleared by cutting and burning. Land is farmed until its productivity falls, then new area is cleared. This type of agriculture usually is associated with shifting cultivation.

crown land(s)—The equivalent of federal public lands in the United States. The crown lands were for the most part secured as state succession or as inheritance from the king of Kandy.

Dravidian—Ethnic group; ancient Australoid race of southern India; a language family of India, Sri Lanka, and western Pakistan that includes Tamil, Telugu, Gondi, and Malayalam. See also Tamils.

Durava—Sinhalese lower, minority caste who traditionally worked as toddy tappers.

Eelam—Tamil name for Sri Lanka.

fiscal year (FY)—calendar year.

Goyigama, Govi—Highest Sinhalese (cultivator) caste. Traditional ruling caste and leaders of established order, comprising at least half of the Sinhalese population. Agriculturalists, now challenged for status by Karavas (*q.v.*).

gross domestic product (GDP)—The total value of goods and services produced within a country's borders during a fixed period, usually one year. Obtained by adding the value contributed by each sector of the economy in the form of compensation of employees, profits, and depreciation (consumption of capital). Subsistence production is included and consists of the imputed value of production by the farm family for its own use and the imputed rental value of owner-occupied dwellings.

gross national product (GNP)—Gross domestic product (*q.v.*) plus the income received from abroad by residents, less payments remitted abroad to nonresidents.

Indian Tamils—Tamils whose forebears were brought from India in the late nineteenth century to work the tea and rubber plantations. The Indian Tamils were disenfranchised in Sri Lanka by legislation passed in 1948. See also Tamils.

International Monetary Fund (IMF)—Established along with the World Bank (*q.v.*) in 1945, the IMF is a specialized agency affiliated with the United Nations and is responsible for stabilizing international exchange rates and payments. The main business of the IMF is the provision of loans to its members (including industrialized and developing countries) when they experience balance of payments difficulties. These loans frequently carry conditions that require substantial internal economic adjustments by the recipients, most of which are developing countries.

Karaiya—Caste below the Vellala (*q.v.*) in the Tamil caste system, but still a high caste; original occupation was fishing, although group branched out into commercial ventures.

Karava—Lower Sinhalese (fisherman) caste that became wealthy because of access to English education and opportunities for involvement with plantation agriculture and modern commercial enterprise.

karma—Religious doctrine that each rebirth in the cycle of lives is based on the sum of the merit accumulated by an individual during his previous lives. Karma establishes the general tendency of a life but does not determine specific actions. In each life, the interaction between individual character and previously established karma forms the karma of succeeding lives.

maha—Greater monsoon—the main growing season under rainfed conditions for paddy (rice) and most other annual crops. Sowing is between August and October, depending on the time of the monsoon, and the crop is harvested five to six months later.

nibbana—The release from the cycle of rebirths and the annihilation of the individual being that occurs on achievement of perfect spiritual understanding. More commonly known in the West as nirvana.

paddy—Threshed, unmilled rice, which is the basis of the subsistence economy of much of South and Southeast Asia. It is grown on flooded or heavily irrigated flatland.

Pali—The language of the Theravada Buddhist sacred scriptures. A Prakrit, or a language derived from Sanskrit.

rupee—Monetary unit of Sri Lanka. The official exchange rate (par value) from January 16, 1952, to November 20, 1967, was Rs4.76 per US$1. In 1988 the official rate was approximately 32.32 rupees per US$1.

Salagama—Sinhalese lower, minority caste (cinnamon peelers).

sangha—The total community of *bhikkus (q.v.),* or Buddhist monks, in the broadest and most abstract sense; the *sangha* is composed of all Buddhist sects and residential communities and is the traditional Buddhist elite.

Sinhala—An Indo-European language of the Indo-Iranian group. It was derived from a Prakrit, or dialectical, form of Sanskrit. Majority language of Sri Lanka.

Sinhalese—The largest ethnic group, distinguished primarily by their language. As of 1981, Sinhalese constituted approximately 74 percent of the population; over 90 percent of them are Theravada Buddhists. Their ancestors probably migrated from northern India around 500 B.C.

Sri Lankan Tamils—Approximately two-thirds of the Tamils and those who have lived in Sri Lanka for many centuries. The Sri Lankan Tamils enjoy full voting rights. See also Tamils.

Tamils—Ethnic group, predominantly Hindu, whose language is Tamil, a Dravidian language spoken by the Tamil minority in the Northern and Eastern provinces of Sri Lanka; and which is the major regional language spoken in Tamil Nadu State, southeast India. Sri Lankan Tamils are descendants of settlers and invaders and are a native minority that represented approximately 12.6 percent of the population in 1981. Indian Tamils are descendants of estate laborers imported under British sponsorship to the island primarily in the nineteenth century, and represented approximately 5.5 percent of the population in 1981. The Indian Tamil population has been shrinking because of repatriation programs to Tamil Nadu.

Theravada Buddhism—Literally, the Buddhism that is "the way" or "doctrine of the elders." Sinhalese called their beliefs Theravada. Their tradition, frequently described as Hinayana (Lesser Vehicle), preserves a clear understanding of the Buddha as a man who achieved enlightenment and developed monks as accomplished followers of his teachings. This is in contradistinction to the Mahayana (Greater Vehicle) Buddhism, which often treats the Buddha as a superhuman and fills the universe with a pantheon of enlightened figures (bodhisattvas) who help others achieve enlightenment. The Sri Lankans, with rare exception, speak only of Theravada Buddhism, of which there is no central religious authority.

Veddah—Last descendants of the ancient inhabitants of Sri Lanka, predating arrival of the Sinhalese. Veddahs have not preserved their own language, live in small rural settlements, and have become more of a caste than a separate ethnic group. They are generally accepted as equal in rank to the Sinhalese Goyigama (*q.v.*) caste.

Vellala—Highest Tamil (cultivator) caste, the members of which traditionally dominated local commercial and educational elites and whose values had strong influence on Tamils of other castes. The group comprises more than half of the Tamil population.

wet zone—Area of southwest side of hill country and southestern plain receiving an average of 250 centimeters of rain per year.

World Bank—Informal name used to designate a group of three affiliated international institutions: the International Bank for Reconstruction and Development (IBRD), the International Development Association (IDA), and the International Finance Corporation (IFC). The IBRD, established in 1945, has the primary purpose of providing loans to developing countries for productive projects. The IDA, a legally separate loan fund but administered by the staff of the IBRD, was set up in 1960 to furnish credits to the poorest developing countries on much easier terms than those of conventional IBRD loans. The IFC, founded in 1956, supplements the activities of the IBRD through loans and assistance specifically designed to encourage the growth of productive private enterprises in the less developed countries. The president and certain senior officers of the IBRD hold the same positions in the IFC. The three institutions are owned by the governments of the countries that subscribe their capital. To participate in the World Bank group, member states must first belong to the International Monetary Fund (IMF—*q.v.*).

yala—Lesser monsoon—the secondary growing season for paddy (rice) and most other annual crops with sowing between April and May and harvesting four or five months later. For some foodstuffs and cotton, when grown in the dry zone under irrigation, the *yala* crop is more important than the *maha (q.v.)* crop.

Index

Abhayagiri monastery, 15
Accelerated Mahaweli Program, 123, 126, 128, 130, 131, 142-43, 159, 166, 215
accommodessan, 30
Acquired Immune Deficiency Syndrome (AIDS), 110
ACTC. *See* All Ceylon Tamil Congress: ACTC
Adams Peak, 63
Administration of Justice Law (1973), 256-57, 258
administrative districts, 188-89
administrative reform, 29, 31
Adventist Radio, 149
agricultural products, processed (*see also* food processing), 138, 140-41
agricultural sector (*see also* cinnamon industry; coconut industry; coffee industry; plantation system; rice cultivation; rubber industry; sugar industry; tea industry), 8, 10, 17, 121, 126-37; exports, 119, 126, 129; farming communities of, 67; government policies for, 130-33; shift in development of, 127-28; shift in labor force from, 149-50
Agro-Commercial Bank, 167
AIADMK. *See* All-India Anna Dravida Munnetra Kazhagam (AIADMK)
Aid Sri Lanka Consortium, 166
aircraft, 241-42
Air Force Academy, 242
Air Force Security Force, 241
Air Lanka (airline), 148, 225
Algemene Bank Nederland, 168
All-Ceylon Buddhist Congress, 95
All-Ceylon Buddhist Women's Association, 95
All Ceylon Tamil Congress (ACTC), 37, 44-45
All-India Anna Dravida Munnetra Kazhagam (AIADMK), 205, 208
All Party conferences (1984, 1986), xxxi, 207-8, 210
Alms Bowl, 17
Amarapura Nikaya sect, 92-93
Ambalangoda, 228
American Express, 168
Amnesty International, xxvi, 54, 207

Amparai District, 78, 106, 211
Amsterdam Rotterdam Bank, 168
Ananda College, 35
Anglican Church of Ceylon, 101-2
antidrug legislation, 263
Anuradhapura, 3, 8, 10, 11, 12, 13, 15, 35, 65, 67, 71, 225
apatite, 143
Arabian Peninsula, 100
Arabic language, 101
Arabs, 100, 210
Arasaratnam, Sinnappah, 12
armed forces (*see also* Sri Lankan Air Force; Sri Lankan Army; Sri Lankan Navy), 193, 219-20, 221, 235; awards, 248; conditions of services in, 242-43, 245; detention camps of, 262-63; ethnic composition of, 245, 247; expansion of, 230, 234; increased power of, 255, 260; role in Sri Lanka, 230-31, 232-33, 235
Army Training Centre, 238, 242, 248
artificial lakes. *See* water storage tanks
Aruvi Aru River, 63
Aryans, 180
ASEAN. *See* Association of Southeast Asian Nations (ASEAN)
Ashraff, M., 210
Asian Development Bank, 145
Asoka (emperor), 7, 95, 180, 207
assassinations, xxvi, xxxv, 5, 46, 53, 54, 55, 258
Association of Southeast Asian Nations (ASEAN), 14
Athulathmudali, Lalith, 213
Australia, 237, 239, 240, 249
autonomous homeland, Tamils, xxvi, xxx, 42, 46, 54-55, 204, 222, 226
Ayurvedic Act (1961), 264
ayurvedic medicine, 109, 263-64

Badulla District, 238
Balakumar, V., 205
balance of payments, 160, 161
Balasingham, A. S., 204
Bandaranaike, Anura, 51, 53, 196, 213
Bandaranaike, S. R. D. (Sirimavo Ratwatte Dias), 5, 37, 42, 53, 176, 181,

305

Sri Lanka: A Country Study

Tamil United Liberation Front (TULF), xxx, xxxi, xxxiii, 51–55, 108, 176, 185, 193–94, 198, 199, 204, 207, 208, 209–10, 223
Tangalla, 227
Tangalla naval base, 239
tanks. *See* water storage tanks
taxes (*see also* revenues), 162–64
Taxation Inquiry Commission (1968), 162, 163
tea industry, 32–33, 119, 120–21, 126–27, 129, 134–36, 137, 138, 140–41, 158–59
technical colleges, 106
telecommunications services, 148–49
telephone services, 148–49
television transmission, 149
telex services, 148
TELO. *See* Tamil Eelam Liberation Organization (TELO)
temperance movement, 35
Temple of the Tooth, 8, 93
Tenant, Emerson, 15
Ten-Year Plan (1959), 124
terms of trade, 119, 122, 156, 158
terrorism, 5, 52–54, 211, 213, 219, 225, 255
textile industry, 120, 121, 138, 140, 142, 155–56, 158
Thailand, 16, 180
Theosophical Movement, 35
Theravada, 91
Theravada (or Hinayana) Buddhism, 7, 15, 59, 80, 92–95, 180
Thesavalamai, 24
Thimpu, 210
Thondaman, Suvumyamoorthy, 198, 203
thorium, 143
Three Stars coalition, 224
Thriposha Programme, 112
Thuparama Dagoba (stupa), 7
TNT. *See* Tamil New Tigers (TNT)
Tooth Relic, 7–8, 17, 93
topography, 61, 63
tourism, 120, 154, 160, 164, 169–70
trade, foreign (*see also* balance of payments; deficit, trade; exports; exchange rate system; imports; terms of trade), 157–60
trade liberalization, 123, 156
Trade Union Ordinance (1935), 154–55
trade unions, 38, 154–56; affiliations of, 155
trading corporations, 157

training institutes, 106
Training School for Youthful Offenders, 262
Trans-World Radio, 149
Trincomalee District, xxxiii, 71
Trincomalee naval base, 239, 240
Trincomalee: as port, 22, 24–25, 38–39, 63, 64, 147, 149, 209, 210, 211, 215, 221; as territory, 24
Tripitaka, 7
Trotsky, Leon, 38, 197
truck haulage, 145, 147
trusteeship, 28
TULF. *See* Tamil United Liberation Front (TULF)
Two-Year Plan (1975-77), 125

unemployment, 111, 151, 152, 154
unions. *See* labor force
Union Motors, 140
United Arab Emirates, 160
United Front (Samagi Peramuna) (*see also* SLFP-United Front coalition), 49–51, 227
United National Party (UNP), xxviii, xxix, xxxv, 40–45, 46–55, 142, 155, 175, 176, 184, 188, 193–99, 201, 207, 221, 223, 247, 251–52, 255, 256; economic policy of, 119–20, 122–24; emergence of, 41–43, 194, factionalism in, 206; foreign policy position of, 214
United Nations Children's Fund (UNICEF), 112
United Nations peacekeeping force, 230
United Nations (UN), 43
United States, 49, 159–60, 209, 215, 221, 237, 239, 240, 241, 249
United States Agency for International Development (AID), 112
United States Department of State, 253, 262–63
University of Ceylon, 104
University of Perideniya, 105
University of Ruhunu, 105
University of Vidyalankara, 105
University of Vidyodaya, 105
university system, 60, 105
UNP. *See* United National Party (UNP)
untouchable caste, 15
Upanishads, 96
Up-Country Co-operative Estates Development Board, 133

318

Published Country Studies

(Area Handbook Series)

550-65	Afghanistan	550-153	Ghana
550-98	Albania	550-87	Greece
550-44	Algeria	550-78	Guatemala
550-59	Angola	550-174	Guinea
550-73	Argentina	550-82	Guyana
550-169	Australia	550-151	Honduras
550-176	Austria	550-165	Hungary
550-175	Bangladesh	550-21	India
550-170	Belgium	550-154	Indian Ocean
550-66	Bolivia	550-39	Indonesia
550-20	Brazil	550-68	Iran
550-168	Bulgaria	550-31	Iraq
550-61	Burma	550-25	Israel
550-37	Burundi/Rwanda	550-182	Italy
550-50	Cambodia	550-30	Japan
550-166	Cameroon	550-34	Jordan
550-159	Chad	550-56	Kenya
550-77	Chile	550-81	Korea, North
550-60	China	550-41	Korea, South
550-26	Colombia	550-58	Laos
550-33	Commonwealth Caribbean, Islands of the	550-24	Lebanon
550-91	Congo	550-38	Liberia
550-90	Costa Rica	550-85	Libya
550-69	Côte d'Ivoire (Ivory Coast)	550-172	Malawi
550-152	Cuba	550-45	Malaysia
550-22	Cyprus	550-161	Mauritania
550-158	Czechoslovakia	550-79	Mexico
550-36	Dominican Republic/Haiti	550-76	Mongolia
550-52	Ecuador	550-49	Morocco
550-43	Egypt	550-64	Mozambique
550-150	El Salvador	550-88	Nicaragua
550-28	Ethiopia	550-157	Nigeria
550-167	Finland	550-94	Oceania
550-155	Germany, East	550-48	Pakistan
550-173	Germany, Fed. Rep. of	550-46	Panama